'Lesley Downe—   its mystery
— and peeled it   nmend her
engaging and   rld' Arthur
Golden

'Engrossing an   *imes*

'Lesley Downe   secret and
rapidly vanish   *graph*

'Fascinating a   he geisha'
Sunday Times

'Exquisite . . .   hester

'Intriguing, well structured . . . richly rewarding' *Observer*

'This is the best account among several of the real life of the geisha. Fascinating, cultured and still capable of surprising and shocking a Western audience' *Bookseller*

'A vibrant portrait . . . a masterpiece in subject and

Also by Lesley Downer

On the Narrow Road to the Deep North
The Brothers: The Saga of the Richest Family in Japan
Geisha: The Secret History of a Vanishing World
(published in the US as Women of the Pleasure Quarters: The Secret
History of the Geisha)

MADAME SADAYAKKO

THE GEISHA WHO SEDUCED THE WEST

LESLEY DOWNER

review

First published in 2003
by REVIEW
An imprint of Headline Book Publishing

10 9 8 7 6 5 4 3 2 1

Cataloguing in Publication Data is available
from the British Library

ISBN 0 7553 1030 6 hardback
ISBN 0 7553 1031 4 trade paperback

Typeset in Weiss by Palimpsest Book Production Limited,
Polmont, Stirlingshire

Calligraphy by Kishi Yamamoto

Printed and bound in Great Britain by
Clays Ltd, St Ives plc

Headline Book Publishing
A division of Hodder Headline
338 Euston Road
London NW1 3BH

www.reviewbooks.co.uk
www.hodderheadline.com

To the memory of my parents,
Gordon and Lilian Downer

CONTENTS

ACKNOWLEDGEMENTS

By the time I began my research, Sadayakko's daughter, Tomiji, was too old and ill to meet me. Her granddaughter, Hatsu Kawakami, together with Hatsu's son, Shinichiro, generously shared time and memories with me and showed me her precious collection of photographs and souvenirs. Hatsu ensured that I was warmly received at Teishoji Temple. Otojiro's cousin's grandson, Hiroshi Kawakami, who continues the Kawakami family line, welcomed me into his home in Hakata, and I spent a fruitful afternoon with Momosuké's grandson, Kakumasa Fukuzawa. It was a great excitement and privilege for me to meet them all.

Thanks to Saketa-san at Teishoji Temple and Masao Okumura, who showed me around the Garden of Evening Pines in Unuma. In Midono, Takashi Toyama was full of expertise and enthusiasm and took me to the Momosuké Memorial Museum, Oi Dam and several of Momosuké's Art Deco power stations. Thanks also to Ryokichi Matsusei for his memories of Sadayakko, and the staff of Nagiso Town Office for providing introductions. Mr Yasuda of the Nagoya City Office shared his knowledge of Futaba Palace. Thanks to Fumi Noguchi of the Fukuoka City Museum, who organised a wonderful exhibition on the Kawakamis at the 1900 Paris

Expo and introduced me to Koh Egashira, author of the most up-to-date biography of Otojiro. In Tokyo, thanks to the owner of Hamadaya and to Hisamatsu and Hiro of the Yoshicho geisha community.

I would also like to thank Junichi Yano of the Foreign Press Centre in Tokyo who gave me help far beyond the line of duty and came up with all sorts of extraordinary information. He tracked down Hatsu and pointed me towards Ito's birthplace, among much else. Keiichiro Asari, author of a recent biography of Momosuké, introduced me to Kakumasa.

Jun Kanai of Issey Miyake International introduced me to Akiko Fukai of the Kyoto Costume Institute, where I handled the only surviving Yakko kimono (wearing white cotton gloves). Nancy Knox introduced me to Issey Miyake, who gave encouragement and materials on Sadayakko's connections with fashion. Michiyo Sato, the Isadora Duncan dancer, was full of inspiration and introduced me to the dance scholar Kazuko Kuniyoshi.

Hiroaki Sugita, recently retired from the *Kyoto Shimbun* (newspaper) and author of many scholarly works, first drew my attention to Sadayakko and lent me a book about her, from where my fascination grew.

Of the several biographies of Sadayakko in Japanese (listed in the bibliography), Hatsu commended *Actress Sadayakko* by Reiko Yamaguchi as the most accurate. I made much use of Nobuo Shirakawa's magnificently comprehensive collection of clippings covering Sadayakko's and Otojiro's careers to the end of Otojiro's life. There is also a scrapbook of clippings at Teishoji Temple which, to my joy, turned out to cover Sadayakko's later years.

I could never have made use of any of this material without my trusty readers, who ploughed through acres of archaic Japanese and put it into English for me. Chieko Tsuneoka, my long-time friend and ally, gave up evenings and weekends to pore over barely legible photocopies of hundred-year-old press clippings. She shared my adventure with me, taking a weekend out to travel to Teishoji Temple. Midori Hanabusa generously took time off from her normally far more high-powered work to decipher hundreds of pages of ancient press clippings at amazing speed and read Otojiro's diaries. This book would not exist without their help. Tomomi Sherlock, Naoko Takayama and Sara Roche in Tokyo and Satoko Shimazaki in New York also provided sterling help with translation.

The small but enthusiastic community of Sadayakko scholars generously shared their knowledge with me. Ayako Kano sent me the manuscript of her *Acting like a Woman in Modern Japan*, the only book on Sadayakko in English. J. Scott Miller loaded me down with materials and gave me a recording of the Kawakami troupe which he had unearthed in Cambridge. It was thrilling to hear the troupe twanging their shamisens and speaking to me from a century ago while I was driving across Utah in a rainstorm. Professor Peter Pantzer, my generous host in Bonn, not only shared the results of his formidable researches but took me on a boat ride up the Rhine. Thanks too to his excellent assistant, Nicole Zingsheim. Yoko Chiba shared much material. And in Kyoto I had an entertaining and informative dinner with Jonah Salz, whose seminal work, *Intercultural Pioneers: Otojiro Kawakami and Sada Yakko*, formed the backbone for my research.

Professor Drew Gerstle of the School of Oriental and African Studies in London kindly read the first draft and gave me the benefit of his great knowledge of Japanese theatre and the floating world (though all mistakes, of course, are my own). Liam Browne, Elizabeth Handover, Dea Birkett and Scott Miller also read the first draft and contributed valuable suggestions.

I had great fun discovering the resources of excellent libraries around the world. In Japan, I used the Tokyo Central Library in Hiroo and the Waseda Theatre Museum and International House libraries; in Paris, the Bibliothèque de l'Arsenal; in London, the School of Oriental and African Studies' library, the Theatre Museum, the British Library including the National Newspaper Library, Colindale, and the Westminster Public Libraries; in New York, the New York Public Library and the Bobst; and in Chicago, the Chicago Historical Society. Thanks also to Ria Koopmans-de Bruijn of the C.V. Starr East Asian Library at Columbia University.

I owe a bottomless debt of thanks to my wonderful agent, Bill Hamilton of A.M. Heath in London, who was, as always, there all the way through the project, giving wise advice and support. Profound thanks too to Heather Holden-Brown, Jo Roberts-Miller, Celia Kent, Lucy Ramsey, Peter Newsom and everyone at Headline Books, who have been full of support, enthusiasm and patience when required.

Thanks to picture researcher Emma Brown for taking a weight off my shoulders and to John Richardson and Marilyn McCully, and to Emma Page at James Roundel for helping me track down pictures. Thanks to Pieter C.W.M. Dreesmann for permission to use the Picasso pastel in his collection. Many thanks to Kishi Yamamoto for the beautifully brushed characters which form the chapter and section headings.

Lastly thanks to my brother and sister-in-law, Geoff and Clare; my nephews, Chris and James; my recently discovered extended family in Canada – the Chans, Chins, Aitkens and others; and to my supportive network of friends in London, New York and Tokyo who continue to be my friends despite my regular disappearances for months on end and refusal to take phone calls while working.

Note on pronunciation

Japanese words are pronounced as they are spelt, with each syllable distinct and with clean vowels and non-aspirated consonants, rather like Italian. All syllables are equally stressed.

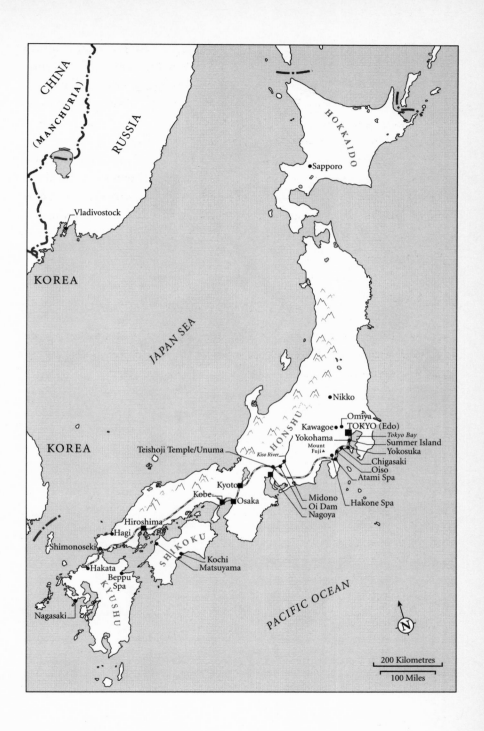

CHINA
(MANCHURIA)

RUSSIA

HOKKAIDO

•Sapporo

•Vladivostock

KOREA

JAPAN SEA

KOREA

H
O
N
S
H
U

•Nikko

Omiya
Kawagoe• • •TOKYO (Edo)
Yokohama ■ *Tokyo Bay*
Teishoji Temple/Unuma *Kiso River* Mount Summer Island
Fuji▲ Yokosuka
Kyoto Chigasaki
Kobe Oiso
Osaka Atami Spa
Midono
Oi Dam Hakone Spa
Nagoya

Hiroshima S
Hagi H
Shimonoseki I
K
Hakata O
Beppu K
Spa U Kochi
K Matsuyama
Y
U
S
H
U

Nagasaki

PACIFIC OCEAN

N

200 Kilometres

100 Miles

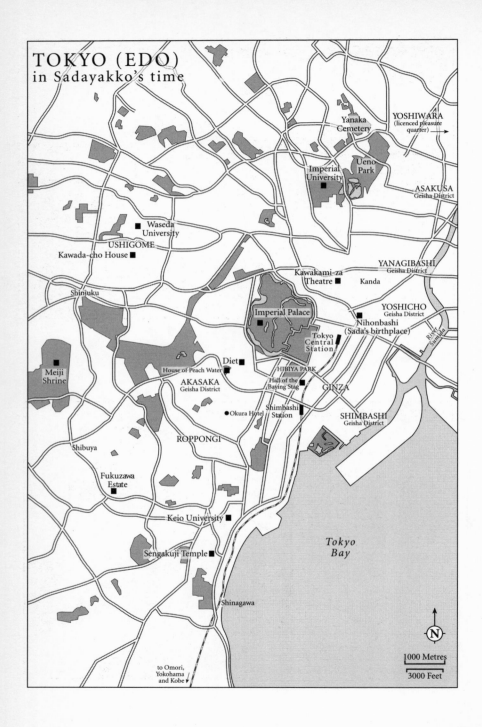

TOKYO (EDO)
in Sadayakko's time

YOSHIWARA
(licenced pleasure quarter)

Yanaka Cemetery

Ueno Park

Imperial University

ASAKUSA
Geisha District

Waseda University

USHIGOME

Kawada-cho House

Shinjuku

YANAGIBASHI
Geisha District

Kawakami-za Theatre

Kanda

YOSHICHO
Geisha District

Imperial Palace

Nihonbashi
(Sada's birthplace)

River Sumida

Tokyo Central Station

Meiji Shrine

House of Peach Water

Diet

HIBIYA PARK

Hall of the Baying Stag

GINZA

AKASAKA
Geisha District

Okura Hotel

Shimbashi Station

SHIMBASHI
Geisha District

ROPPONGI

Shibuya

Fukuzawa Estate

Keio University

Tokyo Bay

Sengakuji Temple

Shinagawa

N

1000 Metres

3000 Feet

to Omori,
Yokohama
and Kobe

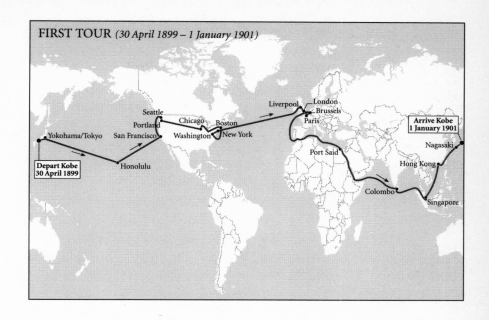

FIRST TOUR *(30 April 1899 – 1 January 1901)*

Yokohama/Tokyo

Seattle
Portland
San Francisco
Chicago
Washington
Boston
New York

Honolulu

**Depart Kobe
30 April 1899**

Liverpool
London
Brussels
Paris

Port Said

Colombo

Hong Kong

Nagasaki

Singapore

**Arrive Kobe
1 January 1901**

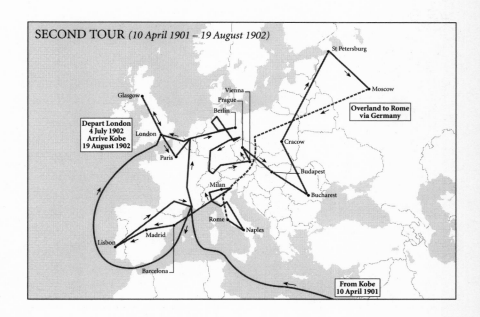

SECOND TOUR *(10 April 1901 – 19 August 1902)*

St Petersburg

Moscow

Glasgow

Vienna
Prague
Berlin

**Overland to Rome
via Germany**

**Depart London
4 July 1902
Arrive Kobe
19 August 1902**

London

Paris

Cracow

Budapest

Milan

Bucharest

Rome
Naples

Lisbon

Madrid

Barcelona

**From Kobe
10 April 1901**

PROLOGUE

IN SEARCH OF SADAYAKKO

Sada Yacco resembles the loveliest ivory bas relief, radiant in
soft brocades and silks. And how this Geisha dances! Flexible as
a little willow wand, the scarlet and white Kimono clinging to
her lithe form and, with every movement, enveloping her like
tongues of flame, she takes the most exquisite poses, recalling
those graceful figures which have 'decorated' our choicest
specimens and curios. No wonder the Geisha bewitches all
travellers in the Flowery Kingdom, for this actress represents her
as the epitome of sweetness and grace.[1]

'The Chatterer', *Boston Herald*, 13 December 1899

On 20 May 1899 the *San Francisco Chronicle* carried an article
breathlessly headlined 'Madame Yacco, the Leading Geisha of
Japan, Coming Here'. The article announced:

Mme. Yacco, until two years ago the leading Geisha of Japan, is a
passenger on the steamship Gaelic from the Orient. While still a
Geisha, Yacco demanded and received an income which would not
be despised by a modern prima donna, the time of her appearance
being regulated by the burning of an incense stick. She is of the best
type of Japanese beauty and a lady of social position, gifted with
musical ability.[2]

It is hard to imagine the storm of excitement Sadayakko created when
she toured the United States and Europe at the turn of the nineteenth
century. In those days people in the West knew very little of Japan; but
they had heard much. And here, for the first time, was a real geisha –
not just that, but the most celebrated geisha in Japan who, at the age of
twenty-eight, had launched herself into a new career to become Japan's

1

first actress. Apart from those who had been to Japan – very few in 1899 – no one had ever seen a geisha before, neither had they ever seen Japanese drama; and they could not possibly have seen a Japanese actress. For 250 years, women had been banned from performing on stage in Japan; all parts had been performed by men.

In that era before film and television, the great stage actresses were the world's idols. Sarah Bernhardt, Ellen Terry, Eleonora Duse and Gabrielle Réju – 'the divine Réjane' – were as celebrated and adored as Hollywood stars, pop singers or supermodels today. Audiences thronged to see the plays in which they starred. They were photographed and interviewed incessantly and pursued by gossip columnists. They were weavers of dreams, larger than life.

Many people said that Sadayakko was the greatest of them all. She was called the Japanese Terry and the Japanese Bernhardt, though in reality, perhaps, she was more like Bernhardt combined with Anna Pavlova, a glorious dancer as well as an actress. The writer Max Beerbohm declared that if, like Paris, he were forced to choose the most beautiful of all these sirens, he would award the golden apple to Sadayakko.

But who was this mysterious, seductive being who appeared like a shooting star, bedazzling America and Europe for a few brief years? Westerners in thrall to her exoticism and beauty, and absorbed in their own preconceptions of what Japanese women were like, had no idea of the real person behind the stage persona. The world she came from was more different than anything they could ever imagine.

We know what the West thought of her; but what did she think of the West? Where did she come from? How did she achieve her brilliant success? And what became of her after she went back to Japan? Who was the real woman behind the painted mask?

On 11 March 1900, a critic wrote in the *New York Times*,

It is difficult to think of the Japanese woman of any age, rank or character as anything but a pretty, dainty little creature, sitting in her toy house, arranging her single branch of cherry blossoms or amusing herself in her miniature garden. . . . No one would have expected to find an emotional actress in Japan, for who would have expected to find an emotional woman there?

Had he known anything of the real life of the flower-like creature on stage, he would have been astounded.[3]

I first came face to face with Sadayakko in Kyoto. I was in a café beside the river, chatting over tea and spongy cheesecake to a grizzled Japanese writer who had studied the life of a famous nineteenth-century geisha.

'But have you heard of Sadayakko, the geisha who became Japan's first actress?' he inquired. 'She was the greatest celebrity of them all.'

The next time we met he brought a book. On the cover was a picture of her. The face I saw was bewitchingly beautiful, heart-shaped with porcelain skin and a long straight nose. Her luxuriant black tresses, swept into an oiled coiffeur, had a reddish tinge. Her eyebrows were crescent moons, her mouth full and sensual. A Mona Lisa smile hovered on her lips, as if she held the key to some secret knowledge. Most mysterious and alluring of all were her large, luminous eyes, dark as pools and deep enough for a man to drown himself. One was flat like a Japanese eye, the other rounder and lidded like a Western one.

A hundred years after she toured the West, Sadayakko still has the power to allure. From that first encounter, I was intrigued and wanted to find out more. I set out in search of her, yet at first she always seemed to slip away. I found myself more and more beguiled. As I searched out articles and interviews and visited places where she had been, little by little she began to come alive. One by one the pieces of her story began to fall into place.

Sadayakko was not only beautiful but feisty and full of life. At a time when the ideal for a Japanese woman was to fulfil the roles of 'good wife and wise mother', Sadayakko took her life into her own hands. From humble beginnings she rose to become the most famous woman in Japan. She carved out her destiny by herself. With nothing but her natural beauty and talents, she created a glittering career, opening the door for generations of Japanese women. She also found time to have a tempestuous love life involving some of the most powerful, charismatic and wealthy men in the country. The way she ran her life, her work and her men made her one of Japan's first modern women. She was as far as it was possible to be from the fictitious Madame Butterfly and utterly different from Westerners' conceptions of Japanese women as docile, submissive and oppressed.

Wherever she went she was news. Seeking Sadayakko, I thumbed through old newspapers and magazines. In the New York Public Library I tracked down a 1900 copy of *Harper's Bazar* (spelt thus) and fingered the fragile paper, musty and dusty with age. Filling the whole cover was a photograph of her. I scoured crumbling copies of the *San Francisco Chronicle* and the *Seattle Post-Intelligencer*, the *Morning Oregonian* and the *Boston Herald*. In Chicago I studied the *Chicago Daily News* on microfiche and found the original location of the hotel where she had stayed and the theatre where she had performed. In London I turned the crackly pages of *The World*, *The Sketch* and *The Queen: the Lady's Newspaper*. In the Bibliothèque de l'Arsenal in Paris I sorted through theatre programmes, reviews, interviews, photographs and cartoons. I was transported back a hundred years to the era of the Boer War and the Boxer Rebellion.

Sadayakko was an adept at manipulating her own story. To use a modern term, she knew the power of spin. In the West no one knew who or what she was. She could recreate herself and project any image she liked. Released from the social pressures of her own society, she enjoyed a brief taste of freedom. She no longer had to fit in. She told and retold her story, changing it as she saw fit. She created her own myth.

In Japan, she was inescapably imprisoned within the stifling social world there. Everyone knew not only who she was but where she stood in the hierarchy. As a geisha, actress and star, she was simultaneously adored and despised. She had a very ambivalent status, at the top and the bottom of society.

Across the world there is a long tradition of men writing with hostility, ribaldry and disrespect about women who step outside the roles society has prescribed for them – courtesans, actresses and other members of the *demi-monde*. Sadayakko sometimes suffered a hostile press in Japan, written by male journalists who felt threatened by her freedom, feistiness and independence. I had to take this into account when I looked at the way events in her life were reported.

4

She and her husband Otojiro were Japan's first celebrity couple. Journalists hovered about them like vultures wherever they went, eager to capture their discomfitures as well as their triumphs.

At the Theatre Museum at Waseda University in Tokyo, I studied century-old magazines and newspapers and pored over yellowing programmes, leaflets and adverts. I was thrilled to discover that Otojiro, a charming rogue and tireless self-promoter, had kept a detailed diary of their journey to the West, with the exact times of departure and arrival at each port and railway station along the way. The cover features an illustration of him on stage, posing on wooden clogs in a man's kimono with a sword tucked into his belt, holding a fan. As well as the Japanese title he gave the diary an English one, *Mr Kawakami's Travels Round the World*. He had it published almost as soon as they got back.

There were volumes of newspaper articles covering her entire career, with photographs, titbits of gossip and long interviews with Sadayakko in which she told her own story. She was so celebrated that her name was used to advertise brands of make-up. Speaking to Japanese readers, she was humorous and self-deprecating. She chatted about her thoughts and feelings as well as her acting techniques. Takeo Azuma interviewed her for *Engei Gaho* (*Performance Pictorial*) magazine. 'When I'm on stage, I'm full of nervous energy,' she told him.

It's quite different when I have time off; I sleep till noon. But if someone wakes me or if I'm disturbed when I'm getting ready to go on stage, I tend to forget my lines. When I'm on stage, if I think it hasn't gone well, I feel terrible all day. I even have sad dreams about it. But when everyone is applauding, I feel happier than if I had made tens of thousands of *ryo* [dollars].[4]

I was eager to visit all the places connected with Sadayakko – the houses where she lived and loved, the theatres where she had her triumphs. I wanted to breathe the air and absorb the atmosphere, to try and imagine myself back into her world. Above all I wanted to walk the streets of Yoshicho, the district which had been her home when she was starting out in life as a young geisha. I knew it was around Nihonbashi in the

5

mercantile heart of the old city, near the Bank of Japan and the Tokyo Stock Exchange. But no one seemed to have heard of the area and I could not find it on any map.

Then one day I was chatting to a man whose family had run a traditional inn in Tokyo for generations. He inhabited the same world as the geisha. It is a kind of parallel universe coexisting with the world of everyday life but accessible only to those who have the key. Outsiders walk the same streets but see only nondescript houses, shops and passers-by. But those in the know can tell which of the anonymous houses are geisha houses and which of the ordinary-looking women blossom into geisha at night. Its inhabitants call it the 'flower and willow world'. In the past courtesans in their lavish silks and brocades were the 'flowers'. The chic geisha in their stylish but subtle kimonos were 'willows', trained to be graceful and pliant but strong of spirit, like a willow tree. Nowadays the courtesans have disappeared but there are still geisha for those who know where to look.

Sadayakko's name, I discovered, opened many doors. The innkeeper too did not know Yoshicho, but when I told him that I was researching Sadayakko's life, he arranged for me to meet a couple of geisha in the Nihonbashi area. The rendezvous was in a quiet corner of Tokyo where no one would go unless they had business. There in a coffee shop two women were waiting for me.

At first sight they might have been simply two elderly women in kimonos. But they had a certain piquancy to them. The skin on their hands was becoming transparent but they were still exquisite. They carried themselves with the assurance of women used to receiving homage as beauties. Their glossy black hair was immaculately smooth, swept up and back into the bouffant style which geisha favour. Tiny, birdlike, they chirped and chattered, holding a manicured hand over a beautifully lipsticked mouth when they laughed. Beneath the artless exterior they had the steely quality of women who had fought to survive.

They told me their geisha names; like Sadayakko, they used only a first name with no family name. One was Hisamatsu, the other Hiro. They were thrilled to hear that I knew of Sadayakko and wanted to write her story for Western readers. Like her, they told me proudly, they were Yoshicho geisha. She had lived nearby. Somehow I had stepped through the looking glass. I was no longer in workaday Tokyo but in the world of flowers and willows. Over tea and ice cream they talked about Sadayakko.

'She was the most sought after geisha in Tokyo,' they told me:

She was always flitting from teahouse to teahouse; everyone wanted to see her and have her appear at their parties. In the flower and willow world we all know that Prime Minister Ito took care of Sadayakko. He was her first lover.

Her 'mother' in the geisha world arranged it. You had to have a *danna* [lover cum patron], otherwise you'd have been poor. She was a great 'mother'. She knew how to do the best for Sadayakko.

In those days geisha came from poor families and were sold to geisha houses. This area was right next to the stock exchange, so we had good business. The customers were high class; geisha had to behave like high-class people themselves, otherwise they wouldn't have been able to entertain.

Lots of men must have liked Sadayakko. We would all say how much we liked a guy, it was that sort of atmosphere. But it was never really love. You might have had a secret fancy for someone; but you always had to remember that it was all a game. There was no time for love.

Life was hard in those days. People put up with whatever destiny put their way. They suffered; they didn't expect tomorrow to be the same as today.

Far too many years had passed to be able even to imagine I could meet people who remembered Sadayakko as a geisha. Hisamatsu and Hiro had been young girls when she was already old. But sitting with these dainty women, chatting prettily in their birdlike voices, I felt I could glimpse her world.

They asked me if I wanted to see the place where Sadayakko had lived. The house was no longer there; but I could see the original location. Pattering along on silk-covered sandals, chattering in high-pitched voices, they led me through the labyrinthine streets of Yoshicho.

It is a part of Tokyo that has remained unknown and unchanged. We walked along quiet streets shaded with plane trees, leaves tinted gold in the first chill of autumn. We passed a tatami-maker's shop where a couple of old men sat stitching thick rice-straw mats and piles of mats leaned against a wall. In a lacquerware shop a craftsman was slicking red lacquer onto wooden bowls. We strolled past kimono shops stacked with bolts of shimmering silk.

'My mother was a geisha,' chirped Hiro. 'I grew up here.'

Hisamatsu reminisced:

When we were young, it was all geisha houses and teahouses.' It was a geisha town, like Gion in Kyoto. There were rivers here lined with willow trees and five or six boathouses. People would go out in boats with little roofs. There'd be fishing. We'd sit there eating sweets, watching. In summer we used to go cherry blossom viewing by boat. Then the rivers went underground and disappeared and little by little ordinary people moved in.

We came to a small temple with a cast-iron lantern outside. In the shadowy gloom fresh flowers had been placed in vases and candles glimmered. There we turned down a sun-dappled alley, just wide enough for a bicycle to wobble through. There were potted plants and small trees in tubs along one side, outside red-plastered houses. On the other, bushes and greenery sprouted exuberantly over a bamboo fence. Cats darted across our path and curled around the plants. A couple of bicycles and a red motorcycle were propped to one side.

At the end of the lane was a rundown little house with sand-coloured walls. The windows had small wooden balconies outside and were shaded with bamboo blinds. Vines and foliage twined luxuriantly around the door and up the door posts.

'The Hamada house used to be here,' said Hisamatsu. 'This is where Sadayakko used to live.'

I was quite lost. Only the geisha had the key. Without them these streets would be anonymous and indistinguishable. I would never be able to find this place again. Then the door slid open and a slender young woman in a kimono slipped silently out. It was as if we had whirled back in time to an autumn day more than a hundred years ago.

Sadayakko's name

Sadayakko went by different names and her name was spelt in different ways in the course of her career. When she was in the West it was usually spelt Sada Yacco and people assumed that Yacco was her surname. Her name is part of her story and the details will emerge in the pages which follow. Sometimes readers will find her referred to as Sada or Yakko or Sadayakko or Sada Yacco or even other variants. But it is all the same woman.

The brushed charachters at the beginning of each section and chapter together make Sadayakko's name. The character marking each section is *sada*, which means 'constancy' or 'chastity'; the character marking the chapter headings is *yakko*, meaning 'a low-ranking retainer of a samurai'.

I
GEISHA

貞

1

THE GEISHA AND THE FARM BOY
1871—1885

O ne fine autumn evening in 1885, a young man was strolling
along the banks of the River Sumida in Tokyo. It was a beautiful
place thick with grasses and wild flowers, lined with cherry
and willow trees. On the water, junks and fishing boats bobbed, while
high-prowed boats like gondolas carried merrymakers to the teahouses
along the banks or the pleasure quarters in the northern suburbs.

Anyone who passed the boy would have turned to have another look.
He was strikingly handsome. He was tall and slight, fair-skinned with fine,
rather delicate features. His large, calm eyes were set wide apart and he
looked about him with a pensive, slightly disdainful gaze. He had what
is called in Japanese a 'high nose', meaning that it was long, straight and
larger and more defined than the average Japanese nose, though still neat
and small to Western eyes. It gave him an exotic, rather distinguished
'foreign' look. His hair was cropped short and neatly parted. He was
dressed head to foot in the Western mode – lapelled jacket, trousers,
shoes and high-collared shirt. He was every inch the student.

By the time the last rays of light were piercing the branches of the trees,
he had strayed a long way out of town. In front of him was grassy moorland

broken with copses, wild and forlorn. Behind, on the other side of the river, stretched the teeming hills and flatlands of the city. Smoke rose from a million cooking pots while all across the city oil lamps, gas lamps and the occasional new-fangled electric light were beginning to twinkle. On the horizon the dark silhouette of Mount Fuji soared serenely against the golden clouds of the evening sky.

The boy was about to turn back when he heard the pounding of hooves swishing through the long grasses accompanied by a cacophony of fierce barking. Then came a shrill scream.

Clinging helplessly to the neck of her dun horse was a young girl, barely out of childhood. The horse was rearing frantically, trying to dodge the fangs of a pack of mangy wild dogs that surrounded it, snarling and snapping at its legs. The girl's hair was flying and her skirts fluttered wildly yet somehow she managed to stay in the saddle.

Without a second's thought the young man grabbed a couple of rocks, heaved them at the curs, then charged into the mêlée, lashing out at the brutes with his stick. The snarling turned to yelping as the dogs turned tail and ran. Then he grabbed the reins, calmed the horse and helped the girl dismount. She was shaking so much she could barely stand. He stood by respectfully while she caught her breath.

She was fourteen years old. She was tiny, a good foot shorter than he, with a heart-shaped face and translucent white skin. Her lustrous black hair, shot with a reddish hue, had come loose from its fastenings and tumbled to her waist. The story has it that she was dressed in a Victorian riding outfit of a scarlet blouse and full riding skirts. She too had a certain foreign cast to her features. Her nose was unusually straight and long, her lips full, delicately shaped and rather sensual. But it was her large eyes that were most extraordinary. The left was flat like a Japanese eye, but the right had a crease, like a Western eye. She was the most exquisite creature he had ever seen.

Finally she began to recover her composure. Taking the reins from him she patted and stroked her horse, talking to it and soothing it.

'Are you all right?' he asked in concerned tones. 'Thank the gods you didn't fall!'

'I lost control of my horse,' she gasped. 'I was so frightened! Where

could they have come from, those awful dogs? I might have been killed!'
She smoothed her clothes and tied her hair back into a long ponytail. She
seemed unusually confident and assured, like one who is already a beauty
and used to admiration. She had the chirpy rapid-fire speech of an Edokko,
a person born and brought up for three generations in the city of Edo, as
Tokyo used to be called.

'My name is Momosuké Iwasaki,' the young man told her, bowing
politely. 'I am a humble student at Keio University.'

'I am Ko-yakko of the house of Hamada in the geisha town of Yoshicho,'
she replied, blushing prettily as she bowed in return. Then she swung
shakily onto her horse and, bowing again and again, cantered off along
the path towards the city. Her red skirts fluttered like a flower petal.

He stood watching until she disappeared from view. He could not help
noticing her sweetness and pride and the skill with which she handled her
horse. But such a woman, he knew very well, was not for him. There was
no point even thinking about it. Taking the same path he started on the
long walk back to the university and his studies.

There were many reasons why she could not be for him. In those days
young people were not in control of their destinies. They did as their
elders told them. They studied what they were told to study and married
whom they were told to marry. Added to that, she was a geisha. That
made her all the more alluring. But it also put her far beyond his reach –
and beyond the pale.

Ko-yakko was not the girl's real name but a geisha name, like a stage
name. Her birth name was Sada Koyama. As a child she was known as
Ko-yakko, which means Little Yakko. When she became an adult geisha,
she was given the name of Yakko. Many years later, when she first took to
the stage as an actress, she put together her birth name and geisha name
to make 'Sadayakko'.

Sada was not born to be a geisha. She came from a well-to-do
samurai family who made a living by doing business. As such, she might
have been expected to make a good marriage and lead an unevent-
ful life as the wife of a respectable businessman. But that was not
to be. Life in Japan at the time was changing at an extraordinary

rate – which was to have a cataclysmic effect on the life of little Sada.

In later years she was interviewed many times. In a Japanese newspaper she described her origins thus:

> My grandfather on my mother's side was an assistant magistrate and rather famous, I hear. Our house was in Nihonbashi, right where the Bank of Japan is now. People say that you can call yourself an Edokko if your family has lived in Edo for three generations. Well, I can claim to be an Edokko. We had a perfectly prosperous life. But then when I was seven my father died and our fortune declined. That year I was adopted by the Hamada house in Yoshicho.[1]

Sada's mother's family, the Kogumas, lived right in the heart of downtown Edo, a couple of hundred yards from Nihonbashi, 'the bridge of Japan', from which all distances in the empire are measured to this day, in an area called Ryogai-cho – the Money Changers' District. It was a bustling, lively area. The city's fish market spread along the quays, where the fishermen unloaded their slimy catch, and spilled through a labyrinth of back alleys lined with tiny shops and stalls pressed roof to roof. Nearby were the great white-walled warehouses where the hugely wealthy rice, grain and sugar merchants stored their goods. There, for generations, the family had run the Echizen-ya, a large store which incorporated a currency exchange and a book shop. They were town officials, pillars of the local community.

Sada's mother, Otaka, was a notable beauty. In her youth she had worked for a time in the mansion of a *daimyo*, a provincial lord. There she acquired airs and graces and an aristocratic style. Sada's father, Hisajiro Koyama, was such a placid, saintly man that he was nicknamed 'Buddha'. When he married Otaka, he moved into the family house and eventually inherited the business.

We do not know exactly when they married, but it must have been not long after 1853, that momentous year when the American Commodore Perry arrived with his Black Ships off the coast of Japan and demanded that Japan open her doors to foreign trade and friendship. Suddenly everything turned topsy-turvy.

For more than 200 years Japan had been a closed society under the strict rule of the Tokugawa shoguns. They had established peace after years of civil war, but only by establishing a system of extremely tight controls. There was a rigid class system with the samurai military at the top, from the highest-ranking daimyo to the humblest foot soldier, followed by peasants, who performed the essential task of producing food, then craftsmen. Merchants, who produced nothing and were thus regarded as parasites, were at the bottom of the social pecking order, though many had become hugely wealthy.

To ensure that no subversive ideas entered and disturbed the delicate balance, the shoguns sealed off the country from the outside world. It was a capital offence for Japanese to leave the country or for foreigners to visit. There were no wheeled vehicles and no gunpowder. Isolated from the rest of the world, Japan developed a sparkling hot-house culture – the culture of the floating world of courtesans and geisha, celebrated in woodblock prints and the plays of the kabuki theatre. Only one small window was left open – the remote southern port of Nagasaki, where Chinese junks brought their goods and a small enclave of Dutch merchants was allowed to live and trade. Through this porthole, news of some of the developments transforming the outside world filtered in.

By the mid-nineteenth century, the country was ripe for change. The merchants had grown rich and frustrated at not being able to change their status and the military government had turned into a rambling bureaucracy. The samurai still strutted around carrying two swords, but most had little or no experience of using them for anything except sport. They spent most of their time balancing account books.

The great powers of the West, ceaselessly looking for new territories to conquer and new areas in which to extend their influence, had long been interested in the fabled riches of this closed country; they wanted to prise open the treasure box.

Commodore Perry's Black Ships were the foot in the door. Perry was an emissary from the American President, Millard Fillmore. His mission was to open Japan to trade and diplomatic contact with the West, by force if necessary. He demanded that the shogun should allow foreigners to live and trade in the country and open some ports to foreign ships.

Soon there was an unstoppable flood of red-haired barbarians on Japanese soil. Their presence destabilised the whole crumbling system. It proved the spark that set the country aflame. Over the following years there was growing unrest. Young disaffected provincial samurai saw their opportunity to rid themselves once and for all of the decadent shogun and his hated government. Finally in 1868 the shogunate was overthrown in a coup d'état. That November, Emperor Meiji – only fifteen years old at the time – came down in a grand procession from Kyoto and was established with much pomp as the figurehead of a new government, dominated by those same samurai. Up until then he had been a purely ceremonial figure living in seclusion in his vast echoing palace. Thereafter too, he remained a figurehead with no real power. Edo was renamed Tokyo ('Eastern Capital') and became the official capital of the country.

On the other side of the world the American Civil War was not long over and a railroad had finally been completed linking the country coast to coast. Queen Victoria had been on the throne of Britain for over thirty years and was nearing the middle of her long reign. Abroad the Western powers were grabbing more and more colonies and at home life was being transformed by the industrial revolution, with Britain in the lead. Everyone was arguing over Charles Darwin's controversial book, *On the Origin of Species*, Count Lev Nikolaevich Tolstoy was completing *War and Peace* and Fyodor Dostoevsky had just published *The Idiot*.

Burning with enthusiasm, Japan's new rulers set about creating a country that could deal with the West on equal terms. The original plan was to absorb the new technology so as to beat the West at its own game. But people soon became seduced by the wonderful things that the West and its industrial revolution had to offer. The slogan of the day was 'Civilisation and Enlightenment'; and everyone was in hot pursuit.

Young Japanese steamed off on P & O liners to Europe and America to study and foreign experts came to teach – British engineers to share the secrets of the industrial revolution, French to explain their system of law and military affairs, Germans to teach the Japanese about their parliamentary system and Americans to teach commerce, agriculture and technology. A British engineer arrived to oversee the building of the first railway, the Tokyo-Yokohama line. Within a couple of years after the coup there was a postal service, a telegraph service, a banking system and a growing, well-equipped modern conscript army.

All this, however, was hugely expensive. Inflation soared and there were cripplingly heavy taxes. For many of the established families who had prospered under the old order, the changes spelled ruin. Among them were the Koyamas.

In 1871 Otaka discovered she was pregnant again with her twelfth child. It was the worst possible time. The new banking system had put currency traders out of business. To make matters worse, according to one version of the story, the head clerk had been caught embezzling funds. Things were so bad that Buddha was considering selling the ancestral business. Added to all this, the couple were middle aged by now. They already had eleven mouths to feed.

Little Sada was born on 18 July 1871. For a few years Buddha managed to keep the family together. They moved to a grander part of town and set up a pawnbroking business, providing cash to impoverished aristocrats who had lost their privileges after the change of government. They still had money from their previous business and for a while were able to keep up their lifestyle.

The stories of Sada's earliest years are a little confusing. According to one version of events, by the time Sada was four, the family was already feeling the pinch. Daughters were expendable, little more than commodities. They sent her off to the Hamada geisha house to work as a maid. Not long after, there was a plan to bundle her off to yet another household. But the little girl had a mind of her own.

In later years, when she was sitting over sake with her daughter, Tomiji, Sada liked to recount the story of her narrow escape. One of her brothers, Sokichi, had been apprenticed to a metal sculptor called Matsuo Kano and it had been arranged that he would marry Kano's daughter that winter. Little Sada too was sent to stay at the Kano house.

There were two boys there who were her playmates. The five-year-old was lively and full of fun. But the older one, who was ten, was rather dull and quiet. One day all three were splashing about in the bath together. The older boy suddenly said, 'You're going to be my wife, little Sada.' Young though she was, she knew very well what that meant. Horrified at the idea of marrying such a dull boy, she ran away from the house first thing next morning.

But where was she to run to? In the bustling thoroughfares and back alleys of Nihonbashi, full of fishmongers yelling their wares, the child was completely lost. She spent all day wandering the streets until she finally spotted the dark wooden walls of the Hamada house. The Kanos may have been customers there; most likely it was Kamekichi, the proprietress of the house, who had arranged the 'marriage' with the intention of selling the child on and recuperating her costs. The Kanos sent a messenger to bring the little girl back. But she clung onto Kamekichi's hand and refused to leave.

Her granddaughter Hatsu has a picture of her at that age, around four or five, with some of her brothers and sisters. She looks rather poised, confident and very determined. She is an exquisite little girl with a delicate heart-shaped face and none of the plumpness of childhood. Her hair is swept back in the traditional child's style, a complicated knot, oiled and held in place with combs. She wears a multi-layered flower-patterned kimono; the dark satin under-collar is visible at the neck.

In later years, anxious to conceal the ignominy of her upbringing, Sada insisted that 'my mother loved music and sent me to have dancing lessons from the age of four'.[2] But in fact there is a contract which shows that her father had entered into an agreement with Kamekichi which was really a disguised form of indentured servitude.[3] This did not reflect on Buddha's reputation as a good man, for in those days there was nothing unusual about such a course of action.

Officially Sada was never 'sold'. The sale of persons had been outlawed in 1872 by a new government eager to appear as Western and modern as possible. But in fact the law changed nothing but the terminology. Sada's family 'borrowed' a sizeable amount of money from the Hamada house in exchange for their daughter. The process and the sum involved was probably much the same as Algernon Mitford (the grandfather of the famous Mitford sisters, who spent many years in Japan) described in a book published in 1871:

Children destined to be trained as singers are usually bought when they are five or six years old, a likely child fetching from about thirty five to fifty shillings; the purchaser undertakes the education of his charge and brings the little thing up as his own child.[4]

No doubt the little girl shed bitter tears, sent away from her mother and family at such a tender and impressionable age. But of course there was nothing she could do and nothing she could say. She was part of a culture where one took the worst life had to throw at one and bore it in silence.

When Sada was seven, Buddha died. Otaka had no idea how to cope. By now the family had fallen deep into poverty. Perhaps before his death there might have been some thought of eventually redeeming the little girl. But instead she was officially taken into the Hamada geisha house as Kamekichi's adopted daughter.

Just as Norma Jean Baker became Marilyn Monroe and took on a glamorous new persona along with the name, so when a child joined the ranks of the geisha she took a new name to mark her new station in life. It is an apt comparison in more ways than that. For the geisha of those days really were like the movie stars or rock stars of today. They were showgirls who danced, sang and entertained the privileged and wealthy few at exclusive teahouse parties: the word 'gei-sha' literally means 'arts person'. But the most beautiful were also stars whose names were on everyone's lips. Ordinary folk who could not afford to enjoy their company could buy woodblock prints or hand-tinted albumen photographs which depicted them. Townswomen emulated their fashions and hairstyles and everyone avidly followed their exploits, which were endlessly recorded in the gossip columns of the day.

Yet no one quite knew what went on at those private parties; and people had little doubt that the geisha were 'no better than they should be'. It was very similar to Europe and America in that same licentious yet prudish Victorian era, where everyone admired and adored the great actresses of the day but, as the old song went, would never dream of putting their own daughter on the stage.

The Yoshicho geisha district which was to be Sada's home for many years was a bustling community of over 300 geisha. The streets were crammed with two-storey wooden houses with steep tiled roofs and bamboo shutters, packed roof to roof along shadowy alleys. Cutting through the area were thoroughfares where hundreds of rickshaws clattered madly along on metal wheels, while their drivers bawled warnings to pedestrians who got in their way. There were streets of geisha houses, where the geisha lived; *ryoriya* teahouses where they entertained over a formal dinner; *machiai* 'meeting houses' where customers went to relax after dinner with a favourite geisha; and streets of tiny shops devoted to geisha paraphernalia – clogs, kimono fabrics, shamisens, fans, combs, cosmetics and hair pomade. In the evening rickshaws crowded at street corners and boats bumped against each other on the canals, waiting to take geisha to their first assignations of the evening.

In those days Tokyo was a city of waterways, a Venice of the East. Canals, rivers and streams lined with willows and cherry trees criss-crossed the city. Boats of every imaginable shape and size – pleasure boats with pointed roofs and horn-shaped prows, great square-bottomed boats with awnings and canopies, sculls, gondolas, the odd paddle steamer, canal boats loaded with goods – bobbed about, transporting rice, fish, vegetables and other produce and carrying passengers of every station in life.

Teahouses had their own boathouses where they kept flotillas of boats. Of an evening pleasure boats would set out laden with geisha and their customers, with brightly coloured paper lanterns hung around the edges of the roof. The plinking of three-stringed shamisens, beating of small drums, reedy singing and merry laughter would float across the water as they drifted by. There were also many smaller boats where inside the makeshift cabin, behind closed paper shoji screens, one might make out two shadows, silhouetted in the yellow lamp light.

Many powerful and wealthy men frequented the Yoshicho geisha houses. The district was in the shadow of the Imperial Palace, a rickshaw ride away from the government offices and the Imperial Debating Hall where the country's new rulers met to argue and plan. A few minutes' walk away from the Yoshicho district were the great merchant houses and currency exchanges of Nihonbashi, where Sada was born. The Tokyo Stock Exchange, opened in 1878, was just around the corner. And in those days when great men wanted to relax, the obvious place was their favourite teahouse.

Today the Hamada house is the only teahouse left in the district. It is still run by distant descendants of Kamekichi, though it has been rebuilt and moved a few blocks to a different location. From outside it is a grand understated mansion in the Japanese style with sand-coloured walls and large forbidding wooden gates. Stepping stones lead through a small garden with neatly trimmed trees, a tiny pond and a couple of stone lanterns. Inside are enormous silent rooms lined with fragrant tatami matting.

In Sada's time, the sumptuous rooms were walled with painted screens covered in gold leaf, which reflected the smoky yellow flame of oil lamps and tapers. There powerful men lounged, chatting, laughing, arguing and tippling sake. When the geisha rose to their feet to sing and dance they clapped their hands to the music or jumped up to show off their own dancing skills.

But while the customers were at play, the geisha were working. As modern day Yoshicho geisha put it:

It was a beautiful dream. As the men left, they'd say, 'I'll come and see you tomorrow.' And we'd say, 'I'll be waiting for you.' In the old days everyone knew it was a game. We'd all say how much we loved them. That was the spell we wove. It was nothing to do with love really.

In the evening it was all glamour. Then in the daytime the geisha took off their make-up and the harsh reality became visible.

Most children who were sent to geisha houses as indentured servants spent their early years dusting, laundering and scrubbing floors until their hands were chapped and raw. They were the lowliest of the low, slapped and beaten for the smallest offence. But Sada was lucky.

'When I was taken in to the Hamada house, it was as a daughter. Even though I was a geisha, I was different from ordinary geisha.'[5] Thus she told her tale. Kamekichi was a perceptive woman who realised that she was an exceptional child. With the proper training she could be a star, the most sought-after, high-earning geisha of the city. She gave little Sada all the love and attention that the child had never had from her real mother and Sada was devoted to her in return.

When she took Sada in as her adopted daughter Kamekichi was thirty-five. The female playwright and theatre critic Shigure Hasegawa, born in the same Nihonbashi district as Sada just eight years later, in 1879, described her as 'a woman with a very powerful personality – tough, strong-willed and rather mannish. She was quite haughty because she came from a good family'.[6] In her day she had been celebrated in the geisha world for her beautiful singing voice. She had been married once but was now widowed. She had, however, been provided – by her husband or perhaps a patron – with the means to buy a property and set up her own geisha house.

Sada told the story thus:

> My adopted mother, Kame Hamada, used to serve as a maid in a nobleman's mansion so she had very high standards. Count Hirobumi Ito and other great men were her patrons. I was brought up very strictly as if I were her own child. I was an uncontrollable tomboy. I wore boys' kimonos and straw sandals just like a boy. Every day I ran off to the ruined mansion where the Meiji Theatre is now. I climbed trees, played tag, jumped around and played with the boys.[7]

It was a struggle to tame such a wild and wilful little girl. But Kamekichi had high ambitions for her. She sent her off to teachers to learn the skills that would make her a star geisha without quenching her spark and spirit. Little by little the child began to absorb the coquettish tones of the Edokko geisha. She learnt how to bewitch a man with a heavy-lidded sidelong glance, how to comport herself with languid elegance, how to chat flirtatiously and glide seductively in a kimono. She picked up the secrets of geisha make-up and coiffeur. She learnt etiquette and how to behave at banquets and weddings. She practised the games that are played at teahouse parties and memorised the words and melodies of the ditties, love songs and ballads of the geisha repertoire. She studied the musical instruments that geisha play – the small lacquered shoulder drum, the larger hand drum, and the banjo-like shamisen which is the geisha's characteristic instrument. She also learnt to perform the tea ceremony elegantly and to make exquisite flower arrangements.

But what Sada really loved was to dance. Every day she went to classes. When she got home, Kamekichi would make her demonstrate what she had learnt. She practised for hours. She had natural poise and grace. She learnt to move crisply, to strike a dramatic pose with precision and to express feeling through the most disciplined and economical of gestures. She learnt the different solo dances which form the geisha repertoire, many of which are taken from kabuki plays. Thus she became adept at telling a story through gesture and body language. It was a discipline as exacting as studying ballet.

By eight or nine Sada was attending banquets, tapping her little hand drum with childish solemnity and filling the drinkers' sake cups to the brim, spilling not a drop. In her butterfly-bright kimono, with her dainty gestures, precocious chit-chat and pretty face, she was the most delightful little creature imaginable. Among those who were charmed was Count Hirobumi Ito, a regular customer at the Hamada house and one of the most powerful men in the realm.

In the winter of 1883 at the age of twelve the child celebrated her debut as an *o-shaku*, literally 'a sake pourer', an apprentice geisha. She also received her first geisha name. From now on she was to be Ko-yakko or Little Yakko, named after a geisha called Yakko who had been one of the most adored in Tokyo. Kamekichi felt sure that Little Yakko would grow up to be as brilliant a star in her turn. But she was still a child with energy to spare and a wild tomboy. As she put it in later years, 'even then I carried on playing with boys whenever I had the chance, and messed about and didn't really concentrate on learning the geisha arts'.

The playwright Shigure Hasegawa remembered her thus:

She had a certain refinement which came from her samurai parents and this quality was nurtured by living in the Hamada house. She also had an innocence that was rare in the geisha world. She was straightforward and very focused. In fact she was a typical Edokko. She learnt all that from her adopted mother and with her support by the age of 14 was one of the most famous geisha in the city.[8]

25

In those days geisha were the heart of high society in Japan. An evening's entertainment would not have been complete without a bevy of geisha to bring sparkle and glitter to the occasion. At theatre openings and first nights, geisha were always invited. The role of a man's wife was entirely different. Her job was to be the matriarch, to stay at home and take care of the family and children. Decent women were not expected to be brilliant conversationalists or witty companions. They had no idea how to flirt; that would have been most unseemly.

It was accepted, however, that men needed charming companions to be seen on their arm at public occasions and for private amusement too. That was where the geisha came in. Many powerful men of the new government who had started out as rough provincial samurai had broken with convention and married their geisha lovers; and all of them had geisha mistresses. Count Ito, for one, was married to an ex-geisha named Umeko; when he later became prime minister, she was first lady of the realm. This gave the geisha a considerable degree of social cachet and at least the appearance of respectability.

The geisha, in fact, posed very serious competition to the faithful wife. As Alice M. Bacon, an American who lived in Tokyo, wrote in 1899:

Without true education or morals, but trained thoroughly in all the arts and accomplishments that please – witty, quick at repartee, pretty and always well-dressed – the geisha has proved a formidable rival for the demure quiet maiden of good family, who can only give her husband an unsullied name, silent obedience and faithful service all her life. The problem of the geisha and her fascination is a deep one in Japan.[9]

Kamekichi's plan for Sada – or Ko-yakko, as we must call her now – was that she should be the *crème de la crème*, the first among this élite group of geisha, groomed to be the brilliant companions of the country's most powerful men. But in order to do so, she would have to learn more than just the traditional geisha arts of dancing and singing.

In those days women's education was in its infancy. The first school for women had opened in 1870, and that was only for noblewomen. The idea of an ordinary woman – let alone a geisha – learning to read and write was outlandish. No matter how many powerful men they kept company with, geisha were still classed as the lowest of the low; romantic though they were, the geisha districts were effectively ghettos, separated from respectable society. For many years after Ko-yakko's time, right up until the end of World War II, many denizens of the entertainment industry – geisha and kabuki actors – were illiterate. Only the highest levels could read or write a billet-doux or compose a poem.

Certainly if Ko-yakko was to mix with the highest in the realm, it was a skill she would have to acquire. Perhaps the idea was sparked by Count Ito, a great progressive and an advocate of women's education. Perhaps it was Kamekichi's idea, or perhaps it was Ko-yakko herself. In any case Kamekichi sent her off to a local Shinto priest to be taught to read and to write beautifully with a brush. It was an extraordinary accomplishment. Geisha were expected to be modern, trendsetting women, but such a skill put her well ahead of the crowd.

From the moment when the Japanese set about their quest for Civilisation and Enlightenment, they had begun to study foreign ways with an insatiable curiosity. A brilliant and handsome young samurai named Yukichi Fukuzawa was the leading advocate of Westernisation. Born in 1835, he had gone to the United States in 1860 as an interpreter on the shogunate's very first mission. He then went to Europe in 1862 and was in America again in 1867.

That same year he published a ground-breaking book entitled *The Clothing, Food and Dwellings of the West*. It was a manual of Western dress and Western ways. Printed on woodblocks, there was page after page of detailed drawings of shirts, undershirts, long johns, trousers with braces, Sherlock Holmes-style overcoats, umbrellas and hats with notes explaining what they were and how to wear them. He also explained how to eat Western style with a knife and fork, described typical Western homes, explained the functions of a washstand, mirror and chamberpot and stressed the importance of learning to consult one's watch rather than listening out for the temple bell to check the time as the Japanese had always done.

The book was a best-seller and hugely influential. According to the *Tokio Times* of 27 January 1877:

. . . in the 2nd and 3rd years of Meiji [1869–1870], the demand for foreign goods remarkably increased. Those who formerly looked upon them with contempt changed their minds and even dressed in foreign clothes. Our males adopted the European style. They put on fine tall hats instead of wearing large cues [topknots] on their heads, and took to carrying sticks after discarding their swords. They dressed in coats of the English fashion and trowsers of the American. They would only eat from tables and nothing would satisfy them but French cookery.[10]

By 1869, trendy Tokyo samurai were rushing to the first Western-style barber in town to have their pomaded topknots chopped off in favour of the fashionable new 'random crop' look. Soon no self-respecting man about town would be seen with his hair in a topknot. Gold watches, diamond rings and Western-style black umbrellas were all the rage. Officials sported beards and moustaches like Western diplomats and in 1872 trousers, frock coats and top hats became the prescribed mode for courtiers and government officers and standard business attire.

That was the men. Women too were gripped with curiosity about the extraordinary 'civilised' and 'enlightened' clothes of the Westerners. Geisha, being by profession bolder and more flamboyant than other women, were the first to try the extraordinary new fashions. In the 1860s a geisha from the Maruyama district of Nagasaki created a sensation by being photographed in a flouncy Western frock and crinoline. In 1872 a Nihonbashi geisha made news by 'pouring sake for customers with her hair in Nanking pigtails and wearing a western dress'.[11]

A bevy of tailors, mainly in Yokohama, turned out lace-trimmed floor-length gowns with bustles and the padding and under-ribbing, a sort of half-crinoline, required to shape the bustle and hold it in place. There were even corsets produced in Japan to enable a slim Japanese woman to attain the requisite hourglass figure. Soon geisha were to be seen bustling about the teahouses and playing their shamisens in flouncy décolletée gowns with huge bustles, gold earrings, bracelets and high-heeled leather shoes, which they sometimes wore even on the tatami matting.

Ko-yakko, being an advanced young geisha, often wore Western clothes. As Kamekichi laced her into her stays, she must have yearned for her soft, comfortable many-layered kimonos. Like other modern women, she abandoned the rigid helmet-like pomaded traditional hairstyles and adopted the looser *sokuhatsu* look, with the hair bunched into a bun on top of the head and framing the face in a flattering way. She continued to wear her hair in this style for much of her life.

Her extraordinary education did not stop at reading and writing. She secretly took lessons in judo, very fashionable at the time. She would summon the *hakoya*, the boy employed to carry her shamisen, take him along to a grassy, unfrequented area, give him a tip and then practise her throws on him, barking war cries in the approved judo manner. She also became a dab hand at billiards. Many a wealthy man, entranced by her lovely face poised studiously over the green baize, failed to pot his balls and laughingly conceded defeat. In fact she was the least ladylike of geisha.

At the age of fourteen she began riding. Until the coming of the Western barbarians, horses had been only for samurai. Japanese women would never dream of being seen on a horse. When Western women were seen trotting side saddle around the streets of Yokohama in their bonnets and long riding skirts, it caused a sensation. Woodblock print artists got their palettes out to depict this outlandish sight.

Ko-yakko learnt to ride at the stables in Honjo, the wild moorlands on the far side of the River Sumida. She became an excellent horsewoman. She was particularly skilled at *horobiki*, a traditional sport in which she would gallop so fast that her long cape flew out behind her like a banner without ever touching the ground. A few years later, as the gossip columnists of the day reported with great excitement, she even took part in professional races. It was another mark of how unconventional and progressive she was.

And thus it was that one day, riding across the Honjo grasslands, she met the handsome young student, Momosuké Iwasaki. The day after their encounter, Ko-yakko set out for Keio University bearing a gift of particularly delicious bean jam cakes, to thank her benefactor. Perhaps she went with Kamekichi, who surely would have kept a close watch over her valuable young charge. Or perhaps she slipped away under the pretext of going to a dancing class.

Keio was Japan's first university. It had been founded in 1858 by Yukichi Fukuzawa, the great proponent of Western ways, who was then just twenty-three years old. His intention was to train up a generation of modern young men. In 1868 it was declared a fully fledged university and established on a spectacular cliff in the south of the city, near the mouth of the River Sumida and the clam beds of Tokyo Bay. The first classes at the new location took place as the shogun's forces made their last desperate stand against the imperial army a few miles away, on the other side of the city. Keio was a prime symbol of the new, enlightened era.

There the first students, most of good samurai stock, swaggered up and down the steep stone steps which led from the street to the campus on the hilltop above. From their caps and cropped hair to their trousers and leather shoes, they represented the hope and pride of the new Japan. They pored over their books in the certainty that they were destined to be the leaders of society, guaranteed success, wealth and power in their adult lives.

Other fourteen-year-old girls might have been intimidated by such bumptious young fellows. But Ko-yakko was used to the company of men. Wandering around the grand Western-style brick and stone buildings of the campus, she sought out Momosuké. She offered him the cakes and apologised prettily, with an irresistible mixture of little girl bashfulness and artless coquettishness. She had been so flustered, she said, that she had failed to thank him properly for saving her. Strolling the streets below the campus, the two began to tell each other their stories.

'My family lost their money,' she prattled in her high-pitched Edokko chirrup. 'So I had to become a geisha. My real name is Sada.'

Momosuké confided that he really wanted to be a poet; but he had had to give up that dream and think about a more practical career. He had to make money to support his family. Momosuké was familiar with hardship. Born in 1868, he was four years older than she. He came from a small village near Kawagoe, a country town many hours by horse-drawn carriage from Tokyo. There his family had been village elders and prosperous farmers for 300 years. But in the economic chaos in the last decades of the shoguns' rule they had lost most of their fortune. As always in Japan, what remained of the family land and fortune was inherited by the eldest son. The second son – Momosuké's father, Kiichi – received nothing but a few paddy fields.

Kiichi was a rather impractical scholarly type, who much preferred sitting at home with his brush perfecting his calligraphy to breaking his back in the fields. Momosuké's mother, a capable woman who, as it happens, was also called Sada, opened a shop to support the growing family; but they were frequently on the verge of bankruptcy.

Momosuké was a smart, ambitious child who excelled at his studies. Under the system of the time, at the age of fifteen his schooling was due to end. But a neighbour, a lower-ranking keeper of the town office, had noticed the boy. *Au fait* with the exciting developments in the capital, he made a revolutionary suggestion to Kiichi. Instead of setting the boy to work in the fields, he should give him a chance in life. He should have him apply to the country's most up-to-the-minute institute of Western learning, Keio. That way he would be in a position to make real money. Kiichi demurred that he could not afford the fees but his older brother, the head of the family, volunteered to come up with the money. The boy passed the formidable entrance examinations with ease.

Momosuké was a cool, rather reserved young man. Fresh from the Kawagoe backwoods, he might have been expected to be full of excitement when he found himself in the great city of Tokyo. But he was far too assured for that. He strolled down the magnificent Ginza Street, the pride of the city, where all the buildings were of red brick or stone with glass windows and curtains just like in the West. He even boarded one of the horse-drawn trams which clattered along metal tracks, driven by natty young men in waistcoats, trousers and caps. He observed carriages and rickshaws rattling up and down, women in bustles and bonnets and men in trousers and overcoats. He took it all in, but he was far too phlegmatic to get worked up about it. Even when the Ginza's much-hailed eighty-five electric street lights – Japan's first experiment with the latest new invention, electricity – flickered on in the evening, he was not mightily impressed.

Lodged in one of the Keio dormitories, he had to suffer the bullying of the arrogant young samurai who were his fellow students. There were frequent brawls. But the willowy, delicate-looking farmer's son had a good pair of fists and soon earned their respect. He became known as the 'pretty boy from Kawagoe who is tougher than he looks'.

Two or three times the ravishing young geisha went to visit the gentlemanly farmer's son at Keio. It was very difficult to avoid being seen. Even then, as her daughter Tomiji recalled, 'Ko-yakko was a very famous geisha. So people noticed her and talked about the fact she had gone to Keio.'[12] Sometimes she invited him to visit her at the teahouses where she worked. In those days geisha often invited impoverished students to carouse with them late at night, once the formal parties were over and the customers had been packed off home to their wives. The students only had to pay for their drinks and sometimes not even for those. Geisha loved the company of these dashing young gallants. They also knew that the young men were destined to become the country's élite. As such, they would undoubtedly patronise those teahouses where they had been treated so kindly. It was well worth striking up a relationship early.

But for Ko-yakko it was far more than that. As the others grew more and more drunk, she would sit longer than was proper with the quiet young student with his soft voice and steady gaze. They chattered about childish things – her classes, his studies, their hopes and dreams. Ko-yakko taught him the foolish games that geisha play. They sang, they danced, they laughed. In each other's company life seemed more vivid than it ever had before. They did not care what they did so long as they could be together. It became harder and harder to be apart.

For Ko-yakko, it was not only his beauty that drew her to him. He had a purity and untutored sincerity. Until then she had known only the practised compliments of men old enough to be her father. Here was a young man who knew nothing of the geisha world of play acting. When he told her in his artless way how pretty she was, she knew his words were from the heart. As for Momosuké, he had never met anyone as exquisitely lovely and exuberant as her, and so full of life. She was on the cusp of adulthood, an enchanting combination of innocent child and coquette, with a streak of barely concealed wildness lurking just beneath the surface. They were two children in a world of adults.

At first they did not understand what was happening. They burned with the ardour of a new and unknown passion. But whenever they became aware of sober reality, they remembered that their relationship could not last. Their lives were not their own. The best they could hope for was that when many years had passed, when they were no longer the property of others but could control their destinies, their paths might cross again.

Maybe they even found an opportunity to sequester themselves in a small room in a teahouse somewhere. But that would have been very difficult indeed to organise. Ko-yakko was old enough to know that her virginity was not hers to give away. Kamekichi had plans for this young woman in whom she had invested so much and those did not involve a poor farmer's son, even if he did have a great future mapped out for him.

2

THE PRIME MINISTER'S FAVOURITE
1885—1888

One of the mementoes that Sada's granddaughter, Hatsu, treasures is a mysterious hand-written document. It is a yellowing piece of paper, handmade and rather fine, dated 20 July 1883, Sada's twelfth year, when she was on the verge of starting her geisha life under the name Ko-yakko. Brushed in sweeping characters in faded black ink is a single cryptic word: *toranai*, 'I will not take'. Then come four names, surnames only: Fujita; Inoue; Utsumi; Ito. Rounding it off is the full name Osuzu Hasegawa. Sada, Hatsu explains, gave the document to Tomiji who passed it on to her. The meaning too has passed down through the family.

The men gathered at the teahouse the day the document was written were some of the most powerful in Japan. Denzaburo Fujita was a hugely wealthy industrialist from Osaka, reputedly ruthless and unscrupulous. He had recently founded a business empire with interests in mining, railways, textiles and electric power. Kaoru Inoue was a name to conjure with, a high-flying statesman, financier and economist and the lifelong friend of Count Hirobumi Ito. Tadakatsu Utsumi has not made ripples in history, but he must have been wealthy and powerful to have kept such company.

The last name was Ito himself, by then senior councillor in the government and the most powerful man in the land. Osuzu Hasegawa, the proprietress of the teahouse where the document was drawn up, added her signature as witness.

As for the word *toranai*, it was code. According to Japanese practice the last signature is always that of the highest ranking person of the group, to whom the others yield precedence. *Toranai* was a pledge by the first three signatories that they would not 'take' young Ko-yakko. They relinquished her to their superior in rank.

Ko-yakko was growing into a strikingly beautiful young woman. She was long-legged and coltish, like a dancer, and in certain lights her hair had a reddish tinge. With her straight nose and extraordinary eyes, she looked not quite Japanese. There was an alluring alienness in her appearance. Rumours began to circulate that she had Russian blood in her veins.

Perhaps, people said, that explained her fiery temperament. By now she was becoming known outside the small teahouse world. More and more customers asked for her by name to entertain and dance for them at their teahouse parties. No matter how powerful they were, no matter how high their status, she was not in awe of them. While other geisha fawned, she did exactly as she pleased. She said what she thought and talked to the highest men in the realm on equal terms. If something annoyed her, no matter how important the gathering, she would get up and leave without stopping to think of the consequences. But such a delicious lack of artifice, such extravagantly giddy behaviour, only made her all the more bewitching.[1]

Kamekichi, being a shrewd woman, was no doubt well aware of Ko-yakko's secret meetings with the dashing young student from Keio University. From her point of view there was one unshakeable condition. The relationship had to remain platonic. It was entirely counter to the geisha code to sleep with someone who was not paying for it. That is not to suggest that geisha were prostitutes. Far from it. They were far too hard-headed to devalue themselves by making themselves available to any but the highest bidder.

She lectured her young charge on the geisha precepts. Ko-yakko took these to heart and later repeated them to her contemporary, the playwright Shigure Hasegawa:

Never sell yourself cheap. Be true to your patron. Keep yourself pure. Always surround yourself with beauty and luxury and avoid people and places where there is neither. When entertaining customers, make sure you are smarter than them but never let them know. Always seem foolish and capricious. And never argue. No one likes a geisha who disputes or talks about intellectual things. Never forget that this is not a solemn business. Your job is to entertain. This is the world of play.[2]

Ko-yakko's virginity was a priceless commodity. As she reached puberty, Kamekichi pondered the all-important question: who should perform her deflowering? She had invested a huge amount of money in her young charge. She had bought her for a large sum. She had supported her throughout her childhood and teenage years, paying for her education, kimono, food and housing, giving her pocket money and taking care of her needs. *Mizuage* – the youthful geisha's formal deflowering – was the primary way in which the proprietress of a geisha house recouped her investment. It generated an enormous amount of money, for the deflowerer was required to pay a fee equivalent to the cost of a small house for the privilege. If the girl was alluring enough to entice someone of the highest prominence, it could also be an excellent provision towards her future. The chances were great that her deflowerer would continue to be her *danna* or patron, providing her with financial support and an indispensable network of connections. This was what all geisha hoped for, to be the mistress of a powerful man.

There were plenty of contenders to initiate Ko-yakko into adulthood. But she was so unusual and irresistible that Kamekichi thought it worth approaching the most powerful man in the realm – her old friend and patron Hirobumi Ito. Ito had been observing the coming of age of the exquisite little girl with great interest. He was also well known as a lover of women and particularly of geisha. No doubt Kamekichi had been cultivating his interest in her charge for some time.

By the time she was twelve, he had staked his claim. That was the real meaning of the yellowing document which the four friends drew up. As for the girl whose virginity was the prize they were bargaining over, no one would have dreamt of asking her what she thought.

Of all the dashing young men of Meiji who battled to overthrow the shogunate and dedicated themselves with patriotic enthusiasm to building the new Japan, Ito was the most colourful, brilliant and successful. Like Ko-yakko, he had started life on the margins of society. He went on to rise through the ranks in a way that would have been unthinkable a few decades earlier under the rigid rule of the shoguns.

When he entered Ko-yakko's life he was in his forties, approaching the pinnacle of his career. He was a short, Napoleonic figure, a strutting bewhiskered playboy and notorious libertine. In photographs he looks forceful and charismatic, despite the stiff Victorian poses. He has a fleshy, sensual face with a broad forehead, high cheekbones and narrow eyes that gaze intently into the distance. His hair is immaculately parted and slicked into place and he has a straggling goatee-like beard framing his full lips. In some photographs he is dressed like a Victorian potentate in a frock coat, high-collared shirt and bow tie. In others he wears full dress uniform, covered in gold and brocade with a ribbon across his chest. But for all his air of weightiness and self-importance, there is an unmistakable twinkle in his eye.

A young woman named Umeko Tsuda, recently returned from the United States, described meeting him at a ball in 1883. He 'came up to me and said, his eyes twinkling with merriment, "Who am I? Can you guess?" I shook my head. He repeated again, teasingly, "But who is it?" Finally he said, smiling, "I am Ito."' It is a perfect evocation of this irrepressible flirt and charmer.

Tsuda had been sent to spend her childhood in a puritan household in Georgetown, Washington DC, and at the time when she returned spoke no Japanese. She was therefore the ideal person to be the governess and English tutor for Ito's children. She went to live with the family but was shocked to the depths of her puritan soul at his behaviour. 'Mr Ito, in spite of his foreign ideas, is far from being moral himself,' she wrote to her American 'mother'. 'I know *he spends nights out [sic].'*[3]

Ito was born Shunsuke Hayashi in 1841 deep among rolling hills and golden paddy fields not far from what is now the city of Hiroshima. His father was a farmer. But while he was still a child the family moved to the castle town of Hagi in the province of Choshu, soon to become one of the centres of resistance against the shogunate. There he joined a samurai household. Eventually the boy was adopted into the Ito family and given samurai status and a new name.

By eighteen he was a swashbuckling young warrior who had already tasted blood in the struggle against the shogunate. He had become a follower of a charismatic young thinker and revolutionary named Shoin Yoshida, who had been in prison for his activities and was under house arrest. At the age of twenty-nine Yoshida was executed. Ito was one of four representatives of the rebel province who, after much pleading, were allowed to retrieve the body and give it a proper burial.

In 1863, when he was twenty-two, Ito was one of five young activists who smuggled themselves aboard a ship bound for London in defiance of the shogunal edict which punished foreign travel by death. When they changed ships at Shanghai, they could not speak enough English to explain their mission. They were mistaken for deckhands and ended up spending the four-month journey manning the pumps, spreading the sails and swabbing the decks. They suffered terrible sea sickness and could barely stomach the diet of salt beef, stale biscuits and sugary tea. When they arrived at Gravesend, they 'looked like hungry crows', according to a Japanese report.

Their samurai topknots, two swords and broad hakama skirts had drawn crowds in Shanghai. So they cut their hair and took to wearing Western clothes in order to look less outlandish. They settled down to study at University College in London and lodged with the professor of chemistry there, Alexander William Williamson, in Chalk Farm. They also visited museums and galleries and inspected the factories and huge shipyards of industrial revolution Britain.

Less than six months later, Ito was leafing through a copy of *The Times* when he saw with horror that his home province had fired on foreign ships steaming through the Shimonoseki Straits. By now he was fully aware that Japan could not possibly defeat the overwhelming military might of the West. A fleet of British, French, American and Dutch warships was about to set sail to attack the town of Shimonoseki in retaliation. Ito and Inoue hurriedly packed their bags and set sail at top speed for home. They wanted to warn their compatriots of the hopelessness of resistance and to try and mediate. Unfortunately their efforts were in vain.

While the Americans were playing out their civil war across the Pacific, Japan launched into its own fully fledged civil war. Ito was one of the rebellion's natural leaders and played a key part in the battles to topple the shogunate. After the Meiji Restoration, with the rebel samurai in power under the titular leadership of the Emperor, he rose with extraordinary speed through the ranks. It was a tribute to his brilliance, undoubted courage and unshakeable determination to make Japan into a great nation, combined with good connections and a dash of luck. He married his geisha lover, Umeko, who had been his loyal support throughout the struggles, risking death more than once to hide him from the shogun's troops. It was a time when all the old taboos were being overthrown; in any case he was of lowly birth himself.

By 1880 he was senior councillor and the most powerful man in the realm. In 1885 the councillors put in place the beginnings of a modern parliamentary system. It was an epoch-making time. The whole future of the country was being discussed and shaped. Ito was appointed Japan's first prime minister and was called upon to form a cabinet. He was far more powerful than the title of 'prime minister' suggests, for he was answerable only to the Emperor and the oligarchy of whom he was the kingpin. It was to be several years before the country held its first elections. He was an unelected potentate, commander-in-chief of the Japanese Empire.

A crucial step in the shaping of the new Japan was the drafting of a constitution in preparation for the country's first elections. Ito was entrusted with the job. When the *toranai* document was signed, he had just returned from a year in Europe, mainly in Austria and Germany, studying their constitutions. He concluded that the Prussian model, as drawn up by the Iron Chancellor, Otto von Bismarck, was most suitable for Japan. It provided for a showcase parliament and monarch but left the real power firmly in the hands of the bureaucrats – Ito and his colleagues. From 1886 onwards, he sequestered himself in one of his seaside villas with his most trusted aides to work on the document.

He also played a key part in developing a peerage system, which had been established a year earlier. Umeko Tsuda, who was working for Ito as a governess, wrote about how confusing it was when people who had been plain Mr So-and-so one day suddenly became Count This or Marquis That the next. Thus Ito the farmer's son became Count Ito. He rose yet higher in rank and ended his days a prince.

Ito had two very different sides to his personality. In public he was pompous, arrogant and inordinately proud of himself and his achievements. He liked to hold court in his brocade dress uniform, his chest covered in medals, a fat Havana cigar firmly wedged in his stubby fingers. But off duty he was happiest among ordinary working people such as he had once been himself. Most of all he loved the company of geisha. 'By nature, I am content with little and give absolutely no thought to saving money,' he said. 'I have no wish to live in a splendid house and so have no urge to heap up wealth. What I like best is a geisha companion to entertain me after work.'[4] Then he could relax and enjoy himself like a schoolboy. While geisha fluttered around him, he would regale them with an endless flow of improvised songs. He particularly liked the ditty, 'When eager lovers get together like this – a simple four mat room, no noise except the kettle boiling – they seesaw like two pine needles in the wind!'

Finally, having set his sights on a particular young woman, he would burst into 'Oh, what a boor and nuisance are you!' The geisha knew very well that it was time to slip out of the room and leave him alone with the one who had taken his fancy. That was the Ito Ko-yakko knew.[5]

Ever since he had first spotted the exquisite little Sada, pouring sake and dancing with childish gravity, Ito had always asked for her to entertain at his parties. Now he took to demanding that she visit him at his villa too. On fine days he would send a rickshaw to pick her up from the Hamada house. The middle-aged prime minister and the pretty teenager would take a boat from Yokohama and sail along the bay to Natsushima, 'Summer Island'.

Today there is a factory where the villa used to be. But in Ito's day it was entirely unspoilt, an undiscovered place where he could enjoy seclusion and privacy. A line of pine trees stretched along the shore. There fishermen set out in their boats or sat all day mending their nets. The tranquil waters lapped at the edge of his garden and rippled clear and blue across to the small islands covered in trees which dotted the other side of the bay.

Ito's summer house was made up of three or four cottages, some thatched, some tiled, surrounding a small courtyard-like garden. Inside, polished corridors led from one to the next. In summer the heavy wooden doors which made up the outer walls were stored away out of sight. The rooms became pavilions with nothing but slender pillars supporting the heavy roofs. Cool breezes wafted through, jangling the wind bells which hung from the eaves.

There, one day in 1886 when Ko-yakko was fifteen, Ito finally claimed his rights. She of course had no say in the matter. The negotiations had been between Kamekichi and Ito. Apart from the cryptic *toranai* document, all the evidence that Ito was Ko-yakko's *mizuage danna* ('first lover') is word of mouth, stories remembered and recorded in later years. But as modern-day Yoshicho geisha say impatiently, that is not remotely surprising. It would be utterly unthinkable to keep an explicit written record of such a thing. Everything to do with geisha and their world was secret and hidden. It was a place of shadows where men who lived their lives in the public eye could retreat to relax. Nothing that went on there was a matter of public record. Nevertheless it is common knowledge in the geisha world that Ko-yakko was the favourite of the great Count Ito and that he was her patron. In geisha parlance, he 'took care of her'.

For Ko-yakko, the fact that her deflowerer was the prime minister was a matter of immense pride. That is why the family treasures the *toranai* document. When she was interviewed, her daughter Tomiji asserted proudly that Prime Minister Ito had been her mother's patron. Sadayakko's contemporary, the playwright Shigure Hasegawa, an observant chronicler of the world she knew, reports in her memoir of Sadayakko, 'When she was sixteen [by the Japanese method of counting age; fifteen by ours] she took on the geisha name of Yakko. Soon afterwards it was revealed that she was supported by Ito Hirobumi, prime minister of the time. So she had nothing to fear any more.'[6]

Throughout her years as a young geisha, Ko-yakko would have known that she would have to undergo an essential and maybe painful rite of passage in order to attain the status of adult geisha. Contemporary geisha, old enough to have been through *mizuage* themselves – a custom that largely ceased after World War II – say that their deflowering was horrible. But it was also unavoidable.

Ito was a kind man and probably prepared her for it. According to a tradition in the geisha world, for a week before the climactic night, the deflowerer spent every evening with the young girl, massaging her thighs with egg white. Each night he reached a little higher, so that when the moment finally arrived, it was not such a shock.[7] No doubt Ito, being greatly experienced in this area, did all that was necessary.

Kamekichi had certainly tutored Ko-yakko in the proper procedures. On the day, she would have bathed and put on her make-up with extra care. The evening would have begun with conversation, sake and dancing. Then the two would have retired to a small tatami-matted room. There Ito would have loosened her kimono; Western clothes would have been unsuitable for such an intimate moment. The act itself was always performed semi-clothed.

Unlike her Victorian contemporaries, Ko-yakko probably did not need to lie back and endure what she had every reason to expect would be an unpleasant experience. On the contrary, the arts of love were highly developed. While our forefathers suffered agonies of guilt as they plunged into the fleshpots of New York's Broadway or the London Haymarket, the Japanese had never until very recently encountered Christian ethics. Far from being a sin, they considered sex a game, the most enjoyable possible form of recreation. And as with any game, adepts devoted themselves to refining their expertise.

Manuals such as the Chinese *Records of the Bedchamber* had been in circulation for centuries. This volume advises that 'the man must always first engage [his partner] in protracted gentle play to harmonise her mood with his and make her feelings respond' and gives ample advice on how to make the woman's yin juices flow. There were also Taoist manuals detailing the many ways in which the Jade Stalk could move over the Lute Strings.[8] Extremely explicit *ukiyo-e* woodblock prints known as *shun-ga* ('spring pictures') were widely available, particularly in the geisha quarters. So Ko-yakko's deflowering may not have been as horrific an experience as modern-day readers might imagine.

Ko-yakko's coming of age was marked by a new name. From now on she would no longer be Little Yakko but plain Yakko. When she wore a kimono, it would be not one of the butterfly-bright, long-sleeved kimonos of childhood but a subtly hued adult one – though in the daytime, she usually wore flouncy Western frocks.

The city's teahouses were hotbeds of gossip. Soon rumours were flying around that Prime Minister Ito was Yakko's patron. She had always been hugely popular. Now this prestigious relationship ensured that she was the star of the Tokyo geisha world. She became what was known as a five-minute geisha. So many customers begged her to put in an appearance at their parties that she was forever flitting from teahouse to teahouse, dropping in for a bare five minutes before moving on to the next. She also undoubtedly from time to time was summoned to dance at Tokyo's high society haunt, the Rokumeikan, the romantically named Hall of the Baying Stag.

Those were the years when the craze for all things Western was at its height. The Tokyo fashionable laced themselves into their corsets, wriggled into their bustles, ball gowns and excruciatingly tight leather shoes and put on feather boas and tippets. Then they stepped out on the arms of gentlemen in swallow tails and top hats to dance the night away to the strains of Offenbach and Strauss.

It was Ito's old friend Kaoru Inoue, by then also a Count and the foreign minister, who came up with the idea of bringing the gay social life of Paris and London to Tokyo. There was a political aim at the bottom of it. Japan was suffering greatly under the unequal treaties that the foreign powers had imposed, which prohibited the government from raising tariffs to slow the influx of foreign goods. The most hated of all was the 'extraterritoriality' agreement which made foreigners immune from Japanese law. No matter what terrible offence they committed against Japanese nationals, they would be tried in a consular court by their own countrymen, who invariably found them innocent or let them off very lightly.

The supposed rationale was that Japan was not truly civilised and could not be considered on a par with the Western powers. Inoue's great idea was to establish a splendid ballroom where foreign dignitaries could mingle with the cream of Japanese society. Thus they would see that the Japanese were just as civilised and enlightened as they and revoke the hated treaties. That was the theory, anyway.

Inoue entrusted the design to a British architect named Josiah Conder. After three years and at enormous cost, the Hall of the Baying Stag opened on 28 November 1883. It was right in the centre of Tokyo, almost across the road from the Emperor's palace, next to where the Imperial Hotel stands today. Set in spacious grounds with trees, a lake and a couple of pavilions, the Hall was a palatial two-storeyed mansion of stuccoed brick in the Victorian hybrid style, with Tuscan colonnades on the ground floor and Moorish galleries on the second. The mansard roof echoed the celebrated new Louvre in Paris. It was the first building in Japan to be lit with electricity and sparkled like a fireworks display. A disdainful French visitor, Lieutenant L.M. Julien Viaud, who under the pen name of Pierre Loti had written a bestseller entitled *Madame Chrysanthème*, said that it reminded him of nothing so much as a second-class casino in a French provincial spa. But to Japanese eyes it was monumental and wonderfully exotic.

There were rooms for dancing, drinking, card-playing, billiards and reading, as well as promenade halls and suites for official state guests. A French chef presided over the dining room, which served strictly Western food to be eaten with knives and forks. Beneath the chandeliers of the grand ballroom, Japanese women in low-cut dresses with unwieldy bustles whirled and twirled in the tight embrace of beribboned and bewhiskered foreign diplomats. The dance was the waltz, which had shocked the aristocracy of Europe a few decades earlier. For traditional Japanese wives, who were not used to spending time in male company, let alone coming into close physical proximity with unknown foreign gentlemen, it must have been a terrible ordeal.

The theory was that the Hall of the Baying Stag was strictly for the *crème de la crème*. Japanese were expected to appear with their wives on their arms, just as Westerners did. In Japanese terms this was truly extraordinary. To this day most Japanese men spend their evenings in the company of other men, with professional women to entertain them. Wives are not invited to social occasions.

A few of the wives, notably Countess Ito and Countess Inoue, were ex-geisha. Trained to dance and to make charming small talk with unfamiliar men, they were in their element. But plenty of aristocratic wives much preferred to stay home. As a result, men far outnumbered women on the dance floor. Sometimes a couple of frock-coated gentlemen were to be seen studiously dancing together, determined to demonstrate how civilised and enlightened they were. And naturally geisha were often smuggled in to swell the ranks of women.

A satirical Parisian artist named Georges Bigot, who was living in Japan at the time, drew many unkind cartoons lampooning the party-goers at the Hall of the Baying Stag. In one, women decked out in bustles and feathery hats squat on a veranda outside the Hall, smoking tiny pipes and stubbing them out on the wooden boards. Their vulgar style marks them out as geisha. In another a gaggle of geisha are on their way to the Hall, ungainly in their unfamiliar Western frocks with rumpled stockings visible beneath their too-short skirts. Another depicts a woman alighting from a rickshaw outside the Hall. She too is in a bustle and bonnet, but clutching a shamisen, the tool of the geisha's trade. Yakko, of course, being a higher class of geisha, would have slipped unnoticed into the glamorous crowd. No doubt her waltz and quadrille were perfection.

Eventually the decadence went too far. The problem was Ito and his uncontrollable libido. On 20 April 1887, he hosted a sensational masked ball at his palatial prime ministerial residence. It was Tokyo's first fancy-dress ball ever. Four hundred guests were invited, including diplomats, dignitaries, foreign residents and the cream of Japanese society.

Ito greeted them dressed as a Venetian nobleman. Countess Ito was in a Spanish gown of yellow silk with a mantilla while Miss Ito, their daughter, was an Italian peasant girl. Foreign Minister Inoue went as a comic troubadour from Japanese folklore. The Home Minister went as his real life self of twenty years earlier – a rebel samurai in black armour with crossed swords. A leading industrialist dressed as an ascetic mountain monk and his wife was a dancer in a butterfly costume. There was a Mary Queen of Scots, several ladies in Louis XIV and Louis XV frocks, a Henry VIII, a King John, several friars, a Dr Faust, two Mephistopheles and an Oscar Wilde. It was, as the *Japan Weekly Mail* of 30 April 1887 reported, 'a gay and motley throng of warriors and peasants, gods and devils, kings and nobles'.[9] The dancing went on from nine in the evening to four in the morning. One guest was heard to observe wearily that he had 'danced for the sake of the country'.

A few days later rumours began to surface. The evening, according to the gossip columns, had degenerated into an orgy of ribaldry and bawdiness. Ito, it seems, had seduced the beautiful young wife of Count Toda, second daughter of Prince Iwakura. Whether or not that was true, ordinary people were disgusted to learn that their national leaders were cavorting about in ridiculous costumes, like low-class actors, and dancing with foreign women. Ito's cabinet was dubbed contemptuously 'the dancing cabinet'.

Worse was to come. For all the display of civilisation and enlightenment, the treaty negotiations were not going well. Far from repealing them, the Western powers extended their privileges. Foreigners were no longer to be restricted to the major cities but would be allowed to travel wherever they wished in the country.

There were violent anti-government protests. Adopting Western garb and aping Western ways now seemed unpatriotic and ridiculous. Men still wore high collars and suits for public life. But many women thankfully went back to the kimono. At the Hall of the Baying Stag, the symbol of the great Westernisation boom, there were fewer and fewer grand occasions. In 1889 it was sold to become a gentlemen's club. Ito resigned from office in April 1888, a year after the fateful ball.

While Yakko rattled through the streets in her rickshaw, whirling from teahouse to teahouse, or waltzed at the Hall of the Baying Stag, she had not forgotten the pale young man who had saved her life and stolen her heart. She might be the lover of the highest man in the realm, but that was business. It had nothing to do with love.

She and Momosuké continued to meet whenever they could manage it though she was now so famous that it was almost impossible to conceal her activities. Sometimes she would disguise herself, scurrying out with her hair tied back in a simple style, in a plain kimono, with a shawl wrapped around to hide her face. No doubt, once Ito had initiated her into the arts of love, she shared her new-found knowledge with the handsome young man. But both of them knew all too well that their love was doomed. In those days no one in Japan imagined for a moment that they would marry for love. Love was a shameful emotion, a brutish stirring in the loins that drove men to behave in dishonourable ways. It was certainly nothing to do with marriage, which was arranged by one's elders and betters with the good of the family in mind.

Momosuké had a duty to his family to marry whomever they proposed. He could never marry Yakko. Like her, he could not afford to be ruled by sentiment. He was too poor to be a romantic. Apart from anything else, she was a geisha. Only the most powerful men in the realm married geisha and then only when they had reached a station in life when they no longer needed to care what anyone thought.

They knew that they would part. But perhaps neither of them guessed how dramatic and final that parting would be. For Yakko was not the only one to have noticed what a very fine young man Momosuké was.

For all his elegant languor, Momosuké was a hard-working student and a natural leader. He was part of a circle who prided themselves on their progressiveness. They ate meat, wielding their knives and forks with enthusiasm, following the precepts of their revered principal, the great moderniser Fukuzawa, who argued that meat-eating would improve the Japanese physique. (Until the coming of Westerners, the Japanese had eaten only fish, vegetables, fowl and game, but no four-legged beasts bred for meat, following the precepts of Buddhism.) They also engaged in Western-style competitive sports. In the past the Japanese had only practised martial arts like jujitsu and karate and skills like horse riding that were an essential part of a warrior's training.

A year after the two first met, in the autumn of 1886, when Yakko was spending time at the prime minister's villa on Summer Island, Momosuké and his classmates organised Keio's first ever athletic meet at the Keio sports ground by Tokyo Bay. Among the guests who were invited were the principal, Yukichi Fukuzawa, and his family. Before they set off for the meet, so the story goes, the family joked that they would watch out there for a husband for Fusa, Yukichi's second daughter.

By then Fukuzawa was fifty-one. Japan's leading thinker and educator, he was one of the most powerful and influential men in the country. Besides writing innumerable books and founding Keio University, he had also started one of Japan's first newspapers. A brilliant businessman, he had become hugely rich. He had several estates dotted around Tokyo. The main Fukuzawa estate was very near Keio University. Even the secondary Fukuzawa estate in Shibuya, in south-west Tokyo, was the size of a small village.

In his books Fukuzawa argued that arranged marriage was a pernicious institution and that Japanese youth should be allowed to marry freely, in the Western way. In the case of his own children, however, he did not put theory into practice. Of his four sons and five daughters, he particularly adored Fusa. She was her father's girl, clever, scholarly, serious and introverted. The only photograph that exists of her shows a plain round-faced woman with her hair pulled into a tight bun. It seemed unlikely that she would ever find a husband by herself.

As the athletes pounded around the sports ground, no one could miss the tall young farmer's son, running faster than everyone else in breeches and a dazzling white shirt with a motif of a lion's head on it. It was Fukuzawa's eldest daughter, O-Sato, who pointed him out. Fukuzawa had noticed Momosuké before. He would, he agreed, make a fine addition to the family.

A professor named Yoshiaki Sakae was called upon to act as intermediary. He summoned Momosuké to his home. Sitting cross-legged on the floor while his wife served green ceremonial tea, he laid out the terms of Fukuzawa's offer. It was a truly extraordinary proposition. The great man wanted him to marry into the family, take the Fukuzawa name, live on their vast estate and eventually be one of his heirs. In the normal course of things, when a young woman married she would go and live with her husband's family. Fukuzawa did not want his beloved Fusa to live with the impoverished Iwasakis. This was a way to keep her with him. He had also presumably decided that Momosuké showed more promise than his own sons.

For Momosuké it was a two-edged sword. To be an adopted son was a very difficult and stressful position. Usually in a Japanese marriage the husband had total power and authority – except in this one case. If

Momosuké were to enter the House of Fukuzawa, he would be perpetually under the thumb of his wife and her formidable father. Momosuké was canny and very ambitious. Instead of leaping at the offer, he bargained. He could perfectly well join the Fukuzawa family, he said. After all, he was the second son; his older brother would carry on the Iwasaki family name. But marriage was not what he had in mind. Above all he wanted to travel. He wanted to go to the glorious West and study. And of course he would have to discuss it thoroughly with his father. It was his duty as the son of a poor family to make the most money he possibly could and support his family.

Soon rumours were percolating through the city's teahouses. The handsome young Keio student, Momosuké Iwasaki, it was said, was to have an arranged marriage with Fukuzawa's daughter. For Yakko the pain must have been intense. She was Ito's favourite. She could confide in no one, least of all Kamekichi, about her illicit romance. She knew perfectly well that Momosuké could never marry her. There was no reason for her to feel betrayed. But she was only sixteen and he was her first love. She must have hoped and prayed that the rumours were not true.

On 17 December 1887 Fukuzawa sent Momosuké a formal agreement to sign. He was to go abroad for three years to study. The Fukuzawa family would pay for everything. When he returned, he would marry Fusa and become Momosuké Fukuzawa. It was a business contract – which was what marriage was in those days.

One icy January day in 1888 Yakko met her handsome farm boy for the last time. She shed not a tear. No matter what she felt, she was determined that he should never know.

'We are destined to lead separate lives,' she told him. 'But let's each of us do our best to be successful, you on your path, I on mine.'[10]

A few days later, on 2 February, he boarded a steamship and sailed for New York. She could not even go to the quay to wave him off. She must have endured the most terrible, gut-wrenching pain, loss and emptiness. Her life had become hollow. Everything had lost its colour and meaning and become utterly pointless. The horror of it was that she could not say a word to anyone. She had to weep alone in secret. In public she had to be cheerful, flirting with old men for whom she cared nothing. She had to keep her tears, sorrow and anguish to herself.

It was a harsh introduction to the realities of adult life. She had learnt the key rule by which geisha led their lives. The geisha world was a beautiful dream where everyone played at love. But for the women who spun that web of fantasy, the secret was always to remember that it was just a game. Real love was too dangerous. It brought only pain.

Perhaps something in her heart turned to ice. She would get on with her life. She would concentrate on her work and perfect her dancing. After all, she was a star, one of the most popular and famous geisha in the city. She had plenty of admirers, even if she did not love them. There would be no more love.

3

THE LIBERTY KID
1888—1896

Love was gone; but at least Yakko's career was thriving. After all, she
had Count Ito behind her.

Her contemporary, the playwright Shigure Hasegawa, gushed in
her flowery prose:

> Yakko had chosen the best possible patron. At home in Kamekichi
> she had a shrewd mother watching over her. Not only that: her face
> was as beautiful as a peony blossoming next to a sleeping lion. She
> was a butterfly playing with a lion's mane. In the flower and willow
> world, she was number one. She was a most unusual geisha, very
> 'high collar'.[1]

Hai kara – 'posh', 'cool', 'fashionable' – was the catch phrase of the time,
in reference to the high-collared suits that trendy young blades sported.

Yakko was still as wild and boyish as ever. In the daytime she loved to
ride along the banks of the Sumida, her glossy black tresses carelessly tied
and flying out in the wind behind her like her horse's tail. She also took
part in several public horse races where she acquitted herself well. She was

often to be found at the billiard table with a plaid shawl thrown around her shoulders, the height of fashion at the time. In the evening she would re-emerge, transformed into the most alluring geisha in the city. People called her 'stylish Shimada Yakko', in reference to her glorious hair, styled into a Shimada coiffeur.

She even had her own rickshaw, one of only two geisha in Tokyo wealthy enough to do so. Her skinny driver, a headband wrapped around his head and a cigarette dangling from his lips, could be seen patiently propping up the wall outside teahouse after teahouse, the shafts of the carriage resting on the ground, ready to whisk her off to the next party.

'When I was going back and forth to school with my textbooks, I heard about the geisha who had her own rickshaw in Yoshicho,' wrote Shigure. 'My father has his own rickshaw, but our family only uses it when he goes to court. My father is an important man [he was a judge], so I realised this geisha must be important.'[2]

Ito showered her with extravagant gifts, exotic Western imports like jewellery and a riding costume. He often took her away with him to the coast. At the time Japan's first seaside resort was just being developed, in a balmy area called Oiso with sandy black beaches and shallow waters, further down the coast from Summer Island. A railway station opened there in 1887. Ito was one of the first to buy land and have a villa built. It was a splendid place with gables, a steep tiled roof and Tiffany-style stained-glass windows. He named it Sorokaku, 'Blue Wave House'. After that he spent as little time as possible in Tokyo.

There one summer he taught her to swim. Swimming was a highly unusual and modern skill in Japan in those days. Like most Japanese, Yakko was used to paddling, wearing nothing but a *koshi maki*, a strip of cotton wrapped sarong-style around her waist. One of the customs which most shocked the Victorians when they arrived in Japan was that women stripped to the waist without a second thought on hot summer days or to breast feed. Difficult though it is for Western readers or modern Japanese to imagine, breasts were not considered erotic or remotely provocative.

Ito, a great promulgator of Western ways, sent to Paris for the latest couture bathing costume for Yakko. The top was like an undershirt with elbow-length sleeves and a scoop neck, the bottom a flimsy skirt which clung to her legs most fetchingly when wet. Perched on the rocks like a mermaid, wearing a wide-brimmed straw hat to keep the sun off her milky white complexion, she made an exquisite picture.

She had also discovered a new talent: acting. Under the shoguns, women had been banned from the stage for two and a half centuries. In those days acting and the selling of sexual favours were inextricably linked. From 1629, in an attempt to maintain order, kabuki was restricted to male actors. Women performers went underground. The entertainers of the pleasure quarters, who later became known as geisha, performed music and dance of the same genre as kabuki, including dance solos from kabuki plays, but only for private, exclusive customers.

So it was a short step for a geisha to act. In 1872, after the Meiji government came to power, the new rulers lifted the ban on public performances by women. Soon many geisha districts began giving occasional dance performances. Initially women were still restricted to appearing in all-female troupes. The ban on men and women appearing on stage together was not lifted until 1891. Even then the tradition of all-women and all-men troupes largely persisted.

Yakko discovered that she much preferred taking the exciting male parts, with plenty of dramatic posing and fighting scenes, rather than playing coy women's parts. 'When I was a geisha,' she remarked in an interview some years later, 'I played Goro [in the violent revenge tragedy *The Soga Brothers*] at the opening of the Yurakukan Theatre near Yoshicho.' This was the first time that geisha had performed their dances as drama, wearing costumes and using props.

After that we did charity performances for three days every December. I had Y1000 worth of tickets to sell. I was very busy. I always liked playing men. Whenever someone didn't want to play a man's part, I took it – old men, villains, I did them all. I was good at fighting scenes and doing hara-kiri standing up. I was a real tomboy in those days! My first role when I was 19 was Kiichi [a famous old warrior who features in the play *Kiichi Hogen's Book of Tactics*]. I went to Mr Terajima [the kabuki actor Kikugoro V] to ask him to teach me. He said, 'I've never done Kiichi but I'm going to soon. You can come and watch.' So I went to the Shintomi-za Theatre and watched Kikugoro rehearsing. That was how I learnt.[3]

In another play she had to strut backwards along the *hanamichi*, the raised walkway which runs through the audience in a kabuki theatre, striking dramatic poses with two huge swords stuck in her belt and dragging along the ground.

'One time I tripped and fell off into the audience. In those days people were more relaxed!'[4]

After three years Count Ito released Yakko from being his mistress, though he remained her friend and adviser. She could not be his for ever. Like modelling today, a geisha's success was predicated on her youth and beauty. Once she had passed her peak, work would not be so easy to come by. She needed to find someone to marry her while she was still desirable.

Like any woman, geisha yearned to find someone to be their love and supporter and stay with them into old age. A *danna* (patron) theoretically provided financial support for the whole of a geisha's life. But in reality *danna* were fickle and temperamental and might easily turn to a younger, more malleable woman as a geisha grew older. In any case, it was a business relationship, not emotional support. The geisha code was never to threaten a man's marriage and always to put his wife first, which meant she could never make demands on her *danna*. Geisha knew that as they grew older, life would become lonelier and lonelier.

Marriage offered a way out. If a geisha married, she had to give up her career in the flower and willow world. Nevertheless, if she wanted to have children it was the most acceptable course. It was a way to step into mainstream respectability and the best chance of a secure position in the years to come.

Over the next couple of years Yakko's name was linked to a variety of different men. By 1891 she was enjoying the favours of two *danna* and two lovers, all at the same time. The *danna* ('patrons') supported her financially, in exchange for which she entertained at their teahouse parties and was available for sex when required. Fortunately the only men who could afford such a role were middle aged and invariably married, and far too busy to make too many inconvenient demands on her. One, a man called Keisuke Hida, was the president of the Second Yokohama Bank. He bought a house and set her up in it. The other was called Shigeo Narahara. She had created a scandal in the geisha world a couple of years earlier by seducing him away from a fellow geisha. He was besotted with her and showered her with gifts and money.

Those were business relationships. For her lovers she turned to the louche world of entertainers – sumo wrestlers and kabuki actors. Like her, they were celebrities, with thousands of fans among people who would never have the chance to meet them. She, of course, was part of their inner circle, she inhabited the same world. In their time off when they were out of the public eye, they relaxed together.

One of Yakko's lovers was a brawny sumo champion named Konishiki; his real name was Jugoro Hatachiyama. Then as now the lumbering wrestlers with their gleaming oiled chests were greatly desirable symbols of manliness. Modern sumo wrestlers consort with models. In those days it was geisha.

She was also much adored by Fukusuke Nakamura, a young kabuki actor already famous for his portrayals of women. A willowy, ineffably elegant young man, he had a long, rather beautiful face and the shaved and pencilled eyebrows and close-cropped hair which marked him out as an actor. He was a heart-throb, hugely popular among the women of the city. He later became the great Utaemon V.[5]

Of all these, he was the most likely candidate for marriage. For all their glamour, actors, like geisha, were outcasts, at the very bottom of the social pecking order. The theatre which became kabuki had first been performed in the seventeenth century by outcasts who had nowhere to live but the dry bed of the River Kamo in Kyoto. They were still contemptuously dubbed *kawara kojiki*, 'riverbed beggars'. This made them the natural allies, friends and lovers of geisha. They often married. In fact they had little choice but to marry from within their circle. Respectable people could be their devoted fans, but to marry them was out of the question.

'In those days Yakko was extremely popular,' Utaemon once recalled.

She was beautiful, talented and wonderfully skilled at *gei* [the geisha arts of dancing and singing]. Not even the Shimbashi geisha could compete with her. She was very wilful. She always liked to have her own way. When we went out together, she used to take her abacus with her. She'd work out her share of the bill and insist on paying it. She wouldn't let me treat her. I wanted to marry her, but I was too sickly.[6]

That year everyone was talking about a flamboyant young man who called himself the Liberty Kid.[7] Along with his troupe he performed seditious political dramas which had been thrilling audiences in Osaka, Kyoto and beyond, throughout western Japan. His trademark was a catchy satirical song he had composed, which was a huge hit. Now the troupe were on their way to Tokyo. Their first appearances at the prestigious Nakamura-za Theatre were heavily booked before they had even arrived in the city.

The geisha were as curious as everyone else to see them. The courtesans of the Yoshiwara pleasure quarters had booked *en masse* and would be there to add their celebrity glitter on one of the first nights. Apparently there was a hilarious scene about the abolition of prostitution which they were eager to see. Kamekichi went along too. She bustled back full of enthusiasm and told Yakko she must go straight away.

The Nakamura-za was one of the grand old theatres of Tokyo. Normally it played host to the traditional drama, kabuki. In those days plays began in the morning and went on until nightfall when, despite the candles and gaslights, it was too dark to see much any more. The audience's 70 sen bought them squatting room in crammed tatami-matted space rather like sheep pens, as one Victorian observer wrote, divided by raised walkways along which attendants scurried carrying sweetmeats. Or you could pay 1½ yen to sit on your knees in a box right over the stage, usually occupied by celebrities such as geisha. Performances were not hushed reverential events as they are today but cheerful community occasions. People sat drinking, smoking long pipes, picnicking on the packed lunches they had brought, chatting, occasionally snoozing and yelling lustily to cheer on their favourite actors at key dramatic moments.

But on this occasion the young men strutting their stuff on the stage were not even professional actors. The plays that they performed were radically different from anything anyone had ever seen before. Noh and kabuki were very stylised with traditions, plots and conventions with which everyone was familiar. But these were shockingly realistic.

The opening play, *The true story of our Itagaki's disaster*, was a dramatisation of a failed assassination attempt on Count Taisuke Itagaki.[8] Itagaki was the leader of the radicals and founder of the country's first genuine political party, the Liberal or Freedom Party (Jiyu-to). In 1882, he had been attacked and stabbed by rightists. As he fell, he shouted the famous words, 'Itagaki may die but freedom never!' He lived to tell the tale and was seated cross-legged at the front of the audience on the first night. With his pale lugubrious face, soulful eyes and long wispy beard, neatly parted down the middle and flaring stiffly out to each side like a walrus, he was instantly recognisable.

Then came the moment everyone had been waiting for, when the play ended and the curtain swept across the stage. A lone figure wearing a jaunty white headband swaggered out and with a flourish knelt in macho samurai style, his knees spread wide apart, in front of a gold leaf screen. It was the Liberty Kid.

He cut an extraordinary figure. He was wearing a red samurai surcoat with exaggerated pointed shoulders above a plaid men's kimono. His bushy black hair burst out around his headband like a hedgehog's bristles. He was no pretty boy; he had a cheeky round face, thick eyebrows, a blunt nose and a defiant set to his mouth. He looked like an overgrown street urchin spoiling for a fight. His cocky self-confidence, combined with a certain self-deprecatingly comical style, was irresistible. His name was Otojiro Kawakami. He was twenty-seven years old.

Flourishing a black fan emblazoned with a red rising sun, he broke into his satirical hit, the Oppekepé song (*Oppekepé bushi*). While a rhythmic shamisen strummed, he spat out the words in a husky rapid-fire patter, improvising verses as he went along. He sneered at the government, the rich and the kind of people who dressed in Western clothes, aped Western ways and spent all their money on geisha. It was nineteenth-century Japanese rap. The catchy chorus imitated the sound of a bugle or a trumpet, like a night watchmen's call: 'Tara, tara! Watch out, watch out!'

In these days when the price of rice is rising,
You completely ignore the plight of the poor,
Covering your eyes with tall hats,
Wearing gold rings and watches,
You bow to men of influence and position
And spend your money on geisha and entertainers . . .
If you think you can get to Paradise
By . . . using a bribe when you encounter
The King of Hades in hell, you'll never make it!
Oppekepé, oppekepeppo, peppoppo.[9]

'After every scene there is loud applause,' reported the *Jiji* newspaper of 24 June 1891. 'Kawakami's style of speech is unique and so is his Oppekepé. The performance is full of variety. Each part has its own surprises for the audience. This is ground-breaking stuff. Don't miss it!'[10]

The first run did not last long. On 6 July, two weeks after the performance had begun, Otojiro was on stage playing the part of Itagaki's assassin. Some actors dressed as policemen ran down the hanamichi walkway to help the fallen Liberal leader. But the theatre manager and his younger brother, convinced that these were real policemen, chased along after them. A brawl broke out. The audience roared with laughter but the play was closed down anyway. By then, however, the streetwise songster had already encountered the high-spirited Yoshicho geisha.

Otojiro was a survivor. He was born in 1864 in the rough port city of Hakata on the island of Kyushu in Japan's deep south. He came from a merchant family, purveyors to their local feudal lord but, like Momosuké, he was the second son of a second son. He had no responsibilities and would inherit nothing.

When he was eleven, his mother died. His father brought a new wife into the house but Otojiro did not get on with her. So he ran away from home, went down to the harbour, stowed away on a cargo ship and ended up in Osaka, penniless and friendless.

Those were Dickensian times in Japan as much as in the West. Children were tough. Young Otojiro made a living by his wits. He took any job he could get and somehow managed to survive in Osaka's labyrinth of dusty, crowded alleys. At eighteen he was a policeman in the neighbouring city of Kyoto. He was so proud of his uniform that he had his photograph taken – a chubby-faced lad looking gravely into the distance in peaked cap and epauletted great coat, holding a pair of woollen gloves and a long policeman's staff. Shortly after that, fired by the political turmoil and the strident calls for democracy, he had joined Itagaki's Liberal Party as a *soshi* agitator.

Itagaki and his followers wanted elections and the creation of a representative people's assembly. As far as many people were concerned, Count Ito and his cronies were every bit as despotic as the shogunate had been. They had used the Emperor's name to claim legitimacy but in reality had simply grabbed power in a military coup. A particular grievance was the swingeing taxes required to pay for the government's modernisation plans and the much-publicised frolics at the Hall of the Baying Stag.

But the Liberal Party quickly became a focal point for all manner of malcontents. The most visible of Itagaki's followers were left-wing agitators, the *soshi*. The fringes of the movement encompassed swashbucklers, fanatics, thugs and hoodlums. During the 1880s there were outbreaks of rioting, violence and even political assassinations.

Otojiro was a natural performer, never happier than when he was haranguing a crowd, the bigger the better. Soon his scurrilous tongue and subversive speeches were getting him into trouble. He was arrested time and time again – 180 times in all, he bragged. At nineteen he was banned from speaking in public in Kyoto for a year and from using the name Liberty Kid. He also went to prison six times. After a particularly long stint in 1886 he declared that his name was now The One Who Got Away. He organised a speech event which he called 'The Secret Lives of Criminals', in which he regaled his audience with all the tales he had heard in the cells.

The following year he chanced upon another outlet for his exuberant showman's instincts. He took to the stage with a troupe of kabuki actors in a play called *Robinson Crusoe of the Orient*. The script, which still exists, calls for the action to break off while Otojiro steps outside the curtain to improvise. Apparently his fellow actors already appreciated the entertainment value of his skill. Then, perhaps realising that he needed training, he apprenticed himself to the Japanese equivalent of a stand-up comic, a *rakugo* master. There he developed his Oppekepé song. The first performances in 1888 caused a sensation.

Meanwhile a young man named Sadanori Sudo, a fellow activist, had come up with a creative way to bypass the repressive laws and get the revolutionary message across: theatre. Political speeches were full of jargon and invited repression; whereas the theatre was not only easy for everyone to understand but uncontroversial, on the surface at least. The new *soshi* theatre aimed at being realistic, just like in the West, and thus could claim to be following government directives to be as Western as possible in every way. Very few Japanese at this point had ever actually seen Western theatre or knew what it was like, so their 'Western-style realism' was entirely experimental.

The first performance of Sudo's *soshi shibai* ('radical theatre' or 'agit prop') took place in Osaka in December 1888. Soon the sheer joy of acting had taken over. The actors did not forget their revolutionary roots, but they started to perform entertaining non-political plays too. They renamed their theatre *shosei shibai*, 'student theatre' or 'amateur theatre'. Far from being career-driven professionals, like the kabuki actors, they portrayed themselves as romantic, devil-may-care Bohemians. Their amateur status freed them from all the constraints and conventions of the traditional theatre.

The scripts of all their plays had to be presented to the police for scrutiny and were heavily censored. Police also kept watch during the performance. If the actors dared to ad lib or deviated by a single line from the approved script, the play was closed down then and there. The audience were sent home and the actors frequently spent a night in the cells.

Inspired by Sudo's example, Otojiro founded a *soshi* troupe of his own. Sudo never had more than minor success. But within a couple of years, thanks to Otojiro's irrepressible energy and drive, he and his troupe were on stage at the grand old Nakamura-za in Tokyo.

Like everyone, Count Ito had heard about the rambunctious young man. Being well aware of his own importance, he expected a private command performance. So Otojiro was summoned to a teahouse party to be introduced. Yakko, as one of Ito's favourites, was there.

Everyone assumed that Otojiro would be honoured and overawed in the presence of the great man. But the young radical was not so easily cowed. After all, the high-living ex-prime minister was one of the chief objects of his barbs. When he was called upon to do his piece, he said brusquely, 'If you want to see my performance, come to the theatre and pay for a ticket.' Ito, who had been a rebel himself, was tickled by his effrontery. The young man stayed and talked and later Yakko showed him to the door. She also invited him to meet her some time at a teahouse.

Otojiro already had a coterie of devoted fans, some of whom followed him from city to city; and he was not averse to taking advantage of the favours on offer from time to time. But for relaxation he and his troupe gravitated to the women of the *demi-monde*. Most of the actors favoured the courtesans and prostitutes of the Yoshiwara. Otojiro, being a cut above the rest, preferred the more refined company of geisha.

Asajiro Fujisawa was Otojiro's drinking companion and fellow woman-iser. The two were seldom apart. He too had pulled himself up by his own bootstraps. He had been a wholesalers' clerk, a lawyer's apprentice and a journalist, rather a gifted one, before joining Otojiro's troupe. There his smooth matinée idol features made him the perfect choice to play women's roles. He became the star and the ladies' man of the company. In later years he recorded his memories of those dissolute days.

One evening five of the young actors were invited to a very grand teahouse called Kiraku, around the corner from the Yoshicho geisha district. Five geisha were there to entertain them. One was Yakko.

Otojiro had set his sights not on her but on another geisha called Oteru. Early on in the evening he went off with her and hid in another room. The young actors, having consumed enormous amounts of sake, came to their senses, noticed his absence and decided he must have gone back to their digs. Relieved, they staggered off to the more raunchy environment of the Yoshiwara. Having given them the slip, Otojiro spent the night there.

Soon Oteru was fussing around Otojiro, bringing meals to his dressing room and welcoming guests there for all the world as if she were his wife. But Otojiro was already getting bored.

One day the actors and their geisha friends went to the mountains north of Tokyo to see the glorious old mausoleums of Nikko. They spent the night there in an inn. Oteru commandeered a cosy room and waited for her beau to join her. But Otojiro was already settled in another room with her rival – Yakko. Humiliated and furious, Oteru sent some of the actors to sort him out. They shoved open the door where the two were sleeping and barged in. Otojiro sat up, enraged.

'What do you want?' he roared. 'If you have something to say, say it before you come in!'

'Kawakami [Otojiro] ruled the troupe like a tyrant,' wrote Asajiro:

He was the law. If he disapproved of someone, he fired them straight away. Yakko saw his power and realised what a strong man he was. At that moment she fell totally in love with him. She thought, 'I'd like to be with someone this powerful for the rest of my life.'

Otojiro was a celebrity, like an up-and-coming pop star today. But in terms of status, he was the lowest of the low. As 'riverbed beggars', kabuki actors were lower in status even than geisha. But at least they belonged to particular acting dynasties. Otojiro came from nowhere, he had no connections. His fame counted for nothing. He was lower even than a riverbed beggar. And he was not even good-looking.

The playwright Shigure Hasegawa remembered seeing him perform in his extraordinary homespun kimono and red surcoat. She wrote:

Even as a child I could understand that Kawakami and his Oppekepé was not a great man. I thought Yakko a much greater person because even though she was a geisha, she had her own rickshaw. I wondered why a woman like her would get together with a man like him.

Yakko was one of Tokyo's top geisha and linked with the most powerful man in the land. To be having an affair with a person like Otojiro was extremely embarrassing. Soon gossip about this odd couple was circulating around the teahouses. Night after night, at every party she attended, she had to endure merciless teasing. Nothing could change her commitment. But, wrote Asajiro, 'she had her pride. She decided she would have to make Kawakami a man. Otherwise she would lose face.'

Soon news began to spread that Otojiro had big ambitions. He was not going to be a riverbed beggar for the rest of his life.

'Acting is not my life's vocation,' he said grandly to the press. 'In the future I intend to become a major figure in politics. The job of prime minister is one I'd certainly be interested in.'[11]

Bombast was all very well. But in the present not only did he have no status, he had no money either. Actors were generally very poor and were expected to supplement their meagre stipends with tips from their patrons, which goes some way towards explaining the persistent link between acting and prostitution. The troupe were just setting out and had plentiful debts; added to which, Otojiro was notoriously hopeless with money.

Yakko had completely lost interest in her two lovers and two *danna*. The enormous sumo wrestler and kabuki heart-throb were left to pine disconsolately. At first she kept her new romance a secret from her *danna* and carried on entertaining them, then gave their money to Otojiro. When Narahara, the besotted *danna*, gave her presents she passed them on to him. She was so absorbed in Otojiro that she flirted shamelessly with him right in front of her lovelorn *danna* and even had a room refurbished in the house that the *danna* had given her so that Otojiro could live there. Eventually even Narahara lost patience and refused to have any more to do with her.

Otojiro responded to all this devotion. In January 1892, six months after the revolutionary players first came to town and just as a new play was about to open, the star of the troupe suddenly went missing. The actors sent a delegation to interrogate Yakko but she denied all knowledge of his whereabouts. Then a letter arrived in the missing Otojiro's handwriting declaring that he had gone into retreat to work on his role and pray for the success of the forthcoming play. This was greeted with derision and disbelief. The opening of the play had to be postponed. Ten days later he reappeared and soon afterwards the play opened to acclaim.

Just after Otojiro's reappearance, the *Chuo* newspaper ran a tongue-in-cheek article headlined 'Oto's Hide and Seek'. In Japan at that time, far from being romantic, to be driven by passion was considered worthy only of the utmost contempt. It was the sort of behaviour that people on the margins of society, such as geisha and actors, indulged in. The press – not much above geisha and actors themselves – reported every demonstration of ardour with fresh hilarity. The *Chuo* wrote:

> People are saying that the head of the Torigoe Nakamura-za, Mr Bushy Eyebrows, Oto Kawakami, uses ninja techniques to disappear. Here's the real story. Boss Kawakami staged a real life love scene with Miss Yakko of the Hamada house at the end of last year. He thought she might become very popular if only she put that cool, stylish beauty of hers on stage. For her part, she thought he was different from the big-spending, flashy kind of *danna* she usually hangs around with. He was a real man, greatly different from other men who were dumb and weak, like jellyfish or women. Apart from which, no one has ever created such a funny song as 'Oppekepé' in the whole of Japan. So she called him to her side and would not let go. Kawakami, as befits a hero, couldn't leave her either. Or perhaps two or three of his bones had melted, disabling him from acting.[12]

A few months later, when Otojiro returned from a long tour in the provinces, Yakko was waiting for him with two gold rings which she had had inscribed with their names. The *Chuo* headlined its story 'Yakko's Kawakami fever'. Just as writers across the world have done, journalists – almost certainly entirely male – felt that women who used their beauty to make a living were perfectly legitimate targets for burlesque and satire. They wrote about the feisty geisha with barbed words:

> When she heard Kawakami was back in Tokyo, she was so excited she stuck her tobacco pipe in her hair and her hairpin in her cigarette holder, put her underwear on top of her clothes and slapped lipstick on her face and white powder on her lips. Then she jumped into her rickshaw and put the ring on Kawakami's finger, then pulled it off again, licking and touching him without caring who was watching.[13]

'Licking' probably means 'kissing'. At the time kissing was so far from acceptable behaviour that there was not even a word for it. It was the sort of outlandish sexual technique that geisha and other professionals engaged in, certainly not something that any decent woman would dream of doing, especially not in public.

By the end of the year rumours were going around that the two were going to get married. 'It was big news,' wrote Shigure Hasegawa.

Yakko's own memory of events is very different. In her account, recorded some eighteen years after, in 1908, she is at pains to emphasise that the decision was not hers but Kamekichi's. Speaking to the Japanese press, she wanted to refute any allegations that she had done something as shameful as marry for love. To have acknowledged that it was true would have put her socially beyond the pale. She said:

When I got together with Otojiro, it was 1890. At the time I was a geisha in Yoshicho, with the name of Yakko. So some might think it was a typical geisha–actor affair and that we just hitched up of our own accord, for convenience; but it absolutely wasn't like that. The fact is, I was taken into the Hamada house as an adopted daughter. My adoptive mother was always saying to me, 'I'm so sorry that you have to work for your living. If I sent you off to be a mistress that would be a terrible thing to do as a parent.' She was always saying she would make sure I got a proper husband, no matter how scrawny or withered he was.

As it happens at that time Kawakami was at the Nakamura-za in *The true story of Taisuke Itagaki's disaster*. Mother went to see it and said, 'It's really interesting. You must go and see it too.' So we went together. That was the first time I saw Kawakami. When he decided to go abroad, Mother went and promised me to him as his bride without me knowing anything about it. It was only when everything had been decided that she said, 'You don't have any objections, do you?'

I was pretty eccentric myself and really liked Bohemian types. I also thought Kawakami would not be an actor all his life. Again, considering my social position, even if I wanted to marry into a decent family, I knew they wouldn't have me. I decided I'd like to marry a real maverick. If Kawakami was kind enough to want to marry me, I said I would accept. So it was settled.[14]

'The person who fell in love with Kawakami was my mother,' she asserted in another interview. 'She said, "That man is a student who will certainly become a government minister in future." She recommended him.'[15]

No doubt in retrospect, as a middle-aged married woman, she persuaded herself of the truth of this. After all, she had started life as a geisha and then became an actress, both professions that had a very ambivalent status, simultaneously an adored celebrity and an outcast. She must have been determined to make it appear that, no matter what people might think, she had led her life according to the norms of respectable society.

Yakko had made her decision. She settled into the traditional wife's role – to be the little woman behind her man, the driving force behind her feckless husband-to-be. She carried on working as a geisha but 'just for fun', as she put it, to keep herself busy. All this meant, of course, was pouring drinks and chatting flirtatiously at parties. She had to make money to support Otojiro and to keep in touch with her wealthy supporters and benefactors. But all her attention was focused now on Otojiro and his career.

With Yakko behind him, Otojiro's star was soaring. He was becoming more and more renowned, not just for 'Oppekepé' but for his thrilling and topical dramas. A newsworthy event had barely happened when Otojiro would have had it transformed into a play and performed on stage. The plays were so realistic that doctors frequently had to be called to bandage up the bruised and battered actors. Once the actor playing Itagaki was slashed across the head. Dauntlessly he staggered on to the end of the play with blood streaming down his face, to the great delight of the audience. Eventually Otojiro arranged to have a doctor permanently stationed backstage.

In his pursuit of the ultimate in realism Otojiro planned to ride around the stage on a real horse instead of the usual 'human horse'. 'Student theatre must show reality as it is!' he declaimed. The police and the theatre manager opposed the idea, arguing that a horse would kick, jump and would most likely urinate and defecate on the stage. The plan was abandoned. One which did go ahead was to have a real fire on stage. The actors made great play of extinguishing it, wielding the latest new-fangled technology, portable fire extinguishers. Otojiro went as far as to ponder the barely imaginable concept of having women acting on stage alongside men. But this was a step too far, even for him.

His plays were so popular that some people queued for two or three days to see them. On one occasion the audience included the prime minister of the time, Count Ito's daughter, a party of 120 Nihonbashi firemen and 150 Yanagibashi geisha. The poet Matthew Arnold, visiting Japan at the time, was taken to a performance and was reportedly impressed. Otojiro's fame grew to such an extent that the Empress herself planned to honour the troupe with her presence. Unfortunately she caught a cold and the imperial visit was cancelled.

But Otojiro had bigger plans still, and for those all the money he could earn and Yakko could give him was far from enough. In January 1893, a year after his first disappearance, he vanished again. But this time he waited until the theatre manager had handed him the advance salaries for the entire troupe. When the other actors discovered his absence, they panicked. Not only had he taken their money, they were due to start a new season in a few days and the star was nowhere to be found.

One, a fierce young man named Mohei Fukui, was in particular trouble. He had agreed to stand surety for Otojiro's debts. He grabbed a short sword and burst into Yakko's house. Yakko had been expecting a visit of this sort.

'Where have you hidden Kawakami?' he yelled.

'I'm so sorry,' she cooed, all sweetness. 'What a terrible thing!'

'Hand over Kawakami or I'll kill you!' roared Fukui, aiming a blow at her. One of the leaders of the *soshi* agitators, he had been in prison more times than Otojiro. Violence was his way of life.

As a geisha, Yakko was used to dealing with all manner of unruly male behaviour. She dodged the blow, took hold of his arm and cajoled in her most seductive warble, 'What can you be thinking of, coming into a geisha house waving your sword – and you from such a good family too! Come on, you're not a *yakuza* hit man. Let's chat about this in a reasonable way. Come upstairs and have a drink.'

Her maid was white with fear. Yakko told her to prepare food and drink for him. Eventually she got him so drunk he forgot his anger for that night, at least.

After this, wrote Asajiro, the troupe decided that they had better take care of Yakko while the Boss was away and moved *en masse* into her house. 'You couldn't tell if it was a geisha house or a students' dormitory. But Yakko wasn't worried. She took care of all of us. We had better food than in our own houses and partied every night.'

Yakko knew perfectly well where Otojiro was. As the others soon guessed, he had gone to Kobe and was on his way to France. The plan had been in the air for some time. Among the couple's powerful friends was a man called Baron Kentaro Kaneko, a high-ranking political figure and Ito's close associate. He was a member of the ruling clan of Fukuoka, where Otojiro's home city was, and had followed his maverick young countryman's progress with interest. The two became good friends. Kaneko had recently been posted abroad as a diplomat and suggested to Otojiro that he should go too.

But the young actors had certainly not expected that he would take all their money. After much discussion as to whether he should be expelled from the troupe in absentia, all agreed that, no matter what, the play must go on. Asajiro became acting leader and the season began on schedule – though, without the star, audiences dwindled.

On 2 May Asajiro announced that the Boss was returning. The troupe hired a cavalcade of rickshaws and went to meet him at the railway station. Most, however, had tucked a sword inside their kimonos. Feigning joy, they clattered down to the east end of the city and went into a teahouse for a drink. There they gathered menacingly around him. It was not a moment for bravado. Otojiro cast pride to the winds. He grovelled. Using all his powers of persuasion he explained that he had done what he did exclusively for the good of the troupe. They would do another season at the Nakamura-za and he would pay them back everything with his earnings.

No one knows much about what Otojiro did in the three and a half months he spent in the wicked and exotic city of Paris. There *fin de siècle* decadence was in full swing. Toulouse Lautrec was painting Jane Avril at the Moulin Rouge, Loie Fuller was swirling her voluminous skirts at the *Folies Bergère* and all manner of degenerates were busy drinking themselves to death while turning out glorious art. The wild living of Tokyo's geisha districts paled when compared to the riotous nightlife of Montmartre. Theatre was at the heart of this explosion of creativity and, in an era before television and movies, the celebrities of the day were the actors and actresses.

Otojiro must have felt a little as if he had landed on the moon, though, as a streetwise young fellow from dissolute Tokyo, he took it all in his stride. He stayed at the Japanese legation, under the protection of Ambassador Yasushi Nomura, a friend of both Kaneko and Yakko, which ensured that he could not indulge in too many excesses. He sent the odd letter home for publication in the press. In one he bragged that he had enrolled in the Paris Conservatoire and was studying theatre and music. This was received with the scepticism which greeted most of Otojiro's claims. 'The letter seems real but the bit about the Conservatoire sounds like an exaggeration,' the editor commented.

Otojiro later told the French journalist Louis Fournier that he had spent his time going 'from theatre to theatre, witnessing play after play, studying, in fact, every detail of the French stage'. He also had the chance to meet the legendary Sarah Bernhardt – 'the divine Sarah' – at the time nearly fifty, and saw her in her role as Marguerite in *La Dame Aux Camellias*. He was so impressed that he bought the play and brought it back to be translated into Japanese.

Trailing clouds of glory after his foreign adventures, Otojiro set to work to apply all he had learnt about theatre. From now on the stage would be lit with electric lights while the auditorium and orchestra would be in darkness. The lights would be dimmed while the scenery was changed. These were ground-breaking innovations. In one of the first productions after his return, *Swordplay (Tachimawari)*, the swords were wired so that when they touched, real sparks flew. Another, *Three Brothers*, was advertised as a French-style drama and involved incest, baby-killing and a courtroom scene. The actors spoke naturally instead of in the mannered staccato of kabuki and had only a light coating of make-up, unlike the thick white paint which made the kabuki actors look like puppets. This could no longer be dismissed as 'student theatre'. It was a radical new drama in its own right – New Wave theatre, *shimpa*.

That October, Otojiro and Yakko were formally married. Baron Kaneko was the official go-between. Count Ito, who by then had started a second term as prime minister, gave the couple his blessing and contributed a magnificent trousseau. There was a huge party, held amid all the splendour of the Yoshiwara, to celebrate Yakko's *hiki iwai*, her formal departure from the geisha world. Otojiro gave extravagant presents to everyone and the partying and carousing went on all night. She also gave up her name. Officially she became Sada again – though both Otojiro and the press alternated her two names, Yakko and Sada. Sada was her private name, Yakko her public name.

There is a wedding photograph of the pair. They look shockingly young, like two innocent children. Both are in formal dress. Otojiro, in a dark haori jacket marked with crests over a pale man's kimono, holds a fan. He looks straight at the camera, his crop-cut hair lightly tousled, his chin jutting defiantly. He is still the overgrown street urchin. Yakko looks softly pretty in a fashionably pastel-coloured unpatterned kimono. She sits while he stands protectively at her side. Her hair is looped back in the soft *sokuhatsu* style and falls delicately around her forehead. Her skin is like porcelain, her huge dark eyes as extraordinary as ever – one lidded, like a Western eye, the other flat like an Asian eye. She looks submissive, pensive and quietly satisfied as if she is looking forward to a placid but happy life in the shadow of her man.

Otojiro had a genius for giving the public what it wanted. He had a string of hits with some spine-tingling melodramas based on contemporary events. First came *Shock!* (*Igai*), based on a recent sensational poisoning scandal in an old family. He followed it up with *Shock Again!* (*Mata Igai*), then *Shock Yet Again!* (*Mata Mata Igai*). A newspaper reported that when he performed a quick change on stage, he revealed that he had an artistic tattoo covering most of his body. Some yakuza gangsters had gone to see the play and placed bets on whether it was real or not. They visited Otojiro backstage and discovered that it was. 'Kawakami is very embarrassed,' declared the paper.

But he could never break free of his money problems. Right in the middle of a successful run, his debtors would appear with a demand or bailiffs would come to seize some of his property.

Then in August 1894 Japan declared war on its gigantic neighbour, China, and laid claim to the Korean peninsula. It was an opportunity to show the Western world just how advanced and 'civilised' Japan had become. The whole nation was galvanised with patriotic fervour. The valiant young soldiers marched off in their European uniforms armed to the teeth with European weapons and everyone waited eagerly for news from the front.

Here was the perfect opportunity for Otojiro's theatre-as-reportage. In an age before television or filmed news, what could be more thrilling than to see real-life battles portrayed on stage? Other troupes applied for a permit to perform plays depicting the conflict but Otojiro was the first to succeed. Kabuki actors, argued the police, were uneducated, effeminate and too interested in appealing to the ladies. At least Otojiro and his student actors had a smattering of education and some ideals. This manly form of drama was more appropriate to stir the nation's fighting spirit.

Less than a month after war was declared, *The Sublime, Exhilarating Sino-Japanese War (Sozetsu Kaizetsu Nisshin Senso)* opened at the Asakusa-za Theatre. Otojiro, ever the opportunist, had done an about turn from anti-establishment rebel to jingoistic supporter of his country. The programme notes exhorted the audience to bow whenever the 'illustrious name of His Majesty the Emperor' was mentioned and pointed out that, to give added dignity, the Japanese soldiers and sailors in the play would fight in dress uniform, unlike in real life. The script was by Asajiro. There were bugles instead of shamisen to provide the music and live gunpowder exploded deafeningly on stage to simulate cannon blasts.

The performance was so realistic that at one point two men in the audience leapt onto the *hanamichi* walkway screaming 'You pigtailed Chinese, you won't get away with this!' and beat up an unfortunate actor playing a Chinese soldier. None of the regular actors wanted to play Chinese, reports Asajiro, so Otojiro employed poorly paid extras. After all, they had no lines to learn. They just had to get killed.

But Otojiro was not content with an imagined re-creation. He wanted authenticity. He applied for permission to the police agency to accompany the troops to Korea and on 22 October set off for the front. A month later there were 500 people in several hundred rickshaws and a band at the station to welcome him back. He had brought uniforms, swords, flags and helmets which he had stolen from Chinese corpses and even a real twenty-three-year-old Korean man who appeared on stage.

When *Otojiro Kawakami's Battlefield Diary* (*Kawakami Otojiro Senchi Kembunki*) opened on 3 December, the crowd, which had been gathering overnight, spilled in. The auditorium was so full there was no room even to stand. The play began at 11.50a.m. and went on until eight o'clock in the evening. A woodblock print of the production shows moustachioed Japanese soldiers in Western uniforms skewering pigtailed Chinese while a handsome clean-shaven Otojiro strikes a dramatic pose in the midst of the mêlée.

The play was such a sensation that the troupe were invited to perform before the Crown Prince, later Emperor Taisho, in a tent in front of the Tokyo National Museum in Ueno. A photographer was commissioned to take pictures to present to the Emperor himself. One shows a dramatic scene with banners waving, uniformed soldiers brandishing swords, a hand-to-hand struggle going on in the foreground and a pigtailed mannequin's head rolling about on the ground. Another accolade came when the troupe was invited to perform at Tokyo's top theatre, the Kabuki-za. New Wave Theatre and its leader, Otojiro Kawakami, had achieved establishment recognition.

By then the war was over. It had been easily won. Despite warnings among Western observers that Japan had no chance against the might and vastness of China, the well-armed, well-trained, well-disciplined Japanese soldiers quickly proved that they were far superior in military might to the Chinese. After a series of victories in most of which the Chinese turned pigtail and fled, the Japanese took Korea and were advancing onto the Chinese mainland. A peace treaty was signed in April 1895 ceding Formosa (now Taiwan) and the strategically vital Liaotung Peninsula, between Peking and Korea, to Japan.

There was rejoicing on the streets. But the ink was barely dry when Russia, Germany and France made a Triple Intervention, 'advising' that Japan return the Liaotung Peninsula to China. A fleet of Russian warships just happened to be anchored nearby and all three countries indicated that their troops were on the alert. It was a galling humiliation. Far from having achieved equal status, Japan was still at the mercy of the bullying Western powers. Within three years Russia controlled the strategic peninsula.

Suddenly the theatres where Otojiro and his troupe performed were empty. Once again Otojiro was swamped with money problems. The newspapers reported his discomfiture. On 13 April the actors were in Nagoya, unable to get back to Tokyo until they found a patron to pay their fares. On 23 April a bailiff was despatched by the owner of the Naniwa-za Theatre in Osaka to seize Otojiro's property for non-payment of debts. 'Kawakami's downfall seems not far away,' predicted the *Yorozu*.

As always Otojiro was ready to bounce back. What he needed was his own theatre in which he was the owner-manager, not a wage slave. Only then would he actually begin to make money. As it happens, the theatre was already well under way. Work had begun two years earlier, just after Otojiro returned from France. The Kawakami-za was to be one of Japan's very first modern theatres, designed on the French model with electric lighting throughout and no *hanamichi*.

It was a hugely ambitious project. Otojiro and Sada had mortgaged themselves to the hilt. Otojiro had no money and no access to any. That was Sada's domain. As the star geisha of the Hamada house and Ito's known favourite, her credit rating was extremely high. All she needed to do was put her stamp – the equivalent of her signature – on a document and she was able to borrow 50,000 yen, a fortune in those days. This was the deposit for the Kawakami-za. By the middle of 1896 the building was finished. The grand opening was planned for June. But a domestic dispute threatened to scupper all their plans.

Yakko, wrote Shigure, was a devoted wife. 'For her, the first thing was her husband and the second thing was her husband. She had given up her geisha status at the pinnacle of her career to devote herself to him.'[16]

Otojiro, however, was beset by temptations. Wherever he went there were geisha, dancers, prostitutes and women of every sort eager to offer their services free to the ebullient young stage star. Otojiro was certainly not the type to pass up an opportunity. Like Ito, he was one of those old-school Japanese men who saw philandering as their God-given right. In those days, it did no harm to one's reputation to be seen as a dashing ladies' man. The newspapers often referred to Otojiro facetiously as 'the male castle toppler' (a 'castle toppler' being a courtesan so seductive that, like Helen of Troy, she could topple kingdoms) or 'the demon lover'.

On one occasion ten geisha hid near a bridge with their faces covered in hoods and ambushed him on his way to the bath house. The geisha house proprietress who had already claimed him for the evening had to beat them off to retrieve her prize. Then there was the chicken restaurant heiress who spent all her family's savings meeting Otojiro at *machiai* (very expensive teahouses used for romantic assignations). Several Shimbashi geisha were 'known' to be in relationships with him. All in all, reported the papers, 'he has caused headaches for several hundred women up to now who have fallen for his charms'.[17]

After his death a geisha remembered him thus:

He had a very merry temperament. But he was always telling the most enormous lies. He was as slippery as a fox on a horse's back. If you thought he was telling lies over here, the next minute he'd be telling different lies over there. That was the tune he played. But he had a sort of magic for a woman. He was a real lady-killer.[18]

Japanese wives were supposed to stay quietly at home, take care of the house and children and be pleased that their husband was wealthy enough to be seen out and about with a beautiful celebrity geisha. Yakko did her best to be a compliant Japanese wife but eventually Otojiro went too far.

One wintry day she was sitting at home beside the charcoal brazier smoking a long pipe when two women slid open the front gate. One, who was strikingly lovely, had the elegant grace of a denizen of the *demi-monde*. Behind her was a woman in the baggy trousers and hempen kimono of a servant. She had a baby wrapped in a quilt tied to her back.

'Where've you sprung from?' inquired Yakko carelessly, turning her pipe upside down and tapping the ash into the brazier. 'New domestics, are you? My husband's out. If you want to talk to him, come back later.'

The pretty woman spoke up. 'You must be that Miss Yakko that everyone talks about,' she said, defiant and nervous at the same time. 'Well, I happen to be Oshizu of the Iroha house and this is Mr Oto's baby. Mr Oto told me that he would take me and my baby in any time. He promised. So I'm moving in. I've come to be his wife. I've got no dowry, but I've got a baby. That's worth much more. I don't need three sips of sake [a wedding]. I just want Otojiro to recognise this child.'

'I've never heard of such a thing!' gasped Yakko, barely able to speak with shock. There followed a couple of hours of arguing and weeping, at the end of which Yakko, her face puffy with crying, pushed the intruders out of the gate and slid it shut with a bang.

At that moment Otojiro returned. Realising what had happened, he sent Oshizu off to stay at a nearby inn while he 'talked reason into Yakko'. Yakko, however, was not to be mollified. She grabbed him by his kimono front and pummelled him. Yakko was not only hurt but humiliated. At first she was too ashamed even to speak to Kamekichi. Finally she confided in her. Otojiro was summoned to the Hamada house to face Kamekichi's rage.

What did he think he was doing? demanded Kamekichi. How could he behave in this way? Yakko was busy morning to night, running his business, applying to her powerful friends to raise money for his theatre. And all the while he had been engaged in this treacherous behaviour.

Otojiro expected his wife to be submissive. After all, he had not the slightest intention of leaving her. There was nothing unusual in fathering a child. Any Japanese man who prided himself on his manliness would do the same. All he had to do was talk reason into her. Then they would adopt the child or hand it over to someone to bring up. It was a minor offence. He would act very contrite and it would soon blow over.

If Kamekichi had not been present he might have behaved differently. In later life Yakko told a journalist that he used to hit her and kick her 'all year round'. As an old-school Japanese man, he was convinced that his wife was his property, not much higher in status than a domestic servant. But Yakko was not that kind of woman.

Confronted by the two of them, he bowed his head, trying to appear as humble as possible, and began to stammer out excuses. But Yakko had had enough of playing the compliant wife. She may have given up her career but she still had the fiery spirit of a geisha. Sweeping out of the room, she pulled the hairpins from her chignon. Her much envied long black hair, bound with a swatch of white paper, swung to her waist in a glossy ponytail. Taking a pair of scissors, she cut it all off. Then she reappeared, holding the long tail of hair still tied at one end, and threw it on the floor in front of the stunned Otojiro.

'I relinquish this marriage. I'm no longer your wife!' she cried, in storms of tears. The remaining locks, shaggily cut, swung loose about her lovely face.

In those days it was impossible for a Japanese woman to divorce her husband. The only way she could escape from a disastrous marriage was to cut off her hair and become a nun. A woman's long hair was her crowning glory. Only a nun or a true eccentric would dream of having short hair. It was a symbol that Otojiro understood perfectly. He was speechless. Looking at his wife, all the more beautiful for her sudden disfigurement, he finally realised how profoundly offended she was. Throwing aside his masculine pride, he apologised in earnest. But words were not enough to salve Yakko's anguish.

'I'm so defiled I can't look my adopted mother in the face,' she whispered. Her head bowed, she rose to her feet and slipped out of the room.

Otojiro begged Kamekichi to intervene but she was far too incensed. Shamefacedly he went off to ponder the best course of action. The proper intermediary was the person who had acted as go-between for their marriage: Baron Kaneko. Moreover as a man and Otojiro's fellow countryman, he could be expected to understand his behaviour. Otojiro went to him and begged his help.

Oshizu was still billeted at the inn. Eventually, worn out, she wrote a note saying, 'Just take care of the baby then!' and sent it along with the baby to the house. Otojiro was buffeted between the two women. He had caused great hurt to Yakko and destroyed her trust in him, but he had also given his word to Oshizu. He went down on hands and knees and begged Yakko's forgiveness, swearing he would never misbehave again. The two were reconciled and the baby was taken in.

By now the affair was public knowledge. Otojiro announced that his son would be named Raikichi. *Kichi* was a standard ending for a boy's name but *rai*, which means 'thunder', was an unusual prefix. Pressed on why he had chosen this name, he explained rather ungallantly:

Any number of men in all the four directions, east, west, north and south, may well have provided the seed for this child. However, he happens to have fallen on me, like a thunderbolt from the blue. So that's why I've given him this name.

But he never denied outright that the child was his.[19]

The Kawakami-za Theatre stood imposingly on a main road just to the north of the Imperial Palace in Kanda, an area crowded with students, bookstores and intellectuals, like the Paris Left Bank or London's Bloomsbury. Instead of being open and welcoming like an old-style Japanese theatre, with slatted wooden doors that slid out of the way and an upper floor displaying colourful posters of the latest production, it was a hefty three-storey brick and stone building in the Palladian style with narrow doors, small windows and a large auditorium. Emblazoned on the proscenium arch above the stage, framed within a frieze of chrysanthemums, was the legend 'Théâtre Kawakami'. It was Tokyo's most up-to-date theatre.

The grand opening took place on 6 June 1896, a couple of months after Raikichi had joined the Kawakami family. Otojiro had planned a spectacular extravaganza attended by more than a thousand illustrious guests. People filled the auditorium and pressed up the staircases.

Instead of sweeping aside, the curtain rose, Western style. To the audience's amazement, there was Yakko standing demurely on the stage next to her husband, in a fashionably decorative kimono. By then the craze for Western dress had soured. Women proudly wore kimono to show their patriotic spirit.

But what could this mean? Everyone knew Yakko as a famous one-time geisha though, apart from those who had been her customers, they would not have had the chance to see her. And of course they read about her in the papers, notably the recent story of the domestic upheavals, which had been reported with much gusto in the press. Why had she stepped from the shadows in this way when wives were expected to stay home?

Glancing around, Yakko picked out many familiar faces. Her patrons from her teahouse days were all there. Otojiro was making one of his interminable speeches about his impressions of drama in France, the evolution of theatre and the development of the Japanese new wave on the model of Western theatre. The culmination of all this, he declared, was the Kawakami-za.

The playwright Shigure remembered the occasion. She would have been seventeen at the time. Perhaps she was there; or perhaps she heard about it from her father who, as a leading judge, would undoubtedly have been invited.

As the speech ended, there was a round of applause. Yakko bowed deeply. Since cutting her hair she had taken to wearing a heavy, oiled wig, like a modern day geisha. It was not soft like a Western wig but had a metal frame which held the shape.

'She was so happy and so engrossed in their success,' wrote Shigure, 'that she had forgotten that she was wearing a wig. She didn't notice that it was falling off. It hit the ground with a thump. Then she heard the audience laughing.'[20]

Suddenly her short hair, oiled to her head and held in place with an unflattering headband, was revealed to all. Burning with embarrassment and shyness she hid behind Otojiro as the stage manager hastily brought down the curtain.

Nevertheless as far as Otojiro was concerned it was a triumph, confirmation of everything he had achieved. He had turned up in Tokyo as an impoverished anti-establishment rebel. Now he was a famous actor and theatrical entrepreneur who had captured one of the most celebrated beauties in the realm as his wife. He was, however, still impoverished. All the money which Yakko had managed to collect had been spent. To fund the launch they had had to borrow another 10,000 yen from a money-lender at a ruinously high rate of interest. They had achieved success but it was perilously insecure. Unless they were very lucky, they were headed for disaster.

II

ACTRESS

貞

4

SETTING SAIL
1896–1899

t last Otojiro had the perfect showcase for the new wave drama he
had pioneered. Just as the kabuki actors had the Kabuki-za theatre,
so the Kawakami troupe would perform at the Kawakami-za,
named after their illustrious leader. The first performances were hugely
successful; on at least one occasion the police had to be called in to
calm the crowds. Fired with enthusiasm, Otojiro spearheaded adaptations
of Western classics tailored to a Japanese audience. One was a version
of Jules Verne's *Around the World in Eighty Days* with a Japanese Phileas
Fogg and Otojiro as the comic servant, setting off from Tokyo on their
journey around the world. It was perfectly judged to fit Japan's increasingly
sophisticated knowledge of the West.

But all the money that Otojiro could generate was no more than a tiny
drop in the ocean of debt that he owed. He had trouble even repaying
the interest. The theatre had been mortgaged to raise the loan for the
grand opening party. Otojiro's creditors were soon threatening to seize
it to recoup their losses. They demanded that it should be rented out to
other theatre troupes. But to Otojiro that was unthinkable. He had not
built his theatre for other troupes to soil the boards.

Struggling to keep his head above water, he decided to turn the theatre into a limited company. He put out advertisements inviting subscriptions. There were plenty of people eager to buy shares and the offer was soon over subscribed. But any amount of money he raised was still pitiful compared to the size of the debt. To add to his troubles, creditors started turning up from his murky past to claim ancient debts. A court ordered some of his property to be seized and sold; but even that generated only enough money to cover a tiny fraction of what he owed. The last straw came when bailiffs barged into his lodgings when he was on tour in Kobe and seized two large leather trunks stuffed with his possessions. Under fire from all sides, Otojiro made an extraordinary announcement. He was going to stand for parliament.

Count Ito's new constitution had been formally presented to the Emperor with enormous pomp on 11 February 1889. It provided for an Upper House, consisting of royalty, peers and major taxpayers, and a Lower House, for which representatives were to be chosen by election. Only affluent homeowners, male pillars of the community aged over twenty-five, who paid at least 15 yen a year in tax, had the right to vote. Out of a population of forty-four million, there were fewer than half a million voters.

This was the national assembly for which Otojiro's old mentor, the fiery and idealistic Liberal Party leader Count Itagaki, had fought. By the time Otojiro made his momentous decision, Itagaki had been gathered back into the fold and given the post of Home Minister. It seemed there might be a chance for something approaching a real parliamentary democracy. So the timing made a sort of sense.

Yakko stood by her man, no matter how outrageous his ideas. Shortly after his announcement, towards the end of 1897, the couple left their home near Yoshicho and moved to Omori, a pretty village near the coast just outside Tokyo, towards Yokohama. Today it is a prosperous Tokyo suburb. In those days it was peaceful, pastoral country 'made beautiful,' as Eliza Ruhamah Scidmore, a 1900 American visitor, wrote, 'by old groves, old temples and shrines, tiny villages, picturesque farm-houses and hedge-lined roads'.[1] At the heart of the area was a grand old temple, much frequented by pilgrims, which stood on a green tree-clad hill ringed by paddy fields and persimmon orchards. On fine winter days the white-capped cone of Mount Fuji shimmered on the horizon. There they set up home in a very avant-garde six-sided Western-style house. Yakko made no complaint. She assented to all Otojiro's plans and quietly packed up and moved.

Otojiro began his campaign by organising an enormous outdoor party. There were jugglers, acrobats, magicians, booths full of trinkets and smoky stalls filling the air with the smell of grilled octopus and squid. Bonfires crackled and strings of coloured lanterns swung. Ten thousand people dropped in to eat, drink and enjoy his largesse. It was, said the papers, as noisy and crowded as a festival at a temple. Otojiro gave an amusing speech, then a bevy of beautiful geisha from the Yoshiwara, Yoshicho and Shimbashi glided gravely onto a makeshift stage to grace the occasion with their exquisite dancing.

Thereafter Otojiro was to be seen dressed in a sober cotton kimono, racing around the quiet country lanes in a black-painted rickshaw, trying to drum up support. After much inquiry he discovered a local issue: Omori was on the line between Tokyo and Yokohama but, inconveniently, the last train out of Tokyo did not stop there. He vowed that, if elected, he would lobby to have that changed.

He gave frequent parties for his constituents, who were all, of course, wealthy male landowners. He went from guest to guest, assiduously pouring their sake and chatting unctuously. He would say:

Honoured sirs, the prime minister can no longer be trusted with the business of running the country. The major political parties no longer represent us. Like you, I am angered at the current state of affairs. Think of me as your boat, the Kawakami line. You, my honourable constituents, must guide me into port.[2]

Then he outlined his platform. He would outlaw, he said, his gravelly voice rising in unfeigned fury, the bloodsucking moneylenders who charged exorbitant rates of interest. He would also promote New Wave theatre and do all he could to raise the social standing of actors.

He used his famous sex appeal to court the wives and daughters of his constituents. The wife of one local grandee, a Mr Yamamoto, threatened

83

to leave her husband unless he voted for Otojiro, the papers reported. He wooed his old geisha girlfriends, cajoling them into soliciting their wealthy patrons on his behalf. For all her professed docility, Yakko was not prepared to tolerate this kind of behaviour and there were regular rows. Nevertheless she also went out campaigning on his behalf. Her fame, beauty and connections were a great asset to him.

The press, however, was implacably hostile. Here was he, a riverbed beggar, an outcast, barely human, daring to think of sullying the purity of parliament with his presence. Even national papers targeted his small local campaign.

'This Kawakami, this ragtag agit prop actor, is only standing for office in order to get campaign funding from the Kuroda clan [of Fukuoka, his home city],' snorted the *Mainichi*. 'Actors need to sell themselves to maintain their popularity. That's the only reason he's doing this.'

'If the Demon Lover is chosen as a representative,' trumpeted the *Yomiuri*, 'it will not only shame the voting populace but will bring down the sanctity of the imperial parliament and dishonour the entire Japanese empire. Voters, exercise common sense!'

The words *kawara kojiki*, 'riverbed beggar', were bandied about. One of his rival candidates was quoted as saying contemptuously, 'He's just an agit prop actor. We all know actors are nothing but riverbed beggars. It's preposterous that someone like that should dare to stand for office of representative.'[3]

The *Yorozu Morning News* launched a relentless campaign against him. This was a famous paper, founded six years earlier in 1892, by a man called Ruiko Kuroiwa. It had become known for its exposés of corruption in high places; though most of its loyal readers bought it mainly in order to keep up with Kuroiwa's gripping adaptations of French detective novels which came out in daily instalments. Kuroiwa was nicknamed Shuroku the Viper. He dug scandals out of Otojiro's past, questioning his reputation and declaring that if he were elected it would defile the Japanese nation.

The vote took place in March 1898. 'It is disgraceful that so many electors are voting for the Oppeké [*sic*] guy,' fumed Kuroiwa as the count began. 'This casts great shame on the entire population of Tokyo.'

Thanks largely to Kuroiwa's vitriolic brush, Otojiro was trounced. Never one to know when he was beaten, a couple of months later he was on the campaign trail again. Finally even he had to acknowledge it was hopeless. He and his faithful Yakko were ruined. He had begged yet more money to fund his absurdly extravagant campaign. Now the creditors were hammering on his door in earnest. He would finally have to give up his beloved theatre. It was a moment of heart-rending disappointment. Everything he had hoped and struggled for had been lost.

Early one morning he opened the door to his theatre for the last time. Clutching a bottle of champagne and a glass he walked slowly through the shadowy auditorium, pausing to gaze fondly at the proscenium arch with its proud legend, 'Théâtre Kawakami'. Then he climbed onto the stage and sat down cross-legged on the bare boards.

As he remembered many years later, relishing the theatricality of it:

I opened the champagne and knocked back three glasses. Then I said my last words to my theatre. 'Well, in the end, with great difficulty, I made this one little theatre, but I had no idea how to support you after that. Now I set you free. Take any lover you like to be your next manager and good luck!' Then I poured the last of the champagne on the floor and said 'Goodu bai'.[4]

It never occurred to him, of course, to credit Yakko with playing even the smallest part in the creation of the theatre.

Hoping to drum up some money, he arranged to perform at the Kabuki-za with his troupe. Then, feckless as ever, he disappeared. When the creditors appeared at the door, Yakko was left to fend them off. 'Please give us a little more time,' she begged. 'My husband will be home soon with the advance for the next performance at the Kabuki-za.'

But several days passed and still Otojiro did not come home. Yakko, who knew his habits all too well, went to the Shimbashi geisha district. Eventually she discovered he had gone to Oiso, the fashionable seaside resort where Ito had his villa. Otojiro had been seen there frolicking in the sea with four youthful geisha, barely in their teens. He was swimming with one of them on his back, laughing merrily. To top it all, he would, of course, have to foot the ruinous bill for all four geishas' time and expenses.

Yakko was waiting for him when he finally got back. She grabbed him by his kimono front and gave him a severe thumping.

Yakko told an interviewer many years later:

Kawakami was a really reckless man. He wouldn't listen to anyone. I married him when I was twenty-two and, when I was twenty-five, the Kawakami-za was established in Misaki-cho in Kanda. I intended to spend my life peacefully and quietly taking care of him as his devoted wife. But in 1898 he unexpectedly ran for parliament and lost. That was the beginning of our unfortunate fate.[5]

It was July 1898 when Otojiro finally abandoned all hope of a political career. He carried on acting with his troupe at the Kabuki-za where they attracted large audiences who felt sorry for them because they had lost their theatre. But both he and Yakko were desperately depressed. Otojiro took to disappearing for a week at a time to drink his sorrows away. 'After I lost the election I suffered so much I thought I'd go mad,' he remembered later.[6]

One night after a long absence, dishevelled and wild-eyed, he burst into the small house in Omori.

'I'm going to kill that Ruiko Kuroiwa,' he stormed. 'I've been following him but he keeps getting away.'

He had a pistol in his belt. He had been walking back and forth between Kuroiwa's house and the newspaper offices, he told Yakko, but had not been able to find him. He had even burst into the offices and made a scene, yelling abuse, scattering inkstones and brushes and smashing furniture.

Yakko was horrified. 'There are protectors all around him,' she told him. 'You can't do it by yourself. Don't think of such a terrible thing!'[7]

Hoping to calm him down, she suggested that they go out and take a stroll along the waterfront, even though it was well past midnight. As they wandered along, they noticed a small boat bobbing in the harbour. It was up for sale. The stars twinkled in the inky sky and the water lapped enticingly. The two looked at each other.

In an interview in 1908, Sadayakko remembered what happened next. 'Kawakami bought the boat, named it Nippon-maru and decided he was going to sail off to some far country. So I said I would go with him.'[8]

It was a very small boat, just fourteen feet long, with a mast, oars and triangular sail but no cabin. Nevertheless Otojiro began daydreaming wildly. He raved about going to the West, going to the Antarctic or just disappearing into the depths of the ocean, where no one would ever know what had become of him. He wanted revenge on the world. If that meant he had to die, so be it.

Yakko had no need to participate in such a desperate mission. As a famous geisha she could make a very good living by herself. It was she who supported him, not vice versa. She did not need to share in his disgrace. Japanese did not do things in couples. If a husband went away somewhere to work, the wife always stayed at home to take care of the house and children. It was a very eccentric and modern choice to accompany her man. Like a Western wife, she had decided that their fates were inextricably bound.

But who really initiated the plan? When Yakko was interviewed in 1908, Otojiro was very much alive. As a devoted wife, it was her job to make sure that she always presented him, to himself and to the world, as the manly decision-maker while she was just the little woman. But in 1937, when he was dead and buried and she had become a *grande dame*, famous in her own right, her memory of events had changed:

I said to Kawakami, 'Why don't you stop planning to murder someone? Let's get on this boat and end our lives together on a desert island somewhere. If we can reach the Pacific maybe we'll be shipwrecked and die without trace, without anyone knowing what became of us.' To my amazement Otojiro agreed. 'Let's buy it right now,' he said.[9]

Perhaps she had just forgotten. Nevertheless it is significant that, towards the end of her life, she chose to recreate her legend with herself as the driving force in the relationship. Thus a plan was hatched to begin a new life, go off to a new land somewhere, anywhere, and start afresh. It was a last throw of the dice. They had nothing to lose.

For a harebrained scheme it was carefully planned. A couple of years earlier Otojiro had obtained foreign travel permits covering China, Korea,

France, England, Germany and America to study the performing arts. They packed ocean maps, a compass, buoys, Japanese magnets, a trumpet to sound the alarm and a lantern to hang at the front of the boat. They stockpiled provisions – rice, sweet potatoes, *miso* soya bean paste, soy sauce, charcoal, cooking pans, bowls and chopsticks – and recruited Otojiro's eldest niece, Shige, who was thirteen, and a dog called Fuku to go with them. As there was no roof they took padded kimonos and raincoats.

Then they waited for the September typhoon season. On a day when the winds were high and the seas rough, they hoisted a Japanese flag and launched their frail craft. Yakko had also stitched an SOS flag as a precaution.

By turns becalmed and driven by the winds, they scudded along the edge of Tokyo Bay. At nightfall two days into the journey, they saw lights and steered for shore. There they dropped anchor and went to sleep. They were woken by the hooting of sirens and the rumbling of steam boats. They had accidentally entered military waters. They were in the Yokosuka naval base.

A boat chugged alongside. Sailors, natty in their European uniforms, attached grappling irons and towed them to shore. There they were arrested by the military police and taken to the office of Rear-Admiral Arai for questioning. Splendid with his moustache and braided uniform, he gazed curiously at the bedraggled little group.

'And just who might you be?' he barked.

'Kawakami,' replied Otojiro in his cockiest tones.

'Not the actor Kawakami?'

'The same.'

'And what do you think you're doing here?'

'We're on our way to Kobe,' Otojiro lied. 'Just to see if we can make it. We took it on as a challenge.'

Behind his officious exterior the rear-admiral was a kind man. He tried to dissuade them from their crazy plan but nothing would make them budge. Eventually he detained them in Yokosuka and telegrammed Yakko's adopted mother, Kamekichi.

Meanwhile the press had got wind of Otojiro's latest escapade. A flurry of articles appeared. According to one he was fleeing his creditors, according to another it was blatant self-promotion. Rumours were rife. Fuku the dog was described as a servant and Shige was said to be Otojiro's mistress; though it was rather unlikely that a mistress would be travelling alongside Yakko in one small claustrophobic boat.

In the *Yorozu Morning News*, Kuroiwa the Viper turned out articles daily. Otojiro was licking his wounds, he sneered. He had failed in his political schemes, the Kabuki-za performance had been a hopeless flop and even his troupe had turned against him. At his wits' end, he decided to flee abroad to study theatre but he could afford nothing better than this little boat. By the next article he had a different theory: Otojiro was fleeing his creditors who had said they would chop him up with their swords. Kuroiwa too thought the fourth member of the party, Fuku, was a servant.[10]

As soon as she heard, Kamekichi took the train along the coast down to the naval base with one of Yakko's brothers. Long arguments followed. Kamekichi tried to persuade Yakko and Otojiro to give up their plan but the two were obdurate. Eventually they agreed to leave Shige and Fuku behind.

Rear-Admiral Arai warned them of the danger of their project. The seas between Tokyo and Kobe were notoriously rough and choppy with cross currents and unexpected squalls, even when the weather looked fine. Nobody sensible would set sail across such seas during the typhoon season, which hit that part of the coast particularly hard. If they survived, they would have to navigate the whirlpools at the entrance to the Inland Sea. To top it all, winter was approaching. They would be risking their lives if they carried on.

Otojiro was beginning to feel distinctly dubious about their foolhardy plan. The rear-admiral's superior knowledge seemed to offer a way for him to abandon it without losing face. Then Yakko happened to see a Tokyo newspaper. The headline was, 'Kawakami plans an ocean trip: he's finally gone completely mad!'

'When I saw this,' she recalled, 'I felt a rush of anger. "If you won't go, I'll go alone!" I said. So one night we cut the chain of the boat and sneaked out of the base.'[11]

For the next three and a half months the two skirted the coast of

Japan, driven by the west wind, heading towards Kobe. Otojiro raised and lowered the sail, operated the broad oar at the stern and occasionally took out a long pole and punted. Yakko, in a thin cotton kimono, was in charge of the rudder. At first the boat followed a zigzag path. Yakko kept confusing port and starboard so they made up their own terminology. Otojiro would shout 'pull' when he wanted to swing to starboard and 'push' for port.

Thus the two were thrown together in their small boat. A few days after they left Yokosuka, they were caught in a typhoon. When they saw the red warning flag, they hurriedly lowered the sail. Yakko roped herself into the boat so as not to be thrown out. The waves rose higher and higher until they were towering over them like jagged grey mountains. The little boat tossed and spun like an autumn leaf. Otojiro was desperately struggling to keep from capsizing, bailing out the water which crashed onto the deck and swirled up to his knees. When the typhoon finally passed they were battered, chilled and utterly exhausted. Otojiro's hands and legs were covered in blood and Yakko could hardly stand. As soon as they could get to shore they dropped anchor. They took shelter in an inn and rested for several days.

Sadayakko remembered:

Human beings are very strange. Even in that little boat we kept quarrelling. I said that the plan was to die, so we should go out to sea. But unexpectedly, Kawakami turned out to be a wimp. He wanted to stay close to land. So we had constant rows about that.[12]

Yakko, who had known only the geisha world, imagined their journey as a love suicide, the traditional recourse of star-crossed lovers in the old romances. They would confound their enemies, restore their honour and be together forever in death. She was the stubborn one who wanted to stick to the script they had prepared for themselves and follow the plan to the bitter end.

But Otojiro was far too cheery a fellow to let anything depress his spirits for long. Soon he had thought up a way of turning this impromptu adventure to his advantage. One day they were cast up on a beach. A fisherman found them sitting disconsolately on the shore, looking at their boat which was firmly wedged on the rocks. He took them to his village, gave them a good meal and begged Otojiro to perform a story-telling. The villagers assembled and listened, rapt, while Otojiro regaled them with tales of the couple's extraordinary adventures at sea.

News spread. Soon they were sailing from village to village, exchanging stories for food and lodging. Whenever anyone asked them where they were going, they always said, 'Kobe'. But in reality they had no idea. They were simply living from day to day. Otojiro, an inveterate self-publicist, sent off letters to the papers reporting their progress and declaring that they were on their way to Korea or possibly Shanghai, to board a ship for Europe. He wrote:

You Yorozu reporters sadly underestimate the prowess of Kyushu men. You can't help that. But you and we are in the same boat. You journalists are scorned as 'beggars of civilisation', we actors are spurned as riverbed beggars. Let's end all this. Abandon this beggarly mentality, stop publishing articles maligning me just so that you can sell papers. You should have loftier intentions. Be fair, be men! Next instalment coming soon. Signed Man of the Sea, Otojiro Kawakami, September 24th 1898.

The last weeks of their journey were an incessant ordeal. It was winter by then. All the padding Yakko could sew into their kimonos was not enough to keep them warm. Once they found themselves in the middle of a shoal of seals who attacked them and tried to nudge their boat over. Otojiro had to beat them off with a stick. And once they were caught in a storm so savage that they were sure their end had come. It lasted for two days. The sail was ripped to pieces. Yakko wrote a farewell note to Kamekichi and tucked it into her obi so that if someone found their bodies they would know who they were.

By the time they reached Kobe it was 2 January. A crowd had gathered to meet them, chanting 'Kawakami! Kawakami!' as they limped into port. A few days later Otojiro called a press conference and regaled reporters with their death-defying adventures. The pair, reported the papers, 'were looking bloated and unhealthy, not at all like their old selves'.

Some of the other troupe members came down by train to join them. They set about planning to make some money by staging shows in Kobe, Osaka and Kyoto. But in the middle of the first performance, Otojiro collapsed on stage. He was very ill. His hands, face and feet turned swollen and blue, he started vomiting blood and he was semi-paralysed along one side. He was rushed to hospital. The doctors diagnosed dropsy and a severe case of anaemia. It was six weeks before he was fit again.

It had been a strange and not entirely comprehensible interlude. At least Otojiro and Yakko had escaped their creditors. Travelling like vagabonds, they had freed themselves from the constraints of society. They had learnt that they had the talent and performance skills to survive wherever they went. They had also discovered each other's strengths and weaknesses. Yakko had shown that she was far from just the little woman. She was a powerful asset. Otojiro was not the kind of man to overlook something like that. They had left their old life behind. It was time for a new start. The only question was what to do next.

Then a man called Yumindo Kushibiki appeared. He was a Japanese émigré who lived in the United States. A graduate of Keio University, he had made his fortune catering to the craze for exotic Japanalia that was sweeping the West. Along with a business partner, he had opened a Japanese Tea Garden in Atlantic City, New Jersey, a few years earlier. It was extremely successful and popular. Even the President, William McKinley, had paid a visit.

It was every Westerner's dream of Japan. The centrepiece was a picturesque teahouse not much bigger than a dolls' house, of wood, bamboo and paper. There visitors could enjoy Japanese tea and cakes served by kimono-clad 'tea girls'. All around were landscaped gardens with a carp pond, waterfalls and bonsai trees. There was also a gallery selling woodblock prints, painted screens, fabric, pottery, fans and more bonsai. To entertain visitors there were shows by Japanese magicians, acrobats and dancers.

In the Japanese scheme of things *tabi yakusha*, travelling players, ranked very low indeed, considerably lower than riverbed beggars. They included wandering minstrels and travelling balladeers, people who owned little more than the tattered clothes in which they stood. Like gypsies or circus artistes, they roamed from place to place, making a living by their skills.

In 1866, when the shogunate, in its dying years, finally decided to issue permits for foreign travel, they were the first to apply. That year, amazingly, all eighteen permits for America and fourteen of the seventeen for Britain were for travelling players. (The other three were students.) The very first to be issued was for one Namigoro Sumidagawa, a magician. Over the decades that followed jugglers, acrobats, tight-rope walkers, spinning-top virtuosi, stilt-walkers, story tellers, musicians, singers and lion dance performers all swarmed to the West. Some never returned, others were cheated out of their earnings and died miserable deaths. But some came back flaunting untold riches and telling of a land of money trees where gold, silver and precious gems scattered the streets.

There had, however, never been a visit by a troupe of professional actors. Kushibiki had ambitions to be an international impresario. He met up with Otojiro in Kobe and suggested that he and his troupe should tour the United States. He offered to be their sponsor and promoter and 'introduce them to the ladies and gentlemen of America'.[13] They would perform initially in San Francisco then tour the country, ending up at his Tea Garden in Atlantic City. The troupe's visit would, he thought, give his business a touch of class. There might even be bigger possibilities. They might be a hit.

Otojiro had been daydreaming of taking his troupe to perform at the Exposition Universelle which was due to start in Paris the following June. He had even made an announcement to that effect to the press, which treated it as just one of Otojiro's big stories. Here was the chance he had been waiting for.

Within days he had selected his troupe members. Besides himself there would be nine actors, including two smooth-featured young *onnagata* who took the female roles. One of Yakko's brothers, Sokichi, went as costume master. There was a props man, a hairdresser who was in charge of wigs, a singer, a shamisen player and a dogsbody. Otojiro's fourteen-year-old brother, Isojiro, and one of the *onnagata*, Shigeru Mikami, spoke some English. They would be the interpreters. Obviously Yakko would go.

They also took Otojiro's eleven-year-old niece, Tsuru, the younger sister of Shige who had been with them at the beginning of their boat trip. She and Isojiro would play the children's roles. Altogether there were nineteen in the company, including the two women.

The sixteen male members of the troupe would be travelling below deck, in steerage class. Otojiro took them along to the foreign ministry to get permits certifying that they were actors, not labourers, and were travelling on Kushibiki's invitation. The company prepared props and costumes and held a series of 'subscription performances' to raise money for the tour. They also took time to plan their programme and rehearse before they left.

'I intended to go only as Otojiro's wife, to help out,' remembered Yakko. 'But just in case I might have to appear on stage, I did some practice performances.' After the troupe had rehearsed *Demon Quelling in Taiwan* (*Taiwan Oni Taiji*), she performed the dance from *The Maiden at Dojoji Temple* (*Musume Dojoji*). One of the most dramatic and spectacular kabuki dances in which a maiden, maddened with jealousy and rage, dies of a broken heart, this is a regular item in the geisha repertoire. Yakko had often performed it in her geisha days; but this was the first time for her to tread the boards with a company of actors, as an actress.[14]

Otojiro was determined to teach her to carry herself like a Western woman:

At that time I was told, 'If you go to the West, you might have to act. It won't be good if you don't look natural in Western clothes.' So I practised acting wearing Western costume many times. The problem was my posture. I stooped and I kept lowering my head. I was told my posture didn't look Western at all. Finally I learnt to push my shoulders back. I made a real effort. I don't have the ideal Japanese body shape with sloping shoulders and a narrow bottom, I have square shoulders. So Western costume suited me.[15]

Before they left the nineteen had a formal portrait taken. Dressed in their finery, they lined up in three rows against a mock-classical backdrop of Grecian pillars. The men, all clean-shaven, are uniformed like schoolboys in high-collared Prussian jackets with gold buttons down the front and military caps with a line of braid. The back row stands stiffly. The front row sits cross-legged on the ground.

Otojiro is in the middle, looking proprietorial, resting his arms on a stick. Yakko is on his left, her shoulders rounded humbly like a good Japanese wife, her hands neatly folded in her lap. Her hair is pulled back into a glossy chignon, held in place with a cord. Her perfectly proportioned face is impassive. She gazes into the distance with her large luminous eyes. Her nose is straight, her eyebrows two shapely crescent moons, her mouth full and sensual. She is dressed in a black kimono with formal crests and a patterned obi. The kimono is loosely crossed, revealing the collar and skirts of a pastel, flower-patterned kimono underneath. Tsuru is on Otojiro's right. She is a plump-faced little girl in a flowery kimono, with her hair drawn back into a bun and decorated with a ribbon. They look wary, as if they are wondering what life has in store for them.

It was noon on Sunday 30 April 1899 when the company finally assembled at Kobe's bustling harbour. The port bristled with tall-masted American sailing ships which arrived laden with kerosene and left carrying a cargo of Oriental knick-knacks – porcelain, bronze, paper goods, lacquerware, fans, lanterns, toys and curios – for the ever-growing Western market. Jostling alongside were mighty ocean-going steamers, small floating towns with layers of decks, masts fore and aft and funnels pumping thick, black smoke.

The actors' home for the next few weeks was to be the 4,206 ton steamship *Gaelic* of the Occidental and Oriental Steamship Company. The bamboo and wooden trunks packed with their props, costumes, wigs, make-up and personal effects had already been loaded. They made their way up the gangplank, the men swaggering samurai-style while Yakko and Tsuru walked with delicate little pigeon-toed steps, like modest Japanese females. At 4.30p.m., the ship's sirens blasted in an ear-splitting chorus, the engines churned and the great steamer surged off across the water.

At half past six the following evening they were in Yokohama. In a single day they had covered the distance which it had taken Otojiro and Yakko three and a half months to travel in their little craft. Asajiro and the others who had stayed in Tokyo came down to the port to wish them luck and see them off.

Otojiro, Yakko and Tsuru shared a cabin. They spent their days enjoying the luxury of the state room, saloon and smoking room or leaning on the rail of the upper decks, gazing across the boundless blue Pacific. In all there were ninety-eight cabin passengers including thirty-seven British missionaries on their way home, according to the *San Francisco Chronicle;* in those days the arrival of a steamship from the East was noteworthy enough to warrant a lengthy article in the paper. The sixteen actors had a less glamorous journey. They were on the lower deck along with 397 Chinese and eighty-one 'Japanese coolies' who disembarked at Honolulu. If contemporary accounts are anything to go by, their miserable journey involved accommodation in a dark, damp hold, seasickness, lice-infested beds, poor ventilation and nearly inedible food.[16]

The steamer was barely underway when it had to be quarantined for seven days in Nagasaki. A case of bubonic plague had been discovered in the steerage section. One unwelcome result of the increase in international travel was the spread of disease. The great liners which linked Asia with the wealthier West carried not only goods and people but fleas from plague-infected rats. Virtually every ocean-going ship was infested.

After a stopover in Hong Kong, the *Gaelic* was held up again at Honolulu because the only wharf in the island's harbour was already occupied. Otojiro took advantage of the delay to go ashore. There was a sizeable Japanese community there. The company gave an impromptu performance at the Japanese theatre and netted $390.

They also put on a performance on the ship. A Mr Harris, who had been a missionary in Japan for many years, acted as interpreter, Yakko and Tsuru danced and the singer and shamisen player performed. The 'foreigners' were surprised and entranced by the sound of the shamisen, Otojiro noted, though the strident tones of the male singer were not at all popular. Perhaps a geisha song sung in a woman's soft voice might be more successful, he thought.[17]

On Sunday 21 May, after three weeks at sea, they steamed under Golden Gate Bridge and dropped anchor at the Mission Street dock in San Francisco. Even then they had to wait five hours before they could disembark because the Federal quarantine officer was nowhere to be found. Two stowaways, who had been on board since Honolulu, were taken into custody.

As they skipped off the ship into this wondrous new world, the troupe were like children, gazing around wide-eyed in awe. Yakko was sparkling and joyous. This adventure was going to be fun. She remembered:

> On the twenty-first day we got to Mulberry Port [the *kanji* characters for San Francisco]. It was the first time I had ever been abroad. I was completely beside myself with wonder. I felt as if I were in some mythical country like India or up above the clouds. I couldn't believe I was still in the same world. There were railways criss-crossing above and below and steam engines and cable cars and automobiles and horse carriages passing by, so all the time you heard *gaa gaa* ['clang clang']. The houses were so high you had to look up and you couldn't even see the sun. Just even to get across the street was so frightening we didn't dare. So we held hands and pushed and pulled each other across, saying, 'Okay, don't get separated, okay?'[18]

In 1899 San Francisco was a gracious cosmopolitan city of 350,000 people, with cable cars that shuttled up and down the steep tree-lined hills between its splendid golden-stoned Victorian houses. Rudyard Kipling had visited a few years earlier and in his *American Notes* of 1891 described the 'mighty streets full of sumptuous buildings four and five stories high, but paved with rude cobblestones after the fashion of year 1'. The Gold Rush days were long since over, though there were still prospectors sailing off from the Mission Street dock, headed for the Klondike and Alaska, where gold had recently been found.

It was a charming city with a distinctive Spanish-Mexican feel and a population which included a tightly knit community of 20,000 Chinese and a sizeable number of Japanese. When Oscar Wilde visited in 1882 the city already prided itself on its West Coast literati. He addressed the San Francisco Bohemians Club and commented sardonically, 'I never saw so many well-dressed, well-fed, business-looking Bohemians in my life.' But it still had a certain Wild West flavour.

Shepherded along by a Japanese manager who had been arranged by Kushibiki, the troupe finally reached their hotels. Otojiro and Yakko had magnificent quarters at the Palace, the best hotel in town. Yakko remembered that they stayed on the twenty-first floor, but she may have forgotten; when Kipling was at the Palace in 1890, he said that it only had seven floors. It was certainly a massive and imposing building.

Right in the middle of the city, a few blocks east of Union Square, the hotel had a spectacular marble-paved lobby with mahogany furnishings, adorned with gigantic spittoons. It boasted four state-of-the-art hydraulic 'rising rooms' (elevators) and an 'electronic call button' in every room. It was where visiting presidents and celebrities like Sarah Bernhardt stayed. Kushibiki had decided that Otojiro and Yakko ought to be treated as international superstars. The rest of the troupe were in more modest hotels.

The actors, remembered Yakko, had put on their best, most formal clothes when they arrived in Mulberry Port. They were all wearing uniforms with stand up collars. When they got to their hotel they saw that the staff were wearing very similar uniforms.

We all laughed when we realised we were dressed like servants. What was even funnier was that everyone was carrying their own bags. When Kawakami noticed, he said, 'Do that and we'll be laughing stocks. Here you're supposed to have hotel staff carry your bags.' Some of the actors just dumped their bags right there on the stairs and went off to their rooms.

But the biggest surprise for Yakko had come as they were walking through the city. There was her own face, blown up to mammoth proportions, made into posters and plastered all over the streets. It had been cut from the group photograph taken before they left, 'enlarged bigger than my own body' and framed within a drawing of stylised bamboo and chrysanthemum. There she was in her black kimono, her hair drawn into a chignon, her lovely features impassive, gazing demurely into the distance with her extraordinary eyes, one Asian and one Western. What on earth was going on? she asked the manager.

'In these foreign countries you have to have an actress,' he said.

Yakko was flabbergasted. She had rehearsed just in case and had been told she might have to act, but she was certainly not expecting to find herself definitely on stage, let alone see her own modest face being used to publicise the troupe. Otojiro had no doubts at all that it was he who was the great star. She was just his humble wife. Whatever must he think!

'That's completely wrong,' she told the manager. 'I didn't come here to be an actor, it's Kawakami who'll be acting. He's putting on *The Sino-Japanese War*.'

'That won't work. In America everyone thinks Japan and China are the same. No one will go and see a play like that. You absolutely have to have an actress; all the roles should be taken by actresses.'

There was no getting out of it, concluded Yakko. She was going to have to be an actress.[19]

The manager knew his job. This was the era of the great actresses. Sarah Bernhardt, Ellen Terry and Eleonora Duse were the three muses whose dramatic genius ensured that any theatrical production in which they starred would be a triumph. In those days before film and television, theatre actors and actresses were every bit as celebrated and adored as the most famous Hollywood stars, pop idols or supermodels today. They were weavers of dreams, larger than life – Marilyn Monroe, Madonna and Kate Moss rolled into one. They had fan clubs; their affairs and scandals were avidly followed by a devoted public and reported every day in the theatre pages of the newspapers. They were superstars.

No one, of course, thought that little Yakko, from the backwoods of an underdeveloped country like Japan, could ever rank alongside such goddesses. Nevertheless, the Kawakami troupe would never succeed in America if they clung to the Japanese custom of populating the stage with men. The theatres would not even accept an all-male troupe, and if they used male actors to play women the audience would surely walk out.

For Yakko it was a revelation. It was not just that the buildings were strange and the traffic frightening. This was a society where women could be publicly worshipped like goddesses and play a more important part, at least on stage, than men. For a Japanese woman, that was almost impossible even to imagine.

Unbeknown to Yakko, Kushibiki had done a fine job of promoting the troupe with her as the star. The day before they arrived, the *San Francisco Chronicle* had featured the same portrait of Yakko, very large, on page four. The whole article was framed within a decorative border. 'Madame Yacco, the Leading Geisha of Japan, Coming Here,' proclaimed the banner headline, romanising her name in a Western way.

'Mme. Yacco, until two years ago the leading Geisha of Japan, is a passenger on the steamship *Gaelic* from the Orient,' began the article. It described the dramatic journey on the small sail boat, saying that the 'adventurous trio' had put off from Yokohama, destined for Paris. The paper reported:

> While still a Geisha, Yacco demanded and received an income which would not be despised by a modern prima donna . . . She first appeared in drama on the stage of the Kawakami Theater at Tokio, and met with marked success from the initial performance. She is of the best type of Japanese beauty and a lady of social position, gifted with musical ability.[20]

The article showed a distinct laxity in regard to the truth. Yakko had given up being a geisha when she married Otojiro five, not two, years earlier and had never performed on stage in Tokyo, let alone meeting with 'marked success'. And she was certainly not 'a lady of social position' in any sense that an American would have recognised. But then again, the aim was promotion, not accuracy. Perhaps Otojiro had a hand in it.

It was certainly a brilliant piece of marketing. Ever since the West first heard of Japan, even before Commodore Perry's ships arrived in Japanese waters, the myth of the exotic geisha had somehow filtered out of that closed country. The very word carried an erotic frisson. It conjured up a submissive almond-eyed Oriental maiden, the embodiment of all the seductive femininity and sexual freedom of some fanciful exotic East dreamt up in the fevered imaginations of repressed, frustrated Westerners.

Everyone wanted a peep beneath the veil. Pierre Loti's 1888 *Madame Chrysanthème* had been a bestseller in French and English despite the fact it was not at all romantic. Loti and his 'bride', Madame Chrysanthème, felt mutual contempt. The story ends with her biting the silver coins he has thrown to her to make sure they are real. Still, it portrayed the Japanese woman as alluringly available. Then came John Luther Long's short story, 'Madame Butterfly', published just two years before Yakko arrived in San Francisco, in 1897. It too was a huge bestseller. The famous playwright David Belasco, a San Francisco man, was even then in the process of transforming it into a stage play.

Fortuitously, Yakko had arrived in the West at the perfect moment. For all the fascination with geisha, no one except those who had been posted to Japan had ever had the chance to see one. To Japanese eyes the portrait of Yakko merely showed a married woman in a formal kimono. But to Americans this beautiful creature in her exotic garb was the very essence of the mysterious East. The stage was set for her to enjoy an unprecedented triumph.

If Yakko was to be an actress, she needed a stage name, something sonorous like Sarah Bernhardt. Plain Yakko was not enough.

Shortly after they arrived, the troupe met up with a banker, an American who had spent time in Japan and loved the country. He was eager to help. He was particularly interested in Yakko and her future role, not just as an actress but possibly the star of the troupe.

'What is your name?' he asked her.

'Sada Kawakami,' she said, giving him her married name.

'Plain Sada is not very interesting,' he said. 'Don't you have any other name?'

'When I used to be a geisha, I was called Yakko,' she told him.

'Yakko, Yakko, Sada, Yakko . . . ,' he pondered, rolling the syllables around with his tongue. 'Sadayakko would be good!'

'So after that I was called Sadayakko,' she remembered. 'My name was born in America!'

Everything was set for a truly thrilling debut. A scant four days after they had arrived, on Thursday 25 May, with barely a pause to settle into their new lodgings, let alone go sightseeing, the troupe launched into a two-week run at the small Turn Verein Hall on O'Farrell Street.

The show was intended primarily for the Japanese community. There were some 10,000 Japanese émigrés in California of whom a large proportion lived in San Francisco. After the Sino-Japanese War, as Japanese became bolder and more confident of their position in the world, the number of Japanese emigrating to the West had increased dramatically. There were now more than 50,000 Japanese living in the United States as official or unofficial immigrants. Homesick for Japanese theatre, they would be a natural audience for the troupe as they travelled across the country.

Otojiro treated his fellow countrymen to a programme of theatre performed just as if they were still in Japan. Most of the plays were from the traditional kabuki repertoire but performed in realistic New Wave style, with fearsomely bloody fights. The performance went on for eight hours, from morning till night. Japanese were clamouring around the theatre long before the doors opened. There was such demand that on the first day 300 people had to be turned away.

'Brilliantly successful,' reported the American press. The Japanese papers reviewed the plays more than a month later, once their correspondents' reports had made their slow way across the Pacific. They were less enthusiastic. The script of *Demon Quelling in Taiwan* was poor and the story itself uninteresting, reported the *Miyako*, though the sword fights were well choreographed and excited loud acclaim. But what redeemed the performance, even the sternest critics had to agree, was Yakko's exquisite dancing. She performed the death scene from *The Maiden at Dojoji Temple*, which she had practised in Kobe, 'so skilfully that there was a storm of applause'.[21]

Playing to a captive audience of Japanese émigrés was not going to satisfy Otojiro's ambition for long. For him the two-week run was a warm up, a chance to try out the plays and hone them for a Western audience. If they were to perform before Americans they would need a beautiful actress as the star. Thus, even though these performances were mainly for Japanese consumption, Yakko had already taken centre stage. The troupe also made some much-needed money from this trial run. They gratefully pocketed $1271.

Ensconced in their luxurious room at the Palace, Otojiro and Yakko were living like celebrities. Between performances they breezed around town, dining in expensive restaurants and admiring the huge array of Western clothes in the shops. Yakko was aware that her strength lay in her exoticism. Wherever she went she wore kimono, no matter how much she yearned for the wonderful gowns with their leg of mutton sleeves and layers of velvet and lace. The pair also went to the theatre. They studied dramas that were playing at the time and scripted new versions of their plays for Western consumption.

They were scheduled to open at the California Theater, the best and biggest theatre in town, on Sunday 18 June. A few days earlier, Yakko gave two ceremonial teas to which the cream of San Francisco society was invited. The guests included the mayor, members of his office, judges, lawyers, members of the Chamber of Commerce, journalists, artists, actors and 'other affluent gentlemen' and their wives. The gathering took place in the Palace Hotel's splendid Maple Room.

While the guests nibbled cake and sipped traditional Japanese green tea, Yakko and Tsuru bewitched them with their dancing, holding baskets of flowers which they swung daintily. Then Yakko glided from guest to guest, smiling her most beguiling smile as she handed out flowers from her basket. Fluttering from each was a silk ribbon with the words 'Madam Yacco' sewn into it.

There was an air of eager anticipation as the audience flocked into the California Theater that Sunday. The press had given the little company an enthusiastic preview. They described Yakko as 'a beautiful dancer from the land of the geisha' and promised dramas 'exciting enough to stir the pulse of the most inveterate lover of melodrama'.[22]

Otojiro, no doubt in consultation with Yakko, had pondered long and hard about what would best suit Western audiences. New Wave drama depended on language and was too tied to current events to travel well. Instead he presented some of the most famous and well-loved scenes from kabuki plays. These were timeless and would be exotic for what he judged to be Western taste. He cut back the dialogue which, being in Japanese, would be incomprehensible to the audience, and beefed up the visual elements, putting in plenty of dancing, exciting sword fights and comic interludes.

He also simplified the plays and cut them to digestible lengths. When the troupe performed to Japanese audiences, two plays had taken up the entire day. For the Americans he had crammed four into two and a half hours. The restless San Franciscans still got bored. The critics noted that 'the pieces had all been materially cut and condensed, but not enough'.

Otojiro was later panned for having offered up bastardised kabuki to Western audiences. But his changes though radical were not entirely outside the spirit of the traditional theatre. There was a movement then afoot in Japan, headed by a stern old actor named Danjuro Ichikawa, to clean up kabuki and turn it into a sort of national theatre, the equivalent of Shakespeare or grand opera, which above all would be presentable to Westerners. But until then kabuki had been a living, breathing, ever-changing drama, dependent not on text but on the charisma of its actors. The naughty riverbed beggars frequently strayed from the script or broke off the action entirely to strike melodramatic poses or ad lib. In the past kabuki had been every bit as subversive as Otojiro's New Wave theatre.

For Otojiro it was obvious that he would create crowd-pleasing theatre, designed to appeal to a specific audience. That was what he was famous for. He must also have been well aware that an American audience needed a divinely beautiful actress. Sadayakko always said that she became an actress by accident. But perhaps the whole story of her shock and dismay at seeing her own face plastered around San Francisco was a kind-hearted concoction. As the little woman and devoted wife, she could hardly agree to have herself presented as the star of the show. That would never have done for a modest Japanese woman of that era. She always took every opportunity to assert that it was Otojiro who was the star, not her. That was her job, as his wife. For, pragmatist though he was, he was also a macho Japanese man. And what could be more galling and humiliating than to be upstaged by 'the honourable indoors' – one's miserable wife?

Nevertheless it was undoubtedly Yakko whom the audience had come to see. The evening began with *The Duel* (*Sayaate*, literally 'Clashing Swordhilts'). A professional American scene painter had been hired to create a spectacular backdrop, a fanciful depiction of the Yoshiwara at cherry blossom time, awash with pink flowers. Two samurai swaggered out, one – played by Otojiro – a comic figure, the other handsome and heroic. Both, explained the English programme, were in love with the same courtesan and were about to fight it out.

Then the courtesan glided out. With a great swish and flurry of silks and clatter and clack of her foot-high wooden clogs, she progressed with infinite slowness across the stage. It was a splendid entry. The audience held its breath, gazing rapt at this extraordinary vision.

Yakko was swathed within layer upon layer of richly brocaded kimonos. The quilted hem of the outermost layer swept the floor. She kicked it aside with a little flourish with each step. Her obi, a swathe of silk brocade, was tied not at the back, in the usual way, but in the front, the mark of the courtesan. The enormous knot swayed in great folds from her waist to her knees. She wore a wig of glossy black hair, swept into loops and coils and studded with sparkling tortoiseshell and silver hairpins as long as knitting needles.

Her face was a white mask, her eyebrows and eyes etched in black and her underlip an intense peony red. But no one could fail to see the exquisite beauty of the features beneath the layers of paint. In her lavish costume she was not a painted doll but a queen. Grave, lovely, she began to dance.

The Duel was followed by *The Royalist* (*Kusunoki*, also known as *Kojima Takanori*). A patriotic drama, it gave Otojiro an opportunity to take centre stage. The play began with a lengthy, heart-rending speech in which he bade a last farewell to his son, played by his real-life brother, Isojiro. Then the troupe gave a thrilling display of fighting, full of hand-to-hand combat, acrobatic judo throws, the clashing of swords and the thud of falling bodies. 'It was absolutely realistic in the modern sense and acted as our battle scenes never are,' enthused the *San Francisco Chronicle*.

The third piece was *The Maiden at Dojoji Temple*, entitled *The Temple at Dojoji* in the English programme. For this the scene painter had created a gorgeous backdrop of a Japanese temple with 'fine perspective and melting distances'. It was Yakko's *pièce de résistance*. Shockingly transformed from a beautiful maiden into a raging fury, she demonstrated not only her heart-stopping dancing but also her ability to step inside a role.

The last piece was an attempt by Otojiro to produce a version of his trademark theatre-as-reportage for his American audience. The hero of the day was Admiral George Dewey, who had overseen the destruction of a Spanish flotilla in Manila Bay at the start of the Spanish-American

War the previous year. *Dewey Day Celebration on the Pine-Fringed Shores of Miho (Miho no Matsubara)* was a series of jolly folk dances with an unexpected denouement; as one reviewer wrote:

> An American man-of-war sailed on in miniature. One of the Japanese girls entered in a blonde wig, with a gray suit, and swinging herself in imitation of the free American woman, greeting the vessel in English, although the only thing we heard distinctly was 'Hoora, Dewey!'

'The audience,' he added, 'quite recognized the kindly intention of the strangers.' Nevertheless the play could not be judged a success.

The blonde-wigged 'Japanese girl' was probably not Yakko but one of the two pretty young *onnagata*, Kurando Maruyama and Shigeru Mikami, billed as 'Miss Maruyama' and 'Miss Shigeru' (inexplicably, Mikami was billed under his given name). The audience had no idea that these coquettish creatures with their lilting falsettos were actually men.

The critics were a little bemused but in general enthusiastic. Peter Robertson, the regular critic of the *San Francisco Chronicle*, had lived in Japan a quarter of a century earlier. He was not bedazzled by the exoticism of the performance, but commented on Yakko's skill and intelligence as an actress.

He wrote of her Dojoji dance:

> Mme Yacco is more than a geisha, as I knew the singing girl. She is a far more intellectual type than they had in the old days, quite, in fact, a different kind of woman, and her work has in it what we foreigners never thought of crediting to those entertainers – brains and invention. I have seen this kind of 'dragon' representation, but never with such evidence of pure artistic meaning as when Mme Yacco did it the other night.

He recognised that what he was seeing was not kabuki:

> The art of acting has been going through the same process of development as our own. [The Japanese plays] held the same relation to the old that the modern reading of the legitimate drama does to the rant and scene eating performances of earlier times.

Another review commented:

> Mme Yacco showed herself a very clever woman. There seemed to
> be a new poetry given to the Japanese, in her performances, and her
> face as well as her acting had the intellect in it which even those who
> have lived in Japan have not credited to the Japanese woman.'

She 'made us realise a poetic value in all those quaint figures we see on
vases which we have always considered fanciful'. She was like the design on
a willow pattern vase, an impossibly lovely painted image come alive before
their eyes.[23]

The *San Francisco Examiner* hailed the couple as 'the Henry Irving and
Ellen Terry of Japan' and published a sequence of photographs showing
how they portrayed different emotions. There is Yakko in her kimono,
lowering her eyes and gazing through long lashes to evoke 'coquetry'
while Otojiro, who had grown a moustache, roars with laughter ('mirth')
and frowns ferociously ('indignation').

Yakko's debut had been a triumph. Her dancing lessons since the age
of four, her years as a geisha which was a form of acting in itself, her
appearances on the stage in charity performances, had all paid off. Even
Otojiro must have recognised that this was no humble little woman. She
was the entrancing Yakko, the most celebrated geisha in Japan, adored by
prime ministers, sumo heroes and kabuki stars. She could bewitch anyone
– even a theatre full of Westerners who could not understand a word
she said.

The critics were kind but the public fickle. As Otojiro hammed up his
forty-five minute monologue in *The Royalist*, Wild West San Franciscans
yawned and shuffled in their seats. No amount of sword play or gorgeous
dancing could compensate. The Japanese in the audience, meanwhile,
complained because the plays had been so savagely cut. Audiences rapidly
dwindled. The show was, as the *San Francisco Chronicle* put it a few days later,
'a frost'.

Then, as Otojiro put it in his diary, 'there was An Unexpected Event'.
On 21 June the fourth day of their run and a month after their arrival
in San Francisco, they arrived at the theatre as usual and began their

preparations for the evening's performance. But as they were putting on their make-up and laying out their costumes, there was a sudden fracas. Yakko remembered:

In front of a great crowd of onlookers, foreign bailiffs came barging into my dressing room. *'Paa paa paa* ['Blah blah blah' – incomprehensible foreign syllables],' they said, and started impounding everything. We were completely stunned, we had no idea what was going on. Kawakami said, 'Where's Mitsusé? Call Mitsusé!' The bailiffs said, 'No,' and didn't listen to him. They grabbed the costumes and even tore down the curtain. They took everything. So we couldn't perform.

From the very start the finances of the tour had been murky. Otojiro for one had been aware that things were not going exactly to plan. For all his grand claims to be an international impresario, Kushibiki was not there to take care of them as he promised. He had had a major loss in his business and could no longer afford to sponsor them. So he handed them over to a Japanese lawyer named Kosaku Mitsusé, who became their manager. It was Mitsusé who hired the California Theatre.

As far as the troupe was concerned, Mitsusé was the villain of the piece. They had been warned by the expat community, remembered Yakko, that he was unscrupulous. They had barely started working together when he was begging for money. Instead of paying their hotel bills, they gave him every cent they had, even selling their jewellery and watches to help him out. He pocketed one day's takings, saying it was for the electricity bill, then the next, supposedly for the advertising. He paid the actors just $2 each, not even enough to buy coffee or cigars. They were in such straits that Kushibiki's business partner took pity on them and gave them another $2 each out of his own pocket. Then Mitsusé disappeared with $2000, without settling the rent for the theatre.

The American view was different. 'The truth was that the Japanese company was insufficiently capitalized and struck the summer solstice,' wrote the *Chronicle*. Despite Yakko's ceremonial teas and glorious dancing, they had not managed to attract large enough crowds. When the brilliant scene painter did not receive his $250 fee, he walked off with his art work. Mitsusé had made an unsuccessful gamble and was out of pocket by $2000. The source of this information, however, may well have been Mitsusé himself, which would cast some doubt on its veracity.

Whatever the truth of the matter, the tour had been madly reckless — an under-planned, under-capitalised, fly-by-night affair. We do not even know who paid the troupe's steamship fares.

Otojiro and Yakko saw themselves as romantic adventurers struggling against betrayal. But to the patronising American press they and their compatriots were pathetic, bewildered children: 'Many little brown ticket holders walked disconsolately away, hands in pockets and a gloomy expression on their countenances . . . The principals returned sadly to the Palace Hotel, chattering and protesting and not understanding precisely what had happened.'[24]

But the theatre was only the beginning of their woes. When the troupe got back to the hotels where the actors were billeted, they found the rooms locked and their possessions confiscated. Their bills had not been paid. They managed to persuade the managers to let them stay one more day. Then they were thrown out in earnest.

Yakko and Otojiro, meanwhile, found themselves virtually imprisoned in their luxury quarters at the Palace. The management demanded immediate payment and, when they could not come up with the money, refused to let them leave. While Yakko stayed as a hostage, Otojiro went to the owner of Shop Ido, a Japanese merchant who had been one of their most enthusiastic supporters. Practically on his knees, he begged for help. Eventually the shopkeeper agreed to make a down payment of $270 on their hotel bill. They left the Palace, though they had to leave behind their possessions until the bill was fully paid.

There was a gut-wrenching sense of *déjà vu*. 'It was like being stung by a bee when you're already crying,' as Otojiro put it. 'All of us were homeless dogs.'[25]

They did not even have money in their wallets to buy food. In the end the troupe pooled their last remaining cash to buy a few loaves of bread. They went to Union Square, sat down on benches and began to discuss how on earth they were to survive in this hostile land.

5

'AND HOW THIS GEISHA DANCES!'
LOST IN AMERICA 1899—1900

'Our experience in America was the bitterest one,' Sadayakko confessed to Yone Noguchi, the brilliant journalist father of the sculptor Osamu Noguchi, in an interview six years later.

We were ignorant about managing, and did not know what sort of play would fit the American taste. We made a flat failure in San Francisco. We landed on the Pacific coast without any funds. You can imagine how hungry, how discouraged we were![1]

With no home, no money and only the clothes they stood up in, they ate their bread and pondered their dreadful situation. Pursued by creditors in Japan, when Otojiro lost the election and his theatre, Yakko had thought they had reached rock bottom. But this was far, far worse.

For a month the pair had led the lives of pampered stars. At a stroke the great Japanese theatre troupe had been reduced to penniless vagabonds. For all their ambitions, they were no better than riverbed beggars after all. Stranded in a big, frightening foreign country, they could not speak the language or read street signs and did not know the customs. Coming from

110

a small closed community like Japan where everyone took care of everyone else, they found themselves without any friends and relations to fall back on. Worst of all, they had lost their manager, the one person who could mediate between them and the large, scary Wild West foreigners. The only thing they could do was to try and survive one day after another.

But there was one group of allies in this alien place. The Japanese émigré community who had warned them about Mitsusé rallied around to help their stricken fellow countrymen. One family offered them their shed. The actors cleared a space in the middle of the furniture and trunks that were stored there and spread thin straw mats on the wooden floor to sleep on. After a few days they managed to negotiate with the keeper of a Japanese inn. He let them have a room and agreed to defer payment until they had some money.

Yakko was as concerned about the indignity of their situation as the desperate insecurity about how they would survive. As the only adult woman in the troupe she had to take on the role of mother hen, reassuring her brood and doing her best to keep up a cheerful façade. But at night she secretly cried herself to sleep.

'We went to people's houses to beg food,' she remembered:

It was the bitterest humiliation. When we were in Japan, we had heavy debts but we always had three meals a day. Then to come to a foreign country and have to bow our heads and be so poor we had to beg for food! And to think it was all Mitsusé's fault! It was so painful that when I went to bed I couldn't sleep. Whenever I thought about it I'd start crying.[2]

The only way out of their hopeless situation was to find a theatre. They borrowed yet more money and hired a small vaudeville theatre called German Hall on O'Farrell Street. They managed to retrieve some of their costumes and spent several days hammering together a *hanamichi* walkway. Then they put out advertisements around the Japanese community.

By 21 July they were ready to give their first show. They entertained their Japanese audiences with day-long performances of tried and tested New Wave spectaculars: *Round the World in Eighty Days, Shock Again!* and

Otojiro's *Battlefield Diary*. Each day Yakko stepped out on stage and danced. Her welcome on the San Francisco stage had done wonders for her confidence. With each performance she grew more assured. The audience were spellbound.

After a week they had netted $766.50, enough to redeem the rest of their costumes and equipment. But their debts were still huge and their creditors clamouring more and more noisily.

Their new-found Japanese friends advised them to cut their losses and go back to Japan. The actors too had had enough of this experiment. It was time to go home. They were family men, they reminded Otojiro. They were not adventurers with no ties, they were breadwinners. They had wives, children and ageing parents back home, dependent on them for support. Here in this harsh hostile world things could only get worse. Supposing they ran out of money and starved to death? That would be the end not only for them but for their families too.

One of the two English speakers, the handsome young *onnagata* Shigeru Mikami, pleaded his case particularly plaintively. He was twenty-seven, from Kobe. He had three dependants – his fifty-four-year-old mother, his twelve-year-old brother, whom he was putting through school, and a nineteen-year-old 'wife' whom he had not yet formally married. He loved her with all his heart, he said, wiping his eyes sadly. At first his mother had not approved of her. He had begged her to allow him to marry her, saying, 'If I return from the west safe and sound, please make us a legal couple.' Finally she had relented. The three had been at the port to see him off. He had stood on the lower deck watching them holding their sleeves to their eyes as the great steamer pulled out. He had left full of hope, thinking he would soon make his fortune and be on his way back; but now, it seemed, they were destitute.

The actors urged Otojiro to divide their pitiful profits. They would use their share to go to Hawaii and perform there until they had earned the money to go home. Otojiro and Yakko could stay on alone in the United States and make another attempt to establish themselves.

But Otojiro was a very stubborn man. His ambitions soared way beyond the likely or possible; added to which he had had his appetite whetted by their brief taste of success. He was determined to make it to Paris with his

Five portraits of
Sada as a child

Ko-yakko at 14, the age at
which she met Momosuké –
a trendy young geisha, with a
modern loose hairstyle and
high collared Victorian dress

Bigot's unkind cartoon of geisha in western dress outside the Hall of the Baying Stag, stubbing out their pipes on the veranda

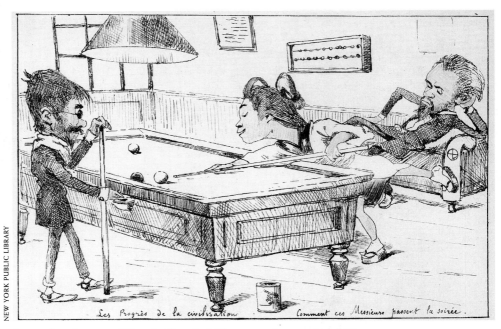

A geisha shows off her billiard skills – another unkind Bigot cartoon

Portrait of Momosuké at 20,
taken in New York, 1888

Otojiro and Yakko's wedding portrait,
October 1893

Count Ito around 1886, when he was
45 and Yakko was 15

MADAME YACCO, THE LEADING GEISHA OF JAPAN, COMING HERE.

Yakko's arrival trumpeted in the *San Francisco Chronicle*, Saturday 20 May 1899

Boston: Yakko plays Portia in the Japanese *Merchant of Venice*, denouncing Sairoku (Otojiro)

Louche world travellers: the troupe in Chicago, October 1899. Yakko is in the middle, Otojiro sitting to her right, with moustache and derby

SPECIAL FEATURES IN THIS NUMBER—MIRIAM ("WOMEN OF THE BIBLE" SERIES), *By Dr. Henry van Dyke;* SADA YACCO'S GREATEST PLAY

HARPER'S BAZAR

PUBLISHED WEEKLY
VOL. XXXIII.—NUMBER 12   NEW YORK, SATURDAY, MARCH 24, 1900   TEN CENTS A COPY
FOUR DOLLARS A YEAR

MADAME SADA YACCO, JAPAN'S GREATEST EMOTIONAL ACTRESS.
FROM A PHOTOGRAPH TAKEN FOR "HARPER'S BAZAR."—[SEE PAGE 232.]

'The ghost of a Mona Lisa smile': *Harper's Bazar,*
Saturday 24 March 1900, celebrates Yakko on its cover

The Geisha and the Knight, Act I. The Geisha, on foot-high wooden clogs, watches as her lover, in white cape and flat hat, challenges the evil Banza to a duel (American tour, 1900)

The Geisha and the Knight, Act II. Sadayakko, as the geisha, tries to persuade the monks to let her enter the temple grounds in pursuit of her lover (New York, 1900)

Diva: a smiling Sadayakko in New York in her tea gown, the height of fashion, 1900

'And how this geisha dances!' Sadayakko as the geisha in an exquisite scarlet kimono, throwing off layer after layer as she dances seductively, Paris 1900

Triumphant return: Sadayakko sweeps through Kobe after the first tour, January 1901

Dinner with the Tsar, 1902. Otojiro is at the front, looking at the camera; Sadayakko, in her kimono, to his left. The Tsar is at the end of the table

'The little Raj': Sadayakko (on the left, in a multi-layered Meiji kimono) with Tsuru and Raikichi in Vienna, 1902

Back home: Sadayakko and Otojiro in Chigasaki, 1903

troupe and perform at the Expo there the following year, no matter what. Oiling his tongue he set to work to win them over. They should not run away from failure, he harangued them. They should fight back, grab life with both hands, push themselves to the limit. They should be heroes, take this opportunity to win everything or die in the attempt:

Let us go on as far as we can! Let us perform as much as we can! When we reach the point where we can do no more, we can always be waiters or shovel coal on the railway. Till that time comes, I beg you, trust in me! Put your life in my hands!

'I couldn't bear the idea of going home showing the white flag,' he remembered. He was also well aware that his creditors were still waiting for him in Japan. For Yakko, it went without question that whatever he chose to do, no matter how hopeless, she would be at his side. Going home was no longer an option.[3]

Somehow he managed to persuade them to stay together, at least for a while. He did, however, make one concession. He decided to leave the two youngsters behind. It was not fair to subject children to the ordeal that was to come, added to which it would mean two fewer mouths to feed.

Sadayakko remembered:

We had no money. If we could just get rid of a mouth or two it would be easier. If we left behind people who were not our relatives there might be bad feelings. So we decided to give up our blood relations, Kawakami's younger brother, Isojiro, and his niece, Tsuru.

By now they had many friends in the Japanese community in San Francisco. An artist called Toshio Aoki, who had no children of his own, was keen to adopt eleven-year-old Tsuru. He had already taken her in to stay with him when the actors became destitute.

In Japan children were often passed around. Childless relatives or even, as in this case, childless friends might adopt a child to bring up as their own. Children could be adopted at any age or even as adults. This meant

113

that children from poorer families could have a better chance in life. The adopting family, for their part, had a child who would become their heir and in time perform the all-important task of tending their graves.

'Aoki said he would love her and take care of her as if she were his own child,' remembered Sadayakko. 'Tsuru said she loved this Mr Aoki as if he really were her father and she wanted to stay with him forever.'

As for fifteen-year-old Isojiro, who could speak a little English, he was left with an American family to be a house boy and get some education. From another point of view it was also a chance for both of them. They would become Americans and perhaps in time even make their fortunes.

Before the little party left they crossed swords with Mitsusé again. Otojiro had managed to track him down. But he swore that he did not have any money to give them. Sadayakko remembered the encounter as if it had been a scene in an old samurai drama.

'Do as you wish to me!' Mitsusé groaned. 'Kill me!'

Otojiro drew himself up majestically and glared at him like a proud samurai warrior. Sadayakko recalled his words:

> If I were the Otojiro Kawakami of old, I could not let you live. But I am a gentleman and a man of honour. So I forgive you. We have had to bow our heads and beg for food and clothing and live in a miserable hut fit only for beggars – and it is all thanks to you.[4]

And, she remembered, he wiped away some manly tears. Perhaps the fact that Otojiro did not press their case suggests that they were not sure any more if Mitsusé really was the villain or what had been the real cause of the débâcle.

On the hundredth day after they had arrived, they left San Francisco. 'The difficulties we had faced during those hundred days were indescribable,' wrote Otojiro in his melodramatic way.

> Soon after we arrived, I felt overwhelmed by the melancholy and depression of being abroad. The émigrés here advised us to take our

tips and go home, but that only made me more determined to stay on. And so we seventeen set off – into the Jaws of Death![5]

With pitiful funds, no manager and only one English-speaker among them, the little band of adventurers prepared to venture into this unknown, hostile land. They had fallen to the level of the much-despised travelling players. Like gypsies, they would keep moving from place to place, travelling as far as they could on whatever money they could get, deciding where to go as they went along, living from day to day.

On 29 August the fifteen actors boarded a boat and set off for 'the little city of Shatoru [Seattle]', 800 miles along the Pacific coast. They arrived on 1 September and put up at a cheap Japanese inn. Otojiro and Yakko followed a couple of days later. They checked into the best hotel in town, strolling nonchalantly through the glamorous stone portals of the Occidental in Pioneer Square, the heart of the city. Otojiro, who now sported a moustache like a fashionable West Coast gentleman, wore a three-piece suit and bowler hat while Yakko shuffled along with dainty steps in an exquisite kimono. No matter how precarious their finances, they were determined to keep up appearances. They were international stars. They would worry about the bill later.

Seattle in 1899 was a booming pioneer city. Cable cars, automobiles and horse-drawn carriages clanked and clattered up and down the streets to each side of the magnificent Occidental, a tall triangular edifice like a West Coast version of New York's Flatiron Building. Mark Twain had swept through on a lecture tour four years earlier. Six years before that Sarah Bernhardt had descended on the town with a huge entourage in a private twelve-carriage train in which she occupied an entire carriage, a luxurious 'palace on wheels'.

In the last couple of years Seattle had grown fat thanks to the gold rush. Thousands of the 'travelling men' bought their outfits there before setting off from Seattle's bustling port for the Klondike and Alaska. Those who were lucky enough to strike it rich returned humping sacks of gold which they dispensed lavishly. They were to be seen propping up bars, sporting their moustaches, bowler hats and smart new waistcoats, flashing gold nuggets as large as a man's fist to pay for their drinks, boots and railway tickets. The more sober ones started businesses and spread their new-found wealth around.

There was also a huge and growing community of homesick Japanese, recruited to work on the railroad and in logging, mining, fish processing and agriculture. Japanese ships steamed in and out of the port and there was a lively Japantown crammed with shops and businesses. So the troupe was guaranteed a ready-made audience.

With Mikami, the lovelorn young English-speaking *onnagata*, as interpreter they managed to hire a theatre. On 9 September, just three days after Otojiro and Yakko had arrived, they were on stage, performing to the Japanese community. Less than a week later they had transferred to the grand Seattle Theatre.

The local press had no idea that these supposed international superstars were actually living a hand-to-mouth existence. Garnering audiences was a matter of life or death. They risked starvation, quite literally, if they failed.

The day after their first performance the *Seattle Post-Intelligencer* featured a large photograph of Yakko on the front page, headlined 'Mme Yacco, Japan's Ellen Terry, Visits Seattle En Route to the Paris Exposition'. She was on tour, said the accompanying article, 'supported by her husband Otto Kawakami and a company of Japanese artists'. It compared her to American stars, concluding, 'As an Oriental dancer, if the customs of the Orient must be accepted as art, Mme. Yacco is truly acknowledged peerless.' The writer added delicately that the troupe's reception in San Francisco had been 'beyond what was expected, although on the whole it could not be classed as enthusiastic'.[6]

Otojiro and Yakko had been thinking hard. They had learnt some lessons from San Francisco about how best to promote themselves to a Western audience. Galling though it was for the vain Otojiro, Yakko was clearly the star. Only her seductive grace and beauty had the power to lure crowds.

In Seattle the company had a modest success. Once they had paid the rent for the theatre, their hotel bills and other expenses, there was still a little money left over. They took the train on to Tacoma, a journey of two hours and thirteen minutes. There they stayed a week and gave a couple of performances which generated enough money to make the overnight train journey on to Portland, Oregon. The critic of the *Morning Oregonian* reported that Yakko was 'the best type of Japanese beauty, bearing a strong resemblance in contour of face and coloring to the Italian style of beauty. Large, brilliant eyes, a face of great expressiveness and charm, and extremely graceful in every movement.'

'The audience was closely attentive and warmly appreciative,' he added after the show.[7]

So far they had stuck to cities with large Japanese émigré populations, ensuring a supportive community for them as well as a natural audience. Then, on 7 October, the troupe turned away from the friendly west coast and headed east into the hinterland. Hereafter Japanese would be thin on the ground. They would, Otojiro recorded in his diary, be travelling through mining country. If all else failed, they could get work in the mines. He had probably not bothered to check whether there really were any mines between Portland and Chicago. He was being humorously hyperbolic, as usual.

To save money, they took the train only for long distances. For short journeys and within the cities, they walked. They tied together their costumes, wigs and props, made them into bundles, heaved them onto their backs and set off. For travelling they wore Western clothes. But while their bodies announced that they were modern Westernised people, on their feet they felt more comfortable shod with home-made straw sandals, the traditional footwear for Japanese travellers. During the Sino-Japanese War, the Japanese soldiers too had been famous for wearing straw sandals despite their smart Western uniforms. Even Yakko wore straw sandals.

Relishing the drama and maybe exaggerating the hardship and length of their journey just a little, Otojiro wrote:

We looked just like coolies! When we got to the theatre, these 'coolies' would slap white powder on their grubby faces, dab on rouge and turn into princesses and princes. We'd even make quick costume changes on stage. In this way from Seattle to Chicago we performed plays and got money to go on to the next place. We didn't suffer great failure. And luckily we didn't have to become miners.[8]

After eighty-nine hours rattling and bumping slowly along, winding through the Rockies and then trundling through unendingly flat prairie land, the little party of adventurers rolled into Chicago's Wells Street Station at 1p.m. on 11 October. The 2312 mile journey had taken nearly four days. Stiff and exhausted they clambered off the train and gazed awe-struck around them.

Long broad avenues populated with sputtering automobiles and horse-drawn carriages stretched as far as they could see in every direction. Massive ornately carved skyscrapers with chimneys belching black smoke soared higher by far than the battlements of the most formidable medieval castle in Japan. Sailboats and steamers dotted the blue waters of the lake. Seattle, Tacoma and Portland had been tiny hick towns compared to this vast, grimy, intimidating metropolis.

Chicago was America's capital of money. With a population of 1.6 million, it boasted more millionaires than anywhere else in the country. Rudyard Kipling, who visited around 1890, found it an inferno of uncultured barbarians 'talking about money and spitting about everywhere'. But it was also riddled with vice, poverty and fearsome slums populated by thieves, gunmen and white slavers. Its brothels were world famous and operated around the clock with police protection. This was the city where three years earlier, in 1896, a low-life character called Mickey Finn had invented his notorious knock-out drink.

There was no friendly Japanese community to be found here and no homely Japanese inn. Instead the fifteen actors checked into a small boarding house. In their usual style, Otojiro and Yakko headed for the best hotel in town, the Grand Pacific. (Otojiro recorded that they stayed at the 'Hapiric', a misspelling which indicates the level of his English at that point.) A magnificent stone edifice in the French style with pavilions and a mansard roof, the Pacific filled an entire city block in the financial centre, near the Board of Trade. It boasted 600 huge, luxuriously furnished rooms, two elevators and sumptuous meals served in grand style. Every president that passed through the city stayed there. Mrs Abraham Lincoln had been a permanent resident in 1875, when she went spectacularly mad.

Otojiro and Yakko were shocked to discover that the rate was $35 a night. The troupe had $200 between them. Nevertheless they took a room.

In this money-mad city there were thirteen top theatres, each larger and more splendid even than the Kabuki-za back home. Here, they thought, they were bound to find the success that had eluded them for so long.

The next day the pair had a good breakfast of two eggs, clear soup and tea, which reduced their funds by $4 a head. Then Otojiro put on his smartest suit, picked up his cane, cocked his derby at a jaunty angle and set off to find a theatre where they could perform. By then, being a man who loved to talk, he had mastered a good few English phrases. He took Mikami, the handsome young English-speaking *onnagata*, along to help.

They pushed through the swing doors of the first theatre they came to and strode into the ornate, velvet-swagged lobby. They strutted up to the box office clerk and explained their mission. He looked at them askance and consulted with the office clerk. The office clerk spoke to the manager and reported that he was too busy to see them. They could try some other day if they really wanted.

It was only after visiting several theatres that they found a manager who was prepared even to speak to them. A well-built man with a buttoned waistcoat bursting open over his well-fed belly, he towered over them. Looking like little Lilliputians in the land of giants, they talked excitedly in garbled English, waving their arms about. The man peered down at them with mild curiosity, then shrugged when he realised what they wanted.

'Fully booked,' he drawled. 'You wanna perform here, you gotta book years in advance.'

At another theatre, a gargantuan bewhiskered man asked them how many actors they had in their troupe. Seventeen, they told him. He stared at them in disbelief.

'Look around you,' he boomed. 'This is a huge theatre. We have casts of two or three hundred here. You can't put on a show with seventeen actors. I'm a busy man . . .'

'You're actors, you say?' scoffed a third. 'So you can dance. Let's see you dance! Let's hear you sing! I'll decide whether to talk to you after you've done your piece.' And without more ado he showed them the door.

A fourth jeered, 'Chinamen, are you?'

'No,' said Otojiro, bridling. 'We Japanese.'

'Chinamen, Japs, makes no difference. We're not interested.'

Wherever they went they had the same response. No one would take them seriously. They were laughed at, scorned and rejected. Some people had never heard of Japan or thought it was part of China. And no one imagined that such a distant, beggarly country could possibly have music worth hearing or drama worth seeing. Everyone called them 'Japs'.

'You telling us Japs got music?' they would sneer incredulously. 'You Japs got theatre?'

Sadayakko remembered:

When they heard we were Japanese actors they snorted *fnn* ['huh'] and turned up their noses and wouldn't even bother to talk to us. All the theatres did shows with casts of 300. We did Japanese plays and, on top of that, there weren't even twenty of us. They wouldn't even bend their noses to look at us.

There was one slender thread of hope. They could always throw themselves on the mercy of the Japanese consulate. There they would surely find fellow countrymen who were bound to help them out. If the consul put in a word for them with a theatre, all their troubles would be over.

A couple of days after they arrived, Yakko put on a formal kimono and Otojiro donned a suit. At the consulate they were ushered into the presence of Consul Fujita. But they had made, it seemed, a terrible miscalculation. Westerners might take them to be international stars comparable to Henry Irving or Ellen Terry. But to Japanese officialdom, no matter how successful they may have been on the west coast, they were still outcasts, embarrassing despicable riverbed beggars. The consul looked at them with undisguised contempt.

'We told him our circumstances and begged his kind offices,' remembered Sadayakko. 'But the consul was a Christian. He said he hated the theatre and wouldn't pay any attention to us at all.'

'Not a single decent Japanese ever comes here!' he snapped. 'You travelling players, you're all the same. You're tricksters. You do something unethical or dishonourable, you get into trouble, and then you turn up asking for help. I have no time for you.'

Perhaps, Yakko ventured, he might at least kindly help them retrieve their luggage. Because of language problems, they did not know how to pick it up.

'I'm not a janitor for actors' luggage!' he snarled and had them shown out.

'There he was, Japanese just like us, yet so utterly unsympathetic!' remembered Yakko in disbelief.

Money was running desperately short. Otojiro and Yakko felt the weight of responsibility heavy on their shoulders. It was they who had insisted that the troupe should make this reckless journey. If they failed, if they turned into beggars or starved to death, the blame would be all theirs.

That day they moved out of their splendid hotel and took a room in a cheap hostelry run by an old couple. The room, remembered Otojiro, contained a *duburu betto* (double bed), 'like a sleeping mat for two'. If only it had been a Japanese inn, they could have dragged in futons and put up the whole troupe there in one room. But Westerners were not so easy going. And they did not even have the spare cash to bribe the staff to turn a blind eye if they moved the others in.

The actors had had to move out of their boarding house. Some of them pitched camp on a patch of grass down by the river; they really had become riverbed beggars. The hard-working Mikami and some of the others drifted in and out of the Kawakamis' tiny double room. They would make great play of being 'visitors', talking and laughing loudly. Then they would spread their costumes on the hard wooden floor and go to sleep. Some even slept under the bed. They listened out for footsteps. If they heard someone approaching they would all quickly wake up and start chatting earnestly. Thus somehow they managed to get some sleep.

By now they were down to their last few dollars. Yakko rationed the money, allocating each actor 5 cents a day for food. In the morning they had coffee, bread, ham and eggs at the cheapest restaurant they could find, then missed lunch and spent the last couple of cents on a coffee before bed.

'After a little while we could barely afford even a 5 sen [2½ cents] piece of bread,' remembered Yakko. 'We were so hungry it was unbearable.'

Their stomachs rumbling, Otojiro and Mikami tramped the windy streets of Chicago. Surely there must be a theatre somewhere where they could perform. It was bitterly cold and they had arrived without winter clothes. To keep warm and drown their misery, the two men drank heavily, frittering away precious money on whisky.

Yakko mothered her brood, trying to keep their spirits up and stop them from losing heart. She remembered:

> Kawakami was at his wits' end, thinking there must be somewhere that would rent us a theatre. Day after day after day he went out patiently. Waiting at home, we kept thinking, 'Surely today he'll come back with good news.' But he'd come back in the evening dazed. We were utterly forlorn.[9]

They had tried everything. It seemed their luck had completely run out. Then, five days after the troupe had arrived in Chicago, Otojiro and Mikami happened to hear of a theatre called the Lyric. There was a new manager there, they were told, a Mr James S. Hutton. An unconventional, kindly person, he was open to all sorts of novel and eccentric ideas.

Hardly daring to hope, they went along to the theatre. As always, they met with a cold reception. The manager was busy and could not see them. But they had no further ideas. This was their last chance. So they waited outside the theatre until the end of the day, asking again and again to see Mr Hutton.

Evening came. Finally the manager himself appeared, curious to see who these persistent foreigners were. He ushered them into his office. With Mikami interpreting, Otojiro explained their mission. They were Japanese actors, the best in the land, in need of a theatre in which to show off their craft. He was hoping, he said, that they might hire the Lyric.

'I'm afraid we're booked out,' said Hutton dismissively, without even pausing to think. They looked at him in blank despair. But as it happened, his daughter was in the room too. She was mad about Japanalia. Along with many fashionable young people at that time, she adored woodblock prints and sought out books on Japanese history and stories. Here before her eyes were some real Japanese who claimed to be actors. She was desperate to see them perform.

'Just for ourselves, can't we see what they can do?' she cajoled her doting father.

He could not say 'No'. The theatre was booked out every evening. But the matinée performance that Sunday happened to be available. He offered the use of the theatre for one show only. Instead of charging rent, he would split the takings. It was a kind gesture. It was all too likely that no one at all would come and he would end up making a loss.

'Your performance will be the first show from the Orient that anyone here has ever seen,' he told them. 'It might well be very interesting, but it'll be completely unfamiliar. Even if you spend a lot of money on advertising, I can't guarantee that a single person will come. But even if no one comes, my daughter and I will be your audience!'

Then, relenting a little, he promised to invite the press, local literati, artists, actors and theatre people as unpaying guests. Exploding with joy, Otojiro and Mikami sprinted back to tell their hungry comrades the good news. Suddenly everyone was bursting with courage and enthusiasm. But their problems were far from over. It was only the beginning of the week. There were five or six days to go until Sunday and they had almost no money left. They no longer had even 5 cents each for food.

The next few days were a horrific ordeal. By the end the troupe were reduced to trying to quell their gnawing hunger pains by filling themselves up with water. They grew pale and thin, with dull eyes and grey sunken cheeks beaded with cold sweat. When they looked at each other they saw not human beings but hungry ghosts. But they had to put their all into this one performance. It was their only chance. If they failed they really would die of starvation.

The agreement was that Hutton would lend them the theatre and cover the cost of electricity and staff. Everything else was their responsibility. Yakko remembered:

All he lent us was the theatre. That was all – no costumes, nothing. We had to use the backdrops we'd brought from Japan. For cherry blossoms I cut up paper and the troupe members pasted them onto branches. It was a real to do!

They also needed desperately to advertise. Otherwise who would come and see them? But without money they could not pay for fliers or posters. Then Otojiro remembered his agit prop days. They would do street theatre. That would cost nothing.

The actors were weak and listless with hunger. Nevertheless, the day before they were due to perform they struggled to their feet and put on their costumes. Otojiro and the other seven players of male parts strapped on black samurai breastplates and ferocious horned helmets with scowling masks over their faces. They slipped their feet into straw sandals. Mikami and Maruyama, the handsome *onnagata*, hid their manly features beneath thick white lead-based make-up, outlined their eyes in black and painted in eyebrows high on their foreheads and girlish rosebud mouths. They put on heavy wigs, wound on silk kimonos and thick brocade obis and shuffled forth in high wooden clogs.

It was a freezing day. The sky was dark and lowering and it was beginning to snow. Banging and thumping on huge drums and blowing conch shells which sent out a long melancholy wail like an alpen horn, the actors paraded through the city streets in the shadow of the looming skyscrapers with their dusting of snow. They carried a banner advertising their performance the following day. They made such a racket that workers came out of their offices to stare. Sadayakko recalled:

> They looked completely mad, as if they were possessed by fox spirits. When I saw them walking along, it was so pitiful that I wept. I would have walked with them, but they said, 'If you get ill, you won't be able to dance and our show will be ruined.'

Everyone realised that she was the key to their success. If she were to catch a chill and be unable to appear, they would be doomed.

On Sunday the doors opened at one o'clock. People began to trickle in, more and more, until the theatre was packed. Their advertising ploy had worked.

But how were the actors to perform? They had not eaten for days. They were so weak from lack of food that they could barely stand up and their exertions the previous day had used up what little strength they had left.

Their faces were pallid and covered in cold sweat and they felt hot and cold by turns. Their top-knotted samurai wigs, instead of fitting snugly, slipped loosely about on their heads. 'We were like invalids,' remembered Otojiro. Nevertheless they would have to make one last effort. It was make or break.

The performance consisted of two plays. First they did *The Royalist* (*Kojima Takanori*) which had been a success in San Francisco for its vividly realistic fights. It ended with a dramatic battle in which swords flashed and the actors leapt around performing agile judo throws. Those who had been thrown were supposed to somersault, spring to their feet and rush back into the fray. But they were so weak that they were already staggering and once they had fallen could not get up again. Otojiro grabbed a couple by their kimono collars, pretending to shove them down whereas in fact he was desperately trying to haul them back on their feet. Sadayakko remembered:

Everyone attacks Takanori, then they're thrown, then in the play they're supposed to attack him again. But none of us had eaten for three days. After they were thrown, no one had the strength to get up. So we just had to close the curtain with all of them lying there on the ground.

Then came *Dojoji*, Yakko's *pièce de résistance*. The painted backdrop evoked the grounds of a Japanese temple, with a pagoda and enormous temple bell housed in a pavilion with a tiled roof. The cherry blossoms which Yakko had cut out so painstakingly fluttered to each side. The actors, dressed as bald-pated monks, performed an introductory dance.

Then Yakko glided out to take centre stage. *Dojoji* is the story of a maiden who falls in love with a handsome young celibate priest. When he rejects her, her rage and jealousy are so great that she turns into a fire-breathing serpent. He hides inside the temple bell but she coils around it and incinerates him. The play begins when, having taken human form, she reappears at the temple gate. The monks have made a rule that no women are to be allowed inside the temple. Like Salome, she sets to work to seduce them with her dancing.

Sweetly pretty, Yakko held the audience with her large dark eyes, then tilted her head at a coquettish angle and slowly, captivatingly, began to dance. She had quickly realised that Westerners did not appreciate the stylised white make-up which traditionally denoted women on the Japanese stage. They said it looked like a death mask. While the *onnagata* still covered their faces in thick white paint, she used much lighter, more natural make-up which set off the loveliness of her face.

She was wrapped in a brilliant scarlet kimono with a flower pattern that scrolled across the long loose sleeves and close-wrapped skirt. The heavy quilted hem swirled as she danced with delicate, graceful movements. On her head she wore a scarlet 'travelling hat', flat like a wheel, decorated with flowers. She held more in each hand, wielding them like fans as she danced. Then she shrugged off the topmost kimono layer, letting it fall to drape around her obi like a second skirt. Beneath was a flower-patterned white kimono, equally sumptuous. Sloughing off layer after layer, she changed her costume nine times, dancing more and more frenziedly while the shamisen strummed and the drums beat insistently.

But as she threw back more and more layers of kimono, the monks were cowering in fear and agitation, for a serpent too sloughs its skin nine times. Finally the maiden reveals her true nature. Yakko had last performed this dance in Portland, Oregon, where 'she tore down her elaborate coiffeur and, with hair streaming to the winds, mad with rage, worked herself up into a frenzy of passion, finally dying with grief at the base of the great sacred bell'.[10]

'I was so excited that I got through my dance and put my whole heart into my performance,' she remembered. 'But looking back on it now, I can't imagine how I even managed to move!'

She was performing her death scene, spinning around and around holding a parasol when she suddenly turned dizzy and crumpled to the floor in a faint. The actors playing monks rushed over to her, making believe this was part of the play. They helped her up and patted her cheeks. Somehow she managed to finish her dance.

The performance had been far from perfect but at least they had acted with passion. They had put their all into the dramas. They were too exhausted and starving to care whether or not they would ever be invited to play again. But as Hutton had said, the audience had never seen Japanese theatre before. Miraculously, they assumed that everything was just as it should be. After all, what could be more natural than to fall over and die in a battle scene or to look pale and ghastly and collapse in a death scene? At the end of the performance there was a storm of applause. As they left the theatre, the audience talked excitedly about the extraordinary realism of the performance. No one realised quite how realistic it had been.

The actors stumbled backstage, barely able to walk. After deducting expenses, there was a net profit of $60. Hutton handed Otojiro half, as promised. Otojiro divided the money evenly between everyone in the troupe.

'Well, we made it!' he said. 'Let's go eat, western food, anything.'

Their legs shaking, they tottered off to the nearest restaurant they could find. There they started ordering – steak, curry, everything they had been dreaming of for the last weeks. Japanese food would have been best, but they were too hungry to care. Besides, as world-travellers, they prided themselves on their knowledge of Western cuisine. But when the waiters came and laid the food on the table before them, they were too overcome by conflicting emotions to pick up their knives and forks. 'We just looked at each other without speaking,' remembered Sadayakko, 'and cried.'[11]

The next day Hutton turned up unexpectedly at the miserable hostelry where the troupe were staying. Ashamed to let him see their room, Otojiro and Mikami rushed down to the parlour to meet him. He had brought a bundle of newspapers. Beaming, he turned to the reviews. All were extremely enthusiastic. The *Chicago Daily News* reported:

The play acting was worth serious attention. A certain earnestness and polish of gesture and richness of costume made up the balance of interest left over after masks of comic and tragic intent had held sway and the chattery, musical lingo of the actors from Japan had ceased its music.

The reviewer admired the actors' 'cunning tragedies and fierce comedies' and thought the theatre 'too small considering their unique entertainment'.[12] Hutton's literati friends too had been greatly impressed. In fact, everyone in Chicago was clamouring for a repeat performance. Had they, asked Hutton, considered doing a season?

Suddenly the situation was reversed. Now Otojiro had the upper hand. Certainly not, he said, if all Hutton was offering was to split the proceeds fifty-fifty. He needed enough money to move into a decent hotel and make sure that all the actors could have a bath, do their laundry and eat proper meals. In the end Hutton agreed on $400 a week plus an allowance of $2 for each actor. Once again Otojiro and Yakko were installed like visiting royalty in the overblown splendour of the Grand Pacific.

The troupe celebrated their change in fortune by having their photograph taken. It is startlingly different from the group portrait taken just six months earlier, before they left Japan. The actors are no longer wearing uniforms like bellboys or standing nervously in three stiff lines. They have acquired a patina of cool. They are a louche-looking bunch. They lounge carelessly like Americans in cravats, high-collared shirts, waistcoats and jackets. A couple sport bow ties, one has a cane, another a gold chain looped across his chest. They all wear derbies, tilted at cocky angles, and sport sullen rock-'n'-roll-star scowls.

Otojiro is sitting on a chair, holding a cane. He gazes arrogantly at the camera. His trim moustache makes him look older, tough and business-like – not a man that anyone would ever dare call 'Jap'. He wears a three-piece suit with a high-collared shirt and a bow tie. His high-crowned derby is tipped well forward on his head.

Yakko is at the centre of the picture. She has blossomed. No longer in the shadow of Otojiro, she stands next to him, one arm resting confidently on his shoulder. She has a smile hovering on her lips. Her face is rounded and dramatically lovely. She is dressed like a fashionable American in a long-sleeved high-necked blouse with a ruffle at the front and an ankle-length skirt with a belt and a big buckle. Her luxuriant hair is swept up into a loosely knotted chignon and she has a straw boater with a flower on the brim perched on top.

These are no longer the naïve innocents who skipped off the steamer at San Francisco. They are older, sadder and maybe wiser. They have experienced the heights and depths together and have somehow survived. They have grown up.

Despite the fact that he had sworn the theatre was fully booked, Hutton managed to squeeze the troupe in for a two-week run of matinées. They also did evening shows at the Chicago Opera. A couple of times they repeated their highly effective advertising routine, parading through the city in their exotic costumes.

They even signed a contract with an impresario named Alexander Comstock of the McCauley Comstock partnership, putting their affairs into his hands for the next forty weeks. Just over a month had passed since they had arrived in the city like beggars. Now they were an established theatre company with an American manager.

Soon Comstock had them shuttling from city to city, doing a couple of nights at each place as they headed east. It was a gruelling schedule. Often they took the sleeper, arrived in the morning and were on stage that same night.

Otojiro recorded their progress in his diary. They took in Grand Rapids in Michigan, then went on to Muskegon, where the two stars stayed at the Occidental; the other actors put up at an inexpensive inn. In Battle Creek they performed at the Hamblyn Theatre, in Adrian at the Colossal, in Tiffin, Ohio, at the Noble Opera House and in Toledo at the Palatine Theater. In Dayton they stayed at the Atlas Hotel and performed at the Victoria Theatre. From there they went on to Mansfield, then Bucyrus, then back to Mansfield and on to Albany in New York State.

On 3 December, after nearly three weeks on the road, they finally rumbled into South Station in Boston at 7.45a.m. Yakko and Otojiro checked into the United States Hotel while the rest of the troupe took a rented house on Columbus Avenue.

But such an exhausting schedule after the terrible hardships that they had suffered in Chicago had taken a toll on their health. The day after they arrived the younger of the two *onnagata*, Kurando Maruyama, collapsed, desperately weak with agonising abdominal pains. He was rushed to Boston Hospital where the doctors diagnosed lead poisoning.

He was only twenty-two, but he had spent years as an *onnagata*, covering his face, neck, back and hands day after day in white lead-based paint. Lead poisoning was an occupational hazard for *onnagata*. It was also a danger for geisha, who often used the same white make-up. Many looked like old women by their late twenties, with hideously yellowed and wrinkled skin. At least they were only required to use it for formal parties, not every day; and they could avoid it by using white powder made of ground rice, though that did not give the same smooth sheen. Yakko was well aware of the importance of preserving her appearance and would have seen the devastating effects of the lead-based paint on the older geisha in the community. No doubt she used it as sparingly as possible.

Despite his pretty face, which was why he had been chosen to play women, Maruyama was a fiercely taciturn young man. For months he had gone on working, never saying a word or revealing his suffering. Gradually his nausea and stomach cramps became unbearable. Otojiro and Yakko, who were like parents to the young actors in the troupe, discovered he was using morphine to anaesthetise the pain. He had scars and lesions all over his body and arms from injecting. The pair threw away the drug whenever they found it but as they travelled across the country he would pay bellboys to buy more for him.

The troupe began their Boston season at the Tremont Theatre without him. Between performances they rushed to the hospital. He was in terrible agony and fading fast. Nothing the doctors could do could help him. Sitting at his bedside, Yakko and Otojiro gently broke the news to him that there was no hope. Otojiro remembered:

> This man was a bachelor. He had no parents and no wife, he was all alone. He didn't care about anything. He was a simple guy. He never had much to say but he hated being beaten. Even at his last hour he showed no unmanly weakness at all.[13]

A week after he had entered hospital, he died. His comrades were gathered around him, with Yakko at his bedside, weeping. He was buried on a hill top outside the city. Everyone was in a state of shock. They had been through so much together, they had become family for each other. Now one of them was gone. They marked his grave with a wooden grave marker and recited Buddhist prayers. It was strange and fearful to think that his bones would be left here in this alien country with no one to tend his grave or offer incense and say prayers there. 'Where is his soul roaming now?' mused Otojiro in his diary.

Maruyama had shared in all the troupe's hardships and suffering. Now he was dead, just as their fortunes seemed to be improving at last. It was a sad irony.

Boston was the first major city that the troupe had visited under Comstock's management. With his help, Otojiro was determined to make it clear that they were serious actors, entirely different from the jugglers, acrobats, tight-rope walkers, dancing girls and other vaudeville acts which were all that Americans had ever seen of Japanese entertainment. Comstock blitzed the local papers with information. A couple of days after they arrived the *Boston Globe* was reporting that 'Otto Kawakami and Sada Yacco occupy the same relative position in their own country as do Sir Henry Irving and Ellen Terry in England.' To compare them to the most famous actor and actress in the English-speaking world was a little audacious, but it was all good publicity.

To establish their credentials, the Kawakami-za theatre was somehow resurrected in distant Tokyo. The paper continued:

Kawakami is the proprietor of a very fine theatre in Tokyo, which is said to surpass in architectural splendour and artistic decoration any other theatre in the world. The company that are to appear today at the Tremont come direct from this theatre and bring with them all the properties they have used there.

Here on the other side of the Pacific, no one need ever know the truth about the theatre's sad demise. The troupe also mysteriously received imperial patronage. They were now billed as the 'Imperial Japanese dramatic company . . . from the Mikado's own theatre in Tokio, Japan'.[14]

Ever since the disaster in San Francisco, Yakko and Otojiro had been thinking hard, trying to fathom what sort of plays would best please their

Western audiences. By the time they reached Boston they had found a formula that seemed to work. Otojiro wrote:

> For foreigners we have to have beautiful costumes and some exotic, extraordinary event. This means it has to be a period piece with dance. And we must show this within a very short span of time. This is Foreigners' Taste. Unless we do it like this they won't come and see Japanese plays.[15]

In San Francisco, Yakko later told the journalist Yone Noguchi, the troupe had been

> . . . so foolish as to appear to an American audience with one of our classical dramas like *Kusunoki*. Nobody could understand, since they had no knowledge of our Japanese history. Immediately we found out that we must play a love play. Love is universal. Then we played *Geisha and Knight*, which was a universal success through America and Europe. It was a queer mixture of Japanese plays, but it appealed to the American mind with love, and delighted with our gorgeous costumes.[16]

The Geisha and the Knight, also billed in mock Japanese as 'Geisha to Somaray', was the highlight of their repertoire. It was a stroke of genius – a knitting together of *The Duel* (*Sayaate*) and the hugely popular *Dojoji* to make a single drama. The new play embodied all their strengths – thrillingly choreographed fight scenes, humour, split-second costume changes and gorgeous scenery. Above all it provided the perfect showcase for Yakko's exquisite dancing and spine-tingling death scene.

The first act, 'The Duel', is set in the Yoshiwara pleasure quarters before a spectacular backdrop showing a street of wooden teahouses fading in sharp perspective into the distance. Cherry trees laden with brilliant pink blossom adorn the stage. A beautiful geisha has rejected the advances of a boorish samurai named Banza in favour of her true love, Nagoya. Banza challenges Nagoya, striking his sword hilt. A fierce battle ensues between the two samurai and their bands of retainers, with plenty of energetic swordplay, hand-to-hand combat and acrobatic throws.

For the second act, 'Dojoji', Yakko's *pièce de résistance*, had been subtly altered so as to merge seamlessly with the first. The backdrop was the temple courtyard with a great bell covered by a tiled roof and mountains in the background. There the geisha has discovered that Nagoya is betrothed to another. He and his bride-to-be have fled into the temple grounds. She dances before the gates, trying to seduce the monks into allowing her to pass. Then the bride-to-be appears and the geisha tries to kill her, but is prevented by the samurai. Loosing her luxuriant waist-length tresses which fly about like a lion's mane, she turns into a raging fury and dies of a broken heart in her lover's arms.

Initially the two halves did not knit very well; but it was honed and improved with each performance. In any case, the drama was performed in Japanese and the audience were following the story from a synopsis in the programme, so it did not need to make perfect sense. It had ample emotional force and a hugely dramatic dénouement.

In Japanese terms, it was not as outrageous to fillet and cobble together two kabuki plays as it would have been to do the same to Shakespeare. In kabuki, the text was essentially a vehicle to showcase the actors' dazzling virtuoso displays. Audiences went to the theatre primarily to see their favourite stars. Actors, producers and managers regularly made free with the scripts, improvising or cobbling together two plays to make one.

Nevertheless, *The Geisha and the Knight* was a rather extreme case. It was unashamedly popular, closer in spirit to an Andrew Lloyd Webber production than classical theatre. Admittedly that was within the spirit of kabuki, which had always been the people's theatre. But this was angled towards a very different audience who knew nothing of Japanese culture. Whether by chance or design, it played up to practically every Western stereotype of Japan: the geisha, the samurai, the pretty, the exotic and a hint of something barbaric lurking just beneath the surface.

As Otojiro put it, 'If a Japanese had seen it, he would have thought it very strange. But it was intended for foreigners, so it was okay.'[17]

Initially reviewers were rather bemused. They had never seen Japanese theatre before or heard the decidedly outlandish music – the strumming of the shamisen and the high-pitched wail of the songs. Most were not sure what to make of it. The reviewer from the *New York Times*, who had come to Boston for the first night of this much heralded new troupe, wrote:

> The actors spoke in their native tongue and they were accompanied by weird and monotonous instrumental music and strident chanting or singing. The chief characteristics of their art were its action and its vividness . . . Yet, in the midst of all this extravagance, there was at times unquestioned power. Mr Kawakami was ever dignified and impressive and Mme Yacco's death scene at the end of the play revealed tragic force.[18]

Strange and barbaric though the drama might be, there was one element that everyone could appreciate. Yakko's beauty, dancing and sheer exoticism enthralled all of Boston. Soon the troupe was playing to packed houses. Reviewers, abandoning their attempts to understand the plays, described this wondrous new phenomenon. One enraptured columnist gushed:

> Sada Yacco resembles the loveliest ivory bas-relief, radiant in soft brocades and silks. And how this Geisha dances! Flexible as a little willow wand, the scarlet and white Kimono clinging to her lithe form, and, with every movement, enveloping her like tongues of flame, she takes the most exquisite poses, recalling those graceful figures which have decorated our choicest specimens and curios. No wonder the Geisha bewitches all travellers in the Flowerey Kingdom, for this actress represents her as the epitome of sweetness and grace.[19]

Another breathless admirer wrote:

> She has conquered us, and she has us grovelling at her feet. She has charmed us with a personality as daintily alluring as the early spring breath of a balmy April day; she has bewitched us with a voice that speaks the unintelligible words of her tongue with a music akin to the soft rippling of leaves just stirred by the passing breeze.[20]

Thanks to Yakko's elegance and style, the troupe succeeded in drawing audiences from the topmost layers of Boston high society. After matinée performances Yakko charmed the local ladies by conducting teas on stage, gracefully moving among them and chatting charmingly. Her interpreter was Mikami who, wrote a reporter, 'also enacts some of the female roles so perfectly that the audience never suspects him to be a man'.[21]

Despite the growing audiences, the troupe was still struggling financially. The arrival of the Japanese notables had come to the attention of Bunkio Matsuki, a Japanese antiques dealer who had become a leading figure in the city. As a man of influence and a fellow countryman, he took on the role of father figure to the troupe while they were in his territory. When they were low on funds he helped them out and sponsored an extended season at a theatre called Copley Hall.

With his patronage they were able to afford new backdrops painted by Japanese artists and new props. The advertisement for a new historical drama declared that 'the stage will be decorated with a unique collection of Japanese curios and bric-a-brac'. Another promised 'the exhibition each afternoon and evening of an elaborate collection of curios, tapestries, arms and armour and rare costumes before and after the entertainments'. All this, of course, provided useful exposure for Matsuki's Japanese antiques. Yakko must have felt as if she was performing in a junk shop. But she knew that a large part of her appeal lay in her exoticism. To be surrounded by picturesque screens, fans and vases could only enhance her charm.

One evening Matsuki hosted a banquet with Yakko as guest of honour. Alexander Corbett Jr of the *Boston Globe* took the opportunity to interview the mysterious dancer. Whenever Yakko met the Japanese press, it was always with Otojiro, who held forth volubly while she sat quietly smiling and nodding. But Americans wanted to hear what the dainty lady herself had to say. In Japanese terms, that in itself was extraordinary. Through Mikami, Yakko commented on her impressions of this foreign land, in which she had now spent nearly six months.

She began by complimenting American women on their elegant clothes, 'hardly as comfortable as our Japanese costumes, but I love to see them, they show off the form so beautifully'. Then she was asked if she would like to live permanently in the United States.

'I would never hesitate a moment to remain here if I could,' she replied. As if to justify this startlingly passionate response, she went on to reflect on everything she had seen of the lives of women in America and to compare it with a woman's lot back home:

You know the women of Japan are not esteemed as they are here. They are not educated or given the opportunities which men have. All my life I have believed that women could do many things as well as men could they but have an equal chance. O, how I have dreamed of one day visiting western countries, where women can do and be something. At last the time came. My friends said: 'Do not go! It cannot be good that you should leave your native country.' But I did not believe them.

And here I am, astonished more than I can ever tell you, at the value with which I see women regarded everywhere. At home, the woman makes every sacrifice and suffering for the man. Here the men love the women so they will suffer everything, do anything for them. At home the woman is nothing in society, here she is everything. I shall never forget how the American women are cherished by the men, and when I return to Japan I hope to have at least a little influence in making my countrywomen a more important factor in the life of the nation.[22]

Leaving Japan had opened Yakko's eyes. There, no matter how much power she really wielded in her relationship with her husband, she was eternally required at least to play act the role of the demure little woman behind her man. In this land where women were cherished and actresses were goddesses, she had been able to step out of Otojiro's shadow. Here the essential rule of a Japanese woman's life – 'a clever woman never lets a man know how clever she is' – no longer applied. She could speak her mind.

She must have known perfectly well, however, that it was a temporary luxury. They were in that wonderful nevernever land known as 'abroad', where the usual rules do not apply. Once in Japan, the prison doors would slam back into place. Once again she would be fixed in her locus at the very bottom of society – ex-geisha and wife of riverbed beggar. That certainty gave her all the more reason to enjoy her freedom while it lasted. Or perhaps, somehow, she might be able to take some of her new-found freedom with her.

A few days later she spoke to another journalist for an interview published on Christmas Eve in the *Boston Sunday Post*. He painted an evocative portrait of the exotic creature who was causing manly hearts to pound across Boston.

> Mme. Yacco is sweet in manner and probably the daintiest actress this country has ever seen. She nods her head of lustrous black hair most bewitchingly and casts her beautiful eyes in a charmingly fascinating way. . . . She has a sweet modulated voice and undoubted grace.

He went on to write breathlessly of her 'thin pencilled lashes and drooping eyelids'.

'The clever actress is rapidly acquiring sufficient command of the English language and throughout the talk took the keenest delight in correcting the interpreter in his pronunciation of several words,' he noted. We can almost see Yakko teasing Mikami as he stumbled over the difficult foreign words.

Delicate and lovely though she was, she was not prepared to conceal her powerful intelligence. She was even more outspoken about the hardships that women had to face in Japan than she had been in the previous interview. It was an opportunity to talk about the suffering she had experienced as a child, though in an elliptical way:

> We Japanese women are most womanly, kind and gentle; but those who are born poor, their misfortune might well cause the generous heart a pang. When a son is born in Japan there is great rejoicing and fetes, even among the poorest, and every attention is showered upon the young child. When a daughter comes, the feeling is different. She is despised and cursed and taught that in all things she is man's slave and inferior. Obedience is the first teaching of our religion. My

parents were very poor and to educate my brother, I was ordered to dance in the streets when I was but ten years old. Even then I appreciated the odium of my position and resolved that I would keep myself clean and free of degradation even if death should be the alternative.[23]

It was a fanciful, almost fairytale version of her childhood, and not strictly true. Perhaps she was re-creating her story, playing up the tragedy to present an image that she thought would appeal to her Western audience. It was also a way of expressing the bitterness she must have felt at having been sold into geishadom. Far from home, among people who could not even speak her language, she was free to tell her story in any way she chose.

By the time the article was published, Otojiro had been rushed into hospital. Most of the actors were in poor health. One, reported Alexander Corbett Jr, had been bed-ridden for several days, 'during which matters were somewhat aggravated by his taking his medicine three doses an hour for nine hours, instead of one dose every three hours'.

Otojiro had been complaining of stomach cramps for some time. Just before Christmas he doubled up with pain. With the help of Mr Matsuki, the antiques dealer, Yakko found a Japanese doctor. He diagnosed acute appendicitis. Otojiro must have an operation immediately, he said, or he would die.

Like Maruyama, he was admitted to Boston Hospital. Yakko was at his side, willing herself not to think about the young *onnagata*'s terrible death. He was wheeled into the operating theatre almost immediately.

The troupe continued to perform with understudies taking Otojiro's parts. Had they been in Japan, the principal male actor would have stepped in as troupe leader. But here everything was topsy-turvy. Yakko was the Boss's wife and the star of the show. For the three and a half weeks that Otojiro was in hospital, she was at his bedside, on stage, engaging in interviews and leading the troupe, making daily decisions.

On 1 January 1900, Boston celebrated the beginning of a new year and a new century (by the Christian calendar; by the Japanese calendar it was simply the thirty-third year of the reign of Emperor Meiji). Boston had always been a sombre, Puritan city, the home of grand old families – the Lodges, the Cabots, the Lowells, the Adamses – who would never have dreamt of engaging in unseemly display. But that year boisterous new immigrants far out-numbered the old grandees. It was the first American New Year's celebration not only for the troupe but also for the city. Tens of thousands gathered in the snowy streets and battled their way through blizzards to go to church. The following day the city rang with the tinkling of bells as thousands of men and women, bundled up in furs, glided through the city in horse-drawn sleighs. Yakko and her little flock of actors crunched across the snow, gazing in wonder at this extraordinary new world.

Mikami was particularly excited. He had had a letter from his future bride, telling him that he was to be a father. By the time he got back, the baby would already be born. Bursting with joy, he ordered sets of baby clothes, all blue. He scoured the shops for toys and talked incessantly about his son.

'How do you know it will be a boy?' Yakko teased him.

'I just know it will,' he said firmly.

But Mikami's health too was failing. As handsome young *onnagata*, both he and Maruyama had received sackfuls of fan mail from American admirers, addressed to 'Miss Mikami' and 'Miss Murayama', in happy ignorance of the fact that they were really men. Now he was thin and gaunt. His skin had a pallid, bluish taint. He stumbled around, complaining of nausea, stomach pains and weakness. As a family man, he did not resort to morphine. Instead he drank heavily. Not a day passed, wrote Otojiro in his diary, when he did not empty several tumblers of whisky or brandy.

Otojiro was barely out of hospital when Mikami collapsed. He too was rushed to hospital. The doctors diagnosed a brain haemorrhage, probably as a complication of lead poisoning. Otojiro put it down to drink. One account suggests that it was syphilis.

Lying in his bed surrounded by screens in a bleak white-walled hospital room, Mikami already looked like a ghost. He had the baby clothes and toys spread around him on his pillow. Yakko did her best to keep up a comforting, hopeful face; but in her heart she was praying fervently to the Buddha, the Shinto gods and her own personal protector, the fierce

Buddhist deity Fudo Myo-o, for his recovery. At least, she prayed, let him live long enough to go home and see his child.

Mikami whispered in a voice so faint they could hardly hear it: 'I can't die. If I die, what will my mother and brother do? They're looking forward so much to me getting home safe and sound! My child must already have been born, I want to see his face. I want to see him in these foreign clothes, this hat, these shoes. I don't want to die in a hospital in a foreign land without seeing my baby's face. But if I do, my soul will come back with you to Kobe.'[24]

It was after midnight. The troupe were gathered around his bed with Yakko by his pillow, all in surgical white. The nurses too were in white. A blue arc light cast a cold light on his face. His hair was unkempt and his unshaven cheeks grey and sunken. He looked so grimy, wrote Otojiro, that no one could touch him.

'I will take care of your mother and your child,' said Yakko through tears. 'I promise. You can be sure of that.'[25]

And, still muttering deliriously about his baby, Mikami died. He had barely breathed his last when a funeral director appeared. Later the actors were called to the funeral parlour. There was a shiny black box as big as a kimono box, like the box that a woman takes to her wedding, with two golden locks.

Otojiro wrote in his diary:

We were wondering what a wedding box was doing in a funeral parlour. As we watched, it turned out to be Mikami's coffin. We were all astonished. A boy came, opened the golden locks and lifted the lid. Inside it was lined with velvet, like a watch box.

They were even more astonished when they looked at the body. Mikami had been miraculously transformed into a gentleman in a starchy frock coat, shiny shoes, stiff collar and smart new neck tie, with his hair neatly trimmed and oiled. His face was plump and clean shaven, his skin white as snow, his cheeks lightly rouged and his lips the colour of coral. He had even had his nails clipped and cleaned of grit, his cuticles trimmed and nail polish applied.

'He was really chic, as if he was going to a wedding in the other world,' remembered Yakko.

When someone died in those days in Japan, the head was shaved and the body washed. Then the corpse was put in a sitting position and squeezed into a firwood barrel bound with bamboo bark, or a large urn for the wealthy, to be buried in a small, deep grave. So it was no wonder they were flabbergasted.

All the time they had been travelling, wrote Otojiro, they had been so poor they could not afford to buy frock coats, so they could never go to official functions. And here was Mikami in a brand new coat, beautifully made up, like a great gentleman.

'We had to laugh. He was the lucky one. He died and got to be a gentleman in a frock coat!'[26]

They buried him on the hill top next to Murayama. The following day the little troupe, down to fifteen members now, were back on stage. No matter what happened, the show had to go on.

6

'THE WITCHERY OF SALOME'S ART'
BOSTON TO LONDON
1900

This flower-like woman, [with] movements like the motion of a lotus flower on the water, or a field of long grass in the wind . . . In the dance we feel the swift curve and flicker of a flame.

Katherine Metcalf Roof, June 1900[1]

The highlight of Boston's Christmas season that year was a visit by the undisputed greatest living actors of the English-speaking world: Sir Henry Irving and Ellen Terry. They were playing at the Knickerbocker Theatre, a couple of doors along from the Tremont. Otojiro and Yakko had been doing their best to live up to their billing as 'the Henry Irving and Ellen Terry of Japan'. They must have been thrilled and unnerved to discover that they were all in the same city.

Almost as soon as they arrived Otojiro, brashly confident, sent Irving a letter inviting him to attend one of their performances. Irving replied with a graceful note, saying that he would be delighted.

Irving and Terry had been the leading lights of the theatrical world and Victorian high society for almost thirty years. Until the middle of the nineteenth century, European theatres had been the haunt of low life, rowdy places full of drinking, swearing, brawling and prostitutes who prowled the pit where the groundlings gathered. Upright citizens went to the opera instead. Actors had been despised as rogues and vagabonds, as they still were in Japan.

Irving had made theatre respectable. With his dedication, artistry and dignified stage presence, paired with the brilliance of his leading lady, Ellen Terry, he had transformed acting into an honourable profession and made actors into stars, adored by every level of society. Theatre buildings became more luxurious, seats were installed in what had been the pit and gentlemen in evening dress and 'ladies in ravishing toilettes' replaced the low life. In London, attendance at the Lyceum, the theatre where Irving was actor-manager, was *de rigueur* among the fashionable classes. Whenever the great man made his entry, the 'Lyceum roar' would resound to the beams. He had been knighted in 1895, the first actor ever to receive such an honour.

Irving and Terry were now on their sixth American tour. Irving was sixty-two, a tall angular patrician with a dramatic pale face, razor sharp cheekbones, sensitive eyes and flowing grey locks. Terry was fifty-one, sparkling with wit and seductive beauty, with a strong though feminine face and a great pre-Raphaelite bush of wavy red-gold hair. Otojiro and Yakko were hugely impressed with the way in which she inhabited her roles. She was, Otojiro noted, 'very skilful at comedies, overflowing with charm, using her body very lightly and delighting the audience with her agile movements'.[2]

The most acclaimed production of these two eminent actors was their *Merchant of Venice* which they had first performed more than twenty years before. Terry as Portia, in gold-brocaded Venetian robes and then a black lawyer's gown, and Irving, as a dignified but implacable Shylock, made an electrifying combination. This was the production that they had brought to Boston, with two other celebrated dramas, *Robespierre* and *The Bells*.

For Otojiro and Yakko, it was a priceless opportunity to see the very best of Western theatre. No Japanese actors before them had ever had such a chance. They went several times. They noted the sophisticated use of lighting, the way in which Irving's face, for example, was spotlit when the rest of the stage was in darkness. They admired the way in which each scene was choreographed and organised. And they were much impressed by the splendid set pieces, one of which involved dozens of real horses kicking up sand, pulling a carriage across the stage.

After the performance, they went backstage to visit the great actor-manager in his dressing room where he sat taking off his make-up, surrounded by mirrors and flowers. Otojiro recorded their conversation.

'What did you think of tonight's performance?' Irving asked, as one actor to another.

'I can't tell you right now,' replied the cunning Otojiro. 'I'm worn out. I'll go back to the hotel, have a rest and think about it. Then I'll tell you.'

'Why are you so tired?' demanded Irving, his curiosity tweaked at such an eccentric reply.

'I used up all my energy, I was so engrossed,' replied Otojiro.

Irving liked this answer very much. He was also so impressed with what he had seen of the troupe's performance and Yakko's dancing that he wrote a letter of introduction for them, referring to Otojiro and Yakko as his 'comrades in art'. He gave it to Otojiro and urged him to take the troupe to London. It was a great compliment and, from a man of Irving's stature and dramatic instinct, an irrefutable endorsement. With such a recommendation, they hoped that doors would open for them when they arrived in that distant and unknown city.[3]

The day after they had been to see *The Merchant of Venice*, posters appeared outside the Boston Theatre where the Japanese company was now playing, advertising a brand new play: *Sairoku: The Merchant of Venice, Japanese Version*. The posters referred playfully to competition between 'the greatest actors of Japan and Britain'. Otojiro had taken the trial scene and transposed it to Japan. Shylock had become Sairoku, an old fisherman on the northern island of Hokkaido. Antonio was Ando Jinzaburo, a merchant who had borrowed money from him. Portia became Princess Osode. Perhaps the fact that Shylock was a moneylender had reverberations for Otojiro, who had suffered at their hands in Japan.

Instead of asking for a pound of flesh, Sairoku, played by Otojiro, demanded nine square inches. He took out a brush, ink and set square and painted a three-inch square on Ando's chest, then raised a large butcher's knife so that light glinted off it. A photograph of the production shows Otojiro with a bush of white hair and a white goatee grasping Ando by the collar, aiming a fearsome knife at his throat. Yakko as Osode, in a severe black robe and fez-like black hat, stands watching in horror. Reviewers commented on how very manly she looked, as if 'she wished to deceive not only the judge and courtroom spectators into the belief that she is a man, but the audience as well'.[4] As a geisha, she had enjoyed playing male parts, an experience that had served her well.

The script had been put together with dazzling speed for the simple reason that there was hardly any. When Yakko asked for a translation of Portia's great speech, 'The quality of mercy is not strained . . .', Otojiro told her, 'Our audience are westerners, so you can say anything you like – *sucharaka poko poko* ['rhubarb, rhubarb'] or *namu amida butsu* [the equivalent of 'Hail Mary']. Just say it forcefully and hit the table.'[5] According to Otojiro's memoirs, Irving and Terry helped him and Yakko with their roles and gave them coaching in Shakespearean acting. Perhaps the great duo were tickled by the charming effrontery of their Japanese friends.

The audience did not realise that the actors were speaking gibberish. The *Boston Herald*, in fact, complained of 'protracted dialogue and insufficient pantomime to clearly indicate what the people were talking about'.[6] Critics applauded the set square scene for its attention to detail, but everyone gasped at the savagery of the knife. According to Otojiro, he saw his version of the play as an indictment of Western capitalism; but in fact all he succeeded in doing was to reinforce the stereotype of the Japanese as barbaric.

Yakko, by now the toast of the town, was being gathered to the ample bosoms of the divas who passed through. The statuesque star of the New York Metropolitan Opera, Emma Eames, who commanded $1500 per appearance, was 'most demonstrative' in her praise. The voluptuous French soprano Emma Calve went to every matinée performance for a week. She swept rustling with lace and silks into Yakko's dressing room, gushing enthusiasm. 'After complimenting that charming little specimen of the womankind of the Flowery Kingdom on her performance, [she] took from her own hair a beautiful comb set with diamonds and fixed it in the raven locks of the Oriental actress.'[7]

In distant Washington DC, the Japanese ambassador, Jutaro Komura, had been receiving reports of the bewitching Japanese actress who was seducing all of Boston. No doubt he had also heard from the stiff consul in Chicago about the riverbed beggars who had come knocking on his door. From the point of view of Japanese officialdom it was a matter of grave concern. Here were these outcasts – a geisha, little better than a prostitute, and a bunch of travelling players – peddling a bastardised form of kabuki and fooling ignorant Westerners, who had never seen Japanese theatre before, into believing it was the real thing.

Ambassador Komura decided he had better find out for himself how these newly famous fellow countrymen of his were presenting Japanese theatre and whether they were making Japan a laughing stock. He boarded a train and made the twenty hour journey to Boston. Without announcing himself, he sat in on a performance.

With Maruyama and Mikami gone, the troupe had lost their *onnagata*. So Otojiro promoted the hairdresser, a man called Hanjiro Takagi, who was in charge of taking care of the wigs. He was the only backstage worker that the much reduced little troupe could spare. Unlike Maruyama and Mikami, he was not at all like a dainty Japanese woman. He was tall for a Japanese and big-boned with a prominent nose, deep-set eyes, well-defined features and a manly bass voice. But once painted up and tricked out in a kimono, he made a rather fetching Western woman. American theatre-goers adored him and soon 'Miss Takagi' was receiving sackloads of fan mail.

Unlike the consul in Chicago, Ambassador Komura was an urbane, sophisticated man. To his eyes, Takagi made an irresistibly comical 'woman'. Every time he appeared on stage the ambassador could not help laughing merrily. But he was well able to appreciate the quality of the performances and the power of Yakko's dancing. The theatre, he noted, was packed and the audience demanded curtain call after curtain call. Although in Japan actors were reviled as riverbed beggars, in the West they received adulation. It did no harm, he concluded, for Westerners to know that Japan too had show biz and stars.

After the performance Komura made himself known to the troupe. He had decided that far from shaming their country, they were deserving of official recognition at the highest level. He invited them to Washington.

On 28 January, nearly two months after they had arrived in Boston, they boarded a train for the overnight journey and set off on the next stage of their adventure. They thought sadly of the two comrades whom

146

they were leaving behind on a foreign hill top. Sueji Kawamoto, the troupe dogsbody, had found a job in a trading house and was also staying behind. Of the original nineteen there were now fourteen.

In Boston they had experienced terrible loss though they had also had the satisfaction of seeing their fortunes rise. But they were still living from day to day. Otojiro was adamant that their destination was Paris. But if Komura had not sponsored them, it was not at all clear how they would have got there.

That year Washington's 300,000 inhabitants were looking forward to celebrating the centenary of its founding. The elegant streets and magnificent white sandstone buildings were blanketed in snow. Ladies in full skirts and feathered hats and gentlemen in overcoats and derbies stepped gingerly out of their carriages across the snow drifts as they made their way through the grand portals of the Lafayette Square Opera House. The troupe had barely had time to unpack when they were on stage.

The *Washington Post* was in raptures. Their dramas, declared the reviewer, 'compare favourably in most respects with the work of American Thespians'. Yakko was every bit as talented and adorable, he said, as the great international stage sirens – the Briton Olga Nethersole, the legendary Italian Eleonora Duse and the New York star Annie Russell. 'She is a dainty little woman, petite and wonderfully graceful and possessed of the true dramatic fire.'[8]

Komura decided to throw a couple of lavish parties to show off the talents of these celebrated representatives of his country. He called in carpenters to build a Japanese stage in the legation's grand banqueting hall, complete with *hanamichi* walkway and a striped Japanese curtain. Then he sent out invitations to the luminaries of Washington society.

It was an astonishing mark of confidence in the troupe and their work. Perhaps having lived so many years in the West Komura had imbibed something of the American progressive spirit and the new-found Western respect for actors. It was also a subtle way to point out to America's leaders that Japan was a civilised country with a theatre just as sophisticated as theirs.

The two successive evenings were splendid occasions. On the first, the carriages that drew up at the legation's doors held 400 of the city's most

147

wealthy and influential people: old money families, grandees, dignitaries, university presidents, professors, writers, artists and journalists, most accompanied by their wives.

On the second evening, President William McKinley and the First Lady were the guests of honour, joined by members of the cabinet, ministers of state, ambassadors and consuls. An even more glittering crowd mingled beneath the legation's chandeliers. The press reported breathlessly on the ladies' exquisite and occasionally rather *risqué* gowns, the extravagant diamonds and pearls and the fashionable tufty feathered aigrettes. The eager representative of the *New York Herald* was on the phone to New York every five minutes, updating his paper.

Performing before an audience of the nation's élite, the troupe put aside their more experimental concoctions and offered a programme of shortened versions of pure kabuki. They began with *Takanori*. Originally anglicised as *The Duel*, it was now usually billed *The Royalist* on the programme. On this occasion, 'R' and 'L' being indistinguishable in Japanese, it was renamed *The Loyalist* and given a suitably patriotic slant. Then Yakko performed her *Dojoji* dance in its classic form. Lastly the troupe played *Soga* (*The Soga Brothers*), the classic revenge tragedy which Yakko had performed as a young geisha many years before.

Before the show Ambassador Komura advised Otojiro that the distinguished guests had requested 'a Japanese-style hara-kiri'. The Soga brothers were historical figures who did not commit ritual suicide and there is none in the drama. Otojiro was taken aback. He was prepared to make free with the text to a considerable degree but this contradicted the facts. Nevertheless, if the president wanted to see it, his wish had to be obeyed.

Before the last scene, Otojiro secreted across his stomach a sack of gooey red laver seaweed, the usual stage 'blood' in Japan at the time. After his character had completed his vendetta and killed the last of his enemies, he manfully took out his sword, plunged it into his stomach and swept it across in a melodramatic suicide with 'blood' oozing and spurting. The spectacle was so thrilling that it even overshadowed Yakko's dancing.

At the banquet that followed, the American potentates were eager to talk to the exquisite Japanese dancer and her outspoken husband. Afterwards

Ambassador Komura gave Otojiro a very acceptable sum of money, discreetly wrapped in paper in the usual Japanese way, in recognition of the troupe's sterling efforts.

On 8 February the troupe boarded the 2.30a.m. train for New York. Eight and half hours later they rumbled into the Central Railroad Station and stepped out onto the snow-covered streets of that thrillingly glamorous city. They were all nursing colds. Otojiro and Yakko took a carriage to their hotel, one of the best in town. (Otojiro phoneticised it, impenetrably, as the 'Barthology'.) The rest of the troupe boarded a horse-drawn trolley which clanged and clattered to their lodgings on East 27th Street.

Home to 3.4 million people, New York was a ferment of noise, dirt and activity. People swarmed like ants along its canyon-like streets, vertiginously walled with looming skyscrapers. The newly completed Park Row Building was the tallest in the world, soaring an unthinkable thirty-three storeys into the sky; though there were plenty of others nearly as tall bristling alongside. Some had express elevators that did not stop until the fifteenth or even the twentieth floor. There was banging and hammering, the clanging of trolleys, the clatter of iron-shod hooves on the cobblestones and the thunder of the elevated trains. From time to time pent-up steam spurted mysteriously out of the manholes, as if the city itself was alive and throbbing beneath its streets.

New York was also home to unimaginable wealth. Along Fifth Avenue were palatial mansions staffed by valets, butlers, ladies' maids, parlourmaids and flunkies in court costume. Inside, the opulent rooms were crammed to their gilded ceilings with tiger skins, Persian rugs, Oriental knick-knacks, tapestries, paintings and priceless antique furniture. The 'people of standing' who inhabited these palaces enjoyed splendid parties where they mixed with others of their ilk and displayed their wealth on tiaras, bodices, belts and stomachers studded with spectacular diamonds, rubies and pearls.

Ever since the Japanese victory against China, Japan – the little David that had defeated its giant neighbour – had been a *cause célèbre*. Society ladies invited Japanese business magnates to lavish dinner parties. For a while the height of chic among these grandes dames, no matter how busty or big-boned, was to drift about languidly in a kimono. 'Many American women wear them to parties, though they are most unbecoming,' a Japanese newspaper reported with amusement.[9]

Otojiro and Yakko were fortunate enough to make contact with the doyenne of these society ladies, one Mrs Robert Osborne. She was charmed by the exotic newcomers who had already found such favour among the Washington élite. After a première for the Japanese community at the Vienna Hotel, she arranged a ten-day run at the Berkeley Lyceum on West 44th Street. She turned the event into a grand social occasion 'with society men for ushers, and, after the performance, tea, served by the graceful and pretty Mme. Yacco'. She also ensured that the cream of New York society went along to see them perform, including many 'well-known theatrical people'.[10]

The timing could not have been better. The craze for Japanalia was at its height. On Broadway there was a revival of *The Mikado* and a play called *Broadway to Tokio*. Then, five days after the Japanese troupe began its run, a much-awaited new play by the celebrated playwright David Belasco opened at the Herald Square Theater. It was called *Mme. Butterfly*. The star, the vivacious Blanche Bates, had approached Yakko and asked her to coach her to walk and talk like a Japanese woman.

'We were too busy working all the time,' remembered Otojiro. 'So the actress came every day for a week to the performance and studied and I believe she was good.'[11]

Bates gave a humorous interview about the difficulty she had 'tying on the funny little Japanese clothes' and sitting on her knees Japanese-style. She played Cho-Cho-San as the most passive, pathetic of Oriental butterflies. Meanwhile Yakko, the only real Japanese actress in the city, was shocking and fascinating New Yorkers by depicting Japanese women to be as complex as Americans. She did not even have 'the pretty roundness' which Japanese were supposed to have; she was slim and delicate-looking.

'It is difficult to think of the Japanese woman of any age, rank or character as anything but a pretty, dainty little creature, sitting in her toy house, arranging her single branch of cherry blossoms or amusing herself in her miniature garden,' wrote a reviewer in the *New York Times*. In *The Geisha and the Knight* Yakko, conversely, portrayed a woman consumed by passion. The critic described her famous death scene. She has found her lover's bride-to-be and drives her out of the temple:

> She follows her, her long black hair streaming down her back, the short hair around her face standing out stiff and straight, her white face contrasting with the brightness of her Oriental robe, and with a hammer, such a cruel weapon, she strikes at her rival with a cold-blooded hatred that is terrible. She does not pant, she does not speak, she does not make unnecessary motions. But there is such an evidence of well-directed physical force in every blow that it gives great power to the action. Sada Yacco does not understand the methods of English-speaking melodramatic actresses, but she shows plainly that a Japanese woman can love deeply, hate savagely, and then die quietly.[12]

The critic, wedded to his stereotype, doubted that such a depiction could be 'true'. Yakko's performance utterly contradicted the image of the childlike Japanese woman; but ironically, she was also creating an equally simplistic preconception – that of the savage beneath the demure exterior.

A photograph of her as the Geisha emblazoned the cover of the 24 March 1900 issue of *Harper's Bazar* [sic]. She is in the glittering regalia of the courtesan, her hair a stiff coiffeur held in place with tortoiseshell hairpins as long as knitting needles, on wooden patens a foot high. Her face is a perfect heart shape, her nose long and straight. She gazes mysteriously away from the viewer with large impenetrable eyes, the ghost of a Mona Lisa smile hovering on her shapely lips. She is not an individual but an archetype, the Oriental siren, poised, inscrutable, eternally fascinating.

From the Berkeley Lyceum, the company moved to the Bijou, a Broadway theatre where they 'attracted large and deeply interested audiences'. Unfortunately, although more central, it was rather *déclassé*, 'a theatre associated with acrobatic farce of native origin, with mother-in-law, alimony and bar room jokes, "coon" songs and hustlers'.[13] Perhaps, despite their success among New York high society, they were not garnering the audiences they had hoped for, which was why they moved to this less distinguished address.

Yakko was enjoying her celebrity status. She was finally indulging her love of Western clothes. 'I have seen her in a thoroughly modern gown in which she looked most chic and charming, especially when she smiled, which she did with Parisian piquancy,' commented a reporter, though he added that she would not 'seem quite natural to American eyes in any but the Japanese style of costuming, which becomes her so gracefully'.[14]

In a photograph which she had taken in New York, she is every bit the glamorous star. She is dressed in the height of fashion, in a shapely high-collared tea gown with full sleeves gathered at the wrist, a skirt which sweeps the ground and contrasting trim from neck to hem. On her luxuriant hair, piled in a loose chignon, she wears a splendidly beribboned turban. She is poised and confident, smiling that piquant smile. Less than a year had passed since she had posed for a photograph before the troupe left Japan, timid and unsmiling in the shadow of Otojiro. The transformation was astonishing.

Every day invitations poured in. She was guest of honour at an endless round of clubs, receptions and social events. For these formal occasions she always made sure to appear in one of her most exquisite kimonos. She was well aware of the importance of maintaining her exotic image.

She and Otojiro were eager to learn the methods and techniques of Western theatre. The New York Actors' School was a revelation. In Japan actors learnt their trade by joining an acting family and becoming apprentices, in much the same way as geisha were trained. Nothing was explained. Students were supposed to learn by imbibing the master's spirit. Yet here was a school where acting was broken down into its elements and actually taught and where students were not obliged to carry their teacher's sandals, bring hot water or do manual labour.

The Players' Club too proved an education. It had been founded by Edwin Booth, the brother of John Wilkes Booth who had assassinated President Abraham Lincoln in 1865. Back then American actors had been subversives, as Otojiro himself had been. He noted:

According to what we have heard at this club, even in America actors have risen to high position only in the past twenty years or so, before which they were not included in gentlemen's society. In London and Paris also they were seen as riverbed beggars. In Paris, their position improved about ten years earlier than in America. So we can expect improvements in Japan in the future.[15]

Yakko was guest of honour at a luncheon at the Twelfth Night Club, a theatrical society for 'women of distinction'. Through her interpreter, Mr T. Hayashi, she commented on the fact that in Japan society women would not dream of mixing with actresses, let alone entertaining them. 'When I return to Japan,' she said, 'I shall endeavour to make our actresses hold the same position that they do in America.' The members, utterly charmed, made her an honorary member and she was 'besought on all sides for autographs'.[16]

At the time the sultry British actress, Olga Nethersole, was scandalising New York with her production of *Sapho* at Wallack's Theatre, just across the road from the Bijou. Based on a novel by Alphonse Daudet, this was the story of an artist's model, Fanny Le Grand, and a country swain named Jean, a precursor of Lady Chatterley's lover. Nethersole played Fanny as a languid creature in a voluminous gown with a fur-trimmed off-the-shoulder collar and a crown of flowers. Head downcast, she gazed seductively through fluttering lashes.

The scene that had audiences gasping was at the end of the play when Jean, in rustic hat and hose criss-crossed with ribbons to the knees, swept the acquiescent Fanny into his arms and set off up a staircase towards what could only be imagined as her boudoir, there to engage in some unspeakable activity. There was feverish applause as the curtain fell. It rose again for the curtain call, to discover the shameless pair even further up the stairs, gazing into each other's eyes.

In the Victorian West there was plenty of chaste kissing and embracing on stage; but there had never before been anything that even hinted at the carnal. The self-appointed guardians of public morals were horrified. The play was denounced from pulpits, condemned by women's clubs and branded as 'fatally demoralising to young men and women'.

One paper, *The World*, feared for the well-being of the 'Sapho-crazed women' who were flocking to see it and launched a campaign to have it suppressed. After all, as far as ordinary decent people were concerned, it was common knowledge, affirmed by all the medical texts, that women had no interest or pleasure in sex. While men's sexual urge led them to be creators and conquerors, women were dependent creatures who had to be persuaded to put up with sex in order to enter the realm of motherhood. They were brought up to be seductive, in order to snare a suitable husband, but not to be sexual. And no one, of course, imagined that such giddy creatures should be allowed to vote. Such a view entirely failed to explain why 'Sapho-crazed women' packed the theatre; but the paper was concerned with morals, not consistency.

There were certainly plenty of people who disagreed, enough to fill the theatre every night. An inspector for the New York Police Department attended the play five or six times 'in the line of duty' and reported that he 'had not been able to discover wherein it was immoral'. The city – indeed, the whole English-speaking world – was torn apart by the controversy.

Eventually the Women's Club, a society of ferocious battle-axes, brought a charge against Nethersole. The theatre was closed on 5 March and Nethersole was arrested as a 'corrupter of public morals' and briefly imprisoned. The case came to court on 3 April. Nethersole's British lawyers argued for her right to freedom of artistic expression. The judge pointed out that the jury should consider 'not whether the play would shock the modesty of an innocent young girl but whether it shocks the sensibilities of the people at large'. She was acquitted, after less than fifteen minutes' deliberation. Wallack's Theatre reopened immediately to sell-out performances and queues around the block.[17]

Yakko and Otojiro at the Bijou, just across the road, had been following the furore with interest. Japan had no equivalent of the agonised Victorian *mélange* of guilt and fascination regarding sex. There was no puritan morality which condemned sex as dirty. When the Victorians arrived in Japan they were shocked by the relaxed attitudes towards sex and nudity, which constituted appalling licentiousness in their eyes. There was plenty of bawdy, subtle and not so subtle, both in the parlour theatre of the geisha and also in kabuki.

But the great target of the Meiji government – the desire to win Western recognition that Japan was equal to the West and not inferior – had involved sweeping much of the decadence of old Japan under the carpet. For several decades there had been a movement to clean up kabuki and make it into a noble national theatre where Westerners could be taken without embarrassment. As the founder of New Wave theatre in Japan, Otojiro was at the forefront of the movement to create drama that was elevating and uplifting, not to do with low stuff like love and sex. Ironically, as the Victorians were little by little loosening their stays, as the Nethersole case attested, the Japanese were buttoning up more and more tightly.

In Washington, Otojiro had addressed President McKinley on his impressions of American theatre. He talked about the professionalism and technical brilliance of American stagecraft but, he went on, he had been astonished to discover that most American plays were to do with love. In Japan, he said grandly, drama offered lessons in loyalty and filial piety and showed tragedies of great men who died for their lords; but Western theatre seemed to provide material for nothing more profound than the study of 'how a man can win a woman's favour and how he can buy her love'. He was astounded that nearly every act ended with a man and woman kissing.[18]

His description of Japanese theatre was somewhat idealised. Nevertheless he was accurate on one point. In Japan kissing really was extremely shocking. The pressing of lips was restricted to the bedroom, where it was one of the more esoteric of the geisha's armoury of sexual techniques. It was not part of normal human interaction. Wives bowed to their husbands to greet them; they did not kiss them. Yakko had learnt to steel herself to being kissed by women, a disgusting Western habit which, she had come to realise, was a mark of the greatest approbation. When the legendary actress, Mrs (Madge) Kendal, took both her hands and pressed them to her lips, Yakko was so touched that her eyes filled with tears.[19]

The *Sapho* furore was an opportunity to show Americans the Japanese approach to matters of the heart and also, with luck, to boost audience figures, which had been slipping recently. With his usual genius for publicity, Otojiro put up a billboard announcing '*Sapho: The Japanese Idea*' on the very day Nethersole was acquitted. He was not the only one to jump on the bandwagon. There were *Sapho*s all over town, including a vaudeville *Sapolio*, a burlesque and a serious version said to be closer to the original novel.

The first act of the Japanese *Sapho* took place at cherry blossom time in the Mukojima geisha district of Tokyo. The Japanese Jean courted Sahoko the Geisha with folk dances, games and love songs, 'romantic but not overtly erotic and with an elevated air'.[20] Yakko as Sahoko was provocative and seductive but in a delicate, tasteful way. The critic Katherine Metcalf Roof was enraptured by the moment when she feigns illness to lure her lover to her side.

> Over the face turned from him slips a smile that is the subtlest expression of her fascination – a fascination infinitely finer, more complex than any maternal charm – a spell to ensnare the imagination rather than the senses, as removed from the conceptions of Nethersole as the clouds are from the earth.[21]

In the second act, the swain appears with their child, a wooden doll wrapped in a blanket. Repenting of her dalliance, Sahoko holds it in her arms. In an article entitled 'Deeply Affected by the Japs' *Sapho*', the critic Sewell Collins reported that he twice had lumps in his throat, 'a pair more than I did at Miss Nethersole's efforts'. The formidable members of the Women's Club came *en masse* and were loud in their praise of the prim and proper Japanese production.

Nevertheless the theatre remained half empty. There were only sixty-two in the audience for the troupe's last night in New York. They had found fame but not fortune there.[22]

Three years later, back in Japan, Yakko talked of her experiences of America, like Gulliver returned from an almost mythical country that few had ever visited. She painted a portrait of the America she had seen – from the train, in grand hotels, at high society parties, clubs and receptions – and described American women she had met, mainly the wealthy, the privileged and actresses like herself.

America was a country where women were strong, she reported, sometimes, in fact, too bossy and assertive. Unlike in Japan, they never drank or smoked in public. Gentlemen were courteous to ladies. If a gentleman sat next to a lady on a train, he would refrain from drinking or chewing tobacco.

'Why was I not born in a country like this?' she added wistfully.

The women all looked like princesses, tall and elegant with hair dyed blonde, dark or red, depending on fashion. Even housewives painted their eyebrows and applied eyeliner, rouge and highlight before going out. They washed their faces in white wine or milk and sometimes used a facial peel which peeled off 'like a locust shell', leaving them looking radiant. But despite their ladylike behaviour in public, she once stumbled on a beautiful American actress resting in the toilet with a cigar in one hand and a glass of whisky in the other; so they were not as pure as they appeared.

In Yakko's America the women wore rings on all their fingers and thumbs. Some were covered in diamonds from neck to chest, in jewel-studded stomachers 'as bright as the Buddha Amida'. But she also saw women working, as telephone operators, journalists and bank clerks.[23]

Years later, she told the journalist Yone Noguchi:

I owe everything to America. My American trip was my education. America, America, what a great sound America has! . . . After all, the American theatre is the most competent, and the American actresses are the best. And the American critics are generous, not falling into flattery and foolish praise. The American criticism was an education for us. We learned much from it.[24]

Against all the odds, the first Japanese theatre troupe to visit the United States had survived. With only the occasional help of a manager, in a country where they could not speak the language, Yakko and Otojiro had managed to turn a tour which had started disastrously into a triumph. They had embarked with almost no planning, very little funding and no idea how they were going to succeed. They had had some lucky breaks and Otojiro's acting and direction had met with approbation.

But there was no doubt that the foundation of their success was Yakko – her charisma and beauty, the magic of her dancing and the power of her acting. She was frequently billed as Japan's greatest actress. Reviewers did not realise that in fact she had never acted professionally until she reached the United States. She had arrived in San Francisco less than a year before as Otojiro's wife – strong-minded, determined, but still with no ambition other than to be the little woman behind her man. She left a star.

'They begged us to stay longer in America,' Otojiro began his diary entry for Saturday 28 April. 'But as we had Irving's letter of introduction, I wanted to set foot on European soil immediately. Regretfully we left New York, looking back fondly, and set off across the Atlantic.'[25]

The troupe were to travel on one of the new fast transatlantic steamers. Otojiro phoneticised it variously as the 'Ieniya' and the 'Yubenia'; it may have been the S.S. *Ivernia I*, a smart modern vessel of steel construction with one funnel, four masts and twin-screw propulsion which had been launched only seven months earlier and had arrived from Liverpool two weeks before.

At five o'clock in the afternoon the sirens blasted and the engines throbbed as the great ship surged out of the harbour. Yakko and Otojiro must have been among the crowds on deck, watching the famous skyline dwindle in the distance. Eleven days later, on Tuesday 8 May, they were on deck again to see the monumental stone and brick buildings of Victorian Liverpool glimmering against the dawn sky. They dropped anchor at Albert Dock at 6a.m. Without wasting any time they had their trunks transported to the railway station and boarded the first train for London.

Four hours later they were stepping through the massive Doric arch of Euston station, looking around with awe and apprehension. They had made a success of the brash new world of America. But how would they be received in England, the land of 'gentlemen', with its monarchy, class system, long history and huge empire?

At eighty-one, Queen Victoria had been on the throne for sixty-three years. During her long reign, Britain had become the richest, most powerful nation on earth, with an empire that encompassed a quarter of the world's land and a third of its people. British troops strutted the globe, serenely confident of their ineffable superiority and righteousness. That year they were fighting the Boers in South Africa, putting down the Ashanti 'native uprising' in the Gold Coast and keeping a check on the pesky Boxers in

China. British ships sailed to the far corners of the earth, exporting goods produced in Britain's thrumming factories and returning with the spoils of empire – gold, corn, frozen meat and every imaginable luxury.

London was a handsome, supercilious city, full of gracious, well-kept parks, as befitted the capital of a vast empire. The streets were lined with stately buildings and glittering shops. But around the corner from the affluent districts were pockets of poverty, slums and shanty towns full of squalid tenements where the underbelly of Victorian London – labourers, industrial workers, laundrywomen and members of the service classes – eked out short and harsh lives. Foreigners were shocked at the beggars to be seen even on the grandest streets.

Prosperous gentlemen and ladies in elegant day dresses with corseted wasp waists clattered about the streets in hansom cabs, with a top-hatted cabby at the back of each, wielding a whip. They would bowl to the Ritz for lunch or to Harrods to shop, dodging carriages, carts, horse-drawn omnibuses and the occasional terrifying new automobiles which sometimes went even faster than the speed limit of fourteen miles per hour. Artists, writers and other sophisticates gathered at Café Royal to drink, talk and argue. And everyone went to the theatre to enjoy Shakespearean revivals or plays by contemporaries like Henry James, W.S. Gilbert, Henrik Ibsen and Oscar Wilde (by then disgraced and living in Paris) and to watch the performances of the legendary actors and actresses.

Once again Otojiro and Yakko were in a strange city in an unknown land. But this time they had made preparations. They had Sir Henry Irving's precious letter of recommendation and came wreathed in ecstatic reviews. They were welcomed by Arthur Diosy, vice-chairman of the Japan Society, which had been founded in 1891, and a famous enthusiast for all things Japanese. A dapper man with an extravagantly oiled and twirled moustache, Diosy was dubbed 'the Japanner' in society circles. He was lampooned in *Vanity Fair* magazine as 'a very fluent talker in many languages, and especially in English'. The poet Sir Edwin Arnold, who had a Japanese wife, also took the actors under his wing.

General Kamimura of the Japanese Legation found them suitable hotels. If left to their own devices, Otojiro and Yakko would probably have housed themselves in the flashy and ruinously expensive Ritz or Savoy. Instead they were settled in a suite with a living room, dining room and bedroom at the Tudor, in a quiet leafy square in Paddington, at a rate of $15 a day (as Otojiro remembered, translating the rate into a currency meaningful to him); though that still put a considerable strain on their budget. The rest of the troupe stayed at the Norfolk, a few doors away. The general had also arranged a two-horse carriage for them.

Barely pausing to unpack, Yakko and Otojiro bowled through London's clogged and noisy streets to the distant, rather slummy suburb of Notting Hill Gate. They alighted at the Coronet Theatre, a cream-coloured wedding cake of a building with swirling pink mouldings, pillars and a copper-roofed cupola. There they presented themselves and their letter to the owner, the impresario Ernest G. Saunders, whom Irving had suggested they should meet.

Saunders welcomed them kindly but informed them that regretfully there was a performance already in progress. The theatre would not be available for another two weeks. Hiding their dismay they bowed politely and climbed back into their carriage. Once again, despite their success and influential friends, they were desperately low on cash. Otojiro had assumed in his reckless way that they would be starting work immediately. He recorded their plight in his diary:

So we holed up in our hotel for a while. We had wanted to come to London so badly, we'd set off with only enough money for our fares and a few nights at a hotel. All of a sudden we were having difficulty paying the hotel bill.[26]

'In England we had no one to take care of us,' remembered Yakko. 'We were still pitiful travelling players, we had no manager.' But their success and survival depended on keeping up the illusion of being celebrities, no matter what. They were the great Japanese Theatre Troupe. If they let it be known that they were nearly out of money, they would lose all the respect they had won so far.

'For the first two weeks we stayed at the hotel, even though we had no money, deliberately play acting that we were rich,' remembered Yakko. Finally she confessed that she had a little money which she had kept hidden away. Throughout the tour she not only had to act, dance and be the star; she also had to be wife, mother figure and housekeeper for the troupe, taking care of the unruly crew and keeping a tight grip on the purse strings. Well aware of Otojiro's feckless nature, she did her best to keep his spending under control, putting aside scraps of cash to keep it out of his reach.

They were down to their last pennies. Yakko's pin money was not enough to pay the hotel bill. So instead of putting down a deposit, they used it to give the concierge and bellboy generous tips. As they had hoped, the two left them in peace for a week and made no further demands for money.

By now they were so desperate that Otojiro went to their compatriot, General Kamimura, and, feigning nonchalance, asked if he could spare some cash to tide them over. But the general's generosity had its limits.

'Thinking back, we didn't do any sightseeing in London,' remembered Yakko. 'Before we got the contract settled, even when we went out meaning to see the sights, we were so nervous we couldn't concentrate on anything.'[27]

On 22 May the 'Celebrated Japanese Court Company, from Tokio', finally opened at the Coronet Theatre, Notting Hill Gate. Seats were half the price of a West End theatre – 6d (six pence) for the gallery and 1s (one shilling) for the pit to £2 2s for the most extravagant private box. There had been little advance publicity and at first the troupe played to half empty houses. For their first programme, they performed *Zingoro, An Earnest Statue Carver*, the story of a sculptor who carves a beautiful statue of a woman and brings it to life, *The Loyalist* and *The Geisha and the Knight*.

Most of the critics had no idea what they were seeing and the first reviews were somewhat bemused. 'London will probably not go mad over the Japanese players,' wrote the supercilious reviewer of the *Sketch*. Of the traditional wailing singing and plink plonk shamisen music he commented, 'No words could do justice to its horrors, besides which the efforts at cacophony of the domestic pussy cat on the roof are paltry.' But even he was entranced by Yakko and conceded that 'the leading lady, Madame Sada Yacco, made rather a "hit"'.[28]

Despite the discouraging reviews, little by little 'the fashionable and artistic public became aware of the fact that a miniature comedy and tragedy of rare delicacy and charm, as *naïf* as they were beautiful, could be seen . . . in the prosaic neighbourhood of Notting Hill.'[29] Actors and dancers, in particular, flocked to the Coronet to see and learn from a style of acting and dancing that had never been seen on the British stage before.

In *fin de siècle* London, even more than in America, Japan and all things Japanese were the height of fashion. It was a craze that had been going on practically ever since Commodore Perry thrust open the doors of that tantalisingly exotic, mysterious country. Artists like Dante Gabriel Rossetti and the American James McNeil Whistler, along with a catalogue of French masters, from Claude Monet and Edouard Manet to Toulouse Lautrec, Degas, van Gogh and Gauguin, were hugely inspired by Japanese art. They incorporated Japanese themes, *objets d'art*, perspectives and design elements into their work and copied entire woodblock prints. Japonisme, as the movement was called, was a key inspiration for the Impressionists and the Aesthetic Movement and it was the overt origin of the decorative swirls of Art Nouveau.

But it was not just artists who adored Japanese arts and crafts. Arthur Lasenby Liberty shuttled back and forth between London and Japan, lecturing, commissioning work and filling his wonderful emporium on Regent Street with desirable goods. Everyone that could afford it shopped there, filling their homes with screens, fans, lacquerware, blue and white porcelain, kimonos and 'Anglo-Japanese' furniture designed by Edward William Godwin, Ellen Terry's ex-lover. And anyone with the slightest claim to sophistication feverishly admired and collected the woodblock prints of Hokusai, Hiroshige, Utamaro and Sharaku.

'In fact, the whole of Japan is a pure invention,' commented Oscar Wilde in his supercilious way. 'There is no such country, there are no such people. The Japanese people are simply a mode of style, an exquisite fancy of art.'[30] Whether he knew it or not, he was making a very good point. Westerners' image of Japan was almost entirely fantasy, nothing to do with the rapidly modernising and industrialising country on the other side of the globe. They adored everything old and quaint and deplored any evidence of modernisation that came their way.

The Mikado poked merry fun at all this uncritical adulation (although its characters had Chinese-sounding names and the plot was a satire of British, not Japanese, life). It premièred in 1885 and was such a hit that a string of mock-Japonoiserie followed. There was *The Geisha*, a music-hall production, and *The Moonlight Blossom*, a 'Japanese romance', followed by David Belasco's *Mme. Butterfly*, which had just opened in London when Yakko and Otojiro arrived. But these were imaginings of Japan, populated with imaginary Japanese played by big-boned Westerners. London had still to see and hear the real thing. No one had any idea of what real Japanese music, dance or theatre was like or had ever seen a professionally trained Japanese dancer. Londoners knew plenty about Japanese art and design but extraordinarily little about Japanese people.

And here was Yakko, to give sustenance to all those who had been hungry for exotic Japan. She was Japonisme embodied, all the wonder and mystery of the Orient gathered into one petite person.

The Welsh symbolist poet and theatre critic, Arthur Symons, was thrilled to discover that her face exactly mirrored the Japanese women's faces as depicted in woodblock prints. He wrote in ecstatic wonder:

You know the scarcely human oval which represents a woman's face, with the help of a few thin curves for eyelids and mouth. Well, that convention, that geometrical symbol of a face, turns out to be precisely the face of the Japanese woman when she is made up.

He also concluded from the way in which she threw herself into her death scene that Japanese were essentially childlike. That abandonment made her death scene more convincing than anything that had ever been seen on stage before. Theirs, he thought, was:

. . . the emotion of children, naked sensation, not yet clothed by civilisation. . . . With a great artist like Sada Yacco, the effect is overwhelming; the whole woman dies before one's sight, life ebbs visibly out of cheeks and eyes and lips; it is death as not even Sarah Bernhardt has shown us death.[31]

Arthur Diosy, the twirly moustached Japanner, shepherded the newspaper columnist and society wit, Lady Colin Campbell, to Notting
Hill, along with two companions, Carmen and the Dragoon. To Lady
Campbell's eyes the performance was Japonisme come to life. The scenery
evoked a Hokusai landscape, 'dark and sober in colouring, with the cold
blues and greens that he loved and that always seem to have a curious
quality of menace in their tones'. In her courtesan finery, Yakko seemed
to have 'walked out of an Outamaro or Hiroshigé print'.

At first the three were merely curious but little by little found themselves
drawn in. Finally came Yakko's death scene, then the curtain fell.

> I look at Carmen and the Dragoon. She is quite white; he is tugging at
> his moustache; both are silently staring in front of them. The Japanner
> is wiping his eye glasses, and I am aware of a lump in my throat that
> declines to be swallowed. And no wonder, for we have witnessed
> such acting as we have never seen before.[32]

Among the people who made the journey to Notting Hill was a specialist
in Japanese theatre, Osman Edwards. He had come across Otojiro and
his troupe in Japan and knew that this was not kabuki but avant-garde
drama. He quickly saw through their extravagant attempts to promote
themselves.

'There is no "Japanese Court Company",' he pointed out. The only claim
they had to imperial patronage was that 'his Majesty the Emperor was once
present at a performance by Mr Kawakami during a garden party in the
grounds of the Marquis Kuroda'. But when he turned his expert eye on
the performances, he was impressed. 'Good wine needed less bush,' he
observed; they had no need to sell themselves with such absurd hyperbole.
He was bewitched by Yakko. 'Her dances were revelations of the witchery
of Salome's art, her histrionic powers are not less remarkable.' She was,
he concluded, 'not only an ethereal dancer but a tragic actress of real
power'.[33]

The critic of the *Morning Post* was dazzled by Yakko's ability to make
her audience empathise with her despite the fact she was speaking an
incomprehensible tongue. He wrote:

Sada Yacco is certainly one of the most enchanting ladies at present appearing on the London stage. Her dancing was quite delicious and her acting can hardly have been other than superb. One could always follow her, and she made one feel for her and – one cannot help thinking – with her, in a way that none too many of our own actresses could.[34]

Westerners often assumed that what they were seeing was traditional Japanese theatre. In fact Yakko was learning as she went along, quite consciously studying Western theatre and theatrical techniques, deciding what was relevant for her and absorbing it into her work.

There was no precedent in the Japanese theatre for a woman playing women's roles. In kabuki the *onnagata* had perfected a stylised presentation of femininity, walking with mincing steps and talking in a fluting falsetto. When first called upon to act, Yakko used the kabuki methods she had learnt as a geisha together with the more realistic acting style which she, as the little woman behind her man, had helped Otojiro develop in his avant-garde drama. From the moment she arrived in the West, she also took every opportunity to watch great Western actresses and study their naturalistic acting techniques. She told the journalist Yone Noguchi:

I learnt so many things in America. In Japan a laughing face is forbidden while dancing, but in America we must appear smiling and happy in dancing. Japanese art is to make one as a doll. On the American stage we have to show ourselves as living women.[35]

As her confidence increased, she let her own stage instinct shine through more and more strongly. With each performance she was perfecting a unique style of acting, an amalgam of East and West. Her performance was different from both the melodramatic, stylised acting of kabuki and the passionate, theatrical style of her Victorian contemporaries. Compared to the flamboyance of Sarah Bernhardt, the seductiveness of Ellen Terry or the intellectual brilliance of Eleonora Duse, she was mesmerisingly still yet startlingly realistic. She could make her audience feel with her all the more powerfully because her acting was so understated.

She communicated the most profound emotion through a minute movement of the head or flicker of the eyes. A critic wrote:

> To study the face of Sada Yacco is to see what might appear to be the imperturbability of the mask. . . . It is only by an uneasy movement of the eyes – the slightest, almost imperceptible change about the tilted eyelids – that we are made to realise the tragedy taking place within the woman's soul; but it is enough. A more accented expression would have been untrue art.

Above all, she had the uncanny ability to grip her audience and hold them in her thrall.[36]

News of the extraordinary dramas to be seen at the Coronet rippled to the rarefied heights of London society and came to the ears of the vastly wealthy seventy-two-year-old Henri Louis Bischoffsheim and his wife. Mr Bischoffsheim, the owner of Bischoffsheim Bank and a relative of the Hirsch, Goldschmidt and Rothschild banking dynasties, lived in Mayfair, the most aristocratic part of London, in a palatial mansion called Bute House. He loved giving parties. He decided to invite the Japanese company to perform at a reception there at which Edward, Prince of Wales, Queen Victoria's son and heir to the throne, would be the guest of honour.

Arthur Diosy, the ubiquitous Japanner, was the intermediary. Full of excitement at such an honour, Otojiro and Yakko requested an authentic Japanese stage with a *hanamichi* walkway so that the actors could walk through the audience. They submitted a blueprint. Bischoffsheim hired carpenters, who set to work.

On the evening of Wednesday 27 June, the troupe arrived in hastily tailored frock coats and silk hats. The Bischoffsheims greeted them, then lackeys escorted them through the splendid rooms. Perhaps they even took them to the second floor to show them the pride of the house, Giovanni Battista Tiepolo's magnificent *Allegory of Venus and Time*, which swirled across the ceiling of the Blue Drawing Room. Yakko and Otojiro had never seen such evidence of wealth and class, even in New York.

In a marquee in the garden was a Japanese stage, quite the finest they had ever seen. Japanese paper lanterns with delicate designs of flowers and birds, specially brought over from the Universal Exposition in Paris, glimmered with a romantic light.

The cream of London society had turned out. Dukes, duchesses, lords, ladies and the very, very wealthy mingled in the function rooms and strolled about the lawns. The Duke and Duchess of Devonshire were there, 'the Duchess in white lace embroidered in silver over pale blue, with a diamond tiara and necklace'. Lady Randolph Churchill was 'all in black, with her usual "red rose" coiffure', Lady Spencer 'in pale mauve, with diamonds'. Princess Hohenloe was 'in black and white'.

> The pretty women were very many, and included Mrs Menzies, in a picturesque Empire dress, falling in soft folds from under the arms, with embroideries of silver on black and white, and with a silver band in her hair; while Mrs Rupert Beckett was dazzling in black, with a diamond tiara.

The Duke of York, Prince Christian and Prince and Princess Radziwill, the latter 'splendid, in pale pink with diamonds and lace', put in appearances. Mr Alfred and Mrs Leo Rothschild were there, as were the Austrian and Portuguese ambassadors.

'What made the party look so brilliant was the fact that nearly all the women wore tiaras and all the men their orders,' the society magazine, *Vanity Fair*, concluded breathlessly. 'The house was full of flowers, chiefly malmaisons, and dinner was served at one long table instead of several small ones, while a string band played in the conservatory.'[37]

Bearded and genial, the rotund fifty-eight-year-old Prince of Wales exuded majesty, his ample chest glittering with medals and orders. A famous playboy, he had spent the long years waiting to become king indulging in all manner of vices. He ate five large meals and smoked twelve cigars and twenty cigarettes a day and had numerous mistresses. He was a famous lover of dancing and a teller of *risqué* tales. He also much enjoyed the theatre. The Prince's engagement diary for 27 June records, '11 [p.m.] Japanese theatre'.

The troupe members were determined to do their very best for this illustrious crowd. First they performed *The Loyalist*. But when the curtain swept across the stage, there was silence. Fans fluttered, the dukes, duchesses, lords and ladies chattered, but there was no applause. Fearful that they had unknowingly committed some offence, the troupe retreated to their dressing rooms. Then Diosy appeared, beaming with satisfaction. The Prince, he assured them, had enjoyed the play very much; but in court circles it was not done to applaud.

The troupe took to the stage again to perform *The Geisha and the Knight*. As Yakko, as the courtesan, paled and collapsed into her lover's arms, the audience was transfixed. Then there was thunderous applause. It was the first time the court etiquette had ever been breached, Diosy told them afterwards. Still in their costumes, Yakko and Otojiro were presented to the Prince, with Diosy interpreting.

'The prince was immensely pleased, especially with my Dojoji,' Yakko remembered. 'He gave me a kind word and asked me many questions.'

The playboy Prince stroked the exquisite dancer's hair with a plump, beringed hand and told her how lovely it was.

'I'm very happy to have been able to see this oriental art from such a distant land,' he told the two. 'This is thanks to you. What a long journey you have had!'[38]

Strangely, Otojiro and Yakko remembered the occasion quite differently from the way it was described in the British press. While the London papers and the Royal Archives are in no doubt that the troupe performed at Bute House in South Audley Street, Otojiro recorded in lavish detail in his diary and his memoirs that the troupe was received at Buckingham Palace. Yakko was less certain of her memory. In one interview she said that they performed at 'something or other palace'. She, however, reported that she met Queen Victoria, who asked her to take off her wig and commented on how heavy it was. According to another, even more apocryphal, version of events, Queen Victoria was so enchanted by Yakko and her dancing that she wrote to the Mikado to ask him to allow Yakko to perform on the Japanese stage in contravention of the law forbidding women to act alongside men. In fact, of course, that law had been repealed ten years earlier, in 1891.

Undoubtedly Otojiro and Yakko were hugely honoured and excited and little by little, as stories do, this one grew in the telling. It is unlikely that the actors really thought they were in Buckingham Palace. Perhaps it just made a better story. And back in Japan, who would know the difference?

There is another knotty issue. According to every Japanese source, the Prince of Wales gave Otojiro and Yakko a large sum of money: $2000, say some, 2000 yen, say others. But according to the Royal Archives, it is

> . . . exceedingly unlikely that the prince would have given anything like as much as [that]. The sort of thing normally given by members of the Royal Family to actors who had performed before them was a cigarette case bearing, or a brooch in the shape of, the monogram of the member of the Royal Family concerned.[39]

Probably the money came from the Bischoffsheims or from Diosy. Or perhaps this detail too was added in the telling. In Japan, if a potentate summoned actors to perform, it would be unthinkable not to present them with a cash reward discreetly sealed in an envelope. The story would lack credibility without such an ending.

In any case, it was a brilliantly successful conclusion to their visit to London. The next day they packed their bags and at 9.05p.m. were on the train, heading for Dover. There they crossed the Channel and at 6a.m. on 29 June set foot in the magical city of Paris.

7

'AN OPIUM HALLUCINATION OF THE FAR EAST'
PARIS SWOONS 1900—1901

Sada Yakko in Paris! No one ever imagined that those Japanese prints, which were so popular that they even made their way into Clemenceau's portfolio and into Zola's study, that those precious stilted kakemonos [hanging scrolls], would one day come to life.

Paul Morand, *1900 A.D.*[1]

She is an opium hallucination of the Far East, elegant and fragile like an Utamaro print.

Jean Lorrain[2]

'And here I am in Paris, the fairy city. I would never have believed it so beautiful, so vast, so imposing.'

'Sada Yacco Racontée par Elle-meme' in *Le Gaulois*[3]

At the turn of the century Parisians were enjoying the opulent living and shameless extravagance of *la belle-époque*. Paris was the promised land, shimmering and enticing. New York might be brash and exciting, London the capital of the richest, most powerful nation on earth; but everyone was in love with Paris. Like New York today, no one could say they had made it until they had made it there. It was the throbbing heart of art, fashion, poetry and theatre, the creative centre of the world. Frantic, febrile, decadent, degenerate, Paris exerted an irresistible magnetic allure.

Hopeful young artists, writers and poets from around Europe washed up in the seedy garrets, cafés, brothels and dance halls of Montmartre, the labyrinth of alleys which sprawled around Sacré Coeur and the legendary Moulin Rouge. There they dissipated days and nights in a haze of sensual indulgence, inhaling ether, injecting morphine and quaffing laudanum and absinthe, which they dubbed 'the green fairy'. Some disappeared into oblivion. Others turned out hallucinatory works of art.

Inspired by the flat planes and surrealistic style of Japanese woodblock prints, Henri Toulouse-Lautrec created posters of the dancers of the Moulin Rouge and a fashionable can-can venue called Le Divan Japonais. Maurice de Vlaminck was painting the cabaret dancers of Le Rat Mort, Henri Matisse was at work in his garret, Claude Debussy was brooding over his opera *Pelléas et Mélisande*, Erik Satie and Maurice Ravel were at their pianos, Alfred Jarry was creating absurd dramas and the twenty-year-old Guillaume Apollinaire was writing poetry.

The models, dancers and prostitutes of Montmartre (often one and the same) were an essential thread in the rich fabric of life. They were the lovers of artists and poets and the celebrated subjects of painting and verse. *Les grandes horizontales*, the great courtesans of the Second Empire, had grown old; but the city still had its salons presided over by grandes dames of uncertain morals whose jewels sparkled as brilliantly as their conversation. In this decadent world, there was no shame in having started one's upward career as a lady of the night. Coming from the geisha quarters of Tokyo, Yakko must have felt quite at home.

That year the City of Light was celebrating the turn of the century by hosting the largest and most spectacular Universal Exposition ever. Like moths to a flame or iron filings to a magnet, people from all over the world converged on Paris. For the first time electricity was used to light up the entire skyline. The throw of a switch illuminated 6000 light bulbs. The whole city sparkled like a fireworks display. The French novelist Paul Morand captured the spirit of the moment. 'Electricity triumphed at the Exhibition,' he wrote, 'as morphia triumphed in the boudoirs of 1900.'

The 1900 Expo offered thrills and novelty the like of which no one had ever seen before. Overnight a brilliantly colourful world-within-a-world sprang up along the Seine and bustled along the Champs de Mars and the gardens of the Trocadéro. The riverbanks bristled with mosques, minarets, spires, turrets, Oriental domes and fairytale palaces.

Morand was a child at the time. He recalled the exotic mystery and magic of those foreign worlds which had suddenly appeared before his eyes:

> I passed my days at that Arab, Polynesian, negro town, which stretched from the Eiffel Tower to Passy, a quiet Paris hillside suddenly bearing on its back all Africa, Asia, a wide universe which set me dreaming. All this hillside exhaled perfumed incense, vanilla, and the smoke of pastilles that burnt in seraglios, there you heard the scraping of Chinese violins, the click of castanets, the thin wail of Arab flutes, the mystic shrieks of the Aissaous.

The most fascinating street was off limits in the evening to young Morand: the Rue de Paris beside Cours-la-Reine, which runs along the Seine from Pont Alexandre III in front of the Grand Palais. (Both bridge and palace had been built for the Expo.) That was where the *demi-monde* and the more louche inhabitants of Gay Paree paraded and looked for assignations.

It was, according to Morand:

> . . . a street full of theatres, concert-rooms, *cocottes*, actresses, young rakes, elderly Lotharios and Parisian celebrities. There were tents pitched under the horse chestnuts, trestles for strolling players, processions with lighted lanterns. . . . There too was to be seen that pale-mauve, Nile-green night moth, Loie Fuller in her lily dance. She entranced all the artists, a creature wreathed in moonlight, the queen of the impalpable, the goddess of evocation, 'light, flame, flower, star, dragon-fly', waving the polychrome gauzes that fell from her extended arms.[4]

Loie Fuller, an American dancer with buoyant brown curls and the face of an ageing cherub, had conquered Paris almost a decade before with her spectacular dance performances at the *Folies Bergère*. Poised on a plinth, clad in a vast, voluminous, filmy gown, she whirled and undulated, wielding long canes hidden within the gauzy fabric so that it lifted, floated and hovered in extraordinary shapes and patterns. Coloured spotlights dimmed and brightened, throwing subtle light which transformed her flying robes magically into a flower, a flame or a butterfly's wings. The wonderfully fluid visual effects of her dance seemed the embodiment of Art Nouveau.

Besides being a dancer, the thirty-eight-year-old Fuller was a tough businesswoman and budding impresario. Her little theatre, under the horse chestnut trees of the Rue de Paris, was one of the sights of the Expo. Designed by the young Art Nouveau architect Henri Sauvage, it looked like a gigantic version of her vast skirts, swept up in folds at the front to create a doorway. Perched on top was a statue of the lady herself, sleeves and skirts flying like wings. A reporter from the British paper, *The Referee*, considered it 'possibly one of the prettiest and most novel buildings in the show'.[5] Others thought it, at the very least, questionable.

At the beginning of July large signs appeared outside the theatre's lifted skirts, advertising a new attraction: Mme. Sada Yacco and her troupe of Japanese actors. No doubt to his chagrin, Otojiro's name appeared below, in smaller letters. Fuller had heard of the troupe's success in New York and their triumph in London and had rushed across the Channel to book them. They were to be the first troupe to perform in her brand new velvet-walled theatre.

According to her, several hotels in sophisticated Paris were suspicious of these outlandish Orientals with their huge trunks of woven straw. One finally agreed to take them. The next day she found the whole troupe in her garden, waving their arms and shouting 'Hotel! Never again!' She never found out what had happened. In the end she moved them into her own palatial house at 24 Cortambert Street, in the wealthy 16th arrondissement, and stayed somewhere else for the duration of their visit.[6]

Yakko remembered the splendours of the house. 'Such a wonder,' she told Yone Noguchi, 'with four or five carriages and fifty horses.' King Li of Korea had fallen in love with Fuller when he was in Paris and had her living room and bedroom furnished Chinese style. The Chinese furniture provided useful props for the troupe.

For the troupe's first production on 4 July, Fuller sent out invitation cards decorated with crossed flags, French and American, to her glittering network of connections. Her friend Auguste Rodin, the bear-like, bearded sculptor, was there, along with Jules Clarétie, the director of the Comédie-Française and an influential drama critic. Half the audience were her American friends.

'Then I turned Sada Yacco loose,' Fuller later recounted. 'I never saw anything like the way those critics went wild with enthusiasm.'

Rodin was greatly impressed. Later, asked his impressions of the Expo, he replied that he had particularly liked 'the exotic dances, above all at Loie Fuller's, and with her this Sada Yacco, of lively and wonderfully perfected art'. He was eager to sculpt her but Yakko, unaware of his renown and importance, said she had no time.[7]

Initially, despite the publicity provided by Fuller's powerful friends, audiences were rather thin. Fuller had agreed to pay the troupe $3000 a week but told Otojiro and Yakko that she could only afford $1500. (To keep things simple, Otojiro always recorded sums of money in dollars or yen, no matter what country they were in.) Reluctantly they agreed. Something was needed to give the troupe an edge.

One of the most romantic and dramatic plays in the troupe's repertoire was *Kesa, The Faithful Wife*. Taken from a popular kabuki drama and much abbreviated and amended to suit Western taste, it was the story of a young woman captured by bandits.

At the beginning of the play, Kesa, played by Yakko, is forced to dance for the bandits. She does so exquisitely, waving long strips of white silk. Then Morito, a handsome samurai played by Otojiro, passes by. After a ferocious battle involving much clashing of swords and balletic judo throws, the band of brigands piles on top of Morito like a rugby scrum. In a humorous moment, he wriggles out from underneath while the brigands carry on energetically beating up the man at the bottom of the heap. Morito is running off with Kesa in his arms when they discover that the man they have tied up is one of them.

Having finished them off, Morito returns Kesa to her mother and begs her hand in marriage. But before they can perform the ceremony, he has one last knightly mission to accomplish. Three years later he returns, only to find that she has been married to his enemy, Watabane. Enraged, he tries to kill her faithless mother but Kesa prevents him. Then he begs her to run away with him. She replies that she will become his wife, but first he must murder her husband. Giving him a key to the gate, she tells him that she will mark the hut where Watabane sleeps by draping a veil over the lantern.

Night falls. Morito creeps into the garden and sees the hut. He steals up the steps, raises his sword and brings it down, cutting off the sleeper's head. Only then does he discover to his utter horror that Kesa has taken her husband's place. She has given her life for his. A London reviewer commented with amusement that Otojiro made an excellent Morito, 'scattering his enemies in fine style and exhibiting the most acute symptoms of strychnine poisoning on discovering that it is Kesa that he has killed' – which gives us some idea of Otojiro's Grand Guignol style of acting.[8]

When the play was performed in New York, a head spurting blood came rolling out of the shadows after Morito had brought down his sword. But this was too realistic by far for the American audience. Several women fainted and doctors had to be called. The theatre manager told Otojiro and Yakko sternly to remove the blood and gore from their production. Then they performed their blood-free *Kesa* in London. But the strong-minded British expressed their astonishment that there was no blood even though people had been killed. After that Otojiro as Morito wiped copious amounts of 'blood' off his dripping sword and the bloody head once more rolled across the stage.

Watching this drama in Paris, Loie Fuller had a brain wave. Something was missing. Surely the knight should commit hara-kiri. After all, he had murdered an innocent lady. Only that would atone for his offence and prove him a true man. Thirty years earlier, she explained to Otojiro and Yakko, a party of samurai had attacked some French soldiers and cut them down with their swords. The samurai had been ordered to commit hara-kiri in punishment. News of this, together with lurid descriptions, sent an almost erotic frisson of amazement and curiosity through France. French audiences, she cajoled, would love nothing more than to see a demonstration of this bizarre custom.

The couple were bemused. Otojiro explained very politely that Morito was a historical figure. He had, in fact, shaved his head and become a monk in penance for his tragic mistake. He lived for many years and became

175

known for his great wisdom. Everyone in Japan knew the story. To make him commit hara-kiri would be contrary to historical fact. Otojiro might have added, though he probably did not, that in old Japan to kill a mere woman was not an offence at all, let alone one punishable by hara-kiri.

But in Fuller Otojiro had met his match. Stubborn though he was, her will was even stronger than his. The two argued for days. Finally Fuller marched over to the Japanese legation and, priming all her feminine wiles and charms, browbeat Ambassador Kurino into mediating.

'This is not really something an ambassador should get involved in,' Kurino told Otojiro. 'But she wants this so badly. Why not just do it?'

The next time that the troupe performed *Kesa*, Otojiro prepared a sack of gooey red laver seaweed and tied it into his sash before the last act. After Kesa's gory head had bounced across the stage, he declaimed in ringing tones, 'As I have committed this crime, I can no longer allow myself to live!' Then he raised his bloody sword and plunged it into his abdomen, dragging it across so that red 'blood' spurted out. Contorting his face in an expression of acute agony, he tugged the sword upwards, keeled over and died.

In feudal Japan, *seppuku* (the correct term for hara-kiri) was performed in a kneeling position. The condemned man conducted his suicide in dignified silence, with not so much as a wince of pain, then slumped forward. When *seppuku* was depicted in a kabuki play, the Japanese audience understood perfectly that when the character fell forward he had died. But for Westerners, such a quiet toppling over did not indicate death clearly enough. Something sharper and more dramatic was required. So Otojiro performed hara-kiri standing up, which would have been quite a feat if done for real. When he keeled over with a final juddering spasm, the Paris audience leapt to their feet, cheering till the rafters rang. Men threw their hats in the air, women their handkerchiefs.

Fuller pasted notices outside the theatre promising 'Hara-kiri scene today!' The Japanese players were a sell out. There was not even standing room.

On her insistence Yakko added a female hara-kiri. At the end of *The Geisha and the Knight*, instead of simply dying, she committed hara-kiri in the style of a samurai woman, cutting her throat with a dagger. In the end nearly every character in every play committed hara-kiri. When the troupe played *The Soga Brothers*, all three brothers committed hara-kiri one after the other. Every hara-kiri was greeted with delirious cheers.

For Yakko, the hara-kiri hysteria was indicative of the French character. Americans, she told Yone Noguchi, were a gentle people who enjoyed love stories and beautiful costumes and could not bear tragedy. She went on:

> But in France, things are different. The more bloody, the more glad the audience will be. . . . A young lady who looks as if she would not even tease a butterfly would watch our 'hara-kiri' with the coolest face imaginable and be glad at seeing it. Under their grace and beauty, all the French people are hungry for blood and tears.[9]

French academics, meanwhile, settled down to prepare weighty tomes analysing the bizarre Japanese predilection for suicide. Unwittingly Otojiro and Yakko had helped launch one of the most enduring Western stereotypes of Japan.

'Poor old Morito,' commented a Japanese journalist. 'Made it all the way to Paris, only to commit hara-kiri.'

Hara-kiri may have drawn the crowds into the theatre, but what the critics remembered was Yakko, only Yakko. As the city sweated through one of the hottest summers anyone could recall, Paris was at her feet, spellbound. She was beautiful, she was exotic, she breathed life into the woodblock prints which they adored and collected. But there was more to it than that.

The Expo offered an unlimited supply of exotic women. In those pre-politically correct days, Arsène Alexandre, the art critic of *Le Figaro*, wrote a lengthy article cataloguing the many varieties at the fair. He waxed lyrical over the Javanese dancers, the Creole girls from Martinique and the Indian tea-sellers. But he was most captivated by the Japanese dancers at the Trocadéro 'who, with their mothers, their aunts or their chaperones form a large army'.[10]

That year, for the first time, a group of geisha had travelled abroad to represent their country at the Expo. They went at the invitation of the French government which had applied to the Ministry of Foreign Affairs in Tokyo. Ministry officials approached the geisha union in Karasumori, one of the élite Shimbashi geisha districts. For geisha in those days 'Paris was further than heaven or hell', so no one wanted to go. In the end eight brave volunteers stepped forward, ranging in age from sixteen to twenty-seven. Instead of their usual voluptuous kimonos, they dressed like schoolmarms in identical prim male kimonos (*andon bakama*) to discourage any misbehaviour on the part of the foreigners.

In Paris they spent their days penned in the Japanese pavilion, well away from the spectators, doing flower arrangement and tea ceremony and playing the shamisen. But the freedom-loving French raised an outcry, declaring that the geisha were being imprisoned like slaves. The Japanese ambassador, worried about Japan's image abroad, ordered that spectators be allowed in to mix with them. After that the poor geisha had to endure incessant pawing of their hair and kimonos. At least one indulged in a love affair.

But everyone recognised that Yakko was in a different league. She was not a geisha but an actress, on a par with the greatest European stars. Some called her a genius. She may have arrived in the position of Japan's first actress and representative of Japanese theatre by accident but she filled the role brilliantly. She gripped audiences. She moved them to tears and ecstasy. All Paris was 'besotted' with her, wrote Judith Gautier, daughter of Théophile Gautier and a famous Japanophile and expert in Oriental matters. She herself so much admired the plays that she translated *The Geisha and the Knight* into French.

The sophisticated Parisians realised that the Kawakami troupe's dramas were not traditional Japanese theatre. But they were not looking for authenticity. They appreciated the dramatic force of Yakko's unique, individual performances. After sitting through four- or five-hour-long classical Western plays full of lengthy declamatory monologues, it was refreshing to watch a thirty-minute drama in which elemental passions and agonies were communicated through mime and dance, virtually without words. 'No monologues, no couplets: short staccato dialogue,' was how one critic described the Japanese plays with satisfaction.[11]

The audience basked in the hallucinatory unreality of the world which these plays portrayed. They knew all too well that the Japan they depicted was not real. At the 1900 Expo, along with sternly contemporary arts and crafts, the Japanese government chose to exhibit industrial products – tubular boilers, blast furnaces, armour plate and guns – to make the point that Japan was a modern country, on a par with the West.

The imaginary setting in which Yakko moved was very different. It was a vanished Japan, the very Japan shown in those woodblock prints which Parisians so adored. That made it all the more precious and poignant. Gautier wrote:

Sada Yacco brings to us, like a brief and final vision, that feudal Japan which we have not known and which is no more; only the great courtesans and actors piously guard its traditions, which will also be submerged beneath the tide of the new civilisation.[12]

Paul Morand wrote:

Tall on her lacquered clogs, a strange mixture of modern realism and tradition, she acts in a setting of paper, of lanterns, of quaintness, of hallucination, of acrobatics and charm. Her dialogue is tender, feline, lunar, hysterical; her real accent is that of cunning, of wan anger, of madness.[13]

The etiolated thirty-one-year-old writer André Gide, a notoriously stern critic, confessed that he had been to see Yakko perform six times. Of the whole Expo with its pavilions full of treasures, his predominant memory was of her. For him Yakko's stately performance and display of elemental passion evoked the origins of theatre. It was the essence of theatre, theatre in the raw.

'In her rhythmic, measured passion, Sada Yacco gives us the sacred emotion of the great dramas of antiquity, which we seek and no longer find on our own stage,' he wrote in a five-page 'Lettre à Angèle' devoted to the troupe, the dramas and their star. 'Sada Yacco never ceases to be beautiful; she is so continually and increasingly so; she is never less beautiful than in her death, completely stiff and rigid, in the arms of the lover whom such a fierce love has reconquered.'

He was ecstatic about those last scenes in *The Geisha and the Knight*:

In the scene where she metamorphoses three times, three times casting off thin layers of robes, she is a marvel. She is still more so, when, after an instant she reappears in the midst of the disorder created by her violence, pale, dishevelled, wild-eyed, her dress disarranged . . . My dear Angèle, I won't beat about the bush – it was as fine as Aeschylus.[14]

It was an astonishing tribute.

Arsène Alexandre, that great adorer of women, evoked Yakko's extraordinary thin little chirrup of a voice so precisely that we can almost hear it. It was:

. . . like the voice of a timid child or an injured bird, or both together, a tenuous voice, finely caressing, tragically futile, making one want to cry and smile at the same time – adorable, in a word. . . . I hear the prints that we see become animated and come alive like a hallucination. They could not have another voice, if they began to speak, than that of Madame Sada Yacco. When we leaf through our dear albums of Harunobu, of Toyokuni, of Utamaro and of Hokusai, we hear again this sad and childlike warbling.[15]

But more than anything critics were amazed at the devastating realism of Yakko's death scene. 'Her features decompose,' marvelled the Belgian poet Émile Verhaeren. 'Her eyes become immobile, her mouth and lips discolour and become purplish, her hair stands on end, all horror appears.'

'Her nose narrows, her cheeks crease, a sweat of anguish pearls on her temples, her lips tremble and lose colour and go blue and with a cry she falls,' wrote the essayist Adolphe Brisson.[16]

It was so realistic that the anonymous British author of the 'Gossip from the Gay City' column in *The Referee* suspected Yakko of employing the ubiquitous morphia. He wrote:

I was told, and I believe it, that in order to go through her death scene she is drugged to as far a degree as it is possible to go. After the performance, and when the Exhibition grounds were deserted, I saw her helped into her bath chair [her carriage], and it did not surprise me to notice that everyone raised their hats as she passed, for the signs of physical torture on her face made the most casual think of the backstairs of the garish footlights.[17]

We should probably give this unkind slur only as much credence as we would any snippet of gossip in a tabloid newspaper. The last words reflect the prejudice which many still felt about the acting profession. Despite the canonisation of the divine Sarah and her ilk, actresses were still seen as women of dubious morality who flaunted themselves in public for monetary gain. They were thus fair game for journalists who wished to spread unverifiable rumours.

There was certainly plenty of morphine around. But Yakko – exotic flower though she seemed to French eyes – was a sensible woman, most unlikely to risk ruining her performance by dabbling in unpredictable substances.

Adolphe Brisson also saw her leaving the theatre after a performance of her death scene. To him she was 'une petite bourgoise', rather small and awkward in a grey dress, wearing a faded straw hat. 'We saluted with respect,' he wrote. He did not see any signs of dissipation.

Rather than drugs, it was Loie Fuller's flair for drama and mastery of the intricacies of electrical stage lighting that made Yakko's death scene transcendent. Carefully placed spotlights made the colour of her face appear to change. Gradually she was engulfed in shadow, from the feet upwards, until only her face was lit with a ghastly light. One spectator wrote that the performance was so powerful that as she died, a chill seemed to pass through the auditorium, making everyone shiver.

Several aspiring dancers who passed through the city saw Yakko's performance and were hugely inspired. One was the twenty-three-year-old Isadora Duncan, visiting Paris for the first time with her mother and brother. 'One great impression remained with me of the Exhibition of 1900 – the dancing of Sadi Yacca [sic], the great tragic dancer of Japan,' she recalled many years later. 'Night after night Charles Halle and I were thrilled by the wondrous art of this great tragedien.'[18]

Another young American, Ruth Saint Denis, also twenty-three, was on her way back to the United States after appearing in *Zaza* in London. She too was thrilled 'to an unbelievable pitch by the extraordinary acting of Mme. Sadi Yaco [*sic*].

She wrote:

> For the first time, I beheld and understood the beautiful austerities of Japanese art. Here, in her dancing, was the antithesis of the flamboyant, overblown exuberance of our American acrobatics. Her performance haunted me for years and filled my soul with such a longing for the subtle and elusive in art that it became my chief ambition as an artist. From her I first learned the difference between the words 'astonishing' and 'evoking'.

Saint Denis went on to become the mother of modern dance and mentor of Martha Graham. Yakko's performance fired in her a lifelong interest in Oriental culture and dance.[19]

The controversial composer Debussy, who had been much inspired by the music of the Javanese gamelan orchestra, heard Yakko playing her *koto* (the classical six-stringed zither) and incorporated Japanese music into the orchestral study *La Mer*. The ripples of Yakko's presence spread far. She was such a familiar face that she featured in cartoons by the celebrated young Italian caricaturist Leonetto Cappiello. In the magazine *Le Rire*, he drew her in her role as the maddened geisha, with her hair on end like a witch, poised to strike with her candy-stripe hammer.

By now Fuller had restored the troupe's fee to the original $3000 a week. Initially they had been booked for a month; but their contract was renewed again and again. They were so popular that they were giving a gruelling two or three performances a day. The Kawakamis were also much in demand at grand occasions and parties.

On 19 August they were invited to a garden party at the Elysée Palace hosted by President Émile Loubet. (He had recently taken on the post after his predecessor, Felix Faure, passed away in fine French style while making love to his mistress after a heavy lunch.) It transpired that Fuller had promised that they would give a performance without bothering to ask them. This meant that they would have to use the servants' entrance.

Otojiro was outraged. They may have appeared before the Prince of Wales merely as actors, but their ambition had grown since then. Eventually Fuller pulled the necessary strings and obtained formal invitations. When the great day came, they drove across the palace grounds and drew up in front of the colonnaded entrance in grand style in their carriage. Yakko was in a lavish kimono, Otojiro in formal evening dress. Heralded by footmen, they traversed the red carpet and stepped through the great front doors. The riverbed beggars had arrived.

Later Yakko performed the kabuki version of the *Dojoji* dance, shortened to an hour. The assembled ladies and gentlemen were ravished. After the performance, Yakko remembered, 'I had such a lovely talk with Madame Loubet and we walked arm in arm in the garden.' The President personally presented the couple with a bouquet of roses tied with a silken ribbon, inscribed with his signature. 'I have it to this day,' Otojiro recorded in his diary. He also gave them gold pins engraved with their names.[20]

There is a tantalising entry in Otojiro's diary for Thursday 23 August: 'Filmed the action scene of *Takanori* on automatic film, which has become a major attraction at the Expo.' Sadly there is no detail and no further information. To date the film has not been found. There is, however, a fascinating few minutes of footage taken around that time. This begins by showing the rippling 'skirts' forming the entrance to the Loie Fuller Theatre, with a sign advertising 'Mme. Sada Yacco and Otojiro Kawakami'. Inside, female dancers in flowing white robes are flapping their arms energetically. The whole stage is an ocean of fabric, surging and billowing in great waves.

Then the ranks of dancers part. A moustachioed Japanese in a formal black *hakama* kimono makes his way through the dancing throng. He too is waving his arms in vigorous karate chops, hamming it up cheerfully in an eccentric improvised dance of his own. The print is too small to see his face clearly, but surely this shameless character has to be Otojiro.

Around the same time, perhaps on the same day, the rest of the troupe was at a recording session. In 1888 a German immigrant in the United

183

States, Emil Berliner, had invented the gramophone. It had a huge trumpet-shaped speaker and took small wax discs, about the size of modern-day compact discs. Suddenly sound recording was a possibility. Soon pioneering sound recordists were scouring Europe for songs and music. The Expo was the perfect place to collect the exotic sounds of a myriad distant foreign cultures.

Twenty-nine discs were cut featuring the actors of the Kawakami troupe. Strangely, despite Otojiro's genius for marketing, he and Yakko do not feature. Maybe the troupe was moonlighting while the Boss and Yakko were away making their film début. Like the film, the discs disappeared. But, by an extraordinary fluke, they were recently rediscovered. These are the earliest known recordings of Japanese voices.

It is thrilling to hear the actors talking to us over the crackly recording from more than a century ago. Each gives his name as a member of 'the Kawakami troupe, American-European tour'. Then he plays the shamisen and sings a song or declaims a speech. One performs some verses of Otojiro's satirical 'Oppekepé' jingle, another performs lines from the Kawakami version of *The Merchant of Venice*. The thin, stringy notes of the shamisen and the wailing, yodelling singing must have jangled painfully on Parisian ears. Only Yakko's bewitching dance made it palatable.[21]

Yakko was so famous and popular that an exclusive interview with her featured on the front page of the Paris newspaper *Le Gaulois*. In it she spoke of her daily life. In the daytime, she said, she dressed like a Parisian, in ankle-length wasp-waisted dresses with bell skirts. She lived the life of a grande dame:

> I get up at noon. I dine European-style, except that I don't know how to use a fork so I use 'our national sticks' [chopsticks]. I drink excellent tea and rice wine. . . . After lunch I go to the theatre from where, after the afternoon performance, my husband and I take a stroll across the capital. We go home for dinner, then straight back to the theatre. At midnight, after I have feigned death, I really am dead and can think of nothing except going to bed.

Despite her gruelling schedule, Yakko had managed to see much of

Paris. She loved 'your marvellous monuments, your broad boulevards, your sumptuous squares'. Above all she adored the Bois de Boulogne, which bordered the 16th arrondissement where she lodged in Loie Fuller's house. She told the reporter:

> It is delicious, your wood, above all the parts where no one goes. There I know narrow paths where you can feel quite alone in the middle of a turbulent life and surrender yourself to peaceful reverie far from the murmur of the crowds. It's charming!

She was, she confessed, a little homesick and looking forward to going back to Japan.[22]

Only a few months had passed since the troupe had been starving in Chicago. Yakko was well aware of the fragility of their success. With a survivor's instinct, she knew how important it was to maintain an appropriate public persona. She had to be an actress off stage as well as on. To the reporter from *Le Gaulois*, she presented herself as a glamorous celebrity, every bit as cosmopolitan, sophisticated and chic as the great Western stars. The journalist Louis Fournier, who wrote a booklet on the Japanese players, saw her very differently. To him she was an exotic, childlike, irresistibly seductive creature:

> Sada Yacco enters clothed in a long black 'kimono', her delicate and childishly melancholy face lighting up with a smile. She has been ill. I ask if she is better. 'No better, cold! . . . cold!' she says in her caressing voice.

The subject he was eager to hear her talk about was 'Love in Japan'. Perhaps he was hoping for tales of passion, love and suicide. Instead she gave him a rather prim reply:

> 'Different – so different,' she exclaims. 'In this country men and women love each other freely; it is the custom. Japanese girls do not declare their love so frankly. Often they will die rather than confess it. There is a very strict rule in Japan which forbids a girl and boy

after they are seven years old to sit in one another's presence. When once a Japanese girl has taken a husband, she will help him loyally all his life. . . . Ah! to me, my friend, love in Japan is very noble, sublime and sacred!'23

Yakko was happy to reveal that she had begun her career as a geisha; a good part of her mystique arose from that. She knew, however, that Westerners had no idea of the geisha's true role in Japan and suspected that such women had, at the very least, all sorts of *outré* sexual knowledge. She was always careful to emphasise that she had been not a 'teahouse geisha' but a geisha of the very highest class. Thus she polished her image as an artiste and a person of gentility and refinement, as different as it was possible to be from a vagabond travelling player or a 'riverbed beggar'. Her reply was also fortuitously in line with the image of the pathetically devoted Japanese woman portrayed in *Madame Butterfly*.

Both Yakko and Otojiro realised that part at least of their success was due to luck. It would be foolish to rest on their laurels. On one occasion Otojiro lectured the young actors of the troupe and warned them against congratulating themselves, telling them:

The great fame and fortune that our troupe has met with today is by no means due to our own abilities but because, as the Japanese empire won the recent war [against China], many countries have focused their attention on Japan. Our present success is partly due to the fact that foreigners are interested in dramas performed by a victorious nation and also tend to like unusual things. So we should not relax in our studies. We must work even harder!24

Whenever she had time, Yakko went to the theatre to observe and learn from the great actors and actresses. Above all she wanted to see the legendary Sarah. At the Expo, Bernhardt was playing the youthful son of Napoleon I, in *L'Aiglon* (*The Eaglet*) by Edmond Rostand, at the magnificent Sarah Bernhardt Theatre. The fifty-six-year-old actress's performance as the doomed Dauphin was a spectacular *tour de force*. One day Loie Fuller took Yakko along to see it.

Bernhardt had been the unchallenged queen of the theatrical world for decades. Everyone acknowledged her as the greatest actress of the age. The power and emotion of her acting and the pathos of her death scenes, together with her 'golden voice', were unforgettable. Dramatically beautiful, she had a pale, intense face, a mass of frizzy red-gold hair and a fiery personality. Like Yakko, she had emerged from the *demi-monde*. Her mother was a Dutch courtesan, one of *les grandes horizontales* of the Second Empire; the young Bernhardt had been brought up by her father's old nurse while her mother engaged in liaisons.

Yakko 'watched the play in that imperturbable way of hers, and after it was over I asked her what she thought of it', Fuller remembered. '"Think European acting very much speak words; Japanese acting very much act things," she said, and that was all I could get out of her.'[25]

Yakko's observation was astute. One of the qualities that thrilled her *fin de siècle* audiences was the sheer physicality of her own performance. It was all acting, words played no part. When she spoke, her voice, extraordinary though it was, was simply a sound, contributing to the overall effect.

But her reticence was due largely to her lack of English. A decade later, interviewed by a Japanese journalist, she was full of praise for the legendary actress. Bernhardt, she remembered, had given a forty-minute monologue in classical French. The audience, Yakko noticed, were following the script. 'I couldn't understand a word, of course. But I could see the way she expressed the anguish in the lines, with such skill it seemed divinely inspired. I can't forget it, even now.'[26]

At the pinnacle of her career, Bernhardt was unassailable. Nevertheless she must have found it galling to have this Japanese parvenu perpetually compared to her. People were even saying that Yakko's death scene was better. There were rumours that Bernhardt visited the Loie Fuller Theatre from time to time, 'disguised by a thick veil', to watch Yakko perform and perhaps learn something new.

She attended a special matinée at the Comédie Française where Yakko performed before all the great actors of the Paris stage. Louis Fournier rashly asked her opinion of her rival. 'Immediately came a storm of adjectives: "Atroce! abominable! horrible! – a pack of monkeys, my friend, a pack of monkeys!"'

The insult flew back in her face. 'Never mind, exquisite little Japanese' appeared in a well-known French paper the next day, continuing:

It was hardly worth your while giving a *matinée* to be insulted. You are accused of dying like a monkey; go away, little Japanese, and come back in a year or so – before, if you can – and you will find actresses trying to imitate you in every detail. Who will speak of monkeys then?[27]

In all Paris, Bernhardt's was practically the only unkind voice.

'My life in Paris was the most delightful one,' Yakko told Yone Noguchi. 'I can hardly forget it.'

Years later, she remembered how very amused she had been because Loie Fuller always commented on how 'nice' Otojiro was. 'It was so funny to hear that Kawakami was "nice", because all year round he hits me and kicks me. But in the west he always acted "nice" in front of people. There are two sides to everything!'

The pair could not help noticing that, when they were out walking, a gentleman would take a lady's arm and help her along. 'Sometimes Kawakami and I would practise walking like that in the park. It must have looked very funny!' She also noticed that elegant Western women turned their feet out when they walked. She turned hers in, in the manner favoured by chic Japanese used to scurrying along in tight kimonos. That was something else to practise.[28]

Performing two or three times a day, Yakko was running low on Japanese supplies. She needed more white face powder, more toed white cotton socks to wear with kimonos and *bintsuke* oil for her face and hair. So she went to see the Karasumori geisha in the Trocadéro.

She had been away from Japan for more than a year. All that time, she had been the sole woman taking care of her troupe of men. The only other Japanese women she had met had been the wives of ambassadors and businessmen, and then rarely. Usually there were no women for her to talk to. No wonder, as she had told the journalist from *Le Gaulois*, she was looking forward to going home.

In the Japanese pavilion, the geisha inhabited a miniature Japan. They wore kimonos, sat on tatami matting and ate Japanese food. Exotic though they looked to foreign eyes, geisha were working girls who enjoyed a good gossip and had an irreverent sense of humour. Among them, Yakko had no need to maintain a façade. She was one of them.

Among her fellow geisha, she spoke modestly, with proper self-deprecation. It would have been utterly uncouth to boast. Jokingly she played down her success on the Paris stage. She said gaily:

> We were told we had to perform so that foreigners would appreciate us. We could do anything, no matter how ridiculous. But somehow we made it and were invited here. Well, come and see us! If you do us the honour of viewing us, you'll probably burst out laughing!

No doubt, like many successful women, Yakko did not realise her own brilliance and doubted that she deserved her renown. She knew that Westerners rated her as highly as the greatest of their own stars. But she had a shrewd suspicion that her novelty and exoticism had contributed mightily to her fame. For her it was not real success. She had yet to prove herself in her own country among her peers.

Later the Karasumori geisha went *en masse* to see *The Geisha and the Knight*. 'Goodness, it was really different!' they marvelled. 'They did [the kabuki play] *Nagoya Sanzo*, then it turned into *Dojoji*, and in the middle there was some country dancing.'[29]

Otojiro and Yakko assumed that only foreigners would see their plays. But while the troupe were in Paris, the *Yomiuri* newspaper sent the artist and intellectual Beisai Kubota to review *The Geisha and the Knight*. The Japanese were hypersensitive to how both they and their drama were presented to Western eyes. Here was this troupe performing, without official sanction, plays that Westerners were all too likely to take as authentic Japanese theatre. Worse, far from presenting the modern, Western Japan, they were full of geisha, samurai and hara-kiri. What on earth would this distinguished critic make of it all? Unlike the French audience, he was familiar with the original kabuki plays and realised what travesties these were.

'*The Geisha and the Knight*,' he began sternly, 'is a preposterous hodgepodge of *Sayaate* and *Dojoji* with inappropriate costumes and incomprehensible dialogue.' Throughout the play, he complained, there was hardly any speech. The actors gabbled what few lines there were to make way for the next bit of fighting or dancing.

But even Kubota found it hard to resist Yakko's Katsuragi. 'She is extremely attractive and beautiful,' he wrote. However, he pointed out rather sarcastically that in the original play she is an *oiran*, a glamorous high-class courtesan. In *The Geisha and the Knight* she has become a geisha; but, strangely enough, she still wears the sumptuous kimonos of the *oiran*. But when she spoke, instead of talking like a medieval courtesan, she had the cute little-girl voice and east end lilt of a modern-day Tokyo geisha.

'Then again,' he wrote, 'this *Dojoji* is not about a courtesan but the geisha Katsuragi; so I guess it's acceptable if the odd geisha intonation creeps in.' His conclusion was disapproving: 'There is always commotion without unity and the lines are spoken in a low monotonous tone.' Nevertheless, he had to acknowledge that the French loved the play. He was the only person in Paris who had noticed its flaws and inconsistencies. But perhaps his pedantic insistence on how the play 'ought' to be done blinded him to the power and beauty of Yakko's performance which her French admirers, coming to the play with fresh eyes, could see.[30]

As the troupe continued their triumphal run, Otojiro and Yakko were showered with medals and awards. They appeared at a flurry of gala Exposition soirées. They also signed a contract with Loie Fuller for a second tour, to begin on 16 June 1901.

This time the troupe would receive $1000 a week ('$1000 or £200 or 4000DM or 5000 francs, according to the market in money of each country where they perform', the contract specified) to perform six evenings and two matinées a week, with Sundays off, for a guaranteed six months. If the tour was extended, the fee would rise to $1500 a week. Fuller would plan the route, book theatres and cover all expenses 'on condition that Otojiro Kawakami, Sada Yacco and other female actors always, both on ship and train, travel first class'. She also gave them an advance to enable them to go back to Japan and fetch new actors. The Japanese ambassador witnessed the contract and verified that the translation was accurate.

Their last performance was on Saturday 3 November. In their 123 days in Paris they had given 218 performances of *The Geisha and the Knight*, eighty-three of *Kesa*, twenty-nine of *Takanori* and thirty-four of *Zingoro* – a total of 369 performances, averaging three plays a day. The reviews, noted Otojiro in his diary with comical vexation, were almost entirely about Yakko. 'Kawakami did not receive much acclaim. This was also true of the way we were treated. Kawakami was heard to say, "I want to go back to Japan!"'[31]

On Sunday 4 November the troupe boarded a train for Brussels at 9.05a.m. They arrived at 7.30p.m. (Perhaps they stopped somewhere on the way.) They gave a performance at a reception at the Japanese embassy, hosted by Ambassador Motono. The Japanese literati may have had doubts about the troupe; the country's representatives had no problem.

The following day they gave a gala performance in the park in front of the Royal Palace. More than a thousand people crowded to see them. Judith Gautier, the distinguished Orientalist, introduced them and gave a synopsis of *The Geisha and the Knight* and *Kesa*. The reviews in the Belgian newspapers were ecstatic.

A reporter for the *Yomiuri*, writing under the pen name 'Hokkuo', was present. Pondering Yakko's performance, he felt strongly that the sour response with which Japanese greeted her success was nothing but mean-minded prejudice.

'Has there ever been a Japanese who has received such applause among Europeans as Sada Yacco?' he demanded. 'Is there anyone else who can compete with or even surpass their European peers? I can't think of any.' He went on sarcastically:

Of course, Japan has 'great politicians', 'courageous military men', 'learned academics', 'successful entrepreneurs', heroes, schemers, and haughty people who don't consider actors to be human. These are all big shots – within the island called Japan. Once they set foot in Europe, they're nobodies.

More than 500 Japanese visited Paris for the Expo. Most are so-called 'famous people'; the Japanese government paid for their visits. The Kawakami troupe did not brashly set off for Paris all alone. Still, in Paris we never hear about these 'famous people'. But wherever Sadayakko sets foot, she leaves her mark. Even children know her name. She has succeeded in giving Europeans a profound impression of Japan. Could a bearded man do better?[32]

The journalist Louis Fournier summed up the French perspective. At every Expo there was a *clou*, a 'star attraction' which outshone all the others. It might be a stupendous architectural feat, a dazzling new discovery or a landmark invention which epitomised the energy and spirit of the Expo. At the 1889 Expo, the *clou* had been the newly built Eiffel Tower. Visitors to the 1900 Expo argued endlessly over whether there was a *clou* and what it might be.

Passing Loie Fuller's Theatre with, as usual, waiting crowds clamouring outside, Fournier had a sudden realisation. 'There certainly was a *clou* to the Exhibition of 1900. It was not a great mechanical enterprise, or a tower erected to a startling height. It was a woman – Madame Sada Yacco.'[33]

On 7 November the troupe set out on the last stage of what had turned out to be a round the world trip. They left Brussels by train at 9.05a.m. arrived at Ostend at eleven o'clock and took a paddle steamer for Dover. At five o'clock that evening they were in London.

Two days later, at noon on 9 November, they set sail from Albert Dock on the *Kanagawa-maru*, a 5837 ton, high-speed steamer. Ambassador Kurino, who had become a friend, travelled with them. They sailed past Gibraltar, through the Mediterranean Sea and dropped anchor at the bustling Egyptian town of Port Said. Then they steamed along the Suez Canal, through the spectacular desert vistas of the Red Sea, round the tip of India and stopped off among the dazzling white-washed buildings and palm trees of Colombo, the capital of Ceylon.

From there they sailed on to Singapore, then Hong Kong, then Nagasaki. Finally, at eight o'clock on the morning of Monday 1 January 1901, after a voyage of nearly two months, more than a year and a half after they had left Japan, they dropped anchor in Kobe.

It had been an extraordinary adventure. Less than fifty years earlier, Japanese had been prohibited from leaving the country on pain of death.

Even in their day, very few ever had the chance to go abroad. Otojiro, Yakko and the troupe had circled the world. They had travelled the wealthy West and imbibed the steamy air and tropical scents of an extraordinary variety of exotic places. They brought with them the glamour of that great unknown world outside Japan.

At Kobe, the port was decked with flags and a band was playing. Thousands of relatives, friends and spectators were waiting to greet them, huddled in thick overcoats against the crisp winter air. The *Kanagawa-maru* was too vast to berth. While a gangplank was set up, the more impatient climbed into steamboats and bobbed out to the ship.

Otojiro and the actors were resplendent in frock coats. But all eyes were on Yakko as she shimmied down the gangplank. Referring to her by her western stage name rather than Mrs Kawakami, the Chuo newspaper reported breathlessly:

Sada Yakko is in a new dress in the latest Paris fashion. In the old days her hair was as black as crows' feathers and she wore it geisha-style in a *takashimada* or *ichogaeshi* knot. Now it is as blonde as the hair of aristocratic ladies abroad, and loosely coiled Parisian-style with a few strands curled around her delectable cheeks. Even her skin seems to have become milky white with a touch of rouge. With her double eyelids and bell-shaped eyes, she looks just like a Western lady. She is so dramatically changed! She is by far the most radiant and exotic of the troupe.[34]

There is a photograph of Yakko in her spectacular gown, an up-to-the-minute chiffon dress with a fashionably high lace collar, a V-shaped frilled bodice, tiny corseted waist and bell-shaped skirt. Another shows her with Otojiro driving through the streets of Kobe in a horse-drawn carriage. Yakko wears an extravagantly huge, frilly, lacy hat, perched well forward on her head like the chic Parisian lady she has become. Her hair, incidentally, is not noticeably blonde. Maybe that was in the eye of the journalist.

Before going on to Tokyo, the couple spent a few days at Arima Spa, a famous resort in the hills to the north of Kobe. Otojiro had never fully recovered from the appendicitis he had had in Boston and needed to rest. They arrived in Tokyo on 19 January. The railway station there was mobbed. Friends, patrons and several hundred spectators had turned out to meet them, including all the Yoshicho geisha, from the lowest to the highest in rank. Otojiro and Yakko were in the middle of the crush, bowing to left and to right, greeting admirers. But the celebrity was Yakko. Murmurs went through the crowd: 'How beautiful she is!' 'How large her eyes are!' 'She looks just like a westerner. Amazing how people's skin turns white when they go to the west!'

One patron had ordered a Western-style carriage for them but Otojiro turned him down. 'If actors had high status in Japan, like in the west, and were treated with respect, I'd accept your kind offer,' he told him. 'But we are still despised here, so we should walk barefoot.' And he asked for rickshaws to be called.

The troupe was finally back in the dusty streets of tile-roofed wooden houses, few more than two storeys high. The Asakusa Twelve Storeys, the so-called Cloud Scraper, a six-sided red-brick pile, was the highest building in the city. It contained the city's only elevator, which went all the way to the eighth floor. After the wonders of New York, London and Paris, Otojiro and Yakko must have felt as if they had stepped several centuries back in time. But at least they were home.

Asajiro Fujisawa, the ex-journalist and the troupe's most popular actor, had stayed behind in Japan as acting leader of the remaining members of the troupe. They had carried on performing New Wave drama, earning money and maintaining the Kawakami troupe's profile in the competitive Japanese theatrical world.

When Otojiro and Yakko left for the West, it had been the most reckless of ventures. It would have been madness to have taken the whole troupe on such a harebrained voyage. But now the pioneers were old hands. They were established, they had laid the foundations, they had the measure of the West. This time, they would take their best players, including, of course, the handsome Asajiro.

Otojiro's debts had not disappeared in his absence. The troupe did a series of performances, partly to raise money and also to establish his credentials as the maestro of modern theatre techniques. Nobody but he could claim to have first-hand experience of Western drama. They incorporated innovative props, scenery and inventive lighting, no doubt learnt from Loie Fuller.

Yakko appeared in only one piece, *The Tragic Tale of our Western Travels*. The first act was the melodramatic story of how the troupe nearly starved to death in Chicago. The second was a tribute to their lost comrades, Mikami and Maruyama, and depicted their last moments in heart-rending detail. By the end the spectators were sobbing into their handkerchiefs.

Apart from that, Yakko refused to step on stage. She was happy to perform in front of Westerners but her own people would see that she had no training. She reverted to the role of the little woman. She ran around preparing for the next tour, organising props and costumes. As always, she was in charge of the whole complicated financial side of things. She saw her friends among the Yoshicho geisha and spent time with Kamekichi, her 'mother' in the geisha world, who was like a real mother to her.

It was a brief refreshing breath of normality before she returned to the clamour and mad fame of the West. For all her celebrated beauty, Yakko was fundamentally down to earth. All her fame abroad, she assumed, was merely a temporary phenomenon; ultimately it was just a way of making a living. She was not going to let it go to her head.

An important task was to find women to join the troupe. After searching and auditioning, Yakko selected five. One had performed in an all-women troupe; the rest were geisha. Of these, one was a niece of hers, Tsuru Koyama, and another was a relative of Kamekichi called Tane Hamada. Having visited acting schools in New York, she gave them some basic stage training, an unheard of concept in Japan where actors learnt by imitation and practice.

The couple were reunited with Otojiro's son, Raikichi, the Thunderbolt child. He was now five and the cutest, most wilful little boy one could ever meet. He had Otojiro's cheeky face, round with big eyes and a pointed chin. Otojiro and Yakko decided to take him along as their child star.

In those days children were bundled from home to home with no thought for their emotional well-being. After his mother had handed him over to Otojiro and Yakko, he had spent his early years with them. Yakko always referred to him as 'Otojiro's son'. Somehow it is hard to imagine that she treated him like her own child. No doubt, like all Japanese homes in those days, there were plenty of relatives and staff who lived in. Yakko probably supported some of her brothers and sisters once she became successful. There were plenty of people around to take care of the little boy.

On 10 April Otojiro and Yakko boarded the luxury 6000 ton *Sanuki-maru* with their new troupe. There were now twenty actors plus Raikichi along with musicians, dressers and hairdressers. A theatre critic named Tohi Shunsho accompanied them, intending to spend his time studying and researching foreign drama. They stopped in Singapore, Penang and Colombo, steamed across the Red Sea and the Mediterranean and stopped over at Marseilles. At 6a.m. on 4 June, they dropped anchor at Tilbury Docks on the Thames at the edge of London.

Imperial London was as splendid and wealthy as ever and, for many of the troupe, reassuringly familiar. Since their last visit, Queen Victoria had died. The playboy Prince of Wales, who had admired their performance and stroked Yakko's hair, had become King Edward VII, ushering in a new era of glittery extravagance.

Loie Fuller was there to meet them. Instead of the backwater of Notting Hill, they were to perform at the Criterion in Piccadilly Circus, the throbbing heart of the city. The theatre was small but magnificent, replete with gold cornicing, swagged velvet, chandeliers, statues and ornate tile work. The troupe began their season on 18 June. Between the Japanese dramas, Fuller performed her floaty, swirling dances. But everyone knew she was not the main attraction.

Tohi Shunsho, the theatre critic, found himself roped in as the troupe's interpreter, despite his comically limited command of English. He was also expected to be stage manager, props manager and dogsbody. In fact, he had no time at all for study. In a despatch to the *Chuo*, he reported that every performance was a sell-out, adding:

> The theatre is rather small, but its location and status are top level and the audience is very high class. Standing at the entrance, watching them come in, you see semi-naked ladies with their shoulders bare,

wearing evening gowns with long skirts studded with diamonds which shine like stars. The gentlemen wear silk hats. Old and young, men and women come streaming in.

Being a country of manners, he went on, people were so polite that they were careful not to tread on the ladies' skirts, quite unlike Japan.[35]

Years later, Yakko spoke light-heartedly of her memories of Britain and of British women. She found that they had 'a rather old-fashioned mentality', though they were graceful and elegant. Higher-class women, she recalled, dyed their hair blonde like Parisians; but the lower classes favoured a rather extraordinary hairstyle with their hair coiled around the head like a snake, a style which, strangely enough, had been worn in Japan in ancient times. The British, she noticed, were very proud of their birth and rank, which made arranging marriages difficult. And, perhaps because of Britain's long history, people were haughty and unsociable. It was difficult to make friends, unlike in America. But on the positive side, there was plenty of whisky and even ladies drank and smoked quite openly in public. 'And,' she concluded, 'they are very good at horse riding.' As an excellent rider herself, she was well equipped to judge.[36]

After her triumph in Paris, Yakko was an established star, and the critics treated her as such. There were photographs and reviews in all the papers.

'The new cast reveals the pleasant fact that Mme. Sada Yacco is not the only pretty actress in Japan,' commented *The Times*. They could also now distinguish between real Japanese drama, as portrayed by the troupe, and the fake Japonoiserie of *The Mikado* and *The Geisha*. The same critic complained that music from these productions was played during the intermission. 'With real Japan before us, the last thing we wish to be reminded of is the sham Japan of cockney invention,' he wrote.[37]

The greatest compliment came from the critic Max Beerbohm. Pondering the difficulty of assessing the beauty of actresses of different nationalities, he mused:

What is the secret of Sarah's appeal to us? Why do our hearts go out to Sada Yacco? Why is Réjane [the celebrated French actress]

197

enchanting? If I, Paris-like, were called on to decide which of these three goddesses was most admirable, the apple would (I think) be adjudicated to Sada Yacco.[38]

More beautiful and alluring even than the women who had been judged the most beautiful and alluring in the world – until her arrival! It was an astonishing accolade.

They were so successful that they stayed far longer than Fuller had originally planned. They also went north to Glasgow, where they made a brief appearance at the splendid International Exhibition being hosted there. Finally, towards the end of August, they set off for Paris. For Yakko it was almost like a home-coming.

8

THE REAL MADAME
BUTTERFLY
EUROPE 1901–1903

Sada Yacco is truly endowed with oriental charms. Everything about her is soft, delicate, expressive and ingenuous. . . . Her grace is infantile, the emotion she arouses in us at moments of furore and at death is the same as that aroused by a little domestic animal.

Corriere della sera[1]

The Expo was over and the theatres and tawdry parlours beneath the horse chestnut trees of the Rue de Paris had been tidied up and cleared away. The Kawakami troupe was ensconced in one of the city's most fashionable theatres, the Théâtre de l'Athénée, in the establishment heart of the city, close to the Opéra. There, to supplement the plays with which they had enthralled Paris the previous year, the actors performed Otojiro's version of *The Merchant of Venice*, a historical drama called *The Shogun* and *Kosan and Kinkoro*, a Japanese *La Dame Aux Camellias*. Paris thrilled once again to Yakko's seductive acting and mesmerisingly realistic death scenes.

In the teeming alleys of Montmartre, a mile or two to the north, a short, ambitious, fiercely macho Spanish youth was frantically turning out painting after painting. Among the myriad paintings are some of himself. Sometimes bearded, sometimes beardless, he is dressed like an anarchist entirely in black, wearing a crumpled black *pavero* 'turkey-breeder's' hat. He looks at the world with piercing black eyes and a bold, cool gaze.

The young man's name was Pablo Picasso. He was not yet twenty but had already exhibited a painting at the Expo. This was his second visit to the city. He had begun his Paris life living in rat-infested squalor in a Montmartre garret but had been befriended by a gossip columnist and critic called Gustave Coquiot.

Coquiot knew everybody and everything. He arranged a commission for Picasso to do posters and illustrations of cabaret dancers and a series of portrait drawings of entertainers and members of the *demi-monde*. Thus Loie Fuller came to hear of him. She asked the up-and-coming young artist to design a poster of her star, the bewitching Japanese dancer, Sada Yacco.

Unlike the critics, Picasso did not perceive Yakko as 'an exquisite figurine of art' or a woodblock print come to life. He could sense the powerful, passionate woman behind the doll-like features. He empathised with the wild excess of her death scene. He sketched her in motion, with multiple flailing arms like an Indian goddess. The right hands clutch a knife which she is thrusting towards herself. Her body is all violent movement; but her face is impassive, quite beautiful in its stillness.

In the finished ink and gouache poster she is dancing, her head and arms thrown back in abandon. Her blood red kimono coils about her feet as if she is sloughing it off to reveal her serpent nature. Her face is expressionless, absorbed in her ghastly transformation. There are some mock Japanese characters to one side, in a half-hearted attempt to emulate a woodblock print. It is, according to the Picasso expert John Richardson, one of the maestro's less inspired works.[2]

Neither Yakko nor Otojiro ever mentioned it. The nineteen-year-old artist, it seems, made little impact on them, perhaps because he painted Yakko but not her vain husband. The pair were far more impressed by a sculptor named Bernstein. He cast a life-size bronze head of Yakko in her courtesan head-dress and one of Otojiro as the stern-faced samurai. Otojiro informed the Japanese press that it was a rare honour for an actor to be invited to sit for a sculptor. The busts were shipped to Japan and now have pride of place in Yakko's memorial museum in Teishoji, the temple that she founded.[3]

Yakko's glittering fame and her image as the essence of alluring femininity sparked a kimono boom. An elegant shop called Au Mikado bought the right to use 'Yacco' as a brand name. Besides the main shop at

41 Avenue de l'Opéra, it had branches at 8 Rue de la Paix and 35 Boulevard des Capucines, all three in one of the grandest parts of town, very near the Opéra. The Au Mikados stocked 'Yacco' perfume made by Guerlain, 'Yacco' skin cream and even 'Yacco' candy. But their most popular item by far was the 'Kimono Sada Yacco'.

Kimono-like garments had wafted in and out of fashion for decades. They had always been hugely expensive. Gorgeous couture items, lavishly embroidered and worn by the wives or mistresses of the very wealthy, they cost upwards of 150 francs. But now ordinary women too wanted the Yacco look. The 'Kimono Sada Yacco' was a mere 12 to 18 francs. Au Mikado sold them by mail order not only to Parisians but all over the country.

There is a 'Kimono Sada Yacco' in the Costume Institute in Kyoto. Rather shockingly, it has been cut to knee length. It is a silky garment of cream-coloured pongee with a design of phoenixes and has long draped kimono sleeves and a cross-over kimono collar. To Western eyes it is clearly a kimono. But there is something odd about it. The silk has been cut and pieced to make the pattern symmetrical. The left and right sides of the kimono match, an unthinkable breach of Japanese aesthetics. The sleeves are rather narrow and there is no under-arm opening. There is no centre seam and the collar has been strangely stitched into place. It is not so much a kimono as a Westerner's notion of one, made by Western seamstresses for Western wearers.

Yakko probably never saw the Yacco kimono. If she did, she would no doubt have taken it for granted that the form would be altered to suit Western taste, in the same way that she and Otojiro adapted their plays. She might even have thought the garment benefited by being re-created as a Japanesque form of French couture.

When she was interviewed once by a journalist from *Femina* magazine, she was full of knowledge and enthusiasm about the French way of life. She also revealed her enduring love of fashion:

It would be foolish to repeat what everyone knows, to the four corners of the earth, that Parisian women possess to the highest degree the art of dressing with style and of making the most of their beauty. Thanks to them fashion never descends to the grotesque, because they have the gift of making anything look charming: hats large or small, worn in front, behind, on the side, precariously balanced or crammed on the head; dresses simple or absurdly fancy, sleeves exaggeratedly huge or too short; everything suits them, everything makes them look deliciously pretty, they make the best of everything. . . . Everything in Paris is exquisite taste, every Parisian is an artist, even if not by profession.[4]

Among the journalists who came to interview the great actress was G. Montignac from *Le Monde Illustré*. He visited Yakko in her dressing room backstage at the Athénée. The room was full of flowers, carelessly thrust into vases or in lavish bouquets still in their wrapping on the floor. There were mirrors everywhere and pots of make-up lined up on the dressing table. Lustrous kimonos, richly embroidered with thick rolls of quilting at the hems, hung along the wall.

Loie Fuller acted as interpreter despite the fact she did not speak Japanese. She must have interpreted Yakko's limited English or her even more limited French; or, more likely, she simply made up what she guessed Yakko must have said. By the time Montignac came to interview Yakko, she had told her story dozens of times. Fuller knew it as well as she did.

Otojiro was also there. Yakko had barely managed to warble a few words in that fascinating birdlike little voice of hers when he butted in and started making a long speech about his importance in the transformation of Japanese theatre. Then Raikichi came bounding into the dressing room. He stopped short when he saw the reporter, then solemnly held out his hand like a born Frenchman and said 'Bonjour' without a trace of accent. Laughing merrily, he climbed onto a chair and reached for a candy.

Besides acting, dancing, taking care of the feckless male members of the troupe and dealing with the finances, Yakko now had an added responsibility: Raikichi. In Tokyo, she had never bothered to devote much time to the child. Now, in this tiny Japanese-speaking bubble which they inhabited, she began to feel more and more motherly towards the little boy.

Raikichi posed for photographs for *Le Monde Illustré*. One shows him with Loie Fuller, outside her house. In the other, he and Yakko are in a meadow, standing among long grass and leaves. She is behind him with her hands on his shoulders, restraining him while he struggles to run off. Her hair is piled in a loose knot and sweeps prettily around her face. She is looking down at him, smiling affectionately.

He is a fine, handsome little boy with a bright, intelligent face and childish wide eyes. His hair is cut straight across in a fringe. He is in a striped, pleated *hakama* (men's kimono), tied at the front. He has the look of a child who knows he is cute enough to get away with anything. He is posing self-consciously, his hands held straight at his sides, his feet turned slightly in. His head is tilted cheekily to one side.

The caption reads, 'Sada Yacco in an intimate moment with her husband's son.' It seems a rather cruel way to describe the child. Even in France, where no one would have known the difference, she refused ever to accept him as her own. The hurt of Otojiro's infidelity must have been etched so deep it could never be erased.[5]

Raikichi spent his time drawing. One day Loie Fuller noticed that he drew people's eyes popping out of their heads, like billiard balls. She asked Otojiro, 'Don't you think that is an odd way to draw eyes?'

Otojiro explained gravely that to Japanese people, European eyes looked very much like fishes' eyes. Shifting his zoological comparison, he added that 'All Europeans resemble pigs', which silenced even the ebullient Fuller.[6]

The handsome Asajiro Fujisawa was now the troupe's main male lead. He took most of the starring roles, such as the samurai in *The Geisha and the Knight*. Otojiro played some parts; but mainly he concentrated on directing, planning and negotiating with Fuller.

For the young actors, Paris was a glittering paradise of temptation. As Japanese males they took for granted that they could get away with whatever they pleased. In Japan there were no moral limits on a man's night-time activities and no social stigma against paying for sex. Turn-of-the-century Paris offered more varieties of vice than even these youthful libertines could imagine. But it also had hidden hazards. Yakko told a Japanese journalist when they were back from their travels:

France is known as a country of art, famous for its gold and silver, its fabrics and silks. You see a lot of beautiful women there. French women are very charming. Even if they say just a word or two, they hold your attention. I'm not surprised men praise Paris so much.

But when it comes to coquetry, French women could put to shame even the most seasoned Japanese professional, be she a geisha or a prostitute.

Every night, she remembered, after the performance, the actors would head off to Paris's myriad dance halls and brothels. The next morning they would be bursting to tell of their successes.

'I really hit it off with that one,' they would brag. 'She was head over heels in love with me!' But later the young Casanova would notice that a tie pin was missing or a cigarette case had disappeared. There would be a big fuss while he searched for it. Finally he would realise.

'No!' he would say. 'It couldn't have been then . . . !'

'Fujisawa for one had his best diamond tie pin stolen,' concluded Yakko with her silvery laugh.

Maybe there was an unspoken subplot. Rumour has it that Otojiro often joined the nightly excursions. It would not be surprising, given what kind of man he was and the fact that such behaviour was perfectly acceptable for a married Japanese man. Yakko would have just had to endure it, as every Japanese wife did. Still, it might have given her Paris triumph a bitter edge.[7]

The troupe played to full houses for sixty days. Two days after their last performance, on 10 November, they set off for Berlin by way of Holland. Just before they were due to leave Paris, Loie Fuller met a young American dancer. 'She danced with remarkable grace, her body barely covered by the flimsiest of Greek costumes, and she bade fair to become somebody,' Fuller remembered. Full of enthusiasm, she invited her to join the tour in Berlin. This young woman was Isadora Duncan. She was thrilled at the opportunity of touring with Sada Yacco 'whose art I admired so much'.

When Duncan arrived in Berlin, she found Fuller ensconced in a magnificent apartment in the Hotel Bristol,

. . . surrounded by her entourage. A dozen or so beautiful girls were
crowded about her, alternately stroking her hands and kissing her . . .
I was completely taken aback by coming upon this extreme attitude
of expressed affection, which was quite new to me.

If the young American was shocked, what must Yakko have made of
such showy displays of tenderness? In Japan even husbands and wives never
touched each other in public. As for love between women, sisterly warmth
was perfectly acceptable, but Fuller's displays of unabashed sensuality went
a lot further than that.

Yakko happened to have fetched up in the West at one of the most
wacky and Bohemian times in its history. The artists and writers of
turn-of-the-century Paris believed in excess. They were eager to try
anything and everything in the name of freedom and creativity. That
was Fuller's milieu. She may have turned into a businesswoman and
entrepreneur; but at heart she was a dancer and a free spirit. She was
also Yakko's closest Western friend. Thrown together as they toured,
Yakko must have seen plenty of displays of outrageous behaviour.

There was, for example, an intense young woman called Gabrielle Bloch,
with whom Fuller enjoyed a mutual passion. She dressed like a man in a
tailored black suit with her black hair slicked back and 'circulated around
the bevy of brightly coloured butterflies like some scarab of ancient Egypt',
Duncan recounted. There was also a young redheaded woman who took
a fancy to Duncan. Duncan was woken one night by a passionate kiss. A
few days later, this young woman tried to strangle her, sending Duncan
screaming down the hotel's plush corridors. It is most unlikely that Yakko,
staying in the same hotel and spending every day with these people, was
unaware of these extravagant goings on. But maybe she was too busy to
pay much attention.[8]

Berlin was a triumph. 'Yacco charms Berlin,' ran a headline in the *New
York Journal and American*. 'Large Audiences Greet the "Empress of the
Japanese Stage" and pictures of her lovely face are everywhere.'[9] Almost
all the Berlin papers, some twenty or thirty different ones, ran ecstatic
reviews by the city's most distinguished critics.

Otojiro had never fully recovered his health after the hardships of

Chicago and his appendicitis in Boston. In Berlin he was regularly unwell and in pain. At those times Yakko took on his duties as well as all her own. She was also inundated with invitations.

Once the troupe was invited to a reception at the Japanese legation. Yakko's old friend and lover, Hirobumi Ito – now Prince Ito – happened to be in Europe, having just completed his fourth stint as prime minister. Their paths had crossed in Paris, where he had made a point of seeing her perform. In Berlin he was to meet Kaiser Wilhelm II. Now sixty-one, Ito was a grand old man and international statesman, negotiating with the major powers at the highest possible level. But he was as much of an Epicurean as ever and Yakko, whom he had introduced to the arts of love so many years before, was still his favourite. That evening Yakko was overjoyed to sit down to a full Japanese meal with plenty of excellent sake. Drinking, songs and games went on well into the night.

During their stay the dentist to the German imperial family befriended them and invited them to his home several times. He would greet Yakko at the door with a huge bouquet of flowers, take her arm and usher her into the drawing room. Otojiro would stand looking awkward, aware that as the man, he was expected to do something, until the dentist's wife sweetly took his arm and indicated that he should lead her into the room. Such gracious living was a revelation.

The kind dentist arranged a party for Raikichi full of welcoming and noisy children, who taught him German games. The little boy quickly became fluent in German and sometimes interpreted for the actors.[10] The troupe now had a new star. 'Within this ensemble there is a lovely child,' gushed one newspaper, reporting that he was brilliantly talented. 'He is always composed and performs his roles perfectly. He is adorable!'[11] An illustration of *The Geisha and the Knight* shows Raikichi as one of the geisha's attendants, in a pill box cap and long-sleeved kimono. He also performed a masked dance at a party held by the Japan-German Society.

The papers called him 'the little king' or 'the little Raj'. There was no question, they wrote, as to who was the real boss of the Kawakami household. One journalist started playing with him and discovered it was very difficult to beat him off.

Behind Sada Yacco's husband, someone very little, I discovered, had slipped into the room. The little son. A dainty, cute little fellow with an oval face, hair combed forward and flashing black eyes. And the little fellow immediately began to play trustingly with the unknown man, slapped his hand on my hand and smacked and jumped and followed me through the corridor like a squirrel and hammered on my head with his little fists, when I grabbed him and took him back to the room. Oh, you cute, temperamental fellow! You showed me the best of your father and mother. I see that your parents, as artists, do have the sparkling devil in their bodies, without which no Sorma or Duse, no Mittwurzer or Kainz can exist.[12]

Otojiro and Yakko must have been on their best behaviour. It was only through wild little Raikichi that the journalist could see their spirit – as fiery as that of any of the great creative artists he names.

Raikichi was no longer described as Kawakami's boy but 'Sada Yacco's son'. A photograph published in a Berlin paper shows the family with Loie Fuller in a grand Berlin drawing room. Yakko wears a fashionably voluminous, multi-layered kimono, each layer a differently patterned fabric. She is looking down at little Raikichi, smiling with motherly warmth. He is in a sailor suit with a sword tucked into his belt. All his attention is on the newest member of the family – a dachshund, sitting nonchalantly beside Otojiro on the tapestried German sofa.

The troupe performed in Berlin without a break for more than a month. From there they went on to Hanover, Bremen, Hamburg, Leipzig, Dresden, Frankfurt, Baden Baden, Basle, Zurich, Stuttgart and Munich. The days passed in a blur of railway stations, horse-drawn carriages, palatial hotels, flower-filled dressing rooms, spotlit stages, salons and grand drawing rooms where they mingled with princes, princesses, lords and ladies. In Dresden they performed at the most prestigious venue in the city, the Royal Opera House, where the King of Saxonia saw a performance. In Munich King Otto of Bavaria was among their audience. On 1 February they arrived in Vienna.

When the troupe checked out of the opulent Hotel Bristol in Berlin, the hotel had impounded their trunks because Fuller had not been able to settle the bill. Her resources were stretched to the limit; she was perpetually on the brink of disaster. In Berlin, surrounded by her entourage of beautiful young women, she had led a life of heedless extravagance, ordering lavish champagne dinners from room service. But instead of blaming herself for her financial embarrassment, she put the blame on Yakko. Duncan reported that 'Sada Yacco . . . had made failures and Loie Fuller's receipts were drained to pay the deficits.'

In Leipzig, Fuller and her party were so strapped for cash that she had to send one of her beautiful young women (the redhead who had fallen for Duncan) back to Berlin to negotiate the funds to take them to Munich. Once there, Duncan volunteered to beg money from the American Consul for their train fare on to Vienna. In Vienna they checked into another palatial Hotel Bristol where, Duncan recalled, 'we were accommodated in a most luxurious apartment, although we had appeared with practically no baggage'. Then the Viennese theatre manager whom Fuller had been relying on cancelled his contract, putting her out of pocket by more than 100,000 francs.

Fuller laid her financial problems squarely at Yakko's door. Wherever they went, they had to take along 'an enormous car laden with Japanese delicacies, rice, salted fish, mushrooms and preserved turnips – delicacies necessary to support the existence of my thirty Japanese, including Sada Yacco herself'. Every time they moved on, she complained, she practically had to get down on her knees to beg to have this car attached to the train. During the tour she spent 375,000 francs on transportation alone.

Naturally, in their reports to the Japanese press, Otojiro and Yakko made no mention of all this drama and turmoil. To judge by their accounts, the tour was one long triumphal procession; though they could hardly have been unaware that their trunks had been impounded. Understanding little of what was said, perhaps they were bewildered as to the cause of all the fuss. Even if they were not, it was certainly politic to pretend to be. So they turned a blind eye and concentrated on their plays. After all, the financial side of things was Fuller's headache, not theirs. As far as they were concerned, on the first tour they had been beggars; now they were kings. That was clearly part of the problem. Nevertheless,

Ink and gouache poster of Sadayakko by Pablo Picasso, 1902

Japanese rap star: programme and words for Otojiro's 'Oppekepé' song at the Nakamura-za, 1891

Japanese look to the west...
Woodblock print depicting
Japanese at the seaside. One wears
a Victorian bathing costume, such
as Ito bought for Yakko

... and westerners look to Japan.
Poster of Yakko by Otto Muller, 1900

Kimono
Sada Yacco,
all the rage in
Paris, 1905

KIMONO SADA YACCO

*Élégante Robe de Chambre en étoffe authentique du Japon, de
coupe et de forme telle qu'elle est portée par les Dames Japonaises*

Palais de la Femme 1905 ⚜ Médaille d'Or ⚜
Exposition universelle de Liége 1905
Médaille d'Argent
✦ ✦ ✦ *MARQUE DÉPOSÉE* ✦ ✦ ✦

KIMONO en Crépon ramages multico-
lores et or . . . . **12** fr.

Le même doublé pour l'hiver . . . **18** fr.
En Crépon lavable diverses nuances, col **20** fr.
satin . . . .
En tissus broché fond crème, dessins cigognes imitant
la broderie, rouge, rose, ciel, mauve, marron et
noir. Doublé col satin, modèle de la photographie de gauche . . . . . . **30** fr.
En très belle soie de **NAGASAKI**, nuances
diverses, doublé en soie, modèle de la **65** fr.
photographie de droite . . . . .
Le même existe pour deuil.
Très richement brodé sur satin, **150** à **350** fr.
crêpe de Chine ou pongée . . .

MESURE de la NUQUE à TERRE
Expédition franco contre mandat o fr. 85 en plus
CATALOGUE SUR DEMANDE
*Accompagner les commandes du mot
MISURA pour recevoir une surprise*

HENNÉ de Perse pour la teinture des cheveux. Le paquet
franco domicile **3** fr.
EL KOHOL. Collyre du Harem, hygiène et éclat des
yeux, franco domicile **3** fr. **50**
EL CHEBABIA. Savon naturel et hygiénique des
Orientaux, recommandé pour le teint. Bouquets, les
3 pains : **1** fr. **65** ; Rose et Violette : **2** fr. **50**. Port **0** fr. **45**

Mlle WELSONN, du Vaudeville. (Cliché Boyer.)
Mlle DELAROCHE, du Théâtre Sarah-Bernhardt (Cliché Boyer.)

AU MIKADO
35, boulevard des Capucines et 8, rue de la Paix
Pour le Gros et les Commandes : 41, AVENUE DE L'OPÉRA

Parisian chic: Sadayakko with her dog Mary, Paris 1902

As Salome, Tokyo 1914

On stage in Japan in the 1910s

Opposite: 'Uncanny beauty': Yakko's bewitching Ophelia, 1903

Momosuké in his 40s

Lady of the house: Sadayakko at home
in Futaba Palace, around 1920

Futaba Palace

Momosuké's wife, Fusa

Together at last: Sada in fur stole, crested kimono and wooden clogs with Momosuké

Grand opening of Momosuké Bridge, 1922. Momosuké in straw hat, umbrella and straw sandals is on the left, Sada in the middle. In front are the 'old couple', to the right the Shinto priest who will bless the bridge

1900 OCTOBRE - II No 44

LE THÉATRE

DIRECTION ET RÉDACTION :
24, Boulevard des Capucines.

PUBLICITÉ :
DUHAMEL et COMMUNAY, seuls concessionnaires
19, Boulevard Montmartre.

CONDITIONS DE L'ABONNEMENT :
PARIS : 1 an ...... 40 fr | DÉPARTEMENTS : 1 an 44 fr.
ÉTRANGER (Union postale) 1 an .... 52 fr

ABONNEMENT ET VENTE :
Librairie du FIGARO, 26, rue Drouot.

THÉATRE LOIE FULLER (Rue de Paris). — Mme SADA YACCO. — Rôle de la Ghésha. — *LA GHESHA ET LE CHEVALIER*

ÉDITEURS : Manzi, Joyant & Cie, 24, Boulevard des Capucines, Paris. — PRIX NET : 2 fr. ; Étranger, 2 fr. 50

Dazzling the west: Yakko at the Paris Expo,
pictured on stage on the cover of *Le Théatre*, October 1900

Loie Fuller was if anything even more extravagant in her lifestyle than they were.

Turn-of-the-century Vienna was a glamorous, decadent city where the strains of the waltz wafted across the streets of majestic buildings. The capital of the Habsburgs, rulers of the Austro-Hungarian Empire, it was a hive of artistic and intellectual ferment. Gustav Klimt was creating his ravishing Art Nouveau paintings and had recently broken away from the Vienna Academy of Fine Arts to found the Vienna Sezession, an association of avant-garde artists. Sigmund Freud had just published *The Interpretation of Dreams* and *The Psychopathology of Everyday Life*. Gustav Mahler was composing sublime symphonies and conducting at the Vienna Staatsoper.

While Otojiro and Yakko stayed at the Bristol with Loie Fuller, the rest of the troupe was billeted at the Golden Lamb. Kaiichi Yamamoto, one of the troupe's leading actors, had recently joined them from Japan. He sent a despatch to a Japanese paper reporting that the performances were a sell out and the actors in high spirits.

Vienna had been eagerly awaiting the troupe's arrival. English, French and German papers circulated freely in the city's coffee shops and the journalists, writers and painters who hung out there, talking and arguing, had eagerly devoured the glowing reviews. As president of the Vienna Sezession, Klimt approached Yakko and invited her to give a private performance for them. But Yakko was on stage without a break every night and was too exhausted. The troupe did, however, give a splendid performance at the venerable Staatsoper where the seventy-two-year-old Emperor Franz Josef, with his snowy white muttonchop whiskers, observed from the royal box.

Isadora Duncan had disdained to perform in Berlin, declaring herself indisposed. In sophisticated Vienna she recovered and Fuller set about launching her upon the world. She called on her glittering social network – the wives of the British and American ambassadors, the Princess of Metternich, artists, sculptors and critics – and arranged for a début performance. Fuller's guests gathered in one of the hotel's grand ballrooms, where Duncan kept them waiting for half an hour. When she finally floated in, she was wearing a gauze garment so flimsy that she was virtually naked, unthinkably shocking at a time when hemlines had not risen even above the ankle. But her dancing had her audience in raptures.

The group moved on to Prague, then Budapest. There Duncan, having made full use of Fuller and her connections, flounced back to Vienna. Fuller sent a telegram asking if she was planning to return to which she replied, 'Only in case you will deposit to my credit ten thousand francs in a Viennese bank before nine o-clock tomorrow morning.' Poor Fuller felt utterly betrayed. That was the end of Isadora Duncan's connection with Yakko and the Japanese troupe.[13]

In Budapest, according to the local press, there were arguments between Fuller and Yakko over money. The Kawakamis thought that Fuller was taking more than her fair share of the proceeds from their performances. Apart from anything else, they had a whole troupe to feed. Perhaps she was trying to recoup some of the money which she thought they were costing her.

The troupe, complete with their cargo of rice and salted fish, continued their whirlwind tour of Europe. In Bucharest, the capital of Rumania, they performed before Prince Ferdinand and Princess Marie, a granddaughter of Queen Victoria. Then they travelled on to Cracow and St Petersburg.

Russia was an unforgettably romantic place for Yakko. The gallant young Russian men treated her like a goddess. On the streets they cast their coats on the ground where she was to tread as a gesture of welcome, so that they could treasure the imprint of her little foot. When she left a banqueting hall or stepped out of a carriage, she would be amazed to find the ground black with overcoats. Even the snow-white marble floor of the hotel was pitch black, covered in overcoats, when she walked in once.

In the heart of Russian winter, Yakko was shocked that horses were forced to walk through the snow without even a blanket to cover them. She remembered that they had icicles hanging from their noses. She was amazed at the huge coachmen, bundled up against the bitter weather. She recalled:

When I first saw a coachman, I thought he was a woman. He had on a hat that looked exactly like a sea otter and was wearing what I thought was a twelve layer kimono. He was as big as a horse![14]

Otojiro and Yakko were invited to the Winter Palace where they were presented to Tsar Nikolai II at a grand reception. There the Tsar gave Yakko a watch set with diamonds, which she treasured. A photograph shows them sitting in the places of honour to each side of him in a magnificent banqueting hall. Yakko is in an exquisite kimono with a design of bamboo. Russian women in high-necked gowns laden with heavy jewellery and ornate hats sit alongside her. Otojiro, clean-shaven, is in a dress suit with a white bow tie. He cocks an arrogant eyebrow at the camera as if he takes it for granted that he should be entertained by royalty wherever he goes.

In Moscow the troupe went on a country outing in a cavalcade of horse-drawn sleighs. Yakko was in the first sleigh, behind the coachman with his Cossack hat and big beard. Photographs show her in a black coat with a thick fur collar up to her ears and a fur hat prettily framing her heart-shaped face. Raikichi is on her knee, well wrapped up in a cap, scarf, leggings and an overcoat with the collar turned up. Otojiro has grown a manly beard and sports a Russian fur hat and great coat. The dachshund is running alongside on its stubby legs, its belly brushing the snow. In another photograph, the actors are lined up in the dazzling white landscape with ghostly trees behind them. Raikichi is in front of Yakko, pressed against her legs. One of the actors is making a face, opening his mouth wide and pretending to eat a snowball while the little boy stares at him.

From Moscow the troupe headed south by way of Germany to the rolling hills and opalescent skies of Italy. There had been a radical change of plan. According to the original contract they were supposed to continue to Vladivostok and go back to Japan from there. However, they had now extended their contract for another six months, so clearly they had to go on performing. Otojiro was ill and stayed behind at a spa in Germany to recuperate so Yakko was in charge of the troupe; it was the Sada Yacco troupe, not just in name but in reality.

In Rome Yakko made the acquaintance of Hisako Oyama, the wife of the Japanese ambassador. Both were delighted to have a Japanese woman friend in whom to confide. Mme Oyama, a lively, outgoing woman,

211

arranged for carriages to transport the troupe around town and to the legation and invited them for Japanese meals.

She was learning the piano and sometimes sang Western songs for Yakko. One day she asked her to teach her some Japanese dances to perform when they had parties. The two women pushed the heavy furniture back until the huge drawing room seemed as empty as a Japanese room. They were practising the elegant Spring Rain dance when the ambassador walked in, in his dark suit and top hat. He looked startled to see the two kimono-clad women cavorting like geisha in the legation's grand drawing room. 'You're back early, dear,' said Mme Oyama, waving her fan nonchalantly as if nothing untoward was going on, and the two returned to their dance.

Mme Oyama took a keen interest in the theatre and used to drop into Yakko's dressing room in the intermission between performances. 'You need a bit more rouge on your cheeks,' she would say. 'Your face is a bit pale.' Once she said, 'Fujisawa might be good-looking but his acting isn't very good.' She told Yakko that Westerners would not be satisfied unless the sword play was really convincing. After that the actors ended every performance covered in bruises.[15]

The distinguished composer Giacomo Puccini had been following the troupe's progress with interest. At the time he was writing an opera based on David Belasco's play, *Mme. Butterfly*. His librettists had sketched out the first draft of a three-act work and Puccini was composing with great intensity. But some key elements were missing. He had the bare bones of his plot but he needed to flesh it out. He wanted to incorporate Japanese melodies, timbres and tonalities into his work and was searching for samples of Japanese popular music. He also wanted to see real Japanese women moving and speaking and even get some idea of how they thought.

So he was thrilled to discover that the first Japanese theatre troupe ever to tour abroad was passing through Italy, led by a charismatic actress who was receiving rave reviews. It was an unmissable opportunity. He rushed to Rome and arrived on 16 March. But to his intense frustration, they had already left. He had just missed them.

From Rome the troupe went on to Naples, Florence, Livorno, Genoa and

Turin, performing in each city. On 25 April they arrived in Milan for their first show. Puccini had made sure he was there too. He wanted to interview Yakko but discovered that she did not speak any European language well enough to communicate with him and there was no interpreter available. Nevertheless he stayed in Milan for several days, attending the troupe's performances and paying close attention to their acting and music.

Yakko, a fine musician, was a virtuoso on the *koto*, a classical instrument rather like a zither or a harp. Her playing was so beautiful that a recording had been made of it while the troupe was in Berlin. Puccini was particularly impressed by a famous *koto* piece called *Echigo jishi*. Yakko played it in the third scene of *Kesa* when Morito, who has rescued her from the bandits, returns from his knightly mission and finds her picnicking with her mother and new husband.

Besides the music, Puccini was struck by the vigour and dramatic thrust of the plays. Cut right back for Western audiences, each seemed to proceed with unstoppable momentum to a dreadful end, almost always suicide by hara-kiri. 'The Geisha and the Knight,' wrote a Milanese reviewer, proceeded 'with such simplicity of means and with such terrible efficacy as to make a shudder run down the spines of the audience.'[16] The action, said another, had 'that type of insane and uncontrollable intoxication characteristic of primitive peoples'.

The critics, of course, had never seen Japanese theatre before, and in 1902 Westerners laboured under the arrogant assumption that all non-Western people were 'primitive'. Yakko's performance in *The Geisha and the Knight* unintentionally reinforced this belief. In the early part of the play she seemed to their eyes as innocent as a child, an effect enhanced by her diminutive size and doll-like porcelain beauty. This made her transformation into a wild-eyed raging fury all the more shocking. To one patronising Italian reviewer she appeared barely human: 'Her grace is infantile; the emotion she arouses in us in moments of furore and at death is the same as that aroused by a little domestic animal,' he wrote.[17]

Puccini was greatly inspired by the extraordinary timbres and rhythms of the Japanese music and by Yakko's stage performances. The troupe had barely left Milan when he was back at his keyboard. Four days after seeing them, he had written the music to accompany Butterfly's entrance with her wedding party to marry the fickle Lieutenant Pinkerton. He wove into his composition the *Echigo jishi* melody. Some months later, he suddenly decided to discard an entire act. He cut the opera from three to two acts, simplifying it so that it focused with great intensity on Butterfly's personal tragedy and the inexorable progression towards her death. 'The drama should race towards the end without interruptions, tightly knit, efficacious, terrible!' he explained in a letter to his publisher, using the same words – 'terrible efficacy' – with which the Italian reviewers had described the Japanese dramas.

Butterfly's personality closely conformed to the reviewers' response to the women whom Yakko portrayed on stage. Butterfly is a simple, sweet child-woman. The stage directions call for her to behave with 'infantile coquettishness' and 'infantile grace'. She smiles 'like a child' and when she weeps it is 'infantile crying'. It is all the more shocking when this childlike creature breaks into 'savage' rage.

Lieutenant Pinkerton, her faithless husband, is not portrayed as a 'typical American' but a complex, rather unpleasant individual. Butterfly, conversely, is not an individual. This sweet submissive child-woman, finally driven to primitive savagery by the strength of her passion, was the ultimate Westerners' stereotype of the Japanese female.

Yakko's stage performance enabled Puccini to give life to the bare bones of his plot. She provided him with a model for a flesh and blood Japanese woman to give reality to his imagined Madame Butterfly. The irony was, of course, that she herself was not remotely like this sweet, helpless little creature.[18]

Cheerfully unaware of the impact they were having upon Western music, drama and the perceptions of Japan in the West, the troupe boarded the train for Venice. There a budding young artist named Paul Klee, touring Italy after completing his studies, saw Yakko at the 'small, noble' Teatro Pergola and was enchanted.

'Sada Yaco [*sic*] has the dimensions of a Tanagra figurine,' he recorded in his diary, comparing her to the tiny, ancient Greek pottery figures of women swathed in drapes:

Everything about her is as lovely as the way she chatters. Nothing is left to chance! Not the least little fold in her dress. The way she weeps indicates the high quality of her taste (what unappetising tears I've seen on our stages!). The way she goes to bed, sheer enchantment. A sprite or a woman? In any case, a *real* sprite.[19]

By May the troupe was in Barcelona, shocking the Catalan bourgeoisie and delighting the Bohemians of Els Quatre Gats, the tavern where Picasso hung out with his dissolute comrades. There the young artist, now deep into his Blue Period, no doubt reminded the Japanese diva of their meetings in Paris the previous year and renewed their friendship.

In Madrid the Japanese ambassador took the troupe to a bullfight. Yakko was so shaken that she was hardly able to go on stage that night. She was, however, impressed with the beauty of the proud, raven-haired Spanish women. Here was a feminine aesthetic which Japanese could appreciate, close to that of Japan. Spanish women, she remarked, lacked the features which made Western women ugly, like eyes and eyebrows too close together and big ungainly noses. 'Spanish women have huge eyes like the most admired Japanese beauties and long black tresses. If a Japanese gentleman cast eyes on them, he'd be swept off his feet,' she declared.[20]

From Madrid the troupe went on through Portugal, to Toulouse, Marseilles, Lyons, Antwerp, Brussels and thus back to London. On 4 July they watched as their trunks were loaded onto the steamer *Awa-maru*, then filed up the gangplank and settled in for the long journey back to Japan.

The tour had been a triumph. The reviews had been overwhelmingly positive. Despite the occasional argument with Loie Fuller and her complaints about the car full of rice and salted fish, she had happily extended their contract for a second six months. In a year and a month they had performed in a staggering seventy-one cities, performing seven days a week with no break at all. It was an epic tour for a major troupe, quite possibly unprecedented to this day.

Before they left, Yakko was interviewed by a French journalist who reported that the troupe had earned the phenomenal sum of a million francs.

'What will you do with all this money?' he asked her. She replied:

We will build in Yeddo [Tokyo] an ultra-modern theatre, with all comforts. We will call on Viennese architects to draw up the plans. Yeddo is not the end of the world. These gentlemen who have built a theatre in Bombay, in India, will no doubt also want to build one in Japan. There we will perform the masterpieces of European theatre, translated into Japanese. We will play Corneille, Molière, Victor Hugo, Shakespeare and introduce modern dramas too.

The journalist inquired of Tadamasa Hayashi whether Sada Yacco had been celebrated in Japan before coming to Paris. Hayashi was an immensely urbane Paris man about town. A famous dealer in art and antiques, he had lived in the city for almost a decade and more than anyone else had been responsible for making Japanese art known in the West.

'Not at all,' was his reply. 'We hardly knew her. But you found so much talent in her in Paris that now she is *tout a fait* illustrious among us too in Japan. You have made her fortune twice over!'[21]

After a six-week journey, on 19 August 1902, the *Awa-maru* docked at Kobe. The epic journey was over. It was time to come back to earth.

For all her brave words, Yakko must have wondered what fate had in store for her in Japan. There, she was not a diva, a superstar or the idol of the theatre-going public but an ex-geisha, spurned by decent society. Otojiro was a riverbed beggar who lacked even the dubious honour of being a member of a kabuki family. They were thorough outsiders.

It was obvious that her acting career would have to end. It was all very well performing simplified kabuki for foreigners who had no idea of the real thing. But in Japan, where actors were initiated as children into the arcane secrets of an exclusive and closed profession, she could not possibly go on stage.

Moreover, in Japan it would never do for a woman to be more famous than her husband. Yakko's superstar status had been galling enough for Otojiro while they were abroad. Back in Japan, she doubted if their relationship could stand the strain. She would have to step quickly back into the role of 'little woman behind her man'.

At Kobe they boarded a train pulled by a great black steam engine.

Yakko, Otojiro and the female members of the troupe travelled first class with the rest of the actors in second or even third. They rattled through a landscape of woods and streams broken by flat plainland covered in neat emerald green paddy fields laid out like a chequerboard. Here and there were villages of wooden houses with steep thatched roofs and the occasional factory chimney puffing out smoke in the distance.

Yakko slipped her shoes off and curled her feet up under her on the tatami that lined the seats of the little wooden carriage. One of the actresses picked up the kettle and small teapot thoughtfully provided on the floor between the seats and poured everyone cups of green tea. It was blissfully familiar. Their exotic foreign travels had already become a jumble of distant memories.

After many hours they rounded the graceful flank of Mount Fuji and craned to look up at the mystical mountain. Later still with much hooting and puffing they chugged into Shimbashi station in Tokyo. Porters piled their wicker trunks onto carts as they stepped out into the odorous Tokyo night.

Tokyo sweated in the baking August heat. After the grandeur of the imperial West, it was like stepping back into an earlier age. People drifted languidly about in thin summer kimonos, fanning themselves and dabbing sweat from their faces with handkerchiefs. The roads were unpaved. There was dust everywhere, prickling between toes and getting into eyes. The hazy air was laden with the pungent smells of sweat, of food, of charcoal burning and of sewage. It was not until many years later that Tokyo developed a sewage system. Every night the sewage collectors would be out with their carts, buckets and dippers, shouting 'Owai! Owai!', buying human waste to sell as fertiliser.

Most of the great city was still a tinderbox of low wooden houses, crowded together along alleys so narrow that only a single rickshaw could pass through. Every night the night watchmen did their rounds, clacking wooden sticks together to warn the people of Tokyo to beware of fire. Trams clanked and rumbled by and street sellers offering goldfish, tofu or sweet potatoes sang out their wares.

At first glance everything was reassuringly unchanged. Yet even in the year and a half that they had been away, the city had become bigger, more crowded, more bustling and prosperous. The first electric trolley buses rumbled along laden with passengers, grinding to a halt whenever there was a sudden power cut. Electric cables and telegraph wires looped along the streets. There were beer halls on the Ginza. The first had only just opened when Yakko and Otojiro set off on their voyage to the West.

A month after they got back, Yakko bought a large tract of land in Chigasaki, an exclusive seaside resort between Tokyo and Oiso, where many years before Prince Ito had taught her to swim. Presumably the intention was for the couple to live there together, though the deeds were in her name. Chigasaki was a rapidly developing area where politicians and property magnates were buying up land to build country retreats. Their illustrious neighbours would include the great kabuki actor Danjuro, the real 'Henry Irving of Japan'.

There they acquired a beautiful wooded estate full of pine trees in a very desirable location, on the main road between the railway station and the sea. At the top of the gentle hill in the middle they had a villa built. It was a spacious dwelling, mainly Japanese in style, with heavy wooden 'rain doors' which slid together to form the outer walls and elegant tatami-matted rooms. Gnarled pines peeped over the tall wooden fence. After three years moving from hotel to hotel, it was time to settle down and have a home. Yakko was thirty-one, Otojiro nearly forty. They could afford to slow down.

Prince Ito chose a name for the new house. He called it Bansho'en, 'The Garden of Evening Pines', a phrase taken from a Chinese poem. He inscribed the words with a flourish on a paper scroll which they hung in the entrance.

Yakko's plan was to raise animals. She acquired a large dog, a donkey, a goat, pigs and ducks and hired staff to take care of them. The second floor of the house was given over to raising silkworms. There she imagined her life stretching peacefully out into old age.

Otojiro, of course, had no intention of spending the rest of his life as a gentleman farmer. He was dogged by ill health, perpetually in and out of bed. Nevertheless he quickly set to work on the next phase of his grand project to reform Japanese theatre. No doubt Yakko was involved, offering suggestions and ideas; perhaps she was the brains behind the whole project.

But in a male-dominated country like Japan, everyone assumed that Otojiro was the driving force and she was just the 'little woman'.

In the West the pair had introduced Japanese plays in a palatable form with stunning success. Now they intended to repeat that success at home, by introducing Western plays in a palatable form to Japanese audiences. Having already produced their own *Merchant of Venice* to surprising acclaim in the West, they decided to begin with Shakespeare.

Japanese intellectuals read Shakespeare in the original, along with John Stuart Mill, Herbert Spencer, Dickens, Byron, Victor Hugo, Kant and Nietzsche. But that was a very small élite. Only four of Shakespeare's plays had been translated into Japanese. Shakespeare had never been produced on stage for theatre audiences. The couple wanted to make Shakespeare's powerful dramas accessible to everyone. With these startlingly new, realistic and up-to-the-minute plays, they hoped to lure into the theatre new audiences, who had been put off by the stylisation and old-fashioned conventions of kabuki.

This new form of theatre, Otojiro announced, would be light years ahead of *shimpa*, New Wave drama, and, of course, aeons ahead of kabuki. He called it *seigeki*, 'true drama'. Unlike kabuki, where dance and mime were a key part of the total effect, it would focus on the spoken word, like Western theatre.

For the first production he chose *Othello*. With Yakko he set about revising it so that it would make sense in a Japanese context. To show Othello as a Moor would mean nothing to a Japanese audience. Foreigners were foreigners; the gradations between them were of far less importance than their basic foreignness.

In his Japanised plot, Othello became Lieutenant General Washiro Muro, a low-caste Japanese who has managed to raise his status through military victories. The Cyprus of the play is the Japanese colony of Taiwan, taken in the Sino-Japanese War. Muro has put down an insurrection there and is now governor, giving the play a note of topical relevance. Desdemona became the noble samurai lady Tomoné. She has committed the unthinkable offence of marrying below her class and for love, without the consent of her parents. The implication was that if she would betray her parents, it was logical to suspect that she might betray her husband too.

They started rehearsals with the smooth-faced matinée idol Asajiro as Desdemona. But Otojiro was troubled. How could it be 'true' with a man playing a woman? Desdemona should be played by an actress; added to which the public were clamouring to see the divine Sadayakko.

He begged Yakko to perform one last time, as a grand finale for their European tour. But Yakko was, she said, perfectly happy in Chigasaki, breeding pigs and growing silkworms. She was also afraid of the reception she would have if she, an untrained actress and ex-geisha, stepped on stage. In desperation Otojiro turned to Viscount Kentaro Kaneko, the distinguished politician who had performed the crucial role of go-between for their marriage.

Viscount Kaneko wrote Yakko a stern letter. 'I gather you decided to give up acting when you returned to Japan,' he wrote. 'But what about your mission to reform Japanese theatre? I hear the Kawakami troupe's production of *Othello* will be played entirely by men. That would mean your overseas tour had been a complete waste of time.'[22]

Yakko had no choice but to consent. Having made her decision, for several weeks she went down to the beach at Chigasaki every day and stood facing the ocean, declaiming her lines over the roar of the waves. Being untrained as an actress, she had never learnt to project her voice. When they performed in the West, speech had been unimportant. She had said her lines quietly and used gesture and facial expression to communicate her meaning. The actors, she remembered, were amazed when she attended the first rehearsal and spoke out in her big new voice.

Otojiro, meanwhile, had reverted to his old ways. Whenever he had the chance, he slipped away to see women without the slightest attempt at concealment. Yakko tried to turn a blind eye and be sweet and compliant, as was expected of a Japanese wife. But she found it almost unbearable. She had worked so hard and received such acclaim in the West; yet Otojiro still spent his time visiting low-class geisha. Perhaps that was why she hid herself away in Chigasaki while he spent most of his time in Tokyo.

Yakko always knew when Otojiro had been out with other women. When he came back, she would go to the other end of the house. Instead of using his bath water in the Japanese way, she made the servants throw it away. She was disgusted by him.[23] But in spite of everything, she couldn't help feeling profound love and loyalty towards him. After all, he was her husband. His infidelity was normal in a Japanese man and especially for someone with a libido like his. It didn't mean he didn't love her. To forget her pain she threw all her energy into acting and into taking care of Raikichi and the rest of the troupe.

Othello opened on 11 February 1903 at the Meiji-za Theatre on the edge of the Yoshicho geisha district. The geisha community was out in force to applaud the first appearance of their old comrade who had had such success in the West.

According to one story – probably, but not necessarily, apocryphal – Otojiro was in the middle of a torrid affair with a Shimbashi geisha called Kyoka at the time. He had fallen quite in love. Night after night he slept at Shimbashi and came in late for rehearsals. On the opening night, she was at the front of the audience, kneeling coyly in her kimono, her pretty young face illuminated in the lights from the stage.

It was the final ignominy. When they reached the climactic scene where Otojiro, as Othello/Muro, was to strangle Desdemona/Tomoné, Yakko, according to the story, refused to die.

'I don't want to die, I'm innocent,' she screamed.

Otojiro was horrified. The theatre was packed. The audience, who had no idea of the plot, were on the edge of their seats, gripped by the drama. Maybe they sensed that it had suddenly become even more 'true' than advertised. In a flash Otojiro guessed the problem.

'I'm sorry,' he hissed desperately. 'I'll talk to you later. Please die!'

Later he promised never to see Kyoka again and kept his word – though the promise did not extend to other women.

Photographs show Otojiro as Lieutenant General Muro scowling ferociously in a flashy dress uniform with heavily braided cuffs and a feathery plume in his peaked cap. Strangely enough, he seems to be in black face. Another photograph shows Tomoné in her boudoir, willowy and feminine in a trailing kimono, pulling the hairpins out of her hair with a look of gentle resignation in preparation for her bed scene.

Some of the more snobbish critics were fiercely hostile to these adventurers. Their success abroad, they asserted, proved nothing more than Westerners' intellectual inferiority. It was nothing but brazen cheek to show their vulgar product to the far more sophisticated and knowledgeable Japanese. One complained that the public would have been better served with an authentic production of *Othello*. Japanese audiences were thirsty to see real European theatre and Otojiro and Yakko were in the ideal position to provide it.

Others were more favourable. Some admired the innovative scenery and lighting, others enjoyed the dance scenes. But all agreed that Yakko, in her début on the Japanese stage, was undoubtedly the star of the show.

The rising young theatre critic, Shigure Hasegawa, remembered those first performances. Almost no one in the audience had ever before seen a woman on stage; and this was not just any woman but Sadayakko. For most it was also their first experience of Western drama. Her transcendent beauty and inspired acting stirred them to the depths of their souls. She engraved herself unforgettably on their hearts.

She had a mesmerising stage presence, wrote Hasegawa, and a beauty so vibrant that even in a huge theatre it never diminished. She had a fascinating soft smile and a natural allure; but she also had a sweet vulnerability. She had the frail yielding beauty of a willow tree. 'That's her secret,' asserted Hasegawa, 'and no one else can compete.' She went on:

> Her Desdemona was truly remarkable, utterly different from any of the actresses who came after her. I can't describe how she moved the hearts of young people, seeing an actress and a western play for the first time, through her beauty.[24]

The audiences voted with their feet. The troupe played to packed houses every night and then toured the provinces, playing in Kobe, Osaka and Kyoto with huge success.

The suave Parisian art dealer, Hayashi, wrote a review of the drama for the French press. After describing the miniature unheated theatre with everyone squashed in side by side on their knees, he mentioned that the drama lasted for six hours, a considerable feat of endurance for the audience.

The secret of the play's success, he reported, was unquestionably Yakko's

Tomoné. Entirely different from Shakespeare's Desdemona, she was the very embodiment of idealised Japanese womanhood. Yielding, sweet, uncomplaining, she always maintained the calm resignation proper to a samurai lady without ever stooping so low as to complain or protest her innocence.

'Sada has succeeded in giving Desdemona the Japanese spirit,' he wrote. 'The critics, initially greatly prejudiced against this artiste, have been obliged to recognise her inspired mastery.'[25]

For Yakko, this was the real beginning of her acting career. Whenever she was interviewed, she always said she had begun acting in 1903, when she was nearly thirty-two. Her fame in the West was a little like Gulliver finding fame in Lilliput or Brobdingnag; it didn't count. But acting was in her bones. Once she had trodden the boards in Japan, she couldn't stop.

9

SECRETS OF A WOMAN'S HEART
PERFORMING IN JAPAN 1903–1911

I was sick with love for her. Sadayakko's Ophelia . . . ! When
she came out singing, 'Little robin, little robin', in her jewel-like
voice, everyone in the audience held their breath, utterly
spellbound by this woman on stage; and when she laughed her
high-pitched laugh, the uncanny beauty sent a shiver down
everyone's spine.

Ujaku Akita[1]

N

o matter how lonely or betrayed Yakko felt, she was expected
to suffer in silence. There was so much in her heart that she
could never express. When she was interviewed she was down
to earth and humorous. She would chat about her acting techniques or her
make-up secrets in a modest, self-deprecating way. But on stage she was
transformed. She expressed her passion through her acting. She became
the Geisha, burning for revenge. She became Tomoné, the gentle samurai
woman, suffering without ever complaining or revealing the tiniest inkling
of her pain. She acted from the bottom of her heart.

Shigure Hasegawa dropped into her dressing room from time to time.
She remembered how intensely forlorn Yakko seemed once the lights of
the stage had dimmed and the curtain had fallen, writing:

After the performance was over, she would put away the flowers she'd
been given and sit in the empty room and didn't seem to go home.
When I saw her like that, for some reason I felt moved to tears.[2]

After *Othello*, Otojiro and Yakko produced an even more daringly contemporary play. It was called *The Mousetrap*. It opened memorably with a young man dressed as a Tokyo University student in a peaked cap and crisp blue uniform, pedalling through the audience along the *hanamichi* walkway on a bicycle. The character, played by Asajiro Fujisawa, was Toshimaru Hamura – Hamlet in Japanese guise. A flabbergasted French reviewer commented that, besides the uniform, his wardrobe appeared to consist largely of elegant suits from the most fashionable tailor in New York or Boston.

Otojiro played the ghost of Hamlet's father. He had a mop of grey dishevelled hair and wore an admiral's jacket with gold epaulettes, cuffs glittering with braid and the Order of the Chrysanthemum on his chest. He appeared to the accompaniment of a virtuoso display of lighting effects, no doubt borrowed from Loie Fuller. Claudius wore a swallowtail coat and stove pipe hat, Hamlet's duel with Laertes was fought in evening dress and Hamlet was sent not to France but to Manchuria and Siberia, giving a topical slant.

By now Western critics, following the progress of the celebrated Sada Yacco, had begun to discover what the Kawakami troupe was doing to their revered classics. They were shocked. *Hamlet* was sacrosanct. The ghost of Hamlet's father was supposed to stride the ramparts at Elsinore in the moonlight with his armour glittering, trailing a long shroud, not dressed as a Japanese admiral. It was to be another fifty or sixty years before the first experimental or modern dress productions of Shakespeare were even thought of in the West – Yakko and Otojiro were way ahead of their time.

For decades afterwards purist Japanese intellectuals and Western commentators on Japanese theatre dismissed the Kawakami productions as mere second-rate spectacle and relegated them to a footnote in the history of Japanese drama. Critics were particularly scathing of the entry on the bicycle, which they condemned as a travesty of the original.

But as far as the public was concerned it was vibrant contemporary theatre. After all, in kabuki the text was not treated as sacred writ. It was a platform for virtuoso displays of bravura acting. It is only now, when experimental productions of Shakespeare are taken for granted, that critics are beginning to appreciate how fresh and exciting the Kawakami dramas were. They made *Hamlet* accessible to a huge audience and paved the way for later performances which were more faithful to Shakespeare's original.

The Mousetrap was certainly wildly experimental. But what lifted it to the level of the sublime was Yakko's Ophelia – 'Orié'. In photographs of the mad scene she looks transcendently beautiful. She would wander onto the stage distractedly, her long black tresses tumbling to her waist and her face pale, like a lovely lost child. She wore a soft blue gown, the colour of water, trimmed with pristine white lace. There were flowers scattered in her hair and bunches of flowers in her hands. In a thin, birdlike warble, she sang snatches of nursery rhymes.

'Rain is falling on his grave,' she trilled. 'No, not rain, it is tears of blood.'

'When she tottered out swaying on unsteady feet with her child-like voice, it was indescribably poetic,' swooned the critic of the *Yomiuri* newspaper.[3]

A generation of impressionable young university students had never seen an actress work her magic before. They were utterly smitten. One impoverished student went to see her obsessively night after night even though he could only afford a place up in the gods on the third floor. Little by little he sold his possessions to buy tickets until he had nothing left except his desk and his books. He even sold the tatami mats that covered his floor.

Yakko received innumerable love letters, far more than she could answer. A particularly besotted letter from a Kyoto University student found its way into the hands of the press:

I had never seen a play in my life before. My goddess! I was so touched by your portrayal of Ophelia, and the tragic way she died. You have never left my mind since. On autumn evenings when I go out for a stroll, I see you before me, so pure and proud. I see you in the shapes of the clouds and wonder where you are. I wet my pillow with tears, yearning to see you again. . . . From this lovesick man in his mortarboard, to my dear Ophelia, Miss Sadayakko of the flowers.[4]

In the midst of her triumph, Yakko received terrible news. Her adoptive mother, Kamekichi, had suddenly died, on 19 August 1903, at the age of fifty-nine. Yakko had not even known that Kamekichi was ill. She had been away on tour and had not seen her for several weeks. She was utterly shocked and distraught.

Kamekichi had taken in the little girl and loved her as if she were her own daughter. She had made her into the country's most sought-after geisha and had ensured that she had the best patron in the land – Prince Ito. Most of what Yakko had achieved she owed to Kamekichi. It was the first time Yakko had lost someone for whom she cared so much.

There was a grand funeral a few days later at Tsukiji Honganji, a cathedral-like Buddhist temple at the heart of the Shimbashi geisha district, with Kamekichi's son leading the rites. Afterwards Yakko retreated to Hakone, an elegant spa near the base of Mount Fuji. There she sat drinking sake or wandered the narrow mountain streets in a daze, hardly knowing where she was. From time to time she started to feel a kind of suffocation in her heart, making her finger nails and lips turn purple. A doctor diagnosed it as cyanosis. She had become Ophelia, driven to distraction by the loss of a parent.

In the months that followed, Yakko and Otojiro began to try some revolutionary changes in the way they presented their plays. They drastically cut the length of their shows. Usually performances lasted most of the day, sometimes from dawn to midnight. The Kawakami productions lasted a mere four and a half hours, including a half-hour interval. They also attacked the stranglehold which teahouses around the theatre had over patrons.

Everyone had to buy a place and rent a cushion through a teahouse, which took a huge cut. Teahouses also made profits selling food and drinks during the long intermissions. Yakko and Otojiro proposed a radical new system of tickets, to be sold direct to the public at a third of the price. Shockingly, they even suggested prohibiting eating and drinking in the auditorium. At least one disgruntled theatre owner beat up the Kawakami representative who came to discuss all this with him.

Going to the theatre had always been a happy way to while away a day, eating, drinking, smoking, snoozing, wandering around, chatting to neighbours and occasionally even watching a bit of drama. At Yakko and Otojiro's 'true' theatre, you arrived at a certain time, sat in your seat without walking around, watched the play properly without eating or smoking and then left. All in all, it was a much more 'modern' activity, economical of time and money. Theatres even bought rickshaw tickets to sell to the audience to pack them smartly off home. Amazingly, people loved it.

Yakko and Otojiro also introduced children's theatre – *otogi shibai*, 'fairy tale theatre' – to Japan. Their first production was the German play *The Trial of the Fox*, performed largely by children. Yakko played a boy called Fred, scandalising everyone by wearing shorts on stage and showing her knees at the age of thirty-two. Otojiro and Asajiro were foxes. Seats were very cheap, with children and students allowed in free. Like all the Kawakami ventures, it was a huge success.

Meanwhile the country was gearing up for war. A couple of years earlier, Pierre Loti, the supercilious author of *Madame Chrysanthème*, had reported that 'War proclaims itself inevitable and imminent. . . . The most insignificant porter in the streets talks of it as though it had begun and reckons insolently upon victory.'[5]

Japan was rapidly turning into a powerful, highly industrialised nation, demanding to be accepted on equal terms with Europe and America. Every major power had colonies and footholds all over the globe. Japan wanted control over its neighbouring territories of Korea and Manchuria, a comparatively modest aim. But Russia had already pushed in and established a presence in both. The Russians had also wrenched the strategically vital Port Arthur out of Japan's grasp after the Sino-Japanese War, then moved in and taken it over themselves.

Britain too wanted to keep a check on Russian power, to stop Russia encroaching on the British 'sphere of influence' in China. In 1902 Britain and Japan had signed the Anglo-Japanese Alliance, finally recognising Japan's status as a major power, on a par with the Western nations.

On 8 February 1904, Japanese troops attacked the Russian naval garrison at Port Arthur. Two days later the newspapers announced that Japan was at war. A month later there was a Japanese army tramping across Korea and another battling in Manchuria.

The Western powers firmly backed the little David fighting the Russian Goliath. The Americans sent consignments of hominy grits for the Japanese troops and eight nurses from Philadelphia arrived in Tokyo; the Japanese embassy in London was besieged with gifts and offers of help. A cartoon in a Western newspaper showed the plucky Japanese cockerel, with the moustache and beaky nose of Emperor Meiji, digging its claws into the back of the great Russian bear and drawing blood.

In Japan everyone fervently supported the war effort. Even the oldest and poorest donated their savings. *Daimyo* aristocrats made the unimaginable sacrifice of selling their carriages and travelling in lowly rickshaws to save money to send to the War Fund. Ethel Howard, an English governess in a *daimyo* family, gave up six months' salary, with the money to go to the Red Cross Society.[6] Women took to wearing dark blue 'victory colour' kimonos printed with classic Japanese motifs.

Less than two weeks after the war began, Asajiro was on his way to Korea on a research expedition with a photographer and a painter. In April Yakko and a bevy of young trainee actresses visited Tokyo's Red Cross Hospital. They donned crisp white uniforms and tall pleated white hats with a red cross on the rim and practised bandaging and unbandaging wounded soldiers. The ministrations of these beautiful women must have done much to boost morale. In May the Kawakami troupe produced *The Battle Report Drama*. It was so popular that they were asked to perform for the Crown Prince. Every theatre in the country, old or new style, was showing patriotic war plays.[7]

After an epic siege of eleven months, the Japanese took Port Arthur on 2 January 1905. Tens of thousands of Russian and Japanese soldiers had been killed or wounded. The Russians were starving, dirty and battered and many nursed unhealed wounds. They were disarmed, though officers were allowed to keep their swords in token of their gallant stand. Nearly 6000 were shipped to Japan's first ever prisoner of war camp, near the romantic old castle town of Matsuyama on the island of Shikoku, a rural backwater full of orange groves, where rice grew in sparkling green terraces sculpted along the flanks of the hills. The people of Matsuyama had not been expecting to house prisoners of war. They had no facilities so they put them up in Buddhist temples, dozens of prisoners sleeping packed together in dark tatami-matted rooms.

War was still raging across the water in Korea and Manchuria when the Kawakami troupe arrived in Matsuyama on tour. Perhaps remembering the happy time she had spent in Russia, Yakko decided to visit one of the camps. She was walking through the temple grounds crowded with listless, unshaven prisoners when she heard the notes of a plaintive ditty, beautifully played on a violin. Turning a corner, she came upon the player. He looked at her and gasped. Putting down his instrument he rushed to her as if he was about to gather her in his arms.

Despite his sunken cheeks, unshaven beard, bare feet and white prison issue cotton robe, Yakko recognised him. It was a young nobleman, the son of a count, who had been her greatest fan in Russia. Seeing her perform in St Petersburg, he had fallen completely under her spell. He had organised a splendid ball for her, showered her with gifts and attended all her performances.

After Yakko left Russia, he could not stop thinking about her. Whenever he saw people dancing or played his violin by moonlight in the stricken port, he thought of her. When he was captured and taken to Japan as a prisoner of war, his only consolation was that at least he was in her country, treading the same soil and breathing the same air. He poured out his love to her. He disarmed her with his passionate declarations of undying devotion, thrillingly different from the Japanese way where the deepest feelings always remained unspoken and unexpressed.

Yakko wept, her heart melting at his youthful ardour and sorry plight. She went straight to the office of the camp commandant, Colonel Takano, and begged for a few days' leave of absence for the count's son and his closest comrades.

In Matsuyama the prisoners were treated with remarkable kindness. The populace had been informed that 'prisoners are not criminals but honourable men who fought for their country'. Many Matsuyama women volunteered to tend the wounded and those who died were buried with military honours. No matter what they felt about the great Russian bugbear, the people of Shikoku were sorry for these pale young men, so far from home. So the colonel gave his permission on condition that Yakko be responsible for returning them to the camp.

She took them to the little spa town of Dogo with its narrow streets lined with ornately tiled wooden buildings, just outside Matsuyama. There she had arranged rooms at the lovely old Funaya, the best inn in town. She hired local geisha to come and entertain them. They all relaxed together in the steaming pools of sulphur-imbued water, drank sake and enjoyed a few happy hours. There, according to a Japanese newspaper, she 'consoled the lonely heart of this young man imprisoned in a foreign land'.

Who knows what that consolation consisted of? The 'local geisha' undoubtedly offered more than just singing and dancing to the young man's comrades; that was their job. As with all the stories that accumulate around famous people, we will never know whether this one is true or contains a nugget of truth or whether it has been spun from nothing and become hugely embroidered over time. It is certainly not entirely apocryphal. The visit of the Russian prisoners of war is entered in the annals at Dogo Spa town hall. It would be nice to think that Yakko had a brief but intense affair with the lovelorn young Russian count.

As to Otojiro, he was ill again. His appendix trouble had come back; he was in hospital in Takamatsu, at the opposite end of Shikoku island, with inflamed appendicitis. The tour had had to continue without him. The show always had to go on.

Throughout their season at Matsuyama, the young Russian bombarded Yakko with flowers. Accompanied by a prison guard, he attended every performance. It was the talk of the town. But eventually the troupe had to move on to Kochi, in the south of the island. Instead of sailing, they took the mountain route. The besotted young Russian followed by bicycle, pedalling furiously behind Yakko's carriage, accompanied by his dogged prison guards. At the mountain pass where they crossed into the next province the guards told him he could go no further. Weeping, he kissed Yakko's hand and bade her farewell.

The troupe had arrived at Kochi and Yakko was resting before the night's performance when there was a hubbub outside the gate. In a boat in the harbour was the young Russian officer and two other prisoners of war, accompanied by two military police and a local policeman. The young man, it transpired, had said he would starve himself to death unless he could see Yakko one last time. Eventually the long-suffering Colonel Takano had given in. Yakko arranged for them all to stay in the same inn as her for the three or four nights that the troupe was in Kochi and 'consoled the young man as much as possible'.

When the war ended, the young man was sent to Kobe from where he would set sail for Russia. Yakko happened to be performing there. The day before he was due to embark, he sent her a box of chocolates. When she opened it she found two huge diamond-shaped pieces of gold below the top layer of chocolates.[8]

The war had come to a dramatic and terrible end on 29 May 1905 when the Japanese navy, under the command of Admiral Heihachiro Togo, 'the Nelson of Japan', sent the entire Russian Baltic Fleet to the bottom of the sea. More than 12,000 Russian sailors died. A couple of generations earlier Japan had barely had a navy. Now for the first time it had defeated one of the mighty European powers which had seemed unstoppable not so long before. It was the moment of glory the Japanese had been dreaming of ever since the humiliating days of half a century earlier.

In the negotiations that followed Japan won control over Port Arthur, the South Manchurian railway, which would allow free movement into China, and half of Sakhalin, the Russian-owned island to the north of Japan. Russia also recognised Japan's paramount interests in Korea. Japan had done well. Nevertheless the public had been expecting Russia to pay a huge indemnity and felt cheated of the full spoils of victory. On 5 September mobs spilled onto the streets of Tokyo and for a couple of days there was uncontrollable rioting.

Nevertheless Japan's standing in the world had soared. A Japanese diplomat commented with weary irony that . . .

his people had been sending artistic treasures to Europe for some time, and had been regarded as barbarians; but, as soon as they showed themselves able to shoot down Russians with quick-firing guns, they were acclaimed as a highly civilised race.[9]

Besides their repertoire of Shakespeare, the Kawakamis had begun introducing Japanese theatregoers to contemporary European drama. In 1906 Yakko starred in Maurice Maeterlinck's *Monna Vanna*, the dramatic tragedy of a suffragette era New Woman. She also played Dona Rafaele in *Patrie* by Victorien Sardou, the author of *Tosca*. Both were parts that Sarah Bernhardt had made her own. Yakko, still Japan's sole actress, was determined to prove herself worthy of her billing as 'the Sarah Bernhardt of Japan'.

Otojiro's health continued to cause him trouble. Finally he was forced to retire from acting. But nothing could dampen his burning ambition and incessant plans and projects. With Yakko he was determined to build Japan's first truly modern Western-style theatre. Prince Ito, Viscount Kaneko and other leading national figures promised support. The pair also planned another foreign tour, to Argentina and America.

Yone Noguchi, the poet father of the sculptor Osamu Noguchi, had returned two years earlier after more than ten years in New York. He went to Chigasaki to interview Yakko for the *New York Dramatic Mirror*. They sat together on the sandy white beach, admiring the graceful sweep of Mount Fuji, 'that white dome of beauty and art' rising before them 'like a ghost'.

Yakko 'appeared perfectly graceful and bewitching', he wrote in his flowery, slightly stilted English.

The golden sun fell luxuriously over her flowing hair. She left off dressing her hair in the stiff Japanese mode ever since she returned from her foreign trip. She is adopting every American and European custom, not only in her hair dressing. I fancied that even her eyes sparkled like an American actress.

Yakko described the hardships of their American tour but declared she had loved the country. 'Why, I should like to go there again,' she smiled, adding coyly, 'This is a secret. How funny woman has so many secrets.'

Performing a three-hour play in America, she told him, was far more demanding than acting for six hours for a Japanese audience because Americans were 'serious and study and criticise'. She wanted, she said,

233

to make the Japanese too realise that 'the theatre is the holy dome of art and humanity'.

'Art is nothing but heart. Heart, only heart,' she declared. For Noguchi and his Western readers she slipped comfortably into the persona of international diva.[10]

Yakko and Otojiro did not go to Argentina or America. Instead they decided to make a lengthy visit to Paris to make a formal study of every aspect of Western theatre – theatre design, stage management, scenery, props, music and acting techniques. They assembled a party of eight: Otojiro, Yakko, Yakko's niece Tsuru, another trainee actress, two male musicians, a scenery and props specialist and an interpreter. There is no mention of Raikichi. He was eleven by now, so perhaps he stayed in Japan to continue his studies.

On Sunday 24 July 1907, after lavish farewell parties, the travellers boarded the steamship *Hakata-maru* and set sail from Kobe. A few weeks later they were bowling through the Bohemian streets of Paris.

The city was as exuberant as ever. It had not sobered. In Montmartre Picasso and his friends carried on their decadent, wildly creative, drug-fuelled lives. Now twenty-six and living with his first great love, Fernande Olivier, the young Spanish artist had emerged from his Blue and Rose periods. In his squalid mouse-infested studio at the Bateau Lavoir, he was working feverishly on a breakthrough masterpiece, *Les Demoiselles d'Avignon*.

For Yakko it must have been thrillingly nostalgic to find herself back, after nearly six years, in this city which she adored and where she had found such adulation and success. The party settled into a stylish apartment in the pretty and very exclusive Villa Montmorency in Auteuil, Yakko's favourite part of Paris, near the Bois de Boulogne where she loved to stroll. The villa had been the home of André Gide and the Goncourt brothers, among others.

The two younger women enrolled at the Paris Conservatoire, the musicians found professionals to teach them and the interpreter set to work to brush up on his European languages. The scene painter enrolled at the Atelier in the Théâtre Français. Yakko, too, attended the Conservatoire. There she honed her acting, studied Western techniques and closely observed the teaching methods. She also joined Otojiro on his excursions to acting schools and theatrical institutions and to talk to architects and designers about the practicalities of theatre building. With actors they discussed the current state of theatre in the West and the hard road which European actors had travelled to achieve respectability. Every evening they went to the theatre, often going backstage after the show to chat.

On their previous European tours, they had spent all their time surviving, performing every day without a break. This time they were determined to devote themselves to learning and gathering information. Initiated into the secrets of Western dramatic arts, they would be in the perfect position to create a new theatre for the new Japan.

News soon leaked out that the legendary Sada Yacco was in town. Marie Laparcerie of *Femina* magazine pestered Yakko's great friend, Ambassador Kurino, and eventually obtained an interview. The November issue of *Femina* featured a photograph of Yakko on the cover, resplendent as 'The Geisha' in a kimono with a dramatic chrysanthemum design, wearing an archaic headdress knotted under her chin. Her alabaster face was as smooth and impassive as a mask with her mouth, eyes and eyebrows in dramatic contrast.

Under the shrill headline 'Mme Sada Yacco is in Paris!!!', Laparcerie described her four-hour meeting with the reclusive star. She took with her two interpreters, one Japanese, one English. Yakko greeted her in a sumptuous multi-layered kimono with sleeves to the floor and a bold design of bamboo, pine and plum blossom around the hem. Mary, one of two small pug-faced chins (Japanese spaniels) which she had brought from Japan, yapped at her feet.

'In fact, I'm hiding, in retreat, so to speak, in my villa in Auteuil,' she told her. 'I've come to Paris not to show myself or to act but to study in order to perfect myself in the dramatic art.'

Most of the photographs in *Femina* show Yakko in a variety of exquisite kimonos. But in one particularly striking picture she looks quite different. She is dressed like a pageboy or a medieval troubadour in pantaloons and a jerkin with a huge floppy cap on her bushy hair. Laughing heartily, wickedly seductive, she is holding a violin and striking an exaggerated

235

pose. She looks completely relaxed and confident. She is a major star at the pinnacle of her career, with nothing to prove and nothing to fear.

Laparcerie asked her if Japanese women lied about their age. 'Sometimes,' she confessed gaily. 'I would add, "For myself, I always tell the truth," if I wasn't afraid that you'd smile and think, "Every woman, Japanese or French, always says she tells the truth!"'[11]

News of Yakko's presence made its way across the Channel. An article in the November issue of *The Queen* reported that 'Mme. Sadayacco, the most tragic of tragedians, is again among us, but not, unfortunately, with the object of reinitiating us into the mysteries of her wonderful art.' Instead, wrote the reporter, they had come with the extraordinary aim of studying Western drama. '"I think," I observed to them, "we have more to learn from you than you from us."'[12]

The news even filtered across the Atlantic. In January the *Chicago Record* gushed that 'Japan has a Sarah Bernhardt on the stage at Tokio, whose fame as a wonderful actress has spread through England and France and for whose future everything bright and starry in the histrionic sky is prophesied.' Yakko conceded that 'it may not be impossible that we will appear on the stage before returning to Japan'.[13]

It was the celebrated actress Réjane who lured her out of her seclusion. Yakko had given a performance of *Momiji-gari* (*Maple-viewing*), titled *Le Dragon des Erables* (*The Dragon of the Maples*), for a women's university in Paris. Like *Dojoji*, this is the story of a beautiful maiden who is really a dragon in disguise. She seduces the warrior who has set out to kill her, befuddling him with drink. Just in time he regains his senses and, after a ferocious battle, kills her.

Réjane heard of this and begged Yakko to perform in her glamorous new theatre, the Théâtre Réjane. It had opened just a year earlier. It was the most splendid playhouse in Paris with a grand wood-panelled bar and a smoking room with a famous chandelier whose 120 electric lightbulbs cast their yellow light on the huge brocade armchairs. The newspaper *Le Figaro* claimed that the opening party was the most sensational event since the opening of the Suez canal in 1869.[14]

Yakko gave two performances there of *Momiji-gari* and *The Geisha and the*

Knight. The critics were out in force. 'No one knows how to die as well as Sada Yacco!' swooned one.[15]

On 31 January there was a magnificent reception at the Japanese legation, now promoted to an embassy after the signing of the Franco-Japanese Alliance. Ambassador Kurino was also made a baron, so there was a double reason to celebrate. Avenue Foch was jammed from end to end with gleaming automobiles and carriages. The ladies wore softly draped lacy creations with flowing trains or elaborately embroidered kimonos, the height of fashion, in honour of the occasion. The gentlemen were in top hats and formal evening dress. Among the 2000 guests who mingled beneath the crystal chandeliers were the President of France, Armand Fallières, European royalty, ambassadors and ministers of state.

Rumours had been circulating Paris for months that the reclusive Sada Yacco might appear. Towards the end of the evening she took the stage with her small troupe. They surprised everyone by performing Anton Chekhov's *The Three Sisters* and a comedy called *The Cat's Mew*. The performance was the highlight of the evening. The guests were ravished. The following month she was persuaded to play a brief season at the Théâtre Moderne. A French paper revealed that she commanded the phenomenal sum of 2500 francs per appearance.

At 10.30a.m. on 12 May 1908, the travellers were disembarking from the *Hakata-maru* in Kobe, having visited Brussels and Amsterdam on their way back. Otojiro and Yakko spent a few days resting at a spa. Then, burning with enthusiasm after all they had seen and done in Europe, they set to work to put their plans into action. Otojiro announced that he was giving up acting to manage the Sadayakko troupe. It was the first time he had recognised the troupe as hers, not his.

While they had been away, work had begun on their new theatre in Osaka. It was a hugely ambitious project. It would not be a small-scale 'Kawakami Theatre' like their last ill-fated venture into theatre building. It was to be known as the Imperial Theatre (*Teikoku-za*) and would be the leading Western-style theatre in Japan and the home of 'true theatre'.

Yakko had her own pet project. Having seen the freedom which women enjoyed in the West, she wanted to start a school for actresses. 'Having seen how actresses there are highly educated and well read, and how society welcomes them and heartily supports their development, I . . . would like to train accomplished actresses, who might come to be called the Sarah Bernhardts of Japan,' she said.[16] In the West it might have seemed a simple idea but in Japan it was revolutionary, even subversive. Women had only just been allowed back onto the stage after having been banned for centuries because acting was so closely associated with prostitution. Nevertheless she was now famous and successful enough to try and make it happen. She sorted out finance and lined up powerful supporters.

Otojiro's Imperial Theatre Company Limited was to provide 500 yen capital plus 100 yen per month. Five leading members of the business community agreed to be 'founding members'. They were listed in the *Miyako* newspaper of 7 August 1908: Eiichi Shibusawa, the famous entrepreneur; Kihachiro Okura, a leading industrial magnate and head of the hugely rich Okura family (his son later founded Tokyo's grandest Western-style hotel, the Okura); Tsunenori Tanaka and Taro Masuda, both financial heavyweights; and the so-called 'Wizard of the Money Markets', the enormously wealthy stock market wheeler-dealer Momosuké Fukuzawa.

Twenty years had passed since the lovely young geisha had said goodbye to the handsome farm boy. Momosuké had long since given up his surname of Iwasaki. He was married to the daughter of Yukichi Fukuzawa, one of the most famous and prominent founders of the new Japan, and bore his illustrious name.

The willowy student in his shirt with the lion-head motif had grown a little gaunt though he still had the huge eyes and almost ethereal beauty he had had as a youth. But somewhere along the line he had lost his *joie de vivre*. In photographs of him as a young man he looks out at the world with inquisitive, hopeful innocence. At forty he seems a little sad and withdrawn. His eyelids droop wearily as if life has disappointed him.

After that sad parting, Momosuké had left Yokohama aboard the steamer *City of Rio de Janeiro* on 2 February 1888. He landed in San Francisco, then took the train across the country via Chicago to New York. Fukuzawa's sons were already established. With their help he found somewhere to live and enrolled in business school. The plan was that he would spend three years there. Later he became an intern in the Pennsylvania Railroad Company, the largest railway company in the United States. The company president took to the handsome young Japanese lad, put him up at his home and introduced him to his friends and contacts, including the President himself, Glover Cleveland.

Everything was going brilliantly. But then Momosuké received terrible news. Back home in Japan, his father had died suddenly at the age of forty-eight. Momosuké was still trying to recover from the shock when he heard that his mother had died too, of a brain haemorrhage. He had set off for America thinking that he would provide for them and make them proud of him. But in fact he had completely failed them, or so he thought. He had not even been there to care for them when they were dying.

'I had always thought that if I came here my parents would be happy,' he told a Japanese friend in New York. 'My mother especially had a very hard life. She died so young and I couldn't do anything to make her life better.'

The double blow when he was so far from home was more than the young man could bear. His life fell apart. He started drinking and spending money recklessly. He began to suspect he had made a terrible mistake in agreeing to the devil's pact he had made with Fukuzawa. He told his New York friend:

It sounds a foolish thing to say, but the 17th is a tragic day for me. It was December 17th when I joined the House of Fukuzawa and November 17th when my father died. If I hadn't become a Fukuzawa and been sent abroad, I could have taken care of my father and been there when he died.[17]

But it was too late. Miserable, he decided to leave New York earlier than planned. He arrived back in Yokohama on 11 May 1890. There he fulfilled his side of the bargain and married Fukuzawa's daughter, the plain, frumpish Fusa.

Fukuzawa sent the newlyweds off to Sapporo on the remote northern island of Hokkaido. The Japanese had begun colonising it twenty years earlier and it was still frontier country. Fukuzawa had arranged a position for Momosuké with the pioneering Hokkaido Mining and Railroad Company on the preposterously high salary of 100 yen a month. But for the young couple Hokkaido was a terrible exile. Fusa was pregnant and desperately homesick. The last place a nicely educated samurai girl expected to find herself was in an American-style clapboard house in Sapporo, the lone outpost of civilisation in the untamed wilderness of Hokkaido. So they moved back to Tokyo. There she had a son whom they called Komakichi, in January 1891. Shortly afterwards they had a second son, Tatsuzo. He was rather strange and had difficulty connecting with people. Today we might say he was autistic. They decided that was enough.

Momosuké worked in exports at the Tokyo office of the Hokkaido Mining and Railroad Company. He was sharp, clever and diligent and the company's profits soared. But he pushed himself too hard. One day in 1894, when he was twenty-seven, he was on the deck of a ship in Yokohama when he collapsed, coughing up blood and suffering near fatal haemorrhaging. He had tuberculosis, usually a death sentence in those days. Fukuzawa called in the best doctors and Momosuké spent the next eight months in hospital.

Confined to bed he pondered how to escape Fukuzawa's clutches. He hated being under his thumb and desperately needed to become financially independent. Without telling Fukuzawa, who considered trading in stocks and shares no better than gambling, he invested 1000 yen in stocks. In a year they were worth 100,000 yen.

It took him some years to recover completely. He took various positions, meanwhile secretly continuing his stock-trading. Then in 1899, he started his own business, a trading company called Marusan Trading, with his friend Yasuzaemon Matsunaga. But he still needed Fukuzawa's help. Fukuzawa invested 25,000 yen on condition that he also appoint one of the directors. This man's real job was to keep an eye on Momosuké. He soon reported back that the husband of Fukuzawa's favourite daughter was spending all his spare time in teahouses seeing geisha. Fusa too complained to her father about her husband's behaviour.

Fusa was extremely well educated, as befitted the daughter of the nation's great educator and founder of its first university, Keio. She was scholarly, intellectual and very studious. She spoke with the refined tones of a samurai and, among many other accomplishments, spoke excellent English. But, according to the traditional Japanese way of looking at things, maybe her head had been educated too much and her heart not enough. She wasted no time making herself attractive or doing wifely things. She put all her time into her children and her studies. Being very shy, she was quite inexperienced in the ways of the world. Japanese wives were expected to tolerate their husbands' peccadilloes, but she could not forgive Momosuké's infidelities. She was her father's girl. Whenever anything went wrong, she went straight to him.

Fukuzawa decided to punish Momosuké. A year after it had been launched, in 1900, Marusan Trading was about to complete a hugely profitable deal with a major American trading company. But Fukuzawa was the grand old man of Japanese business. He had connections with American business moguls going back almost forty years to 1860, when they were all youngsters and he had been on the first official mission to America. He let it be known that the financial underpinnings of Marusan Trading were suspect. The deal fell through. Shortly afterwards the company went bankrupt.

Momosuké had had such high hopes, but everything had turned bitter for him. His marriage was miserable, though that was not unusual; Japanese of that era did not go into marriage expecting to find happiness. In his work and in his life he could not escape the baleful eye of his father-in-law. He had sold his soul for nothing. The pact he had made had brought him only misery.

He pondered suicide. He told his friend and business partner, Matsunaga, that he was going to quit the House of Fukuzawa and take back his real surname. He got into his automobile and was heading west for Osaka when he started coughing and found tell-tale spots of blood on his handkerchief. This time the disease was less serious though it was enough to stop any desperate moves he might have planned.

Then on 25 January 1901 Yukichi Fukuzawa had a stroke. He was sixty-eight and had been in ill health for some time. He died on 3 February. For the entire nation it was the end of an era. Fusa was heart-broken. The family had ostracised Momosuké. But, as Fukuzawa himself had seen, none of his children had Momosuké's brilliance. Now they turned to him, expecting him to take care of them.

As far as Momosuké was concerned the pressure was off. He had done his duty and fulfilled his side of the bargain. He was thirty-three and free at last to take control of his life. He relaunched Marusan Trading and also took a position with the Hokkaido Mining and Railroad Company. But his real genius was in stock transactions. Over the following years he accumulated a huge fortune through inspired dealing. No doubt there was some insider trading along the way. It was not illegal. In turn-of-the-century Japan, anything went. Thus over the years Momosuké became extremely rich and known as a brilliant and not altogether scrupulous manipulator of the stock market.

He no longer concealed the fact that he always had geisha lovers. He was a very handsome man, as everyone said, and like most Japanese businessmen liked nothing better than to relax in the evening in the company of geisha. He found his consolation, joy and pleasure in the floating world of the teahouses.

And at some point he met up again with his first love, Yakko. We don't know exactly when and how. Maybe they never completely lost touch. They were part of a very small world. The movers and shakers who spent their evenings in teahouses had known Yakko from her days as a celebrated geisha and had followed her progress as she blazed on the international stage. Inevitably Yakko and Momosuké would have crossed paths. But it was only when Yakko broached her plan for an acting school that Momosuké stepped out of the shadows.[18]

Yakko named her school the Imperial Actress Training Institute. Within a few weeks she had found premises near the Imperial Theatre offices in Osaka.

She laid out stringent conditions. Applicants were to be aged between sixteen and twenty-five, educated to at least junior high school level and with two guarantors who were Tokyo homeowners. The curriculum would include history, script-writing, traditional and modern acting skills and Japanese and Western dancing, as well as the playing of musical instruments such as the flute, shoulder drum, shamisen and *koto*.

The course would last two years. There were no fees but students would be expected to perform at the Imperial Theatre as part of their practical training. Anyone who left without completing the two years would be charged for the tuition they had received. If they then took up acting or used their training to practise as geisha, they would be fined.

Everyone apart from Yakko and her enlightened supporters expected that only geisha and other such loose women would dream of taking up such a disreputable occupation as acting. In fact there were over a hundred applications. Many were from very well-educated, rebellious young women of good family who did not want to fritter away their lives as the unloved wife of some rich man. Yakko interviewed and auditioned and eventually selected fifteen.

The grand opening took place on 15 September, less than four months after she had returned from Paris. The five founding members were present, including Momosuké. Yakko slipped modestly onto the stage followed by the students, all in formal black kimonos. Baron Shibusawa, the energetic entrepreneur who had a finger in every imaginable business venture, made a forty-minute speech.

In Japan's recent past, he said, actors had been spurned as 'riverbed beggars'. But in modern times those rigid social barriers had begun to break down. Tradesmen of humble birth, like himself, Mr Okura and Mr Fukuzawa, had been able to rise to influential positions at the top of society. Actresses suffered discrimination twice over, as 'riverbed beggars' and as women. The Imperial Actress Training Institute would enable the profession to rise in society, as merchants had done. It was a timely development now that women were demanding more rights.[19]

There was still a long way to go. For all Shibusawa's fine words, the very next day a newspaper branded the school 'a training camp for hussies'.

One of Yakko's most committed students, Ritsuko Mori, came from an upper-class family and was the daughter of a leading politician.

'For women who wanted to become actresses, this was the only route,' she remembered in later years. 'It was the only oasis in the desert – though we continually had to suffer the sand of criticism blowing in our eyes.'[20]

Mori's first gesture of rebellion was to cut her long flowing hair. She was expelled from her college alumni association as a result of her decision to take up acting. Her younger brother committed suicide rather than live with the taunts of his schoolmates over his sister's shameful profession.[21] It is a hint of the opprobrium that Yakko too must have suffered despite her glowing reviews. In spite of everything, Mori's determination was unshakeable. She went on to become one of the leading actresses of her generation.

Shortly after the school opened, the Kawakami troupe put on a comedy called *Dumb Journey*, featuring actresses from the new school. It was a wonderfully absurd tale making full use of the Kawakamis' much vaunted experiences abroad. It is the story of two Japanese men, one a sophisticated cosmopolitan, the other a bumbling but lovable fool, who fetch up in London. There they are effectively struck dumb because they can't speak the language.

The backdrop consisted of realistically depicted London scenes. An orchestra of foreign musicians, hired in Yokohama, performed a programme of songs currently most fashionable in that exotic city. Everyone said it was almost as good as going abroad oneself.

Splendidly garbed in a huge hat and lacy frock, Yakko played an imperious British actress. The script for the London scenes was entirely English, spelled out phonetically in the Japanese alphabet for the benefit of the actors. No doubt for Otojiro, Yakko and the troupe members who had shared their adventures, it was also a trip down memory lane, a comical rerun of all the mishaps and misunderstandings they had suffered on their own 'dumb journey'.

Meanwhile workmen were swarming around the bamboo scaffolding as work proceeded on the neighbouring Imperial Theatre. One of the most powerful backers was Prince Ito. Now a white-bearded patriarch approaching seventy, he was still a merry, garrulous, self-important, Napoleonic little man who strutted around wielding a gold-tipped cane. After all these years he still had a twinkle in his eye.

Chuo Koron magazine reported that the reason why Ito supported the establishment of the Imperial Theatre was because Otojiro had begged him to. But the real reason, said the magazine, was to be found in his fondness for Yakko. When Ito went to Hakone Spa with the Kawakamis, Otojiro had to request very humbly to speak with him whereas Yakko went in and out of his room freely. 'Anyone who wants a favour or a note of recommendation from Mr Ito would be well advised to ask Sadayakko. Mysteriously she can obtain a letter or whatever else you need very easily,' the magazine concluded.[22]

After the Russo-Japanese War, as Japan's leading diplomat and statesman, Ito had become deeply embroiled in complicated negotiations to extend Japanese power over Korea. Russia had already recognised Japan's interest. Now, with the support of Britain, the United States and France, Japan declared Korea a protectorate. The Western powers, great colonisers themselves, saw it as a way of bringing order and progress to a supposedly backward people.

Ito was sent to Seoul to negotiate with the King of Korea. Reluctantly the King agreed that Ito would become Resident-General, responsible for 'managing' Korean affairs, thus binding Korea more and more closely to Japan. A couple of years later, when the King protested against Japan's growing power, he was forced to abdicate in favour of the young prince, his son, who was mentally retarded. The Korean army was disbanded. As Japan's representative, Ito assumed dictatorial powers which could only be enforced by brutal military suppression. Unhappy with the way things were developing, he eventually resigned. But he was already branded as the embodiment of Japanese oppression.

A month after he turned sixty-nine, he left his villa in Oiso, travelled across Japan and took the ship to Vladivostok. He boarded the luxurious VIP train on the South Manchuria Railway to make the long journey across the freezing northern plains to the city of Harbin. There he was to meet the Russian Finance Minister to discuss the Korean question. The train roared into the station puffing black smoke at 9.30a.m on Tuesday 26 October 1909. There were snow clouds blackening the sky and an icy north wind blasting. A cameraman was on the platform to film the illustrious statesman as he stepped gingerly down from the carriage, leaning on his cane.

He looks frail and old but very determined. He is in a black great coat buttoned to his neck and a black bowler hat. His broad face and wispy beard show white in the flickering film and we can see his breath, steamy in the winter air. He is in the middle of a mélange of officials, all in black, milling about in front of the huge black train carriage. He takes a step forward away from the group. Then the picture blurs and freezes. A young Korean had pushed through the crowd and fired several shots at point blank range.

The following day, under a photograph of 'His Excellency Prince Ito' looking magnificently statesmanlike, the *Japan Times* breathlessly reported on the confusing and contradictory telegrams received from Harbin. Ito, they confirmed, had been 'on the point of alighting from the railway car at Harbin' when he was 'shot at by a Korean and sustained a severe wound in the abdomen'. The consul general and the director of the South Manchuria Railway Company were also wounded. 'The ruffian was arrested on the spot,' the paper added.

Ito lived long enough to be told the identity of his assassin, a thirty-year-old Korean freedom fighter called Ahn Joong Gun. The old man breathed his last words – 'What a fool!' – before passing away. Ahn was executed the following year and in Korea is venerated to this day as a hero and a martyr. There is a statue of him on the site of Ito's Seoul residence.

That same year Japan annexed Korea, making it into a Japanese colony. The assassination of the country's elder statesman had given the government the justification it needed.

It was not unusual for politicians to meet with violent deaths. The Japanese public was shocked but not surprised. Ito was accorded a magnificent state funeral. On 4 November the urn containing his body was borne through the city in an ornately decorated palanquin, like a small portable palace gleaming with brass, with tassels swinging, on the shoulders of twenty sombrely clad bearers. His old comrades provided the guard of honour, striding alongside in full military regalia, with cocked hats and swords, their chests glittering with medals.

Crowds filled the streets to pay their respects. The ceremony took place in Hibiya Park, in the centre of Tokyo, within sight of the moat surrounding the Imperial Palace. Across the road was the dilapidated building which had once been the Hall of the Baying Stag where, almost a quarter of a century earlier, the dashing prime minister had partied so furiously and danced so merrily with Yakko, the most beautiful geisha in Tokyo.

Along with the many other women who had been part of Ito's life, Yakko would certainly not have been able to attend the funeral and she was far too famous to mingle with the crowds who lined the streets as the palanquin went by. She had to mourn in the privacy of her home. She never spoke of her feelings; but we can assume that she wept many tears for the old man who had been her first lover and had continued to be her friend and support throughout his life.

The grand opening of the Imperial Theatre in Osaka was on 15 February 1910. It was a magnificently playful piece of architecture, like an Edwardian music hall transposed to Japan and embellished with Japanese flourishes. Built of brick and stone, it had decorative mock-Ionic pillars, three imposing arched entranceways topped with balconies, and a motif of the rising sun in white stone splashed across the rounded tops of the windows at either end of the building.

Inside there was an area of tatami matting and rows of rather hard wooden benches. The upper circles were narrow, like promenade circles, with swagged velvet drapes reminiscent of the Criterion Theatre where the troupe had performed in London. The domed ceiling was adorned with curvaceous Art Nouveau motifs. The curtain featured an elaborate portrayal of a Shinto goddess performing an erotic dance, a famous scene from Japanese mythology. The lighting and stage machinery were the very latest Western imports but there was also a *hanamichi* walkway, a revolving stage and an orchestra box, as in a kabuki theatre. It was Japan's most up-to-the-minute theatre.

The first week's programme featured displays of dancing by Yakko and her students, performed to Japanese and Western music. Tickets were by invitation only. Each night a capacity audience of 1200 guests filled the auditorium. Geisha from Kyoto, Osaka and Kobe fluttered about like butterflies in brilliantly colourful kimonos, their gleaming waxed coiffeurs sparkling with silver ornaments. The air was filled with the rustle of silk, the cooing of girlish voices and silvery laughter. Great men from the theatre and the political and business worlds mingled under the chandeliers of the foyer.

It was the crowning moment of Otojiro's career. He was the master of

247

his own theatre again, and one far grander and more magnificent than the much-lamented Kawakami-za. As he stepped on stage to make his opening remarks, he was fairly bursting with pride and happiness.

The first production at the new theatre was *Around the World*, loosely based on Jules Verne's *Around the World in Eighty Days*. Yakko donned trousers to play Takeo Fukuhara, a Japanese gentleman out to prove his samurai credentials and win a bet that he can circle the world in seventy days; as a Japanese, of course, he has to outdo Verne's hero and travel faster. Otojiro took to the stage as the comic servant. When the travellers reach London, they find a troupe of Japanese actors performing *Dojoji*, *The Geisha and the Knight*. After a glimpse of the dance that had thrilled Western audiences, they rush on to India, where they rescue a widow from the *suttee* funeral pyre where she is about to be burnt alive. She turns out to be Japanese and vows to remain at Fukuhara's side for ever after.

In an interview with *Engei Gaho* (*Theatre Pictorial*) magazine, Yakko playfully discussed the problems of cross-dressing and playing a man. She had to clomp around with inserts in her shoes, she said, to make herself taller and found it extremely difficult to project her voice while keeping it deep and low. But her biggest problem was when, as Fukuhara, she had a love scene with her niece, Tsuru, who played the Japanese maiden. It was extremely strange, she said, to behave like a lover when she felt like an aunt.[23]

November featured *Star Worlds*, a science fiction revue, with dazzling lighting effects to give the audience the sensation of travelling through space in a hot air balloon. The travellers met angels, the long-eared inhabitants of the moon and beautiful Martian women with red-tinted skin.

The troupe also performed a play called *The Korean King* which combined the Kawakamis' penchant for topicality and controversy with their policy of reproducing Western plays in Japanese form. A version of Wilhelm Meyer-Forster's *Alt Heidelberg*, also known as the musical *The Student Prince*, it told the story of a young Korean prince studying at Kyoto University who falls in love with a beautiful Japanese waitress. The lovers have to part when he returns to the dusty, antiquated Korean court.

It was a light-hearted romance, with the Koreans depicted as a backward, primitive nation in need of modernisation by their colonising Japanese masters. But it was still far too risqué for the Japanese censors. Romantic love of any sort was highly subversive, let alone love between a Korean and a Japanese. The play was heavily censored and eventually performed with all references to Korea deleted and replaced by the bland term 'New Nation'.[24]

The following year Yakko performed Sarah Bernhardt's most famous role, Marguerite in *La Dame Aux Camellias*. Audiences were moved to tears. Never before had she touched their hearts so profoundly. Critics noted that the play was particularly natural and moving for the very reason that this was a woman playing a woman.

That summer the troupe went on tour through Japan. They ended up in Otojiro's home town, the rough southern port city of Hakata. Ever since he had run away to sea many years before, Otojiro had kept in touch with his family. He was particularly close to his cousin, Iwakichi, who had become the manager of the Kawakami troupe after the end of the Russo-Japanese War.

Whenever he breezed into Hakata, Otojiro would fetch up in Iwakichi's house with a gang of twenty or more actors. He would cajole Iwakichi's long-suffering wife, Tsuru, into cooking his favourite dish, rice cakes in broth, for all of them. He and his friends would settle in for days, sprawling on the tatami-matted floor, drinking, eating, joking, laughing and eventually falling asleep crammed together on futons filling the room from wall to wall. Then they would disappear without offering to pay a penny.

But that year he did something rather strange. Through inheritance or purchase he had acquired a block of four small houses in the centre of town. The family's place of worship was Kushida Shrine, the city's most venerated Shinto temple, akin to a cathedral. When they were born, members of the Kawakami family were always taken there to be blessed. Otojiro bequeathed the four houses to the shrine, which would thenceforth collect and receive the rents. He paid to have prayers recited for his ancestors and for the longevity of the family line.

'Now I've done my duty,' he said. 'There is nothing left for me to do.'

He was only forty-seven. It seemed absurdly young to have discovered piety; but no one thought much about it. He and Yakko went to the elegant resort of Arima Spa, in the hills above Kobe, to prepare for the October season. Sequestered in an inn there, Otojiro stayed up till the small hours every night working on the script for their next production, a Japanese version of Ibsen's *The Enemy of the People*. But then, just as they got back to Osaka, his abdomen began to swell. It grew more and more distended, then the swelling spread to his back and became hard. His face was the colour of clay. He lay groaning on his futon, complaining of dreadful weakness and nausea. Yakko rushed to call the doctor. He diagnosed abdominal dropsy complicated by the inflammation of the appendix area which had troubled Otojiro for so many years. He ordered him to rest. Otojiro had been looking forward to performing in *The Enemy of the People*. Advertisements were plastered all over town, the play was about to open. He was fine, he groaned, perfectly capable of going on stage.

'If you're going to be so difficult, then I won't act,' said Yakko sternly, desperate with worry. He finally agreed to abide by doctor's orders. Another actor took Otojiro's role and the sick man stayed at home. But he was so stubborn and unmanageable that the nurses did not know what to do with him. So Yakko had him brought to the theatre office where he lay on futons and she could rush to his side between every scene.

Otojiro was deteriorating fast. He was certain he was going to die. Three days after he was taken ill, Yakko was at his bedside as usual. With difficulty he began to speak. She leaned forward to catch his words. He wanted to talk about reforming Japanese theatre. His life's work had only just begun, he whispered.

The Imperial Theatre has been born, as an exemplar for theatres to come, but we still need to train actors capable of performing on its stage. This has been my ideal. If I die, carry on my work. I've done nothing for personal profit. Do not distort my ideals and turn them towards money making.[25]

Thus he passed his mission on to Yakko. To the end, Otojiro never seemed to appreciate that they had done everything together. Yakko too, as a good and devoted wife, would never for a minute, to the outside world, to him or even to herself, suggest that things had been in any way different from the way he saw them.

Then tears welled in his eyes and began to slip down his grey, clammy face. 'Autumn evenings make me feel so lonely,' he groaned.

Soon the inflammation had spread to his diaphragm. He became feverish and delirious. All night long Yakko was kneeling silently beside his futon, tending to his every need, gently pressing cups of lukewarm green tea to his dry lips. She had become pale and haggard. At dawn a relative or one of the actors would take her place for a few hours so that she could sleep. In the evening she was still performing. She was so exhausted that she had begun to forget her lines. The doctor warned her that she would become ill too if she did not rest. That day she closed the theatre and cancelled all performances.

There were now four specialist doctors dealing with Otojiro's case. It was vital to operate but they were apprehensive because he was so weak. He had eaten nothing for days. Listening to the whispered conversation flittering around him, Otojiro opened his eyes and, through bloodless lips, muttered, 'If I'm going to die anyway, just do it!'

The operation took place in Osaka's top hospital. Otojiro had insisted that he wanted to watch. The doctors administered a partial anaesthetic, then propped him in a sitting position so that he could see as they cut open his abdomen. A bucketful of foul-smelling water came gushing out. Otojiro gritted his teeth like a samurai and made not a sound of complaint.

A few days later he was sitting up, sipping rice gruel and turtle soup. He smiled weakly at his family and the actors gathered around his bedside.

'I think he's going to be okay,' Yakko whispered, hardly daring to hope. 'We can breathe again.'

Otojiro's recovery lasted a few days. Then, quite suddenly, he slipped into a coma. The doctors broke it to Yakko that the inflammation had reached his brain. The prospects of recovery were very poor. But he still held on. Asajiro anxiously telegrammed from Tokyo inquiring after his old friend. Yakko telegrammed back, 'No change'.

At 3a.m. on 11 November he seemed on the point of death. Yakko was thin and ashen-faced after more than three weeks of sleepless days and nights. Raikichi, now a gangly lad of fifteen, was at his side along with relatives who had rushed from Hakata. In a low voice she said, 'It doesn't look as if he's going to make it. I'd like him to take his last breath in his theatre.'

With doctors and nurses in attendance they put him on a stretcher and carried him out into the icy Osaka air. They walked in silent procession through the dark, windswept streets of the city to the Imperial Theatre. The actors had placed screens around a corner of the stage. They carried Otojiro in and gently laid him there on his futon. Yakko, Raikichi, relatives and actors knelt around him and kept watch. In the sleeve of his gown was a string of prayer beads which the high priest of a Zen temple which he venerated had given to him personally. He carried them with him wherever he went. Yakko gently put them in his hands. Otojiro seemed to nod and his fingers moved a little.

At 6a.m. he moved his right hand a little. Yakko put her mouth close to his ear and asked him if he wanted anything. He smiled slightly and moved his hand three times, as if shaking the beads. Then he opened his eyes and looked straight at Yakko. With that he breathed his last.[26]

III

MISTRESS

10

WILD CHRYSANTHEMUM
1911—1917

In the end
the wild chrysanthemum
has to bloom in the shade.
Sadayakko 1917

In the moments after Otojiro's death Yakko knelt numbly at his side. Raikichi was hunched over his prayer beads, stammering prayers, his schoolboy voice breaking with tears. As word spread, wailing and sobbing echoed through the darkened theatre.

At first Yakko could do nothing but weep. Twenty years had passed since she had met Otojiro. Since then they had done everything together. Even when he set off on his first mad voyage, she was at his side. Now that he was gone, all his roughness and infidelities vanished from her mind. She remembered only his love and companionship.

In numb silence everyone set to work. As the sun rose they cleaned the theatre from top to bottom and covered the stage in white cotton sheets. Undertakers came to wash Otojiro's body and shave his head. Yakko lovingly shaved off his moustache herself. Then they wrapped the body in white robes and laid it in a coffin in the middle of the stage, with a window in the lid so that everyone could see his face.

The whole stage was a sea of white roses and bouquets. In front of the coffin they stood a wooden prayer stick etched with his posthumous name. (In Buddhist practice, everyone received a new name after death;

Otojiro's is not recorded.) On the wall behind was a large photograph of him looking stern and handsome. Visitors began to arrive, first by the tens, then the hundreds, to pay their last respects. Huge candles flickered with a yellow flame and fragrant incense smoke wafted in threads above the coffin. Monks beat drums and kept up a monotonous grumble of prayer.

Otojiro's funeral took place seven days after his death. It was a bleak November morning. The arches at the front of the theatre were curtained in black. At half past nine a cavalcade of rickshaws drew up and fifty monks stepped out, their purple and gold robes glistening in the gloom, carrying huge dark red, oiled paper umbrellas. Ponderously they climbed onto the stage, settled on their knees around the coffin and set up a drone of chanting.

At half past ten the coffin, swathed in white fabric, was lifted inside a bamboo palanquin and decorated with bouquets of white roses at each corner. Fifteen or twenty bare-legged bearers, in white robes, hefted it onto their shoulders and set off, leading the procession.

Osaka had never before seen such a spectacle. People had been filling the streets, jostling for places, since long before dawn. There were mounted police at every corner to control the crowds. The teahouses along the route had red felt carpeting laid out in the upper rooms and were doing a roaring trade. Geisha hung from the windows and balconies, their long silk sleeves fluttering like red and purple banners. Customers pushed between them. There were people squatting on the tiled rooftops, some clutching binoculars.

The long street lined with wooden houses was packed wall to wall with men in dark overcoats and bowler hats or caps jammed next to grandmothers with babies tied on their backs. The procession of mourners, all in stark white robes, snaked through the crowd. At the front were the bearers with the white-draped coffin in its bamboo palanquin. But no one in the crowd was looking at the coffin. Every head was turned, every neck craned, trying to get a glimpse of Sadayakko.

As Otojiro's heir, Raikichi led the procession, holding the wooden prayer stick bearing Otojiro's posthumous name. It was a heavy weight to have fallen so suddenly on the shoulders of the fifteen-year-old boy. Then came Yakko, ashen-faced, her eyes downcast. She was so pitifully thin that her white mourning garb seemed to hang on her. Behind her followed some of the nation's most famous stage idols, led by Asajiro, pale and grim, his handsome face set off by his white robes.

Yakko tottered along feebly, as if in a trance, hardly able to walk. As the procession reached the end of the long street, the colour drained from her face, her legs buckled and she crumpled to the ground. The people nearest her caught her and carried her into a nearby inn. There she rested for half an hour. Weeping, she insisted on rejoining the procession. As they neared Isshinji Temple she fainted again.

The procession arrived at the temple at one o'clock. They laid down the coffin and placed in front of it Otojiro's most valued possessions: the gold watch he had received from the Tsar of Russia and the medals from the President of France. His closest friends read messages of farewell. Some children recited a valediction beginning, 'Uncle Kawakami has gone to far away heaven'. Their piping voices reduced everyone to tears. Supported by two nurses, Yakko took some faltering steps towards the altar. She bowed deeply and lit incense, then stood in prayer, her whole body trembling violently, with tears coursing down her sunken cheeks.

The next morning the coffin was put on a train to be taken to Hakata. Yakko, Raikichi, relatives, actors and many friends accompanied it. There they conducted another funeral. Finally the body was taken to Jotenji, a Zen temple on the outskirts of the city. It was a grey, dreary day. The ground was parched and the trees brown and skeletal. There Otojiro was buried.

He had said he did not want to be cremated but buried in the traditional fashion, curled in an urn. Most temples insisted on cremation. That was one reason why he was not buried in the family tomb with his ancestors. It also seemed fitting that his last resting place should be at the edge of the city, near the railway line, where he could hear the trains passing and look towards Tokyo and the great world where he had lived out his adventurous life.[1]

Some days later the geisha of the Shimbashi district gathered at a temple to have their own wake. Being geisha, as a newspaper put it, the whole affair had the whiff of sex.

'Of all of us, the only ones that weren't the Boss's lovers were me and the mistress of Hama teahouse,' chirped the mistress of Tombo teahouse, beginning proceedings.

A geisha called Sonoko had come along from the Kanoya house to represent Kyoka, the woman who had caused Yakko such grief when she first played Desdemona. 'Big sister is ill so I've come instead,' she trilled.

'That's not true! She's with Mr Ii,' called out another, referring to the famously handsome Yoko Ii, a member of the Kawakami troupe.

But as the ceremony began, they fell silent and one by one began to cry. There was much bowing and politeness over who should take precedence in the offering of incense. Then they all tucked into a delicious meal. Over food and drink reminiscences began to flow. There was much argument over who had known him first and who had loved him best. When they began to count they had to agree that at least sixty geisha in the Shimbashi district alone had been his lovers. They decided to form an ex-lovers' group and get together annually to remember him.[2]

After the funeral, ill from exhaustion and sadness, Yakko stayed in Hakata with Otojiro's family. She lay wanly, barely able to move, looking at his picture and weeping. When she tried to get up she was so weak that her legs crumpled under her. She saw a doctor, half hoping it might be tuberculosis so that her life too might end. He told her it was not serious but that she needed to rest.

In those days there was no place for a widow in Japanese society. The proper course for Yakko was to cut her beautiful hair, become a nun and spend the rest of her life praying for her husband's soul and tending his grave. She did not even have the responsibility of taking care of children. Raikichi had been sent to Hakata for his schooling and was settled with Otojiro's family. In any case, he was nearly an adult. It would soon be his responsibility, as her adopted son, to take care of her.

As a geisha and then an actress, Yakko was used to being an outsider. She had won her place in society not through birth or marriage but her own beauty, talents and fame. But it was a precarious position. While Otojiro was alive, she had always been careful to emphasise that she had engaged in the highly questionable activity of acting not out of choice but simply to support him and help his business. She always did her best to make it clear that she was the perfect Japanese wife, devoted and obedient. That was her only *raison d'être*. Now that she was on her own, however, that excuse was lost. If she were to continue acting, she might well find powerful forces ranged against her. Popularity and fame were not enough to allow her to go against the accepted conventions of society.

There was, however, one way out. Everyone understood that it was her duty to obey Otojiro's last wishes, and he had told her to carry on his work. Instead of cutting her hair short, as widows were expected to do, she simply trimmed it. She explained to a journalist:

> I wanted to become a nun and spend the rest of my days praying at my husband's tomb. But I can't shave my head yet. I have to fulfil his last wishes until I too am a corpse. So I have cut my hair, keeping half and putting half into his coffin.[3]

It was only after weeks of sadness that Yakko finally felt able to face the world. Gradually, in her misery, memories began to float back of everything that she and Otojiro had been working on together – the Imperial Theatre, which had been dark since his death, the actress school and the children's plays. She remembered she had been in the middle of all that. She said later:

> It was obviously my responsibility to fulfil my husband's dying wishes. And for myself, from my own feelings, I hoped to have a bronze statue of Otto made. . . . I decided I must do my work as best I could, as if my husband was going to come back again soon. Once I had decided that, all my pain disappeared and I started feeling better.[4]

At that moment a telegram arrived from Asajiro. The original Kawakami troupe had long since broken up. The actors had gone off to become stars in their own right; some had founded troupes of their own. Now they were eager to get together again as the 'Kawakami all-stars troupe' and tour the country performing in his honour. It was obvious that Sadayakko, his widow, should be the star.

At first Yakko demurred. She was still grieving, she said, she had no energy. But the actors insisted. On 8 February 1912, the ninetieth day after Otojiro's death and the end of the first prescribed period of mourning, the curtain rose again at the Imperial Theatre. Nothing had changed – the areas of seating, the tatami matting, the swagged velvet edging the balconies, the Art Nouveau swirls on the domed ceiling. The audience half expected Otojiro to step on stage, bow and say, 'Good evening and welcome' in his gravelly voice. Backstage, the room that had been his office was dominated by a large portrait of him and a memorial tablet marked with his name, with candles and incense burning in front. The actors laid offerings of fruit and flowers. Two priests droned prayers. Yakko knelt for a few moments, overwhelmed by memories.

Asajiro began by making a speech, paying tribute to Otojiro. As he spoke of his achievements and dedication to the theatre, Yakko, kneeling in the middle of the stage, could not contain her tears. Later, a handkerchief to her eyes, she explained to a journalist:

> I wanted to thank the people of Osaka myself for their kindness and sympathy and for supporting us when my husband was alive. I truly appreciate why my husband chose to build his Imperial Theatre here in Osaka. But when I tried to speak, my heart started breaking. I couldn't stop my tears or say a single word. That's why I asked Mr Fujisawa to express our gratitude. Even when I'm on stage I'm overcome by emotion. I tell myself, 'I'm acting, I must forget real life.' I try and pull myself together but I can't help being a woman.[5]

Every performance was a sell out. Yakko appeared in the last play, *The Beautiful Maiden of the Deep Mountains* (*Miyama no Bijin*). She played the Maiden, a simple peasant brought up far from civilisation who has 'never even eaten rice'. It was a little difficult, she confessed, to play an innocent virgin. Journalists who interviewed her noted how thin her wrists had become and how pale and sunken her cheeks.

After a two-week run the troupe travelled to Kyoto where they performed at the city's top theatre, the Minami-za. They went on to Tokyo and Nagoya, then set off on a nationwide tour. In Kobe they added

David Belasco's *Mme. Butterfly*, performed in English, to their repertoire. Whenever she was interviewed, Yakko always said sadly that she was on stage purely in order to pay tribute to her dead husband. She told a journalist in Kobe:

> I have to do my best, otherwise what excuse can I make to my husband? When I think of that, I worry so much I can't sleep. When I think that Otojiro is watching from the other world, I feel quite nervous.[6]

Theatres were packed and audiences cheered and applauded the beautiful Sadayakko. Nevertheless, there was something a little desperate about the tour. The troupe by now was working its way through a string of provincial cities. Snide critics in Tokyo and Osaka asked whether Sadayakko's career could really be healthy if she was reduced to appearing in small town theatres like a low-grade travelling player.

Late on the night of 29 July 1912, Emperor Meiji died. It was an event every bit as momentous as the death of Queen Victoria ten years earlier in Britain. Few people could remember a time when he had not been on the throne. The nation went into deep mourning. Theatres and shops closed. On the day of the funeral Tokyo was engulfed in silence. People lined the streets to bow to the ground as the hearse rumbled by, drawn by five oxen and followed by a cortège of thousands of courtiers and attendants, some in ancient court costume, others in military uniform.

Meiji was succeeded by his son, the thirty-three-year-old Emperor Taisho. An era had ended and a new one had begun. At forty-one, Yakko must have wondered if her day too was coming to an end. She and her generation were Meiji people, stars of a time gone by. With the coming of Taisho a new generation of stars was rising.

One critic wrote rather cruelly:

> However much her fame precedes her, even though Sadayakko is in good shape, she's getting old. I admire the fact that she is not discouraged by the winds of this fickle world, now blowing cold

towards her; she has great spirit, she even outdoes her husband; and she has certainly contributed a lot to the world of theatre. All the same, if she thinks hard about it, it's probably a good idea for her to pull out of the acting business. The theatre world certainly has a desperate shortage of women, but what it needs is young, lovely, desirable women.[7]

Others clamoured that she should become a nun. Yakko answered her critics, saying in an interview:

Once my husband left this world, I should properly have stopped being an actress. I really wanted to do so. But my karma has not yet run its course. There are various complicated situations and relationships which will not allow me to leave the stage for the next four or five years.

Aware that she was not properly trained, she had decided, she said, to go to Europe in the near future with some of her trainee actresses and study for a year and a half.[8] But first she had to deal with the problem of the Imperial Theatre. The money to build it – a ruinous 40,000 yen – had been stumped up by a wily financier and a construction magnate. The theatre was effectively theirs. After Otojiro's death, articles appeared suggesting that pressure from these two to repay the debt might have hastened his death. One paper suggested that the best move for Yakko would be to seduce Mr Obayashi, the construction magnate.

Yakko was desperate to keep this theatre which had meant so much to Otojiro and enshrined so many memories of their life together. He had expressly enjoined her to take care of it. It was his legacy. But the upkeep was ruinous. Eventually, overwhelmed by debt, she handed it over to the creditors for little more than a token payment. The splendid theatre ended up as a branch of Sumitomo bank.

Her plans to build a statue in Otojiro's memory too were fraught with difficulty. She had commissioned a near life-size bronze from a sculptor who had cast an image of Prince Ito after his death. Her plan was to erect it at Sengakuji, the Kawakami family temple in Tokyo, where a lock of Otojiro's hair was buried. But there was a public outcry. The local worthies were horrified. They did not want a statue of a 'riverbed beggar' defiling their revered temple. It would be a pernicious influence on children, they protested, who might even think of following the same disgraceful profession. The unveiling ceremony had to be postponed while Yakko searched for a new location.

She opted for Tokyo's vast Yanaka graveyard. There, one mild September day in 1914, the statue was lifted on a complicated contraption of bamboo rods and ropes and set on a huge drum-shaped plinth. There stood Otojiro as if alive again, grave and distinguished in a double-breasted great coat, waistcoat and trousers. Top hat in his left hand and cane in his right, he gazed into the distance with visionary intensity. There was not a hint of the irreverent, comical character he had been in real life. At the ceremony of dedication, Yakko made offerings and a bevy of Shinto priests in robes and tall black hats chanted and waved mulberry paper wands. The statue was decked with auspicious paper chains.

The paper chains were not enough to protect it from destruction. It was melted down in World War II to use the copper for bullets. Even the plate with Otojiro's name was taken. But the drum-shaped plinth, eight or nine feet tall, still stands in the peaceful graveyard surrounded by cherry trees and tombstones, with Otojiro's exploits carved on it.

Even before the statue had been settled on its plinth, a succession of strange and terrible things happened. It was Yakko's forty-second year. One day in 1913 she received news that her older sister, Hanako, had thrown herself in a well and died. She had been the mistress of a wealthy man. She had finally found it unbearable to go on living a life hidden from the world, unacknowledged by her lover.

Yakko had barely recovered from that blow when there was another, far worse. Raikichi disappeared. The story that Yakko passed on to Tomiji many years later was that he had had tuberculosis. Perhaps he was desperately ill and thought his case was hopeless. One day he took the train to the desolate Japan Sea coast, where the waves lash savagely at the foot of precipitously high, rocky cliffs. There he threw himself in the sea and drowned. As to whether there were witnesses or how Yakko heard the story, we don't know.

But why should he have gone all that way to commit suicide? Perhaps the real story was too shameful for Yakko to make it known even to Tomiji. The towering cliffs of the bleak Japan Sea coast are the traditional place where star-crossed lovers used to go to commit love suicide. In the days of forced marriages, it was a common last resort. At least they could be together in death.

Raikichi was only seventeen, full of the torments and passions of youth. Maybe he could not bear the stigma of being the illegitimate son of a 'riverbed beggar'. Maybe he had experienced the desperate intensity of first love but had been refused by his beloved's family because of his birth. Or perhaps there was some other reason. Maybe he had heard rumours of Yakko's life after Otojiro's death that distressed him. To this day the family do not know what really happened. They are not even sure that he died. They only know that he disappeared and was never seen or heard of again.

For Yakko it must have been unimaginably painful. He was all she had. He was her family, the son she had been relying on to care for her when she was old. Yet she could not even wail and weep and organise a huge funeral, as she had done for Otojiro. Instead she retreated into silence. She sealed her pain in her heart and spoke of Raikichi only with the greatest reluctance.

For some reason she had never had children of her own. Japanese say that being deflowered in their early teens damaged many young geisha so badly that it made them infertile. Perhaps that is what happened to Yakko. There is even speculation that Otojiro deliberately went to Raikichi's mother to conceive a child so that he would have an heir.

Then news came that something dreadful had happened to Asajiro. He had started mumbling mad nonsense on stage, straying from the script. The lead in the white make-up which he had used to paint his face for so many years had finally gone to his brain. He retired precipitously and died soon afterwards, on 3 March 1914, at the age of forty-eight. Yakko had never in her life been so terribly alone.

In the midst of these terrible events, on 5 June 1913, an article appeared in the *Chuo* newspaper. The headline was 'What will Sadayakko do now?'

Yakko, wrote the journalist, was tasting the pain of life to its bitter dregs.

Having lost her husband Otojiro and handed over the Imperial Theatre, which she regarded as her life, to her merciless creditors, Sadayakko became really forlorn and shook herself like a little bird that has lost its nest. The most humiliating thing for her must have been being called a third rate travelling player.

Lately, however, things had begun to change for the better. 'Recently she appeared at the Tokyo Imperial Theatre in the major role of Tosca, probably the first bright spot since her husband died. Not to mention her relationship with Momo Fuku . . .'

Without elaborating, the journalist asked her plans. She was trying to find funding to complete the plinth of the statue which at the time she still thought would be erected in Sengakuji temple. She had asked her old friends Ambassador Kurino and Baron Kaneko for help. She was planning a splendid ceremony to unveil the statue, she said. She went on wistfully:

You want to know about me? I'm like a floating weed. I have no roots and no leaves, I just drift with the wind. The destiny that was laid down for me has been completed. So for three months – July, August, September – I shall rest. In October, when the autumn wind starts to blow, without being any trouble to anyone, I shall set off alone on my lonely journey to the west. That's my plan. First I shall head for England, France and Germany. But who knows which way the wind will blow?

And she laughed sadly.

'I wonder if she has taken ill fortune for her god,' pondered the journalist.[9]

Nevertheless, as he had hinted, there was one consolation, one reason to prevent her throwing herself on the mercy of the wild winds of fate. We don't know when and how the relationship with Momosuké – 'Momo

Fuku' as the journalist cheekily referred to him – was rekindled. It was such an explosive scandal that the pair did all they could to keep it quiet. Nevertheless news leaked out. Who knows? Perhaps that was the unbearable shame that caused Raikichi to take his own life.

In an article published in November 1912, a year after Otojiro's death, a writer referred colourfully to 'the interesting scandal from Tatsuno which kicked the light out of Yakko's life and sent her spiralling to the black depths of hell. Now,' he wrote, 'she has no way to get her spirits back. She is bitter that she has lost all the sympathy and popularity she had on stage.' He did not elaborate on the 'scandal from Tatsuno' which had made Yakko so miserable. It was such a well-known story that he assumed his readers knew all about it.

Whatever the scandal was, Yakko denied it emphatically. The troupe had performed in Osaka, Kyoto, Tokyo, Kobe, Himeji and the San'in area. Then, she said:

> I was informed that the Emperor had passed away, so we cancelled the rest of the tour and I retreated to my villa in Chigasaki. Because I did that, all of a sudden all sorts of rumours sprang up. But I just wanted to spend some quiet time in the country, preparing my husband's statue and making plans for the future.[10]

But what was this scandal that everyone knew about and what did the mysterious reference to Tatsuno mean? An article published in a local paper in 1914 illuminates the matter. Romantically entitled 'Sadayakko in love: Two shadows entwined with each other', it begins, 'The rumour of a romance between the number one modern actress, Sadayakko Kawakami, and Momosuké Fukuzawa has been flowing down the Iho river of Tatsuno, and has now come quite out into the open.'

Tatsuno was a poetic reference to Kobe; poets sang the praises of the beautiful red and gold autumn tints of the 'maple leaves of Tatsuno'. Yakko performed in Kobe in April 1912. Momosuké must have been there too, which is how the rumours started. So it seems their affair may have been underway as soon as five months after Otojiro's death. So when the *Chuo* newspaper mentioned 'Momo Fuku' in June 1913, there was no need to explain further. Readers knew exactly what the journalist was talking about.

In the terrible days and months following Otojiro's death, Yakko was desperately in need of support and love. As for Momosuké, he had been consoling himself in the company of geisha for more years than he cared to remember. Neither had ever forgotten the intensity of their first meeting as adolescents. Their friendship as adults was touched with the magic of that innocent love. It had never soured. They had been wrenched apart in spite of themselves.

According to one version of events, Yakko had turned to Momosuké for financial help even when Otojiro was alive. The Kawakami finances were always desperately insecure; it was a terrible burden for Yakko to cope with Otojiro's feckless, spendthrift nature. Momosuké, the 'Wizard of the Money Markets', was a very different type of man – pensive, discreet and very wealthy. There is even a story that Otojiro, knowing of their early love, summoned Momosuké to his deathbed and asked him to take care of Yakko after he was gone. When Momosuké had been a poor student, Yakko, as a successful geisha, had paid for him to visit her at teahouses. Now the situation was reversed. She was alluringly vulnerable, in need of love and protection.

They probably met in a teahouse. That was where every sort of meeting requiring privacy and discretion took place; that was the *raison d'être* of the flower and willow world. There, while she kept his sake cup topped up, they exchanged memories of the old days, of the sadness of their parting and the long years that had passed between. They had to be discreet. Yakko was such a celebrity that the press followed her wherever she went.

Perhaps as they looked at each other they became aware that the old magic was still there. It is not hard to imagine that hands met across the table. In the silence and privacy of the tearoom, with the kettle whistling on the hearth, they knew they would not be disturbed. They were adults now, free to do as they pleased.

By 1914 the pair had cast caution to the winds. When Yakko toured the Nakasendo region of central Japan, Momosuké was with her, as close to her as her own shadow.

On 4 January, reported the article on 'Sadayakko in love', the two arrived at the famous and glamorous spa of Beppu, on Kyushu island. There they checked into a beautiful old wooden-walled inn. They booked the whole place and told the innkeeper not to take any other guests. Then they secluded themselves and, as the reporter put it, 'drank the sweet saké of love for two nights'. While snow flurries swirled, whitening Beppu's cobbled, winding streets, they stayed cosily in their room or soaked in the steaming mineral-imbued waters for which the resort is famous.

By then the reporter, 'sniffing the air and sticking his nose in', had got wind of the celebrity lovers. The classy 'high-collar' forty-three-year-old, with her oiled hair piled into a Shimada coiffeur, had the look on her face of a 'young virgin, fresh as a cherry blossom', he wrote. Snow clouds were gathering, threatening a vicious storm, when the pair packed their bags and travelled across the straits to Shimonoseki, on the main island of Honshu. There they checked into the Sanyo Hotel, pulled down the blue blinds and settled in as snow began to fall.

An article in another local paper, entitled 'Tosuké and Sadayakko', has a different version of the story. 'Tosuké' is a familiar way of pronouncing the written characters for 'Momosuké', rather like referring to President George W. Bush as 'Dubya'. The writer declared:

Tosuké Fukuzawa is famous in the flower and willow world as a great lover with geisha girlfriends in the three cities [Tokyo, Osaka and Kyoto]. Whenever he goes drinking he is always surrounded by beautiful women and the scent of face powder. He doesn't hide the fact that his paramour is Sadayakko Kawakami. Plenty of beautiful women are envious of Sadayakko.

Momosuké had merged several businesses to form a company called Kyushu Gas and had also started a Kyushu railway company. He frequently went there on business trips. Early in 1914 he was on his way to Hakata with his business partner, Yasuzaemon Matsunaga. According to the article, 'Sadayakko was feeling sad and pleaded with Tosuké to let her come with him. She was performing in Tokyo at the time but started feeling lonely and wanted to be with Tosuké.' She followed him down by train and arrived at Shimonoseki station at 8.40a.m.

The plan was to cross to Kyushu but the wind was so high and the waves so violent that the ferry had been cancelled. So the travellers checked into the Sanyo Hotel. Momosuké and Yakko went to their room then joined their companions in the dining room. There was a fire burning in the hearth.

Momosuké was standing with his back to the fire, smiling. Sadayakko was wearing red lipstick. Yasuzaemon felt jealous of the two. Morosely he thumped the table, shouting for whisky.

Momosuké was chatting to Sadayakko. His clean-shaven face was so close to hers that his lips and her red lips nearly touched. They dined on western-style food on western plates. They were obviously having a good time together. People around them couldn't help glancing at them.

Kissing or even nearly kissing was shockingly erotic, the preserve of professionals like geisha and still strictly reserved for the bedroom. To behave with such flamboyant intimacy in public was quite outrageous. Yakko and Momosuké were in their forties, rich, good-looking and successful. They were no longer young. Well away from Tokyo, they could afford to relax and flaunt convention. They had no need to care what anyone thought.

With the scandal out in the open, the papers took every opportunity to portray Yakko as a scarlet woman. They made a point of referring to her vulgar, flashy clothes. As an ex-geisha, Yakko dressed with panache in a sexy, alluring way, on top of which she had acquired Parisian flair. Her style was quite different from that of samurai women with their prim kimonos and painstakingly adopted Western fashions.

That day, wrote the reporter, Tosuké was in a snappy suit. Sadayakko, he noted with disapproval, was wearing a fur shawl on top of 'a really gaudy crested kimono and wooden sandals. She looked as if she was trying to hang on to the last of her sex appeal'.[11]

In Japan at the time, men could still do more or less whatever they liked. A man of wealth and power was expected to support a mistress or two and to spend much of his time and money in the teahouses and pleasure quarters. If he did not, everyone would have assumed he had major financial problems or was grossly stingy. But the mistresses were almost invariably geisha. Apart from anything else, geisha knew that their job was to take the pressure off a man's marriage. The geisha code was never to try and tear a man away from his wife. Many geisha even knew their *danna*'s wife and would pop in and out of the house to help with the children or entertain guests.

For Momosuké it was eccentric, to say the least, to pair off with a widow who was not even young. But it was Yakko, not Momosuké, who risked disgrace. Even if she chose not to live out her days as a nun, she ought to have married – not taken someone else's husband. By opting for love, she forfeited respectability.

The theatre critic Shigure Hasegawa often visited Yakko backstage. Once when she was researching a long essay about Yakko for the first of a series called 'Stories of Beautiful Women of Today', she dropped into Yakko's dressing room at the Shintomi-za Theatre during intermission. It must have been around 1914 or 1915. In her essay she described the scene. The room was large as befitted a star, with a dressing table covered with brushes and tubs of make-up along one side. Bouquets and gifts were propped against the walls and piled in the corners.

Yakko was sitting in the middle of the room with a mirror behind her. She had slipped into a simple cotton *yukata* gown tied with a man's obi, with a quilted jacket thrown over the top. With her hair in the gingko-leaf style, she was the picture of *louche* elegance. Her heart-shaped face was a little thinner than in her youth, her cheekbones more pronounced, her jaw a touch more marked; but men could still drown themselves in her huge dark eyes, one flat and Asian, the other lidded like a Western eye.

Momosuké was with her. The pungent smell of dried fish being grilled wafted from the next-door room. Hasegawa wrinkled her nose, a little taken aback. The play was set in a palace; Yakko played a young princess. The smell of grilling fish was likely to jerk the audience back to reality and destroy the illusion. But Yakko didn't seem to care. Momosuké asked for rice mixed with tea (*ochasuké*) and an assistant brought him some in a pretty bowl with a pair of ivory chopsticks. From the street outside came the cry of a hawker selling boiled soya beans (*eda mamé*). Yakko fluttered her eyelashes at Momosuké and said in her high-pitched little girl warble, 'Quickly, won't you go and get me some of those beans – with salt, mind!'

When he brought back the green beans, wrapped in paper, she squeezed the pods and popped a few into her mouth then complained with pretend pettishness, 'They're a bit soft, they're not very nice!'

It was as if the rest of the world did not exist. To Hasegawa, observing all this, 'the two of them were like newly weds playing house together, still in a dream of love. Sadayakko's voice was soft and sweet'.

'Just yesterday I was scolded because I'm so skinny!' Yakko complained, giggling and puffing on a cigarette as she spoke. 'Just the other day Momo Fuku said, "Much too skinny!", that's what he said.'

Hasegawa remarked that she really was thin. Her collar bones were protruding, her hands transparent and her legs almost painfully slender.

'But her face was not so thin, she still looked almost exactly the same as in the old days,' she wrote. 'It's those 1000 ryo [million dollar] eyes of hers. As long as her eyes keep shining, she will be eternally young.'

The sleekly handsome Rokuro Kitamura, Yakko's co-star, dropped into her dressing room in his costume and they had a chat.

'No one except them understands a single word of what they talk about,' commented Momosuké, smiling, to the other people in the room. 'They meet up and exchange a bit of incomprehensible jargon then get together on stage a few days later and everything goes smoothly.'

Hasegawa went back to her seat in the darkened auditorium. As she was waiting for the curtain to rise, some latecomers came and sat down behind her. She couldn't help overhearing their conversation.

'You know, people worry that I care about Kawakami too much.' It was a man's voice. 'They tell me off about that. But let's face it, things go best if a man falls in love with a woman.'

Hasegawa glanced around and saw that the speaker was Momosuké. She said nothing but sat quietly, listening as Momosuké joked:

Look at it this way, supposing it's a man you fall in love with. That's bound to be a disaster. Your reputation's on the line, you risk losing everything. You can't just say, 'I made a mistake, it's time to move on.' A woman is much more straightforward. All she asks is diamonds, kimonos, some time together, maybe a house.

'Then the memory came floating back of Sadayakko's eyes, which seem quite sober and cold, yet enraptured,' wrote Hasegawa. 'So what of Sadayakko when she is white hot?'[12]

With Momosuké at her side Yakko was enjoying a second flowering of her career. Now that Otojiro was dead, she was free to choose her own roles. She opted to play some of the great heroines of the Western stage. In 1913 she starred in the first Japanese production of Victorien Sardou's *Tosca* at the Imperial Theatre in Tokyo. The theatre, which opened a year after Otojiro's ill-fated Imperial in Osaka, had 1700 seats, a smoking room, a powder room, a promenade, a roof garden and not a tatami mat in sight. It was immediately acknowledged as the country's top Western-style theatre. To appear there was an accolade.

In a ground-breaking piece of casting, Yakko played alongside two handsome and celebrated kabuki actors. Baiko Onoe VI was Tosca's lover, Mario Cavaradossi, and Koshiro Matsumoto VII the evil, scheming police chief, Baron Scarpia. It was the first time old and new style actors had appeared together in the same play.

Baiko's wife, Ofuji, had been one of Yakko's closest friends ever since they were geisha together. Yakko had been her 'older sister' in the geisha world and had helped to arrange her marriage.

As a kabuki actor, Baiko had always played opposite men. Now he was performing nightly love scenes with the most seductive woman in Japan. When Ofuji came to watch a performance, Yakko naughtily turned up the passion. Ofuji sat straight backed in the front row, staring fiercely at the stage. Later she passed Yakko's open door on her way to Baiko's dressing room. As she went by Yakko was heard to sigh in a breathy voice, 'I made love so hard to Baiko tonight, I'm worn out!'

Until then Yakko's leading man had always been Otojiro or her old friend Asajiro. Full of confidence and fun, she seemed to have become young again. She was a diva. She could be as frisky and outrageous as she liked.

She thrilled and scandalised Tokyo by kissing Baiko on the cheek. 'The audience applauded,' wrote a horrified journalist, 'but it was really distasteful. If they had been wearing kimonos, hugging and kissing like that, it would definitely have been seen as injurious to public morals and the play would have been closed down.'

Used to the stylised acting of kabuki, audiences found it hard to differentiate what they saw on stage from real life. Yakko was reputed to have had an affair with Baiko many years ago, when she was a young geisha, and many ex-geisha assumed that that was why she was so passionate on stage. One old dame gave her a scolding. Yakko smiled her sweetest smile, widened her big eyes suggestively and piped in her little girl voice, 'Come along tonight and keep an eye on Baiko's cheek . . .' Of course she nuzzled with even more abandon than usual.[13]

Immoral or not, she got rave reviews. Whenever she appeared on stage, her fans yelled, 'Kawakami! Kawakami!' The applause echoed to the rafters. 'How can Sadayakko, who is in her forties, appear so beautiful that you doubt your own eyes?' swooned an admiring critic.[14]

She was now the face of Reito Cosmetics. 'Even the best quality imported creams are not as effective as Reito for Japanese skin,' she claimed in a newspaper advert. 'If you use Reito your make-up will be perfect and your skin soft and beautiful.'[15]

In 1914, war was breaking out in Europe. But in Japan, thousands of miles away on the other side of the globe, the lights burnt on and the dancing continued. Tokyo sizzled to a run of productions of Oscar Wilde's *Salome*. Wilde's outrageously provocative play, written in French in 1891, had been banned in London and never yet performed there. It had become hugely popular in Europe, where Japanese sophisticates saw it. Its fame spread to Japan where it developed into a huge cult. The dance of the seven veils seemed to symbolise Japanese women's growing demand for greater freedom and fitted neatly into the *louche* atmosphere of native permissiveness which underlay Japan's prim Westernised surface.

Yakko was Japan's great *femme fatale* and Salome the obvious role for her. At forty-four she was definitely getting a little old. But then again, as she knew very well, the great Sarah Bernhardt had been rehearsing for the role in London at the age of nearly fifty until the production was banned.

In Europe the actresses who played Salome cavorted in scandalously revealing costumes. Maud Allen, who took the role in 1907, was virtually naked from the waist up, draped in strings of beads which only just preserved her modesty. Yakko, however, kept her body covered. For Tokyo audiences she appeared in a voluminous dress encrusted with gold and silver, swathed from neck to wrist to ankle. She was a brilliant actress and a beautiful woman and her portrayal of Salome was very professional. But the critics – some of whom had seen *Salome* in the West – agreed there was something missing. Her dance of the seven veils was seductive, alluring and beautifully choreographed. But it was too controlled and far too proper. Above all, she revealed very little flesh. Where was the fire, the passion, the wild abandon? She had plenty of that in her own life, but she was too much a woman of her era to reveal it on stage. Nuzzling Baiko's cheek was one thing, an erotic striptease quite another.

'Her flesh is too desiccated, her blood is too dry,' complained the playwright Kaoru Osanai.[16]

'Perhaps it's to do with her age,' suggested a critic. 'The feverish passion is a bit thin, the aroma of flesh is a bit lacking.'

'She can't hide her age which appears on the surface of her skin,' concurred another. 'So she hides her curvaceous beauty beneath a gold and silver costume. Mind you, from the point of view of public morality that is probably a good thing.'[17]

While audiences would happily accept a jowly old man playing a beautiful young maiden in kabuki, in the realistic New Wave theatre they would not accept a middle-aged woman playing a young girl. They had come to watch a real woman, not a man playing a woman. They wanted to be seduced. They wanted overt sexuality.

It might not have mattered had there been no other Salomes. For years Yakko had been not just Japan's greatest actress but the only one. Now there were plenty of contenders. Inspired by her, young women flocked to train as actresses. In one year there were over 300 applications for twenty places at the acting school that Yakko had founded. Other schools too had emerged, rigorously based on the principles of Western theatrical training. Some of the young graduates quite outshone Yakko, despite her international reputation. Unlike Yakko and her contemporaries, they had not risen from the ranks of the geisha. They were nothing to do with the flower and willow world. They were actresses pure and simple.

Until Yakko's time it was the *onnagata* – male players of female parts – who established the conventions of what constituted femininity. Women as portrayed by *onnagata* were far more feminine than any woman could ever be. They were sweet, sexy, vulnerable creatures who scurried about with tiny pigeon-toed steps, hobbled by their tight kimonos and high clogs. They kept their heads modestly lowered and their shoulders rounded and spoke in piping falsettos. As her Western admirers had said of Yakko, they were like the figures in a woodblock print come to life. When Yakko took to the stage, she evolved her own style of acting, incorporating elements of the more realistic European style. Nevertheless, as an ex-geisha, she was steeped in those classical conventions.

The most brilliant of the new actresses was Sumako Matsui. Fifteen years younger than Yakko, she shot to fame with her electrifying portrayal of the feminist icon Nora in Ibsen's *A Doll's House* in 1911. Curvaceous and stocky with a pretty, round, rather fleshy face, Sumako was far from a picture book beauty. She was a real woman, driven and passionate. She blazed with energy and fiery determination and wasted no time moulding herself to men's conceptions of what a woman was. Had there been suffragettes in Japan at the time she would have been their leader. She was the prime example of the Taisho-era New Woman.

Sumako had appeared as Salome a few months earlier. Her Salome smouldered with voluptuous feminine sensuality. She slinked about the stage in a skimpy toga-like creation fastened on one shoulder, draped to give full prominence to her ample curves. The other shoulder and both arms were bare. In her dance of the seven veils she shimmied until most of her torso was exposed. Tokyo was shocked and seduced. Everyone compared Yakko's Salome to hers. It was the battle of the Salomes. It was also an unspoken contest to decide the leading actress of the Taisho-era stage.

Suddenly Yakko seemed to be surrounded by obstacles. She had wanted to make another foreign tour and applied for a travel permit but leading figures in the Salvation Army and the Clean Up the Pleasure Quarters Campaign argued that for her to perform decadent plays like *The Geisha and the Knight* abroad was bad for Japan's international reputation. The permit was refused.

Then a magazine called *New Performing Arts* published a questionnaire asking its readers what should be done about Sadayakko. Suggestions poured in, all of them cruel: she should go back to being a geisha, join a troupe of travelling players, manage actresses at the Imperial Theatre or run a teahouse or an inn. 'She's over forty,' wrote one reader. 'It's painful to see her acting. She should retire while she's still popular.'[18]

It was all too clear that times had changed. Ritsuko Mori, the young actress whose brother had committed suicide in shame at his sister's profession, complimented Yakko on her wonderful performance as Salome. Yakko shook her head. 'An old woman like me is no good,' she told her. 'The time has come for a new generation.'[19]

In September 1917 she announced her retirement. She was forty-six and it was the seventh year after Otojiro's death, a significant anniversary in Japan. For her grande finale, she made a series of farewell appearances in a drama based on Verdi's *Aida*. Momosuké provided financial backing and helped her to organise everything. The greatest actors of the Japanese stage vied to take part. The Tokyo season took place at the Meiji-za Theatre, local to the Yoshicho geisha district. Five thousand people applied for tickets.

On the first night the theatre was almost invisible beneath the cascades of flowers. Bouquets and gifts filled Yakko's dressing room. The wealthy, powerful and famous strutted through the doors, their wives or geishas shimmying along with them, into the glittering flower-bedecked lobby.

Yakko had composed a bitter-sweet poem for the occasion:

> In the end
> the wild chrysanthemum
> has to bloom in the shade.[20]

She brushed it by hand in her spidery calligraphy and had it printed on delicate tea cups to be given to the guests. Shigure Hasegawa analysed the lines. The words 'in the end' perhaps meant 'out of necessity', she suggested, giving a mood of aching sadness. Commentators pondered whether the simile was appropriate. The wild chrysanthemum is a strong plant which grows even in the stoniest soil and blossoms unnoticed on quiet country lanes. But Yakko had been more like a sunflower. She had turned her face to the full blaze of public acclaim for almost twenty years.[21]

Guests also received a pocket-sized souvenir picture album. On the cover was an Art Deco image of a peacock with a long tail, with the inscription 'Sadayakko Kawakami: Farewell Performance'. Inside were two photographs. One is a formal portrait of Yakko in a dark formal kimono with crests with a design of wild chrysanthemums rambling along the hem. The other shows her in her role as the slave girl Aida. She is radiantly youthful and exquisitely beautiful still, and perfectly cast as the captured Ethiopian princess.

She wears a beaded white gown that clings to her figure, fringed along one edge, and holds her hands clasped to her bosom. Heavy bracelets gleam on each wrist. Her dark tresses are loose and bushy, crowned with a jewelled head-dress. With her huge eyes she gazes wistfully into the distance. Both as Aida and for herself, Yakko must have been overwhelmed with longing for the times gone by and doubts and fears for the future.

A writer named Kikou Yamata saw the farewell performance and wrote about it for a French publication, describing Yakko's riveting entrance. Suddenly, without any accompaniment, she began to sing in a strange, hoarse, almost raucous voice, thin and piercing. It had a barbaric quality appropriate for the role. Then she flung herself into the arms of her lover, Radames. Though in Egyptian costume, the actor performed in the stylised kabuki manner.

'My impression was a mixture of the bizarre, the maladroit and of conviction,' wrote Yamata in her elaborate French. 'Nevertheless this archaic, naïve Aida perhaps suited the character of the drama better than a splendid opera production.'

Afterwards Yamata went backstage. She glimpsed Yakko's thin arm, covered in white make-up, reaching from the shadows 'like a ray of light made flesh'. Then Yakko herself stepped out. She looked at Yamata with her shining black eyes, 'the most brilliant I've ever seen', and smiled her soft sweet smile. Yamata noticed her well-defined nose which gave a foreign cast to her features.

She asked her about her memories of Paris. Yakko did not have much to say. It all seemed like a distant memory. Politely she thanked the Parisians for their kindness and for the acclaim she had received there. Yamata wrote:

> I preserve with astonishing clearness the image of this nervy apparition in black and white. This pale, sinuous arm, then this milky robe, then this thin white face made a vertical line in the decor. Finally, beneath her black locks, her brilliant eyes looked straight into mine and she smiled her seductive smile. Thus Sadayakko disappeared from public view.[22]

Yakko's fans abroad had not forgotten her. The retirement of the Japanese diva made news as far afield as the United States.

11

IN THE SHADOW OF THE PEACH TREE
1917—1946

Can it be the rustle of a kite, caught in the branches of the
    peach tree?
Riding the wind, it has the power to uproot the tree.
            'Chojo' (vice-cabinet minister Seiroku Tochika)

Yakko took her farewell production of *Aida* to Hakata and Osaka, the two cities where she had the strongest connections. Then she slipped out of her lavish costume for the last time and took off her thick stage make-up. She gave up her stage name of Sadayakko and her geisha name of Yakko. As plain Sada Kawakami she began a new life with Momosuké.

Momosuké had been the most loving and supportive of partners. Nevertheless he had been gently suggesting to Sada – as we should now call her – that perhaps she should retire. His own business was booming as never before. Their partnership was an inspiration for both of them. Both of them seemed to have become young again. They were rejuvenated by their relationship.

For Japan World War I had been a huge and unexpected bonanza. While fighting raged across Europe, Japanese arsenals and mills were working round the clock, producing ships and munitions to sell to the combatants. As the Western powers switched their economies to a war footing, Japan stepped in to fulfil their needs for civilian goods too. Overseas markets in the Far East and Africa, which had always been dominated by the West, magically opened to Japan. Industrial production soared; exports doubled, then tripled. It was a heady time. People who were prepared to take risks and try out new ideas became fabulously wealthy overnight.

One effect of the war and the growing prosperity was a sudden surge in demand for electricity as a source of power for industry. By 1919 four times as much electricity was being used as in 1914.

Momosuké had gained a reputation as a trouble shooter with an instinct for pulling companies back from the brink and making them hugely profitable. Some years earlier he had been called in to rescue a company called Nagoya Electric Lighting. He turned it into a successful enterprise and also gained insight and expertise in the electricity industry. He began acquiring local electricity companies. Then he had one of those dazzling ideas which are simple and obvious in retrospect but which nobody else had thought of. Japan is a country of steep mountains, deep valleys and plentiful rain. But nobody had yet introduced hydro-electric power. Japan's fast-flowing rivers had still to be harnessed to provide electricity.

In the beautiful Kiso Valley, in the mountains near Nagoya, the valleys were steeper and narrower and the water rushed faster than almost anywhere else in Japan. It was the obvious place to begin. So Momosuké acquired the rights to the water of the River Kiso and moved his base from Tokyo to Nagoya.

He set about tidying up his old life and creating a new life for himself. First he had a rambling Japanese-style mansion built for Fusa on the vast Fukuzawa estates in Shibuya, south-west Tokyo. There was a separate house for him some distance away to use on the rare occasions when he returned to Tokyo and houses for their sons, Komakichi and Tatsuzo. The grounds were as big as a sizeable park with houses for the servants, lawns, flower gardens, orchards, wooded groves and a long drive lined with blossoming cherry trees. He also had a country villa built for Fusa in Hakone spa and made sure she was provided with an ample income.

Then he had a house built for Sada. They commissioned a firm called America-ya (America House) run by an architect who had studied in the United States. America-ya specialised in lavish Western-style homes with Japanese elements, to suit the Japanese lifestyle. The house, initially called Kawakami-tei (the Kawakami Mansion), was in Sada's name. She paid close attention to the planning and made sure every detail was to her liking. Building began in May 1918. The house was completed about a year later.

The house was in Futaba, the grandest part of Nagoya where high-class samurai families had their homes, in the shadow of Nagoya Castle. Sada's neighbours included the Toyota brothers, Sakichi and Sasuké. They had started a loom-making business which became hugely profitable when the textile industry boomed during the war years. The brothers were later to diversify into automobiles.

Sada called it the Futaba House but from the start everyone else called it the Futaba Palace. It was a flamboyantly eccentric building, a jumble of disparate shapes and styles like an assemblage of a child's building blocks on a giant scale. Its tiled roofs were as precipitous as ski jumps, creating brilliant splashes of brick red. One swept down three floors at the front of the house while another created a Swiss chalet effect at the back. There were arches, gables, a cupola roof over the stone-clad bay window of the ballroom and an entrance porch with thick mock-Doric pillars. It might have been a Moorish palace or a Spanish villa transported to Japan. As far as most people were concerned, it was the last word in glamour and perfectly suited Sada's sparkling, rather showy personality.

The fourteen rooms on the ground floor included the grand ballroom, dining room, tea room, study, tatami-matted living rooms, butler's room, kitchens, servants' quarters and guest rooms. There was also a billiards room; Sada and Momosuké were enthusiastic players. Plentiful supplies of sake and wine were stored in the cellar.

Upstairs were Sada and Momosuké's private suites. They had separate bathrooms, dressing rooms with walk-in closets, a make-up room for Sada and a private study for Momosuké. There was a Chinese room ornately decorated and furnished in Chinese style and a room where Sada kept her collection of china dolls.

Besides the main house there were stables, garages, a guard house and a house for the gardener. In the attic was an electricity generator which provided power.

There Sada held court. With Momosuké she would drive through the wooded grounds, past the landscaped gardens with their carefully placed ponds, bushes and stone lanterns, to the porch. There they would alight while the chauffeur parked the car. Momosuké had a Packard, a showy American automobile which he imported privately from the Packard works in Warren, Ohio. He and his son Komakichi, a car fanatic, owned the only ones in Japan and updated them each year. Momosuké's Packard was famous. It was as potent a mark of glamour as a Ferrari is today.

Inside was a splendid entrance hall with a spiral staircase. When they had balls Sada would sweep down to greet the throng. One of the glories of the house was the Tiffany-style stained glass windows. Some depicted flowers and birds, others were stylised designs of the rushing blue and grey waters of the Kiso River, tumbling across rocks.

To launch her life out of the spotlight, Sada founded a spinning and weaving company called the Kawakami Silk Company. The textile industry was booming and she loved fashion, so it made perfect sense. The company produced beautiful silk sold under the brand names Yakko Meisen and Yakko Silk. She invited engineering consultants from Switzerland and France and employed professionals to manage the day-to-day affairs for her; but she laid down the principles.

Having known hardship herself, she wanted her employees to be properly treated. Young women who worked in the mills were usually indentured labourers, virtual slaves. By law they were supposed to work a maximum of eleven hours a day but in reality often worked much longer. Sada employed forty to fifty young women aged between fifteen and twenty. They lived in dormitories, wore black sailor suits and worked a mere eight hours a day with a break every hour. In the evening they learned tea ceremony, flower arrangement and sewing. Sada's enlightened management attracted great attention. Everyone commented on what a classy, 'high collar' concern her company was.

Perhaps because Sada had no children, she liked to surround herself with young women and help them acquire skills which would enable them to be independent. She badly needed an heir. No matter how much she loved and cherished Momosuké and how much he loved her, she was still only his mistress. She needed children to care for her when she got old, tend her grave and ensure that her family line did not die out.

In 1918 she adopted a son, a handsome, studious nineteen-year-old named Hirozo Ino. Hirozo was a relative of Momosuké from his mother's side of the family. The family had sacrificed a great deal so that Momosuké could study at Keio University. Once he could afford it, Momosuké did all he could to repay the debt and helped as many family members as he could, such as by adopting poor relations.

Two years later Tomiji Iwasaki joined Sada's family. Tomiji's grandfather was Momosuké's cousin. Tomiji was the oldest of nine siblings. When her family fell on hard times, Momosuké had taken her and her grandmother to live with him in his house on the Shibuya estate in Tokyo. She had gone to school from there. When he moved to Nagoya he took her to the newly completed Futaba Palace to be Sada's 'daughter-in-training'. She was thirteen.

Tomiji and Hirozo were second cousins; Tomiji's grandmother and Hirozo's mother were sisters. The plan was for them to marry, take the Kawakami name and produce heirs who would be Sada's descendants.

From the start Tomiji and Sada adored each other. Tomiji was a lovely child. She had a fresh, pretty face with a tiny nose, rosebud mouth and narrow eyes. She was rather delicate, so instead of going to school she stayed at home with Sada. She became her shadow. She was always with her and did everything for her.

Although she had retired, Sada had not given up her ambitions in the acting world. Her career might have come to an end in Japan, but she was still a superstar abroad. Besides, as she joked to a journalist, she might be an old maid in Japan, but in the West Ellen Terry had found a thirty-year-old husband at the age of sixty. There was no reason why she shouldn't do the same!

In 1920 she planned another foreign trip. She contacted Loie Fuller and asked her to arrange it but Fuller was discouraging. She had seen the Kawakami productions during the 1907 visit to Europe and was concerned that Sada had absorbed so much of the Western style of acting. Western audiences had recently thrilled to the productions of *Les Ballets Russes*. They were hungry for colour, exuberance, exotic costumes and barbaric dancing. The more realistic Sada's acting became, the less appeal she had for a Western audience.

Sada got as far as applying for a travel permit to tour the United States.

But at the time America was clamping down on immigration from Japan and suspicious of all applicants, no matter how seemingly above board, so the Japanese Foreign Ministry refused it. The door was firmly closed.

That same year – 1920 – Tomiji entered her life. Sada imagined a glorious career for her. She would be the next Sadayakko, Sadayakko II, and would carry on her work. She arranged lessons for her in piano, *koto* (the classical zither, Sada's instrument), traditional Japanese dance and flower arrangement. And whenever they went to the Kiso Valley, Tomiji had English lessons with an American woman called Mrs Fox in the hopes that one day she would go abroad.

Outside the sprawling smoky cities, beyond the perimeters of the towns bustling with manufacturing activity, Japan was still virtually in the Middle Ages. The highways were little more than broad earthen tracks cutting through moorland, scrub and woodland and skirting the occasional village of thatched houses surrounded by paddy fields and vegetable patches. The mountains, dark with forest, rolled range upon range until they merged with the sky on the horizon.

The Kiso Valley sliced through some of the most spectacular country-side in Japan. In the time of the shoguns, when the only mode of transport was on foot or by palanquin, the climb through the Kiso range was the roughest part of the journey between Kyoto and Tokyo. Sheer mountains covered in impenetrable forest plunged to the water's edge. Clouds billowed like smoke in the hollows. In the rainy season the river roared like a waterfall as it surged towards the sea.

At the point where the highway crossed the river, three hours from Nagoya on a noisy smoke-belching train, there was a small town called Midono. There, across the river from the town, Momosuké had a villa built where he could stay while he oversaw the building of his first power stations. He went to New York to raise funding and hired American engineers who were experts in hydro-electric technology.

The villa was completed in 1919. To Momosuké and Sada it was a modest *pied à terre*; but to the people of Midono, who lived in cramped wooden houses, it was a palace. It was a pretty, grey, three-storeyed building, made of rounded stones straight from the riverbed covered in a wash of cement. It had a red, tiled roof with a chimney, an outside balcony upstairs and a conservatory with tables and wicker chairs where Momosuké and Sada could sit and look over the river. There was a dining room and a lounge, with chandeliers and a fireplace, where they entertained a constant stream of guests. There was also, of course, a billiards room. There is a photograph of Momosuké outside the house with his bicycle in a cycling suit and a cotton hat. The huge windows are thrown wide open. Sada and Tomiji are sitting inside. It is a lovely, breezy country retreat.

Just across the road was a sprawling compound like a little America. Seventy or eighty American engineers and their families were housed there with a small primary school for their children and a dance hall. There were also guest houses for the many visitors who came to admire the dazzling new technology and inspect the colossal construction projects. At the height of the building work 2000 Japanese workers lived in huts in the rice fields or rented houses from the villagers. The quiet life of the valley, unchanged for centuries, had vanished for ever.

To the villagers it was as if aliens had descended. Even more than by the bug-eyed foreigners, they were fascinated by the legendary stage star, Sadayakko. They addressed her deferentially as 'Madame Sadayakko'. But they spoke of her as the 'Queen of Kiso Valley'.

One of the village children, Ryokichi Matsusei, now eighty-eight, remembers her roaring along the stony tracks of Midono on her big red motorcycle in her red leather boots. The bike was a classic Indian, developed in the United States in 1901 and world famous for its quality and beauty.

Nobody in the village had ever seen a motorbike before. When the children saw her careering along the gravelly road, dust kicking from the spinning tyres, they would run after her shouting, 'Sadayakko's come! Sadayakko's come!' Once the motor suddenly cut out and the road became eerily silent. The children ran back to the school and summoned the villagers, who flocked out to mend it.

Sada often roared off to look at the building work. When Momosuké wanted to go to a building site, she took him in the side car. Once they went to check a particularly deep shaft in the mountainside. Even the engineers were wary of going down it. But Sada was fearless. Gaily she climbed into the cage alongside Momosuké and was lowered into the blackness. Her verve inspired everyone.

Momosuké and Sada were always together. They went for walks in their Western clothes, she in a long skirt, carrying an umbrella even when there was no sign of rain. All the villagers kept horses. Sada borrowed one and would gallop off along the riverside in jodhpurs and riding hat, her long hair tied in a loose bun.

Most of the villagers were too timid to speak to the grand people from the big city. But Sada was kind to young Ryokichi. She invited him into the villa to play and gave him chocolate, an unknown luxury just imported for the first time. He took it home carefully in its wrapper and eked it out, eating a little each day.

The Americans needed a daily diet of meat so Sada ordered regular deliveries of chicken, which provided a handy source of income for the villagers. Once they ran out of chicken and caught a bullfrog instead, hoping that the ravenous Westerners would not notice the difference. In the evening, after dinner, one of the engineers would pick up an accordion, feet would start tapping and soon people would start dancing. Tomiji used to peek timidly through the window, wondering at the energy of these foreigners who worked all day and danced till so late at night.

Mr Fox and Mr Peace were in charge of engineering operations. In photographs they look a jowly, good-natured pair in their waistcoats, ribbon ties and cowboy hats. Mrs Fox gave Tomiji English lessons – though as neither of them could speak the other's language, progress was slow. Tomiji never progressed much beyond, 'How do you do this morning, Madam?'

The Kiso project was a monumental enterprise. It went on for years. Mountains were gouged out to make tunnels and aqueducts and enormous conduits pushed through to channel water from the river. Power stations were built, American turbines the size of steam engines installed. The beautiful valley became an inferno of grinding, roaring and incessant hubbub.

Besides power stations, Momosuké designed a suspension bridge; before that people had crossed the Kiso by boat. Initially he planned to bridge a narrow stretch of the river, to link the villa to the town with its railway station. But then he decided to build the bridge slightly upriver where it was wider, so that he could make it longer and more impressive.

He named it Momo Bridge, Peach Bridge, *'momo'* meaning 'peach'. But everyone called it Momosuké Bridge. The grand opening was in 1922. A Shinto priest performed a blessing and three generations of couples crossed the bridge to ensure good luck. First came an elderly couple, then Momosuké and Sada, representing the middle-aged couple, then a young couple.

In a photograph of the opening, Momosuké is in a boater, straw sandals and a men's kimono, with his umbrella folded. Sada, at fifty-one, is still amazingly beautiful. She gazes around with bright, youthful eyes. Behind, a horde of guests tramp across the bridge while a mass of people wait their turn on the other side of the river. Nowadays the riverbed which Momosuké Bridge crosses is nearly dry; the river has narrowed to a trickle as a result of Momosuké's building works. The bridge, like a miniature Brooklyn Bridge, rises unexpectedly in the Kiso countryside.

Momosuké built six massive turbine halls along the Kiso River, with gargantuan pipes snaking down the mountainside behind, channelling water. They are elegant 1920s creations, designed with care so as not to impact too harshly on the landscape. But his masterwork was still to come. It was not enough for him to create electricity from the raging waters of the Kiso. He wanted to build a mighty dam that would generate enough energy to send Japan and its industry surging into the modern age.

After several journeys to New York to organise finance, his Consolidated Electric Power Company raised $15 million, to be paid back over twenty years. At the time, America led the world in dam technology. The Buffalo Bill dam, on the Shoshone River in Cody, Wyoming, was the highest in the world. Momosuké hired American engineers to design and build Japan's first hydro-electric dam.

Before work began, Momosuké and Sada, along with friends and helpers, made a pilgrimage up nearby Mount Ontaké, to ask the deity of the mountain for blessing and to pray for the work to be completed safely. They had a photograph taken at the top. Momosuké, in climbing boots, holding a stick, gazes into the distance with a visionary look as if he is already planning his next great enterprise. Sada is in straw sandals and a fur stole. She looks at the camera, unsmiling. She is no longer Yakko the famous actress, out to charm the world. She is Sada, the helpmeet, supporter and love of Momosuké.

For two years builders worked day and night, swarming across the ever-growing face of the great dam shouldering hods laden with rocks, putting them in place by hand. Some lost their lives. At one point the dam began to collapse. But finally in 1924 Oi Dam was completed. Momosuké's seven-year-old grandson, Kakumasa, the son of the rather strange Tatsuzo, pulled the string to unveil it at the opening.

The dam feeds Kyoto and Osaka with electricity to this day. It is a massive, handsome edifice, American Deco in style, reminiscent of the work of Frank Lloyd Wright. Below the dam, the river bursts free and surges as wildly as ever. Above is a huge becalmed lake. The landscape has been transformed for ever.

For the five years that work went on in Kiso, Sada, Momosuké and their entourage regularly made the three-hour train journey, rattling along in the little wooden train carriage through the beautiful mountain scenery between Nagoya and Midono. Momosuké's ground-breaking work had earned him a new nickname: the King of Electric Power. And everyone knew the romantic story of the beautiful actress and the business tycoon. Whenever the pair were in Nagoya, everyone from the prime minister down leapt on the train from Tokyo to visit. They called it the Pilgrimage to Futaba Palace.

While Momosuké focused on the intricacies of his businesses, Sada was unquestionably queen of the house. Every detail of the housekeeping and entertaining had to be perfect. She was the fiery one who scolded Tomiji and the servants while the gentlemanly, mild-mannered Momosuké kept the peace. He joked to guests that he was a guest too. After all, it was Sada's house. She made the decisions and kept the whole operation running smoothly. But no one doubted their devotion to each other. Tomiji remembered her knitting socks for him even when she was at her busiest.

Every morning Tomiji woke Sada at six o'clock. Momosuké rose an hour earlier and went for a bicycle ride around Nagoya Castle. While he read the papers, Tomiji helped Sada oil her hair, put it up and apply her make-up. Then Sada prayed to her guardian deity, Fudo Myo-o. When she was busy, Tomiji prayed instead. For breakfast Momosuké had porridge while Sada preferred traditional miso soup and rice. After he had left for work, she would call the Kawakami Silk Company and deal with the business there by phone.

In the daytime friends from Sada's past sometimes came to visit. Her confidantes were geisha who like her had married powerful men and risen in the world. They would mull over old times. Sometimes they played the shamisen together and sang or danced, gliding with practised grace about the tatami-matted room.

Business entertaining was a key part of Momosuké's work. Every day Sada planned the menus, allowing for ten to twenty guests. There were three chefs turning out four-course dinners of Western food plus simple Japanese fare for Tomiji and Hirozo. Besides the invited guests, an incessant stream of friends dropped by at meal times. On particularly grand or lively occasions, Sada hired geisha and *taikomochi* jesters to provide entertainment.

The parties at Futaba Palace were legendary. The most spectacular was Momosuké's annual birthday celebration on 25 June, at the height of the rainy season. There were always at least a hundred guests, drawing up at the front porch in their automobiles and crowding into the grand ballroom. The great men from the worlds of business and politics made sure they were there, including the presidents of Momosuké's companies, together with their wives. Sada used to rent a stage from the Misono-za Theatre in Nagoya. Everyone knew they would be called upon to perform and practised for months beforehand.

Momosuké was a quiet, haughty, rather inward-looking man. But he had an unexpected talent for letting his hair down. There are a couple of photographs, taken at one of the parties, which show him transformed into an Edo period courtesan. His elegant features are covered in white make-up, his lips red and his eyebrows painted in high on his forehead. He is togged out in an oiled wig, sparkling head-dress and ornate multi-layered kimono, with the obi prominently knotted at the front in classic style, inviting potential clients to untie it. In one picture he is reclining languorously with a sultry pout on his rosebud lips, a quizzical, coquettish look on his face. The other is a close up. With his long nose he makes a convincingly aristocratic, if rather elderly, courtesan.

At one party a prominent member of the cabinet presented the couple with a pair of scrolls. He had brushed a humorous painting on each and added some witty lines of verse, punning on 'Yakko', literally 'a low-ranking retainer of a samurai', and 'Momo', 'peach'. One shows a kite in the shape of a squat, shaven-headed comic-book-style retainer, in samurai skirt and clogs, with wings like a butterfly. He is firmly wedged in a peach tree. The inscription reads:

Can it be the rustle of a kite, caught in the branches of the peach tree?[1]

In the other the determined little samurai, scowling and flapping his wings as hard as he can, has escaped from the tree and is flying high above it, still attached by his string. The poem reads:

Riding the wind, it has the power to uproot the tree.[2]

Both were gentle jokes on how closely and inextricably Momosuké and Sada were bound together and how they nourished each other. The samurai retainer, the poems suggested, might be the stronger of the two.

Mild-mannered though he was, there were times when Momosuké asserted his authority. One was on the question of Tomiji. It was apparent that Sada was grooming her to become another Sadayakko. One day he spoke his mind in his grave, gentlemanly fashion. They had deliberately chosen a sober, well-behaved country girl, he said, in order to provide descendants for Sada. The plan had never been that she should enter the decadent and precarious world of the stage.

'If she becomes an actress,' he said, 'she may not have a child. If she doesn't have a child she won't be able to take care of your grave and the family line will end there.'

Presumably he meant that if she focused on her career she might put off having a child until it was too late and, like Sada, end up childless. So Tomiji's training in music and dancing stopped, though Sada secretly taught her the crane and tortoise dance, her own favourite. In January 1924 Tomiji married Hirozo. She was seventeen, Hirozo twenty-five.

With the opening of Oi Dam, Momosuké's work was completed. He was chairman of more than seventy companies, all established and flourishing. His years with Sada had been the best of his life. With her at his side he had had the courage and confidence to step out, take great risks and win great rewards. Now he was becoming tired. Both he and Sada were aware that they were nearing the end of their lives. It was time to rest and prepare for old age.

Besides Futaba Palace in Nagoya, Sada had a home in Tokyo called the House of Peach Water, named after Momosuké. The pair began spending more and more time there. It was smaller than Futaba Palace but still very grand. It was in a most desirable area, right in the centre of the city, a couple of blocks from the Imperial Palace, just below the hillside where the Diet, the Japanese Parliament, was to be built.

Tokyo was no longer the city Sada had known as a child. In 1923 it had been destroyed by earthquake. The cataclysmic jolts began just before noon on 1 September, when millions of charcoal braziers and gas burners were alight cooking the midday meal. The Asakusa Twelve Storeys, the splendid brick-built Cloud Scraper which had towered over the east end, broke in half; temples crumpled under their heavy thatched roofs; flimsy wooden houses tumbled like packs of cards. Firestorms exploded, lit by the burning braziers. Huge tracts of the older parts of the city were made of wood and blazed uncontrollably for nearly two days though many of the grand Western-style brick and stone edifices in the city centre survived. More than 130,000 people died and 2.5 million lost their homes.

A new Tokyo began to rise from the rubble, hurriedly put together in a frenzy of building. As before there were rabbit warrens of streets lined with flimsy wooden houses, but they were different streets of different buildings. Many of the familiar old places disappeared. Little by little the charming canals down which Sada had wafted as a young geisha were replaced by roads and railways. The old city and the old life had gone.

Emperor Taisho turned out to be mad. He had been removed in 1920 and replaced by his son Hirohito, who became Regent. The period was still called the Taisho era. It was an age of hedonism, of flappers and fast cars, ice cream and movies. Young women sported flapper hairstyles and daringly short flapper skirts, young men grew their hair long. They combed it straight back in the 'all-back' style and devoured the works of Karl Marx until the authorities banned them. People dubbed the mood of freedom and excess 'Taisho democracy'. But there was a disturbing feeling in the air. As a writer of the time put it, they were 'dancing in a town that has no tomorrow'.

Taisho died in 1926. The traditional coffin bearers came down by train from Kyoto, bringing the imperial coffin. Hirohito ascended the chrysanthemum throne. A new era, the Showa era, began.

Sada closed the Kawakami Silk Company. In the aftermath of the earthquake, people had no spare cash for luxuries and the company had begun making a loss; added to which, it was based in Nagoya, not Tokyo. But she still had a yearning for the theatre. In September 1924 she conducted auditions of youngsters aged nine to sixteen. The Kawakami Children's Music and Drama School opened in December in a two-floor house in central Tokyo. The following year she moved it to the Tokyo suburbs and had a building constructed there for the children to board. She took on teachers and staff. Sada and Tomiji had rooms on the upper floor where they stayed when they were teaching. The school crest was a peach.

Every year the students put on dramas and dance displays at the Imperial Theatre. In 1926 they performed *Peach Boy* and *The Crane and the Tortoise*, based on Japanese fairytales. Several pupils went on to become well-known actors.

Eventually, on Momosuké's advice, Sada sent Tomiji back to live with Hirozo in Nagoya. Running Futaba Palace and its staff was a full-time job. In 1930, Momosuké and Sada had a very special reason for visiting Futaba Palace. Tomiji had had a baby two months earlier – an heir for Sada – and Sada had yet to see her. Sada had always told Tomiji that she hated babies. Perhaps because she had never had a child she had convinced herself that that was for the best. She was too wilful to make a good mother, she said. Growing up as a young geisha, she had been taught that becoming pregnant was a disaster and an embarrassment. Rather than having a child of her own, she said, she much preferred adopting people she liked.

So when Tomiji heard cars rumbling along the gravelled drive and pulling up in the porch, she hurriedly tied the baby onto the back of one of the maids and sent her outside so that Sada would not be bothered.

Momosuké and Sada always travelled with an entourage. Whenever they went to Nagoya, Sada sent a couple of maids on beforehand to make sure everything in the house was to her liking. There was great excitement when they arrived. Tomiji was on her hands and knees, bowing to greet them. But the pair had barely reached the entrance porch when they cried out in unison, 'Baby! Baby! Where is Baby?' They used the English word 'baby'. They refused to take a single step until they had seen her. The maid was hurriedly summoned back with the baby and Sada gathered her into her arms. She stood holding her, her face a picture of delight.

'I've never ever held a baby before,' she cooed in her high-pitched warble. 'She's so sweet, so sweet!'

Momosuké too was enchanted. The baby was named Hatsu, 'first'. She was the first of Sada's family line. Hatsu – now a lively, bright-eyed woman in her seventies – remembers growing up at Futaba Palace. Everyone but her was nervous whenever Sada was around, she says. Even the bodyguards, who were judo black belts, were on their toes. But to her Sada was the most loving of grandmothers. She would look at her and her face would wreathe in smiles.

'Ah, Hatsuko!' she would coo, 'Little Hatsu!'

Hatsu addressed her very politely as 'Grandmother', not 'Granny'. Every morning she would toddle down the long tatami-matted corridor, curl her chubby legs into a kneeling position and slide open the door to Sada's room. She would bow politely and squeak in her baby voice, 'Good morning, Grandmother.'

Sada would chirp, 'Morning, Hatsuko. Come in, come in!'

'I just thought she was an ordinary grandmother,' remembers Hatsu. 'When I went to school my teacher and friends told me she had been a famous actress. I said, "*Ah, so! Is that so!*"'

As the years passed, Sada seemed to want to forget she had ever been an actress. Even to Tomiji, she never talked about it. It was as if she wanted to put it behind her. She was absorbed in her new life; and the old life was something about which she felt uncomfortable. It was outside of what was socially acceptable. She told stories from her childhood, about how she had run away from home with nothing but her toy box and gone to live at the Hamada house. She reminisced about the hardships she and Otojiro had suffered in America and how wonderful it had been to taste food after they nearly starved to death. She spoke of how they went to Paris and finally made some money, enough to buy a diamond ring. But she never mentioned that she had been an actress or talked about her days as an actress in Japan.

Tomiji, Hatsu and Sada's biographers always insist that Sada never wanted to be an actress. She began acting, they say, against her will, to save the troupe from failure in America. She was simply an obedient and devoted wife to Otojiro and it was her duty to help his work. In fact, as we know, she rehearsed in Kobe with the troupe before they had even left for America; and when they reached San Francisco they found posters with her picture pasted all over the city.

The family also insists that Sada and Momosuké had a purely business relationship. She was a widow and needed someone to support her; she could not survive on her own. As for him, he needed a manager for his household in Nagoya to help with business entertaining; as an ex-geisha, she was the ideal choice. (The house might have been in Sada's name, but everyone knew that the money underpinning it was Momosuké's.) But they were not lovers, absolutely not. Perish the thought! Contemporary commentators, as we have seen, saw things differently.

Tomiji, of course, did not even enter Sada's life until Sada was nearly fifty and becoming old and conservative. Tomiji herself was a sober country girl and conservative too. After Sada's death she became the custodian of her memory. She was determined that her adoptive mother's lasting image should be decorous and decent.

Momosuké's health had never been good. In 1927 he had a slight stroke. He had a kidney removed, then the other was infected with tuberculosis. In 1928, at the age of sixty, he retired. Sada gave up teaching at the

Kawakami Music and Drama School to take care of him. Eventually she closed it. Their time together was coming to an end. She wanted to be free to enjoy the last precious years in peace. So the years quietly passed and the two grew older together.

At some point Sada sold the House of Peach Water and had a luxurious residence built in Kawada-cho, an exclusive Millionaires' Row in the north of Tokyo. The neighbouring residence was the mansion of Baron Ogasawara, an ex-*daimyo*. Sada's was even larger. It occupied an entire city block. Ever restless, she spent hours with architects and carpenters, discussing every detail of the construction.

Pure Japanese in style, the house was made of top-grade, knot-free cedar specially transported from the Kiso Valley. It was 150 feet from front to back. The rooms seemed to go on for ever. You slid open a set of exquisitely painted *fusuma* doors and stepped into a vast, gracious tatami-matted room only to see another set of *fusuma* doors on the far side leading to yet another room. In summer, when all the doors were taken out so that the breeze flowed through, it was as vast and airy as the legendary harem where the shogun used to keep his hundreds of concubines. The house boasted the very latest luxury, underfloor steam central heating, carried in lead pipes in the basement. There was also a spacious, landscaped Japanese garden.

Several times burglars broke in even when there were people in the house. It was so huge that no one could hear them. So Sada had locks installed at the bottom of the doors. When people went from room to room they had to unlock the doors before sliding them open.

In 1933, when Momosuké was sixty-five and Sada sixty-two, the pair decided it was time for him to move back to his home in Shibuya. In Japanese parlance, Sada 'returned Momosuké to Fusa'. They held a solemn ceremony to mark the end of an era. They had been together more than twenty years. Sada had never hoped for nor expected so much happiness in the second half of her life.

.There are pictures of the two in old age. Sada wears glasses and her face has become a little stern. She is still a fine-looking woman but the pretty softness is fading and her features are growing hard. Her life has been a struggle and her face shows it. Momosuké still has a fey, ethereal look about him. The haughty, aristocratic features, wide-spaced eyes and eyebrows raised in an expression of faint bemusement have not changed. He is an old man, but handsome still.

They parted very formally with no more than bows and polite expressions of good wishes. Their feelings lay too deep for words or tears. Momosuké's bags had been packed. The chauffeur cranked up the Packard's engine, Momosuké climbed into the back seat and disappeared in a cloud of dust to his house on the Fukuzawa estates. It was only a few miles across Tokyo but it might as well have been the other side of the earth. They both knew all too well it was the last time they would ever see each other.

Tomiji explained their decision in traditional terms. 'Sada always walked one step behind Momosuké,' she said. 'She always tried to set Fusa higher. That is why she returned Momosuké to Fusa before his death.'[3]

Fusa was the wife, Sada the geisha mistress. As a geisha, she knew that to serve her man best, it was her duty to preserve his marriage. Along the way she may have forgotten. She may have hoped and prayed it could be otherwise. But in the end she knew she would be called upon to sacrifice her own happiness. Marriage, the socially recognised bond between families, was the rock on which society stood. It was paramount. Sada and Momosuké may have been prepared to shock when they were younger; but as they grew older and more conservative, they wanted to put everything in order. So they took the traditional Japanese path. They put *giri*, their duty to society, before *ninjo*, their personal feelings. They suffered as a result. But they had done the right thing as they saw it.

Momosuké had never broken entirely with Fusa. Over the years he had always fulfilled the minimum requirements of a husband. Wherever he went, whatever he did, he always sent Fusa a note telling her where he was. Before he moved back to Shibuya he often visited and stayed in his house there. He loved spending time with his sons and four grandchildren.

In those days people in Japan seldom divorced. Wives knew that their feckless husbands would eventually return to them when they were old. But Fusa was consumed with rage and anger against Momosuké, and the longer he lived with Sada the worse it became. She would never let him set foot in her house.

Kakumasa, Momosuké's oldest grandson, had been born in 1917. A merry, elfin man in his eighties, he has very clear memories of all the players in the story. He recalls:

My grandfather was a genius at making money. When I was a child he always had the radio right next to him. He would listen to highlights of the stock market and give orders by phone to buy or sell stocks even when he couldn't walk any more. Whenever I dropped in, he'd mention how much money he made that day.

Momosuké never gave up visiting teahouses. He was such an *aficionado* of the geisha world that he took Kakumasa along with him at the tender age of ten. They went to see the famous fireworks spectacular that took place every summer on the Sumida River.

'We went to a teahouse at Ryogoku, just the two of us,' remembers Kakumasa. 'There were crowds of people. Five beautiful geisha sat at our table and played the shamisen and sang.

'But,' he goes on, 'my grandfather's only *aite* [companion] was Sadayakko. He didn't move from woman to woman. He lived with Sadayakko, only Sadayakko.'

Understandably, Fusa was furious at Momosuké for taking the little boy along. Kakumasa remembers:

Grandmother was very serious and intellectual and talked in an educated, samurai way. She probably felt superior because Sadayakko was a geisha and below her. She used to complain about Granddad to me. 'That ne'er-do-well!' she'd say. 'He never comes home.' I heard she used to go to his house and argue. But that was before I was born.

He remembers Sada as a very beautiful woman. Somehow she did not seem old. He called her 'Auntie', not 'Granny', even though she and his grandmother were the same age. He remembers her high-pitched voice and charming, light-hearted chatter. She had the patter and intonation of an Edo-ite born and bred, like a Cockney born within the sound of Bow Bells or a native of the Bronx. Two women could not have been more different.

297

Momosuké spent his last years living very quietly in the house on the Shibuya estate. Tomiji's grandmother took care of him and he had five maids and a cook. He spent a lot of time with his grandchildren, particularly Naomi, Kakumasa's younger sister. Kakumasa was Fusa's favourite. But from early on Naomi lived with Momosuké and Sada. The child flitted back and forth between the two houses and took the role of companion for Momosuké's old age. Perhaps she also carried messages between the two from time to time.

Momosuké enjoyed writing. He used to say he would have become a poet if he had not come from a poor family and been forced to become a businessman. He set to work to write his memoirs. Little by little his health declined. In a picture of him taken the year he died, he looks old and sad. There is a droop to his mouth that was not there during his years with Sada.

Eventually he could no longer walk or talk. He died on 15 February 1938, not long before his seventieth birthday. Naomi was the only person with him. Fusa was not on the estate but at one of her country villas. The little girl instinctively called Sada.

Sada rushed to the house. It was the first and last time she ever went to the Fukuzawa estate. Everyone was in a panic. Quietly and competently she took charge. She did what every geisha knew would be her last duty to her lover: to organise his funeral and support his wife and family. She called priests and informed the family temple so that prayers could be started immediately. She instructed servants to shave and wash the corpse and called Mitsukoshi department store to organise funeral clothes. She drew up the guest list, planned the seating and did everything else required to ensure that the funeral would be correct and in order. Perhaps she also managed to spend a few minutes alone with Momosuké to make her private farewells.

She made sure she left the estate before Fusa returned and went back to her house in Kawada-cho to mourn in private.

The funeral was huge and grand, as befitted Momosuké's achievements and standing in life. A cavalcade of automobiles drew up at the gates of the Fukuzawa estate carrying the nation's wealthiest and most powerful men – the movers and shakers, tycoons and political leaders who had been Momosuké's associates. Sada, who had known them all far better than Fusa, was not there. As the mistress, she could have no place at his funeral. Kakumasa remembers:

> After my grandfather died, whenever the subject of him came up, my grandmother would say ironically that he received the punishment he deserved. But she also used to say that the only great and attractive man in the world was him. She died at the age of eighty-five. Even at the moment of her death, she did not forgive my grandfather.

Momosuké had chosen to be buried near the Iwasaki family home instead of in the Fukuzawa graveyard. By then Sada had a temple of her own. She had a memorial to him installed in the grounds.

After she returned Momosuké to Fusa, Sada began to put her own affairs in order. She sold Futaba Palace. Tomiji, Hirozo and Hatsu moved to a smaller house nearby. The splendid mansion with its steep red roofs became a workers' dormitory for the Consolidated Electric Power Company that Momosuké had founded.

With the money and assets, Sada had a temple built beside the River Kiso, many miles downriver from Oi Dam, where it flowed broad and blue between pyramid-shaped hills densely covered in trees and ferns. She called it Teishoji. *Tei* is written with the character for 'Sada' and means 'chastity' or 'constancy'. *Sho* means 'to shine', *ji* is 'temple'. It was the Temple of Shining Chastity or Shining Constancy, 'Sada's Temple'.

Like having a church built, founding a temple was something that only the very wealthy could contemplate. As a geisha, she was a fallen woman. No matter how rich and famous she became and how loyally she served her various men, she could never erase that stigma. To build a temple was a way of finding not only immortality but a sort of redemption.

Teishoji was a modest, pretty building with a steep copper-tiled roof, set in spacious grounds tucked at the foot of densely wooded hills. Butterflies and dragonflies fluttered in summer, cicadas shrilled and birds twittered. The rushing river, dotted with craggy islands and alive with trout, was a few minutes' walk away.

The temple was dedicated to Fudo Myo-o, the Buddhist deity who was Sada's guardian, and housed an image of him. Sada commissioned an artist to paint scenes of the eight times in her life when she believed he had intervened to save her. She had them carved into wooden tableaux and installed along the outer walls where pilgrims could see them. One shows her as a young girl, being attacked by wild dogs while out riding. Instead of Momosuké, Fudo Myo-o is saving her. In another, she and Otojiro are in a little boat, tossed on mighty waves. In the last she is on her knees in front of Oi Dam, praying fervently, while Fudo Myo-o hovers above.

She had a storehouse built in the grounds to hold her costumes, belongings and all the other precious things she had collected in her life. She also decided on the place for her tomb, in a secluded hollow in the hillside behind the main building, shaded by groves of maple and bamboo. The temple was consecrated in a solemn ceremony on 28 October 1933. Next she had a villa built near the temple, right on the banks of the river. It was an idyllic place. The grounds, fragrant with flowering cherries, maples, pines and swaying bamboo groves, stretched to the river's edge.

There were twenty-six rooms rambling around a central courtyard planted with different varieties of moss. Most rooms had tatami floors and antique wooden doors painted with Buddhist angels, landscapes or legendary scenes. The prettiest section was Sada's suite, with a tiled conservatory with diamond-paned windows looking out across the lawns to the river and the quiet hills. There was also a thatched teahouse, outhouses and garages. The house was spacious enough to accommodate family, servants and the stream of visitors who came to pay homage to the grand old lady.

Sada named it Bansho'en, the Garden of Evening Pines. It was the name Prince Ito had chosen for the Chigasaki villa thirty years before. She hung the scroll on which he had brushed the words in the entrance.

She was still a celebrity. Early in 1937 she gave a series of interviews to the *Asahi* newspaper, telling the story of her escapades with Otojiro. She was sixty-five. There is a picture of her in a wicker chair, very upright, a cushion behind her back. Her hair is black, her skin unlined. Her face is unfathomable. The gay, smiling Yakko of the actress years has disappeared. It is a formal portrait of a dignified dowager.

Otojiro's niece Tsuru Aoki, who had stayed behind in San Francisco at the age of eleven, had recently returned to Japan after nearly forty years. She had had a spectacular career. She had formed her own acting troupe in Los Angeles. When a brilliant young Japanese actor named Sesshu Hayakawa arrived on tour, she recommended him to a Hollywood producer.

Hayakawa became the first Japanese movie star, combining the three qualities that women supposedly found irresistible: 'cruel, exotic and handsome'. He starred in Cecil B. De Mille's *The Cheat* and many years later was to be nominated for an Academy Award for his role in *The Bridge on the River Kwai*. Tsuru also acted in movies. The couple led a glamorous Hollywood life in a mansion called Greystone Castle. It was all due to Otojiro and Sada, who had taken her to America so many years before.

'When Tsuruko came back to Japan, it was just like a dream,' Sada told her interviewer. 'After forty years this little child suddenly appeared in front of me, turned into a plump middle-aged woman. It was a really strange feeling.

'This has turned into an old woman's endless talk, hasn't it!' she added, laughing. She did not once mention Momosuké, neither did the journalist ask.

Sada's life revolved around her three homes: Kawada-cho in Tokyo, the Garden of Evening Pines and a small villa in the hilly, semi-tropical seaside spa resort of Atami, where she went in winter to take the health-giving mineral-rich waters. Hatsu remembers her sitting in her room, arranging flowers hour after hour.

But outside the walls of her peaceful villas, life was growing dark and strange. Japan's flirtation with all things Western had reached its height in the halcyon days of 'Taisho Democracy'. Now that time had disappeared and was replaced by an era which people later spoke of as the 'Dark Valley'.

The nineteen-thirties were marked by a series of assassinations and attempted military coups. The army had grown more and more powerful. In 1931, defying the corrupt and ineffective civilian government, troops occupied Manchuria. In 1932 the moderate prime minister, Tsuyoshi Inukai, was shot in the head by naval officers, one of three prime ministers to be assassinated in these years. In February 1936, 1400 men of the élite First Division and Imperial Guard took over the Diet, the Ministry of War and the police headquarters and sent death squads to execute leading members of the government. The coup was halted and the leaders executed, but senior army officers insisted they needed yet greater powers to maintain order. In 1937 Japan invaded China. The horrific massacre at Nanjing followed.

If Sada read the papers she would have known something of all this, though there were thought police to impose censorship and editors knew better than to antagonise the military. She certainly heard of the thrilling scandal of Sada Abé, found wandering the streets in 1936 with her lover's severed penis tucked into her kimono sleeve; the story was immortalised in Nagisa Oshima's post-war film, *In the Realm of the Senses*. Ordinary people going about their daily lives preferred titillating tales to gloomy news.

But by 1940 no one could ignore the fact that Japan was at war. The government had signed the Tripartite Pact with Germany and Italy. Japanese troops, having occupied much of China, were marching through the jungles of south-east Asia.

Most people's first experience of the war was rationing. The military needed every possible resource and goods on the shelves of shops quickly grew scarce. Anything Western came to seem unpatriotic. People stopped using Western words, smoking Western cigarettes and wearing Western fashions. Women opted for narrow-sleeved kimonos to save on fabric, or traditional peasant garb of baggy cotton trousers and jackets.

In December 1941 Japan launched a surprise attack on Pearl Harbor. The first retaliatory bombing raids by American B-25s came the following April, demolishing swathes of buildings around the edges of Tokyo.

By 1945 life in Tokyo was becoming intolerable. B-29s cruised the sky, raining down firebombs. People fled to the countryside or the coast. Sada retreated to her villa among the peaceful hills and palm trees of Atami.

Hatsu and Tomiji were in Kawada-cho one night when they heard air-raid sirens. They had been preparing to go to the country and had left bundles of photographs, letters and valuables by the front door. Hearing the wail of the sirens, they fled, leaving everything behind. Hatsu was fifteen. She remembers running and running, sliding open the doors of one room and running across it to the next. The rooms seemed to go on for ever. Tomiji had always been sickly and could not walk well. But she managed to escape.

The following day they went back. Searching through a wilderness of ashes, rubble, twisted metal and charred, broken stone walls, they finally found the house. There was nothing left except the lead pipes which had carried the central heating. By the next day those had been stolen. Apart from the few that had been left in the storehouse beside the temple, the photographs and letters which held the memories of Sada's life were gone. They broke the news to Sada that her house had burnt down. 'Tomiji managed to escape, even though she had bad legs,' she said. 'That's all that matters. I don't care about my house.'

The war came to an end on 15 August 1945, after Hiroshima and Nagasaki were obliterated by atomic bombs. Across the country, people turned on their radios to hear the reedy tones of their Emperor, crackling across the air waves. They would have to 'endure the unendurable and suffer the insufferable', he told them.

Sada had seen Japan rise to unimaginable glory. She had seen the great opening up to the West, the discovery of new worlds and new ways of life. She had played a large part herself in transforming Japan and its image abroad. Perhaps she was sorry she had lived to see it all turn sour.

Now she was old and ill. One day she showed Hatsu her tongue. There was a strange growth on it, the size of a bean.

'It doesn't hurt. Don't tell anyone,' she said.

She had cancer of the liver which had spread to her throat and tongue. Hatsu and Tomiji rushed down to Atami and stayed there with her. At the end she could not eat or drink. They sat by her bedside, moistening her lips with cottonwool dipped in water.

Her last words were to Tomiji. 'I'll watch over you,' she said.

Sada died on 7 December 1946 at the age of seventy-five. In those grim days of post-war reconstruction there were far more pressing things to think about than the death of an actress who had been famous decades before. Her demise received no more than a couple of lines in a corner of a newspaper. Three years later her bones were interred in the tomb in Teishoji Temple.

EPILOGUE

The firebombing at the end of World War II destroyed Tokyo. The once-glittering Ginza with its fashionable bars and cafés and the areas around it for many miles were wastelands of ash, stones and twisted metal. The main Imperial Palace burnt down. Roads were pitted with potholes, tram tracks buckled and broken. The city and its inhabitants reverted to an earlier, more primitive age. Across the plain of rubble the cone of Mount Fuji could be seen once again, no longer concealed by buildings, serene and white-capped on the horizon.

One of the casualties of the war was Komakichi, Momosuké's car-mad older son, who had inherited his business empire. He killed himself shortly before it ended, in March 1945. No one knows why. The family speculates that perhaps he felt guilty because he ran a munitions business. Maybe he realised which way things were going and was afraid of what the consequences would be.

The war changed everything. The huge Fukuzawa estate was sold to an insurance company. The great parkland with its three gracious houses, woods and avenues of flowering cherries is now a complex of skyscrapers with a gym, restaurants and bars. A few stone lanterns remain among the trees that edge the grounds.

Sada had made full provision for the family that she had created for herself. Tomiji was thirty-nine and Hatsu seventeen when she died. They carried on living outside Tokyo near the Iwasaki family home. There I met Hatsu, her son Shinichiro and young Makoto, adopted a couple of years earlier at the age of twenty-four to be Hatsu's grandson and heir. Tomiji was still alive but, at ninety-three, in ill health and in hospital.

It was thrilling to hear Hatsu's stories of her grandmother and Momosuké. We sat in the parlour in the smaller of their two houses. The room is dominated by a billiards table, brought from Futaba Palace decades ago. Hatsu had laid out piles of faded photographs and ancient leather-covered photograph albums on it. As Momosuké had wished, Sada's heirs never considered continuing her work by going on stage. Their job is to preserve her memory, casting her life in such a light as to bring it as close as possible to the ideal of 'good wife, wise mother'.

After Sada and Sumako Matsui there was no looking back. Actresses had become an essential element in modern Japanese theatre. Sada's students, notably Ritsuko Mori, became celebrated and thus perpetuated her heritage. Nevertheless, in the years after Sada's death, both she and Otojiro were quite forgotten. Otojiro's New Wave theatre had been a response to kabuki, but it was still within the same tradition. The acting was stylised and the casts included male *onnagata* together with actresses playing the female parts.

At the same time a critic, playwright and director named Shoyo Tsubouchi was creating *shingeki*, 'new theatre', which really was new and bore no relation to kabuki. Tsubouchi's productions of Shakespeare were the first to be faithful to the text, treating the text as sacred writ rather than as a vehicle around which star actors could improvise.

In the years that followed, Otojiro's New Wave theatre dwindled into a minor theatrical form, though it still continues. New Theatre became mainstream modern Japanese theatre. Tsubouchi was opposed to everything that Otojiro stood for. It was he and his followers who were to dominate modern Japanese theatre and write the history books. Otojiro and Sada were reduced to footnotes. After Western critics discovered kabuki, their journey to the West was disparaged as the unscrupulous selling of bastardised kabuki to ignorant Westerners who knew no better.

Zoe Kincaid, writing in 1925, was typical of critics of the time:

Kawakami did much to delay a true recognition of Kabuki and the fine actors of Japan. He was nothing more than an adventurer in the realm of the theatre; his performances were in no sense characteristic; in fact, he was an outsider and an amateur who ignored all that had gone before, building a structure on the sands that collapsed after his death. His countrymen who saw his hybrid plays in England and France and America hung their heads, ashamed at the bold effrontery of the man thus strutting upon the Western stage as a representative actor of Japan.

She also noted scathingly that 'when Kawakami returned from Europe he produced *Hamlet*, but the stage entrance of the Dane was made on a bicycle'. As for Sada, she wrote:

There is no doubt her beauty and attractiveness had much to do with Kawakami's success. Training in dancing and other female accomplishments she had secured as a geisha, but preparation for stage work she had none, and was just pushed before the footlights at a moment's notice to do the best she could.[1]

Most histories of Japanese drama subsume Sada's achievements beneath Otojiro's. As the man, he is credited with the development of New Wave theatre while she is portrayed as the obedient little wife. Some books even state that it was Otojiro who founded the school for actresses and installed Sada as principal. The pernicious myth that Sada went on stage by accident, just to help him out, and was untrained and untalented, persists.

But, as we have seen, her contemporaries, who actually saw her perform, judged her very differently. Everyone, from Japan experts familiar with kabuki and modern Japanese theatre to distinguished actors like Irving and formidable critics like Gide, recognised the originality and passion of her acting. They applauded her ability to grip her audience and take them on an imaginary journey into another world.

Sada and Otojiro were rediscovered in the 1980s. In Hakata, Otojiro was celebrated as a local hero. Near the city centre there is now a statue of him as a young man, wearing a headband, waving a fan and spitting out the scurrilous verses of his Oppekepé song. Several biographies celebrate his achievements as a founder of modern Japanese theatre.

Sada was rediscovered in a different way. More than her pioneering role as Japan's first actress, her romantic story sparked much interest. In 1985 NHK, the Japanese national broadcasting channel, produced a fictionalised drama based on her life in fifty-two one-hour episodes, shown weekly over the year, entitled *Waves of Spring*. Several biographies also appeared, ranging from the academic to the near-pornographic, with lurid accounts of her life as a geisha and deflowering at the hands of Count Ito. Perhaps that is why Hatsu is always so keen to emphasise that her relationship with Momosuké was decent and proper.

Of all the houses Sada built, only a couple are left. The Garden of Eternal Pines, the lovely country villa between the temple and the river, is still there although it is deserted now. There is a caretaker who cleans it and tends the lawns. Bamboo groves still sway and the wind rustles through the pines. The water rushes not far away. The pretty villa made of grey stones from the riverbed in Kiso Valley is now a memorial hall to Momosuké. All the others have long since disappeared.

Seeking to come closer to the heart of this tempestuous, passionate woman, I visited her temple, Teishoji. The storehouse there is a treasure trove of things that were important in her life. The bronze busts made when she and Otojiro were in Paris are there, along with medals awarded by the French President, honouring them as *Officiers de l'Académie*, and pennants celebrating Madame Sada Yacco in French, German and Russian.

There is a mirror stand of lacquered wood, with a design of scattered maple leaves inlaid in gold, silver and mother of pearl, where she used to apply her make-up. There is also a wonderful black kimono with a design of grasses and flowers embroidered in gold and red thread and a floor-length wig, like a mane of matted red rasta locks, which Sada wore when she did the lion dance. There are posters, programmes, books, clippings, photographs, scripts and scrolls of exquisite calligraphy, including one by Count Ito. The clippings include tantalising snippets; one describes Otojiro in his youth, before he met Sada, as 'a little and lovely man' perpetually fighting off homosexual advances.

Photographs, greatly enlarged, adorn the walls. There is the troupe in America; Sada and Otojiro at the Tsar's palace in Russia; and little Raikichi in his cap and muffler, sitting in a sledge on Sada's lap while the dachshund runs alongside through the snow. Otojiro's silk top hats are there, along with a battered leather suitcase labelled Sada Kawakami, a hatbox and two huge straw hats with feathers sweeping from the rims.

There are cabinets containing Momosuké's articles and weighty tomes he wrote on business matters. There is also a memoir published in 1924, the year he completed Oi Dam. It is a rambling work, full of musings about becoming a grandfather for the first time and going climbing in the Japan Alps.

There are no letters or diaries; those all disappeared when the Kawada-cho house burnt down. But there is a scrapbook of ancient crumbly clippings from Sada's last flowering as an actress, after Otojiro's death. They have been collected, dated and painstakingly pasted onto the thick pages, probably by Tomiji.

The temple no longer belongs to the family. It was purchased by a large local temple after Sada's death and is now within that temple's diocese. Every few days a caretaker priest goes to tend Sada's grave, perform prayers, and open the storehouse to the trickle of visitors who come to visit. He is in constant touch with Hatsu.

In the tatami-matted reception room he showed me posters of a drama based on Sada's life, romantically entitled *Overture to Dawn*. It was staged around 1999 by the Takarazuka, a wonderfully camp acting troupe in which, reversing the kabuki convention, all the parts are played by women. 'Sada' is blandly pretty in an exotic Victorian outfit with strings of pearls and a high collar; all the fire and character of the real woman have been air-brushed out. 'Otojiro' is even more of a travesty. Played by a pantomime Prince Charming, 'his' eyes heavily outlined in black and 'his' hair raffishly oiled, 'he' wears a mauve three-piece suit, pink frock coat and bow tie. The real Otojiro would have been utterly outraged had he even suspected he would be represented thus. 'Momosuké', mean and moody in black, broods in the background.

I found Sada's tomb behind the temple, up some stone steps on the other side of a pond and a small graveyard. It is set deep into the hillside. There is a porch-like awning to keep the rain off the candles, flowers and incense burning in front of it. She lies there, eternally separated from the men who played such large parts in her life. They are all three buried alone – Momosuké near the Iwasaki family, Otojiro in the temple grounds in Hakata where he can feel the rumble of the trains.

Apart from the hum of insects and the cries of birds, the place is silent. The stony ground is thickly covered in moss and ferns and shaded by maple and bamboo groves. In front of the tomb is a life-size statue of Kannon, the Buddhist goddess of mercy, akin to the Virgin Mary. The glimmering copper deity looks through a mesh of spiders' webs, across the tranquil tiled roofs of the temple, to the River Kiso and the misty hills covered in woods on the opposite side.

Geisha, actress, mistress: Sadayakko's was a life lived passionately. She managed to tread a narrow path, to follow her heart while trying to play the role expected of a woman in those days. Few Japanese women before or after have created such ripples in East and West.

SELECT BIBLIOGRAPHY

On Sadayakko and her life and lovers: major sources

Books and major articles: English and European languages

Berg, Shelley C., 'Sada Yacco: The American Tour, 1899–1900' in *Dance Chronicle*, vol 16, no 2, 1993, pp.147–96.

Berg Shelley C., 'Le Rêve Réalisé', *Dance Chronicle*, vol 18, no 3, 1995, pp.343–404.

Chiba, Yoko, 'Sada Yacco and Kawakami: Performers of Japonisme' in *Modern Drama* 35, no 1, March 1992, pp.35–53.

Fournier, Louis, *Kawakami and Sada Yacco*, Brentano's, Paris, 1900.

Gautier, Judith, 'La Musique Japonais a l'Exposition de *1900*: Les Danses de Sada Yacco' in *Les Musiques Bizarre a l'Exposition de *1900**, Librairie Ollendorff, Paris, 1900, pp.5–20.

Gautier, Judith, 'La Geisha et le Chevalier' in *Les Parfums de la Pagode*, Charpentier, Paris, 1919, pp.193–223.

'Geisha Sadayakko: The Story of a Japanese Woman who Lived in the Meiji Era' in *The East*, vol 16, nos. 7–8, July 1980, pp.5–14.

Groos, Arthur, 'Cio-Cio-San and Sadayakko: Japanese Music-Theater in Madama Butterfly' in *Monumenta Nipponica*, vol 54, no 1, Spring 1999, pp.41–73.

Kano, Ayako, 'The Role of the Actress in Modern Japan' in Helen Hardacre and Adam Kern (eds), *New Directions in the study of Meiji Japan*, Brill, Leiden, New York and Koln, 1997.

Kano, Ayako, *Acting like a Woman in Modern Japan: Theater, Gender, and Nationalism*, Palgrave, New York, 2001.

Miller, J. Scott, *Lost Melodies Rediscovered: Recordings of the Kawakami Troupe at the 1900 Paris Exposition*, Toshiba-EMI, Tokyo, 1998.

Miller, J. Scott, 'Dispossessed Melodies: Recordings of the Kawakami Theater Troupe' in *Monumenta Nipponica*, vol 53, no 2, Summer 1998, pp.225–35.

Noguchi, Yone, 'Sada Yacco' in *New York Dramatic Mirror*, 17 February 1908.

Pantzer, Peter, 'Kawakami Otojiro und Sadayakko: *Theater, Exotik und Premierenstimmung im deutschen Kaierreich*' in *Kulturvermittler zwischen Japan und Deutschland, Biographische Skizzen aus vier Jahrhunderten*, Herausgegeben vom Japanischen Kulturinstitut, Koln.

Salz, Jonah, 'Intercultural Pioneers: Otojiro Kawakami and Sada Yakko' in *The Journal of Intercultural Studies*, no 20, Kansai University of Foreign Studies Publication, 1993, pp.25–74.

Yamata, Kikou, '*Sada Yakko et le Théâtre Japonais*', La Revue de France, no 19:1, January – February 1939, pp.85–109.

Books and articles: Japanese

Asari, Keiichiro, *Kisai: Fukuzawa Momosuke no shogai* (Genius: The Life of Momosuké Fukuzawa), Nihon hoso shuppan kyokai, Tokyo, 2000.

Domon, Fujii, *Kawakami Sadayakko: Monogatari to shiseki o tazunete* (Sadayakko Kawakami: searching for her story and historical landmarks), Sebido shuppan, Tokyo, 1984.

Egashira, Kou, *Hakata: Kawakami Otojiro* (Hakata: Otojiro Kawakami), Nishi Nippon Shimbunsha, Fukuoka, 1996.

Fujii, Sotetsu (ed), *Jiden Otojiro, Sadayakko* (Autobiography of Otojiro and Sadayakko), San'ichi Shobo, Tokyo, 1984.

Fukuzawa Momosuke ten: Denryoku o (Momosuké Fukuzawa exhibition: King of Electric Power), Denki no Kagakukan, Nagoya, 1994.

Hasegawa Shigure, 'Madamu Sadayakko (Madame Sadayakko)' in *Kindai Bijin den 2 (Stories of Beautiful Women of Today 2)*, Iwanami Bunko, Tokyo, 1939 (first published March 1920).

Inoue Seizo, *Kawakami Otojiro no shogai* (The Life of Otojiro Kawakami), Ashi Shobo, Fukuoka, 1985.

Kawakami, Otojiro and Sadayakko Kawakami, *Kawakami Otojiro O-Bei Manyuki: Mr Kawakami's Travels Round the World* (Account of Otojiro Kawakami's Tour of Europe and America), Osaka, 1901.

Kawakami, Otojiro and Sadayakko Kawakamai, *Jiden Otojiro, Sadayakko* (Autobiography of Otojiro and Sadayakko), edited by Sotetsu Fujii, San'ichi Shobo, Tokyo, 1984.

Kawakami, Sadayakko, '*Meika shinso roku* (Record of the true stories of famous families)' in *Engei Gaho*, October 1908, pp.80–94.

Kawakami, Sadayakko, '*Joyu rekiho roku* (Record of visits with actresses 1)' with Gakusei Azuma (interviewer), in *Engei Gaho*, February 1911, pp.40–6.

Kawakami, Sadayakko, '*Otto ni wakarete nochi* (On being parted from Otto)' in *Engei Gaho*, November 1912, pp.169–72.

Kawakami, Sadayakko, '*Joyu toshite no watashi no kakugo* (Preparing myself as an actress)' in *Bungei Gaho*, November 1913.

Kawakami, Sadayakko, '*Sadayakko omoide hanashi* (Sadayakko talks about her memories)' in *Tokyo Asahi Shimbun*, 23 February to 3 March 1937, eight articles.

Kawakami, Tomiji, '*Gibo Sadayakko no Omoide* (Memories of my foster mother, Sadayakko)' in '*Kawakami-za umi o wataru: joyu dai-ichi go Sadayakko* (The Kawakami troupe crosses the sea: First Actress Sadayakko), edited by Sonoko Sugimoto and Toshio Kawatake, in *NHK Rekishi e no shotai 12* (NHK Invitation to History vol. 12), Nippon Hoso Shuppan Kyokai, Tokyo, 1981.

Noguchi, Fumi, *Kawakami Otojiro to 1900 nen Pari Bankoku Hakurankai ten* (Otojiro Kawakami and the Paris Exposition Universelle of 1900 exhibition), Fukuoka City Museum, Fukuoka, 2000.

Osanai, Kaoru, '*Hongoza no Sarome* (Salome at the Hongoza)' in *Engei Gaho*, June 1915, pp.148–63.

Ozaki, Hirotsugu, 'Kawakami Sadayakko' in *Joyu no Keizu* (Genealogy of actresses), Asahi Shimbunsha, Tokyo, 1964, pp.1–70.

Shirakawa, Nobuo (ed), *Kawakami Otojiro, Sadayakko: shimbun ni miru jimbutsu zo* (Otojiro and Sadayakko Kawakami: their personalities as seen in newspapers), Yushodo, Tokyo, 1985.

Sugimoto, Sonoko, *Madamu Sadayakko* (Madame Sadayakko), Tokyo, Shueisha, 1975.

Sugimoto, Sonoko, and Toshio Kawatake, '*Kawakami-za umi o wataru: joyu dai-ichi go Sadayakko* (The Kawakami troupe crosses the sea: First Actress Sadayakko) in *NHK Rekishi e no shotai 12* (NHK Invitation to History vol. 12), Nippon Hoso Shuppan Kyokai, Tokyo, 1981.

Toita, Koji, 'Kawakami Sadayakko' in *Monogatari kindai Nihon joyu shi* (An anecdotal history of modern Japanese actresses), Chuo Koronsha, Tokyo, 1980, pp.20–37.

Yamaguchi, Reiko, *Joyu Sadayakko* (Actress Sadayakko), Shinchosha, Tokyo, 1982.

Background

English and European languages

Bacon, Alice Mabel, *Japanese Girls and Women*, The Riverside Press, Cambridge, 1899.

Barr, Pat, *The Deer Cry Pavilion: A Story of Westerners in Japan 1868–1905*, Penguin, London, 1988.

Beasley, W.G., *The Meiji Restoration*, Stanford University Press, Stanford, 1973.

Bornoff, Nicholas, *Pink Samurai: The Pursuit and Politics of Sex in Japan*, Grafton Books, London, 1991.

Bowers, Faubion, *Japanese Theatre*, foreword by Joshua Logan, Hermitage House, New York, 1952.

Brandon, James R., William P. Malm and Donald Shively, *Studies in Kabuki: Its Acting, Music and Historical Context*, University of Hawaii Press, Honolulu, 1978.

Crichton, Judy, *America 1900: The Turning Point*, Henry Holt and Company, New York, 1998.

Current, Richard Nelson and Marcia Ewing Current, *Loie Fuller: Goddess of Light*, Northeastern University Press, Boston, 1997.

Dalby, Liza, *Geisha*, University of California Press, Berkeley, 1983; with a new preface 'Twenty-four years later', Vintage, London, 1998.

Dalby, Liza, *Kimono: Fashioning Culture*, Yale University Press, New Haven, 1993; with new acknowledgments, Vintage, London, 2001.

Diosy, Arthur, *The New Far East*, Cassell and Company, Limited, London, 1898.

Downer, Lesley, *Geisha: The Secret History of a Vanishing World*, Headline, London, 2000.

Downer, Lesley, *The Brothers: The Saga of the Richest Family in Japan*, Chatto & Windus, London, 1994.

Duncan, Isadora, *My Life*, Liveright, New York, 1927.

Edwards, Osman, *Japanese Plays and Playfellows*, William Heinemann, London, 1901.

Ernst, Earle, *The Kabuki Theatre*, Secker & Warburg, London, 1956.

Fuller, Loie, *Fifteen Years of a Dancer's Life: with Some Account of her Distinguished Friends*, with an introduction by Anatole France, Dance Horizons, New York, 1913.

Gide, André, *Lettres à Angèle*, Editions de Mercure de France, Paris, 1900, reprinted in Pretextes, Mercure de France, Paris, 1903.

Gold, Arthur, and Robert Fizdale, *Misia: The Life of Misia Sert*, Macmillan, London, 1980.

Hamada, Kengi, *Prince Ito*, Sanseido Co Ltd., Tokyo, 1936.

Jansen, Marius B., *The Cambridge History of Japan: vol 5, the Nineteenth Century*, Cambridge University Press, Cambridge, 1989.

Julian, Philippe, *The Triumph of Art Nouveau: Paris Exhibition 1900*, translated by Stephan Hardman, Phaidon, New York, 1974.

Keene, Donald, *Appreciations of Japanese Culture*, Kodansha International, Tokyo, 1971.

Keene, Donald, *Dawn to the West: Japanese Literature of the Modern Era. Fiction. A History of Japanese Literature, Volume 3*, Holt, Rinehart and Winston, New York, 1984.

Keene, Donald, *Landscapes and Portraits: Appreciation of Japanese Culture*, Kodansha International, Tokyo, 1972.

Keene, Donald, *Modern Japanese Literature: from 1868 to Present Day*, Grove Press, New York, 1956.

Kincaid, Zoe, *Kabuki, the Popular Stage of Japan*, Macmillan and Co., Limited, London, 1925.

Komiya, Toyotaka (ed), *Japanese Music and Drama in the Meiji Era*, translated and adapted by Edward G. Seidensticker and Donald Keene, Obunsha, Tokyo, 1956.

Lista, Giovanni, *Loie Fuller: Danseuse de la Belle Epoque*, Somogy Editions d'Art, Editions Stock, Paris, 1994.

Loti, Pierre, *Madame Chrysanthème*, Calman-Levy, Paris, 1888; translated by Laura Ensor, George Routledge and Sons Ltd, London, 1888.

Mandell, Richard D., *Paris 1900: The Great World's Fair*, University of Toronto Press, Toronto, 1967.

Meech-Pekarik, Julia, *The World of the Meiji Print*, Weatherhill, Tokyo and New York, 1986.

Mitford, A.B. (Lord Redesdale), *Tales of Old Japan*, Charles E. Tuttle Company Inc., Rutland, Vermont and Tokyo, Japan, 1966 (first published 1871).

Morand, Paul, *1900 A.D.*, Flammarion, Paris, 1931, English translation by Mrs Romilly Fedden, William Farquar Payson, New York, 1931.

Oka, Yoshitake, *Five Political Leaders of Modern Japan*, translated by Andrew Fraser and Patricia Murray, University of Tokyo Press, Tokyo, 1986.

Ortolani, Benito, *The Japanese Theatre: From Shamanistic Ritual to Contemporary Pluralism*, E.J. Brill, Leiden, 1990.

Ransome, Stafford, *Japan in Transition: A Comparative Study of the Progress, Policy and Methods of the Japanese since their war with China*, Harper & Brothers, London and New York, 1899.

Richardson, John, *A Life of Picasso: Volume I: 1881–1906*, Jonathan Cape, London, 1991.

Rij, Jan van, *Madame Butterfly: Japonisme, Puccini & the Search for the real Cho-Cho-San*, Stonebridge Press, Berkeley, California, 2001.

Roberts, John G., *Mitsui: Three Centuries of Japanese Business*, Weatherhill, New York and Tokyo, 1973.

Rosenblum, Robert, Mary-Anne Stevens and Anne Dumas, *1900: Art at the Crossroads*, Royal Academy of Arts, London, 2000.

Saint Denis, Ruth, *An Unfinished Life: An Autobiography (with portraits)*, Harper & Brothers, New York and London, 1939.

Sasayama, Takashi, J.R. Mulryne and Margaret Shewring (eds), *Shakespeare and the Japanese Stage*, Cambridge University Press, Cambridge, 1998.

Sato, Tomoko and Watanabe, Toshio (eds), *Japan and Britain: An Aesthetic Dialogue 1850–1930*, Lund Humphries, London, in association with Barbican Art Gallery and the Setagaya Art Museum, 1991.

Scidmore, Eliza Ruhamah, *Jinrikisha Days in Japan*, Harper & Brothers, New York and London, 1902.

Seidensticker, Edward, *Low City, High City: Tokyo from Edo to the Earthquake, 1867–1923*, Alfred A. Knopf, Inc, New York, 1983.

Seidensticker, Edward, *Tokyo Rising: The City since the Great Earthquake*, Alfred A. Knopf, Inc., New York, 1990.

Shionoya, Kei, *Cyrano et les Samurai: Le Théâtre Japonais en France dans la Première Moitié du XXe Siècle et l'Effet de Retour*, Publications Orientalistes de France, Paris, 1986.

Shively, Donald (ed), *Tradition and Modernisation in Japanese Culture*, Princeton University Press, Princeton, 1971.

Symons, Arthur William, *Plays, Acting and Music*, Duckworth and Co., London, 1903.

Tames, Richard, *Encounters with Japan*, Alan Sutton, Stroud and St Martin's Press, New York, 1991.

Toyotaka, Komiya (ed), *Japanese Music and Drama in the Meiji Era*, translated and adapted by Edward G. Seidensticker and Donald Keene, Obunsha, Tokyo, Japan, 1956.

Tsuda, Ume, edited by Yoshiko Furuki, Akiko Ueda, Mary E. Althaus, *The Writings of Umeko Tsuda*, Tsuda College, Tokyo, 1980.

Tsuda, Ume, edited by Yoshiko Furuki, *The Attic Letters: Ume Tsuda's Correspondence to her American Mother*, Weatherhill, New York and Tokyo, 1991.

Waley, Paul, *Tokyo Now and Then*, Weatherhill, New York and Tokyo, 1984.

Japanese

Fukai, Akiko, *Jyaponisumu in fuashiyon* (Japonism in Fashion), Heibonsha, Tokyo, 1994.

Fukai, Akiko, *Modo no jyaponisumu* (Japonism in Fashion), Kyoto Costume Institute, Kyoto, 1996.

Kimura, Ki, *Kaigai ni katsuyaku shita Meiji no josei* (Meiji women who were active abroad), Shibundo, Tokyo, 1963.

Koike, Kazuko, *Roman isho ten* (Evolution of Fashion 1835–1895), Kyoto Costume Institute, Kyoto, 1980.

Toyoda, Jo, *Shodai sori Ito Hirobumi* (Hirobumi Ito, the first prime minister), Kodansha, Tokyo, 1987.

CD

Miller, J. Scott, *Lost Melodies Rediscovered: Recordings of the Kawakami Troupe at the 1900 Paris Exposition*, Toshiba-EMI, Tokyo, 1998.

NOTES

Prologue – In search of Sadayakko

1 'The Chatterer', *Boston Herald*, 13 December 1899, p.6.
2 'Madame Yacco, the Leading Geisha of Japan, Coming Here', *San Francisco Chronicle*, 20 May 1899, p.4.
3 'A Japanese Actress', *New York Times*, 11 March 1900, p.16.
4 Kawakami, Sadayakko, 'Joyu rekiho roku (Record of visits with actresses 1)' in *Engei Gaho*, February 1911, p.41.

PART I   GEISHA

Chapter 1 – The Geisha and the Farm Boy: 1871–1885

1 '*Sadayakko no mi no ue hanashi* (Sadayakko: Her own story)' in *Kyushu Shimbun*, Kumamoto City, 10 May 1913.
2 Ibid.
3 Inoue, p.41.
4 Mitford, p.57.
5 Kawakami, Sadayakko, '*Meika shinso roku* (Record of the true stories of famous families)' in *Engei Gaho*, October 1908, p.80.
6 Hasegawa, p.80.

7 *'Sadayakko no mi no ue hanashi* (Sadayakko: Her own story)' in *Kyushu Shimbun*, Kumamoto City, 10 May 1913.
8 Hasegawa, p.80.
9 Bacon, p.286, 289.
10 *Tokio Times*, 27 January 1877, quoted in Shively, p.82.
11 *Nichiyo Shimbun*, January 1872, *'Yofuku no oshaku* (The geisha in western dress)', from *Kindai Nihon Fukuzoshi*, p.155, translated and quoted in Dalby, *Kimono*, p.81.
12 Kawakami, Tomiji, p.80.

Chapter 2 — *The Prime Minister's Favourite: 1885–1888*

1 *'Mibojin Sadayakko* (Widow Sadayakko)' in *Kokumin shimbun*, 14 November 1911.
2 Hasegawa, p.81.
3 Tsuda, *Attic Letters*, p.127.
4 Oka, p.37.
5 Ibid.
6 Hasegawa, p.82.
7 Dalby, *Geisha*, p.110.
8 Bornoff, p.133.
9 *Japan Weekly Mail*, 30 April 1887, quoted in Meech-Pekarik, pp.155–7; see also Shively, p.95.
10 Kawakami, Otojiro and Sadayakko Kawakami, *Jiden Otojiro, Sadayakko* (Autobiography of Otojiro and Sadayakko), p.15.

Chapter 3 — *The Liberty Kid: 1888–1896*

1 Hasegawa, p.82.
2 Ibid, p.78.
3 Kawakami, Sadayakko, *'Joyu rekiho roku* (Record of visits with actresses 1)' in *Engei Gaho*, February 1911, p.43.
4 Kawakami, Sadayakko, *'Sadayakko omoide hanashi* (Sadayakko talks about her memories)' in *Tokyo Asahi Shimbun*, number 2, 24 February 1937.
5 Kawakami, Otojiro and Sadayakko Kawakami, *Jiden Otojiro, Sadayakko* (Autobiography of Otojiro and Sadayakko), p.242.
6 Ibid, p.17.
7 *'jiyu doshi'*.
8 *'Itagaki-kun sonan jiki'*.
9 Translated by William Malm in Shively, pp.283–4.
10 *Jiji Shimpo*, 24 June 1891, in Shirakawa, p.58.
11 *Jiji Shimpo*, 5 June 1892, in Shirakawa, p.98.
12 A compressed/abridged translation of *Chuo Shimbun*, 20 January 1892, in Shirakawa, p.82.

13 *Chuo Shimbun*, 18 November 1892, in Shirakawa, p.115.
14 Kawakami, Sadayakko, '*Meika shinso roku* (Record of the true stories of famous families)' in *Engei Gaho*, October 1908, p.80.
15 Kawakami, Sadayakko, '*Sadayakko omoide hanashi* (Sadayakko talks about her memories) 1,2' in *Tokyo Asahi Shimbun*, 23–24 February 1937.
16 Hasegawa, p.86.
17 *Yorozu Choho*, 5 March 1895, in Shirakawa, p.186.
18 *Tokyo Nichi Nichi Shimbun*, 11 November 1911, in Yamaguchi, p.74.
19 *Yorozu Choho*, 28–29 March 1896, and *Miyako Shimbun*, 8 April 1896, in Shirakawa, pp.208–11. See also Hasegawa, pp.87–8; and Yamata, pp.93–4.
20 Hasegawa, pp.89–90.

PART II   ACTRESS

Chapter 4 – Setting Sail: 1896–1899

 1 Scidmore, p.134.
 2 *Tokyo Asahi Shimbun*, 29 December 1897, in Shirakawa, p.243.
 3 *Mainichi Shimbun*, 28 December 1897, *Yomiuri Shimbun*, 29 December 1897, and *Yomiuri Shimbun*, 20 January 1898, in Shirakawa, pp.242, 245.
 4 Yamaguchi, p.85.
 5 Kawakami, Sadayakko, '*Sadayakko omoide hanashi* (Sadayakko talks about her memories) 2' in *Tokyo Asahi Shimbun*, 24 February 1937.
 6 Yamaguchi, p.86.
 7 Kawakami, Sadayakko, '*Sadayakko omoide hanashi* (Sadayakko talks about her memories) 7' in *Tokyo Asahi Shimbun*, 2 March 1937.
 8 Kawakami, Sadayakko, '*Meika shinso roku* (Record of the true stories of famous families)' in *Engei Gaho*, October 1908, p.81.
 9 Kawakami, Sadayakko, '*Sadayakko omoide hanashi* (Sadayakko talks about her memories) 7' in *Tokyo Asahi Shimbun*, 2 March 1937.
10 Shirakawa, pp.281–3.
11 Kawakami, Sadayakko, '*Meika shinso roku* (Record of the true stories of famous families)' in *Engei Gaho*, October 1908, p.82.
12 Kawakami, Sadayakko, '*Sadayakko omoide hanashi* (Sadayakko talks about her memories) 8' in *Tokyo Asahi Shimbun*, 3 March 1937.
13 *Miyako Shimbun*, 1 March 1898, in Shirakawa, p.299.
14 Kawakami, Sadayakko, '*Meika shinso roku* (Record of the true stories of famous families)' in *Engei Gaho*, October 1908, p.88.
15 Kawakami, Sadayakko, '*Joyu rekiho roku* (Record of visits with actresses 1)' in *Engei Gaho*, February 1911, p.42.
16 'Ocean and Water Front: The Gaelic Arrives from the Orient', *San Francisco Chronicle*, Sunday 21 May 1899, p.19.

17 Kawakami, Otojiro and Sadayakko Kawakami, *Kawakami Otojiro O-Bei Manyuki: Mr Kawakami's Travels Round the World* (Account of Otojiro Kawakami's Tour of Europe and America), p.9.

18 Kawakami, Sadayakko, '*Meika shinso roku* (Record of the true stories of famous families)' in *Engei Gaho*, October 1908, p.89.

19 Ibid.

20 'Madame Yacco, the Leading Geisha of Japan, Coming Here', *San Francisco Chronicle*, 20 May 1899, p.4.

21 *Miyako Shimbun*, 29 June 1899, and *Yomiuri Shimbun*, 5 July 1899, in Shirakawa, pp.302–3.

22 *San Francisco Chronicle*, Sunday 18 June 1899, p.5.

23 'About Drama and Opera: First Performance of Japanese Dramas', *San Francisco Chronicle*, 19 June 1899, p.5; '"Chimes of Normandy" Well Acted and Sung', *San Francisco Examiner*, 20 June 1899, p.6; 'The Japanese Drama and the Art of the Japanese Actors', *San Francisco Chronicle*, 25 June 1899, p.5.

24 'Japanese Play Ends Abruptly', *San Francisco Chronicle*, 23 June 1899, p.10.

25 Kawakami, Otojiro and Sadayakko Kawakami, *Jiden Otojiro, Sadayakko* (Autobiography of Otojiro and Sadayakko), p.30.

Chapter 5 – 'And How This Geisha dances!': Lost in America, 1899–1900

1 Noguchi.

2 Kawakami, Sadayakko, '*Meika shinso roku* (Record of the true stories of famous families)' in *Engei Gaho*, October 1908, p.91.

3 Kawakami, Otojiro and Sadayakko Kawakami, *Jiden Otojiro, Sadayakko* (Autobiography of Otojiro and Sadayakko), p.32.

4 Kawakami, Sadayakko, '*Meika shinso roku* (Record of the true stories of famous families)' in *Engei Gaho*, October 1908, pp.91–2.

5 Kawakami, Otojiro and Sadayakko Kawakami, *Kawakami Otojiro O-Bei Manyuki: Mr Kawakami's Travels Round the World* (Account of Otojiro Kawakami's Tour of Europe and America), p.15.

6 'Mme Yacco, Japan's Ellen Terry, Visits Seattle En Route to the Paris Exposition', *Seattle Post-Intelligencer*, 10 September 1899, p.1.

7 'Japanese Drama', *Morning Oregonian*, 28 September 1899, p.5; 'Geisha and the Knight', *Morning Oregonian*, 30 September 1899, p.3.

8 Kawakami, Otojiro and Sadayakko Kawakami, *Jiden Otojiro, Sadayakko* (Autobiography of Otojiro and Sadayakko), p.34.

9 Kawakami, Otojiro and Sadayakko Kawakami, *Jiden Otojiro, Sadayakko*, pp.35–42; Kawakami, Sadayakko, '*Meika shinso roku* (Record of the true stories of famous families)' in *Engei Gaho*, October 1908, pp.92–4; Kawakami, Otojiro and Sadayakko Kawakami, *Kawakami Otojiro O-Bei Manyuki: Mr Kawakami's*

Travels Round the World (Account of Otojiro Kawakami's Tour of Europe and America), pp.18–19.

10 'Geisha and the Knight', *Morning Oregonian*, 30 September 1899, p.3.

11 Kawakami, Sadayakko, '*Meika shinso roku* (Record of the true stories of famous families)' in *Engei Gaho*, October 1908, p.94; Kawakami, Otojiro and Sadayakko Kawakami, *Jiden Otojiro, Sadayakko* (Autobiography of Otojiro and Sadayakko), pp.41–51.

12 'Japanese Actors at the Lyric', *Chicago Daily News*, 23 October 1899, p.9.

13 Kawakami, Otojiro and Sadayakko Kawakami, *Jiden Otojiro, Sadayakko* (Autobiography of Otojiro and Sadayakko), p.64.

14 *Boston Globe*, 3, 5, 10 and 11 December 1899.

15 Kawakami, Otojiro and Sadayakko Kawakami, *Kawakami Otojiro O-Bei Manyuki: Mr Kawakami's Travels Round the World* (Account of Otojiro Kawakami's Tour of Europe and America), p.16.

16 Noguchi.

17 Kawakami, Otojiro and Sadayakko Kawakami, *Kawakami Otojiro O-Bei Manyuki: Mr Kawakami's Travels Round the World* (Account of Otojiro Kawakami's Tour of Europe and America), p.16.

18 'Japanese Plays in Boston', *New York Times*, 6 December 1899, p.8:7.

19 'The Chatterer', *Boston Herald*, 13 December 1899, p.6.

20 'Plain Tales of Stage Land', *Boston Sunday Journal*, 17 December 1899.

21 'Japan's Foremost Actors', by Alexander Corbett Jr., *The Boston Globe*, Monday 11 December 1899, p.5.

22 Ibid.

23 'Mme Yacco', *Boston Sunday Post*, 24 December 1899, pp.16–17.

24 Kawakami, Otojiro and Sadayakko Kawakami, *Jiden Otojiro, Sadayakko* (Autobiography of Otojiro and Sadayakko), p.62.

25 'Tragedy Abroad' in Kawakami, Otojiro and Sadayakko Kawakami, *Kawakami Otojiro O-Bei Manyuki: Mr Kawakami's Travels Round the World* (Account of Otojiro Kawakami's Tour of Europe and America), p.14.

26 Kawakami, Otojiro and Sadayakko Kawakami, *Jiden Otojiro, Sadayakko* (Autobiography of Otojiro and Sadayakko), pp.68–70.

Chapter 6 – 'The Witchery of Salome's Art': Boston to London, *1900*

1 Roof, Katherine Metcalf, 'Concerning the Japanese Players', *The Impressionist*, no 8, June 1900, p.10.

2 Kawakami, Otojiro and Sadayakko Kawakami, *Kawakami Otojiro O-Bei Manyuki: Mr Kawakami's Travels Round the World* (Account of Otojiro Kawakami's Tour of Europe and America), p.29.

3 *Kabuki*, July 1903, quoted in Yamaguchi p.110; 'Otojiro Kawakami and Sada Yacco,' *The Era*, 2 June 1900, p.8.

4 Collins, Sewell, 'Japanese Actors Who Visited New York Give Shakespeare to the Oriental Stage.' 'Sada Yacco,' Robinson Locke Clippings File 2663, Billy Rose Theater Collection, New York Public Library.

5 Kawakami, Otojiro and Sadayakko Kawakami, *Kawakami Otojiro O-Bei Manyuki: Mr Kawakami's Travels Round the World* (Account of Otojiro Kawakami's Tour of Europe and America), p.31.

6 'The Japanese Players', *Boston Herald*, 26 January 1900, p.9.

7 'The Japanese Plays', *Boston Post*, 13 December 1899, p.5.

8 'The Stage', *Washington Post*, 4 February 1900, p.24.

9 *Nisshin Kosenroku*, no 38, p.70, quoted and translated by Donald Keene in Shively, p.173.

10 Collins, Sewell, 'Japanese Actors Who Visited New York Give Shakespeare to the Oriental Stage.' 'Sada Yacco', Robinson Locke Clippings File 2663, Billy Rose Theater Collection, New York Public Library.

11 'Otijiro [sic] Kawakami and Sada Yacco', *The Era*, 2 June 1900, p.8.

12 'A Japanese Actress', *New York Times*, Sunday 11 March 1900, p.16.

13 'The Japanese Actors', *New York Times*, 13 March 1900, p.9.

14 Collins, Sewell, 'Japanese Actors Who Visited New York Give Shakespeare to the Oriental Stage.' 'Sada Yacco,' Robinson Locke Clippings File 2663, Billy Rose Theater Collection, New York Public Library.

15 Kawakami, Otojiro and Sadayakko Kawakami, *Kawakami Otojiro O-Bei Manyuki: Mr Kawakami's Travels Round the World* (Account of Otojiro Kawakami's Tour of Europe and America), p.43.

16 'Mme. Yacco a Guest', *New York Daily Tribune*, 21 March 1900, p.5.

17 Material on Sapho and women in America from Crichton, pp.78–85.

18 Kawakami, Otojiro and Sadayakko Kawakami, *Jiden Otojiro, Sadayakko* (Autobiography of Otojiro and Sadayakko), p.85.

19 'The Japanese Players', *New York Times*, 1 April 1900, p.18.

20 Kawakami, Otojiro and Sadayakko Kawakami, *Kawakami Otojiro O-Bei Manyuki: Mr Kawakami's Travels Round the World* (Account of Otojiro Kawakami's Tour of Europe and America), p.40.

21 'Concerning the Japanese players', Katherine Metcalf Roof, *The Impressionist*, no 8, June 1900, p.8.

22 Collins, Sewell, 'Deeply Affected by the Japs' Sapho.' 'Sada Yacco,' Robinson Locke Clippings File 2663, Billy Rose Theater Collection, New York Public Library.

23 Kawakami, Otojiro and Sadayakko Kawakami, *Jiden Otojiro, Sadayakko* (Autobiography of Otojiro and Sadayakko), pp.213–5.

24 Noguchi, 1906.

25 Kawakami, Otojiro and Sadayakko Kawakami, *Kawakami Otojiro O-Bei Manyuki: Mr Kawakami's Travels Round the World* (Account of Otojiro Kawakami's Tour of Europe and America), p.44.

26 Ibid, p.45.
27 Kawakami, Sadayakko, 'Sadayakko omoide hanashi (Sadayakko talks about her memories) 5' in Tokyo Asahi Shimbun, 27 February 1937.
28 'The Japs at the Coronet', The Sketch, 30 May 1900, p.241.
29 Edwards, p.66.
30 Wilde, Oscar, 'The Decay of Lying', originally published in The Nineteenth Century, January 1889.
31 Symons, pp.87–8.
32 Campbell, Mrs Colin, 'A Woman's Walks: No. CLVI: In Far Japan', The World, 13 June 1900, pp.13–14.
33 Edwards, p.66.
34 'The Coronet Theatre', Morning Post, 13 June 1900, p.5.
35 Noguchi.
36 Roof, Katherine Metcalf, quoted in Berg, 1995, p.355.
37 '58 Grosvenor Place, S.W.', Vanity Fair, 5 July 1900, p.10; also The Court Journal, 30 June 1900, p.932.
38 Noguchi; also Kawakami, Otojiro and Sadayakko Kawakami, Jiden Otojiro, Sadayakko (Autobiography of Otojiro and Sadayakko), p.205.
39 Letter to the author from Miss Pamela Clark, Registrar, The Royal Archives, Windsor Castle.

Chapter 7 – 'An Opium Hallucination of the Far East': Paris Swoons, 1900–1901

1 Morand, pp.93–4.
2 Lorrain, Jean, 'Fleurs du Yeddo: Sada Yacco et son Retour', Le Gaulois, 7 September 1901.
3 'Sada Yacco Racontée par Elle-même', Le Gaulois, 9 September 1900, p.1.
4 Morand, pp.88–9.
5 'Gossip from the Gay City', The Referee, Sunday 8 July 1900, p.3:4.
6 Montignard, G., 'Une Visite a des Artistes Étranges', Le Monde Illustré, no 2327, 2 November 1901, pp.340–1.
7 Current, p.142.
8 'The Coronet Theatre', Morning Post, 13 June 1900, p.5.
9 Noguchi.
10 Alexandre, Arsène, 'Les Femmes de l'Exposition', L'Illustration, 13 October 1900, pp.232–3.
11 Fouquier, Henri, 'Sada Yacco', Le Théâtre, October 1900, II, p.9.
12 Gautier, Judith, 'La Musique Japonais: Introduction', in Les Musiques Bizarres a l'Exposition de 1900, p.5.
13 Morand, p.94.
14 Gide, André, 'Lettre VIII', Lettres à Angèle, p.134.
15 Alexandre, Arsène, 'Théâtre de Loie Fuller, Pantomimes Japonaises', Le Théâtre, September 1900, pp.16–19.

16 Verhaeren, Émile, 'Chroniques de l'Exposition', Mercure de France, vol. 36, XI (November), 1900, p.483; Adolphe Brisson, 'Promenades et Visites a l'Exposition: Madame Sada Yacco', Le Temps, 1 August 1900, pp.2–3.

17 'Gossip from the Gay City', The Referee, Sunday 23 September 1900, p.3:4.

18 Duncan, p.78.

19 Saint Denis, p.40.

20 Kawakami, Otojiro and Sadayakko Kawakami, Kawakami Otojiro O-Bei Manyuki: Mr Kawakami's Travels Round the World (Account of Otojiro Kawakami's Tour of Europe and America), p.51; Yamaguchi, pp.124–5. Quote from Noguchi.

21 Thanks to Scott Miller for his pioneering research which unearthed these unique recordings and for sharing his findings. See Miller, Lost Melodies Rediscovered: Recordings of the Kawakami Troupe at the 1900 Paris Exposition.

22 'Sada Yacco Racontée par Elle-même', Le Gaulois, 9 September 1900, p.1.

23 Fournier, pp.19–20.

24 Iwanosuke Fujikawa's diary, published in Miyako Shimbun, 27 July 1900, in Shirakawa, p.320.

25 Current, p.143.

26 Kawakami, Sadayakko, 'Joyu rekiho roku (Record of visits with actresses 1)' in Engei Gaho, February 1911, p.44.

27 Fournier, p.34.

28 Kawakami, Otojiro and Sadayakko Kawakami, Jiden Otojiro, Sadayakko (Autobiography of Otojiro and Sadayakko), p.210.

29 Kimura, p.163.

30 Kubota, Beisai, 'Beisai Reviews the Plays in Paris, I–IV', Yomiuri Shimbun, 1–4 September 1900, in Shirakawa, pp.325–7.

31 Kawakami, Otojiro and Sadayakko Kawakami, Kawakami Otojiro O-Bei Manyuki: Mr Kawakami's Travels Round the World (Account of Otojiro Kawakami's Tour of Europe and America), p.55.

32 Hokkuo, 'Hokkuo Reviews the Performance in Belgium', Yomiuri Shimbun, 29 December 1900, in Shirakawa, p.337.

33 Fournier, p.36.

34 'Kicho no shin haiyu Kawakami Otojiro (The return of the new actor Otojiro Kawakami)', Chuo Shimbun, 4 January 1901, in Shirakawa, p.341.

35 'Dispatch of Tohi Shunsho', Chuo Shimbun, 15 August 1900, in Shirakawa, p.356.

36 Kawakami, Otojiro and Sadayakko Kawakami, Jiden Otojiro, Sadayakko (Autobiography of Otojiro and Sadayakko), p.213.

37 'Criterion Theatre', The Times, 8 July 1901, p.3.

38 Beerbohm, Max, 'Incomparables Compared', The Saturday Review of Politics, Literature, Science and Art, vol XCI, no. 2382, 29 June 1901, p.799.

Chapter 8 – The Real Madame Butterfly: Europe, 1901–1903

1 Corriere della sera, 26–27 April 1902, translated in Groos, pp.54–5.

2 Material on Picasso thanks to John Richardson; see Richardson, especially pp.193–203.
3 'An Actor's Statue', *Miyako Shimbun*, 6 November 1901, in Shirakawa, p.368.
4 Laparcerie, Marie, 'Sada Yacco est à Paris!!!', *Femina*, 1 November 1907, pp.490–1.
5 Montignard, G., '*Une Visite à des Artistes Étranges*', *Le Monde Illustré*, no 2327, 2 November 1901, pp.340–1.
6 Fuller, p.222.
7 Kawakami, Otojiro and Sadayakko Kawakami, *Jiden Otojiro, Sadayakko* (Autobiography of Otojiro and Sadayakko), pp.216–7.
8 Duncan, chapter 10, pp.94–5.
9 'Yacco Charms Berlin', *New York Journal and American*, 5 January 1902.
10 Kawakami, Otojiro and Sadayakko Kawakami, *Jiden Otojiro, Sadayakko* (Autobiography of Otojiro and Sadayakko), pp.208, 211.
11 *Grats* newspaper, quoted in *Chuo Shimbun*, in Yamaguchi, p.143.
12 'Bei Sada Yacco', *Der Tag*, no 513, 17 November 1901.
13 Duncan, chapter 10; Fuller, chapter 18; *Yomiuri Shimbun*, 24 August 1902, in Shirakawa, p.364.
14 Kawakami, Otojiro and Sadayakko Kawakami, *Jiden Otojiro, Sadayakko* (Autobiography of Otojiro and Sadayakko), p.220.
15 Ibid, pp.206–7.
16 *La Perseveranza*, 26–27 April 1902, translated in Groos, p.53.
17 Groos, pp.54–5.
18 Material on Puccini: see Groos and Rij.
19 Klee, Paul, *Italian Diary II*, p.110.
20 Kawakami, Otojiro and Sadayakko Kawakami, *Jiden Otojiro, Sadayakko* (Autobiography of Otojiro and Sadayakko), p.212.
21 'Return of Sada-Yacco and Kawakami', mistakenly dated 20 April 1901. 'Sada Yacco dossier', Clippings File Re 2403, Bibliothèque de l'Arsenal, Paris.
22 Kawakami, Sadayakko, '*Sadayakko omoide hanashi* (Sadayakko talks about her memories) 6' in *Tokyo Asahi Shimbun*, 28 February 1937.
23 Hasegawa, p.62; Yamaguchi, pp.76, 103.
24 Hasegawa, p.72.
25 Hayashi, '*Une Première de Shakespeare au Japon*', *La Revue*, 1 May 1903.

Chapter 9 – Secrets of a Woman's Heart: Performing in Japan, 1903–1911

1 Hasegawa, p.73.
2 Ibid, p.77.
3 *Yomiuri Shimbun*, 9 November 1903, in Yamaguchi, p.188.
4 'University Student sends Love letter to Sadayakko Kawakami', *Miyako*

Shimbun, 27 October 1904, in Shirakawa, pp.431–2.

5 Barr, p.250.

6 Howard, Ethel, *Japanese Memories*, 1918, in Wise, Michael (compiler), *Travellers' Tales of Old Japan*, Times Books International, Singapore, 1985, pp.198–200.

7 Toyotaka, p.275.

8 'Notes for actresses', *Nihhon shogyo shimpo*, 27 June 1914.

9 'Japanese Painting', *The Times*, 10 September 1910.

10 Noguchi.

11 Laparcerie, Marie, 'Sada Yacco est a Paris!!!', *Femina*, 1 November 1907, pp.490–1.

12 'Tout Paris', *The Queen: The Lady's Newspaper*, 16 November 1907, p.910.

13 'The Sarah Bernhardt of Japan', *Chicago Record*, 13 January 1908. 'Sada Yacco,' Robinson Locke Clippings File 2663, Billy Rose Theater Collection, New York Public Library.

14 Gold, p.109.

15 'Ce que nous a dit La Sarah Bernhardt du Japon', *Lectures pour Tous*, March 1908. 'Sada Yacco dossier', Clippings File Re 2403, Bibliothèque de l'Arsenal, Paris.

16 *Jiji Shimpo*, 10 June 1908, translated and quoted in Kano, p.73.

17 From *Fukuzawa Momosuke no O-den*, quoted in Asari, p.107.

18 Momosuké's story: in Asari and *Fukuzawa Momosuke ten*.

19 *Jiji Shimpo*, 16 September 1908, in Shirakawa, p.466.

20 Yamaguchi, p.214.

21 Kano, p.74.

22 *Chuo Koron*, 1908, quoted in Toyoda, p.303.

23 Kawakami, Sadayakko, 'Joyu rekiho roku (Record of visits with actresses 1)' in *Engei Gaho*, February 1911, p.43.

24 Kano, pp.110–16.

25 Yamaguchi, p.233.

26 Newspaper articles, 15 October – 12 November 1911, in Shirakawa, pp.492–502.

PART III MISTRESS

Chapter 10 – Wild Chrysanthemum: 1911–1917

1 Newspaper articles, 11–23 November 1911, in Shirakawa, pp.500–17.

2 'Kawakami no iro kuyo (Putting to rest the love aspect of Otojiro Kawakami)', *Miyako Shimbun*, 30 November 1911, in Shirakawa, p.517.

3 'Sadayakko cuts her hair', *Miyako Shimbun*, 14 November 1911, in Shirakawa, p.509.

4 Kawakami, Sadayakko, 'Otto ni wakarete nochi (On being parted from Otto)' in *Engei Gaho*, November 1912, pp.169–70.

5 'Joyu Kawakami Sadayakko (The actress Sadayakko Kawakami)', *Osaka Mainichi Shimbun*, 11 February 1912, Sadayakko scrapbook, Teishoji Temple, p.7.

6 'Sadayakko no o-cho-san (Sadayakko's Butterfly)', undated 1912 clipping, Sadayakko scrapbook, Teishoji Temple, p.14.

7 *Bungei Club*, March 1912, in Yamaguchi, p.238.

8 Kawakami, Sadayakko, 'Otto ni wakarete nochi (On being parted from Otto)' in *Engei Gaho*, November 1912, p.171.

9 'Sadayakko wa kore kara do suru (What Sadayakko will do from now on)', *Chuo Shimbun*, 5 June 1913, Sadayacco scrapbook, Teishoji Temple, p.30.

10 Kawakami, Sadayakko, 'Otto ni wakarete nochi (On being parted from Otto)' in *Engei Gaho*, November 1912, pp.169–70.

11 'Koi no Sadayakko (Sadayakko in love)'; 'Tosuke-kun to Sadayakko (Tosuké and Sadayakko)' undated, unidentified clippings, Sadayakko scrapbook, Teishoji Temple, p.63.

12 Hasegawa, pp.59–62.

13 'Chie no na ko ni (For children who know nothing)', *Tokyo 26 Shimbun*, 25 June 1913, Sadayakko scrapbook, Teishoji Temple, p.42.

14 'Naniwa-za ryaku hyo (Review of Naniwa-za)', *Osaka Nichi-nichi Shimbun*, 23 June 1914, Sadayakko scrapbook, Teishoji Temple, p.48.

15 'Meiji-za ni-gatsu kogyo (Meiji-za February performance)', *Kokumin Shimbun*, February 1914, Sadayakko scrapbook, Teishoji Temple, p.44.

16 Osanai, Kaoru, 'Hongoza no Sarome (Salome at the Hongoza)', *Engei Gaho*, June 1915, p.155.

17 'Shimpa no Hongo-za (New Wave theatre at the Hongo-za)', *Hochi Shimbun*, 1915; 'Kawai to Sadayakko (Kawai and Sadayakko)', *Yoroi Choho*, 1915, Sadayakko scrapbook, Teishoji Temple, p.59.

18 'Sadayakko o ika ni shobun subeki ka (How should we dispose of Sadayakko?)', *Shin Engei*, March–May 1916, translated and quoted in Kano, p.52.

19 Toita, p.35.

20 *tomokakumo nogare sumu beku nogiku kana*

21 Hasegawa, p.70; Yamaguchi, p.261.

22 Yamata, pp.107–8.

Chapter 11 – In the Shadow of the Peach Tree: 1917–1946

1 *momo no ki ni kakata tako no unari kana.*

2 *kaze ni noreba tachiki hikinuku chikara ari.*

3 Asari, p.264.

Epilogue

1 Kincaid, p.345.

INDEX